Culture in the New South Africa

After Apartheid –

Volume Two

Edited by Robert Kriger and Abebe Zegeye

KWELA BOOKS
and
SA HISTORY ONLINE

This book forms part of the Social Identities South Africa Series and has been produced with the financial assistance of the National Research Foundation, and of the Delegation of the European Commission through the CWCI Fund

Published jointly by Kwela Books and South African History Online

Kwela Books
28 Wale Street, Cape Town 8001;
P.O. Box 6525, Roggebaai 8012
Kwela@kwela.com

South African History Online
P.O. Box 11420, Maroelana 0161
Info@sahistory.org.za
www.sahistory.org.za

Cover and book design by Liam Lynch and Omar Badsha
Cover photograph by Omar Badsha
Set in 10 on 13.5 pt Garamond
Printed and bound by NBD, Drukkery Street, Cape Town, South Africa
First edition, first printing 2001

ISBN 0-7957-0134-9

Social Identities South Africa
General Editor: Abebe Zegeye

The identities of South Africa and its citizens have been undergoing crucial changes since 1994, when the first democratic elections resulted in the demise of statutory apartheid. This has led to an emerging ethos of democratic rule among all citizens of South Africa. But, although changes in South African society are clearly visible in increased social mobility, migration, access to jobs, training and education and general reform in South Africa, the nature and influence of the identities being formed in response is as yet less clear. The SISA project aims to determine the nature of some of these new identities.

The project is shaped by research that indicates that South Africans, while going through flux and transformation in their personal and group identities, have a shared concern about the stability of their democracy and their economic future.

Titles in the SISA Series jointly published by Kwela Books and South African History Online:

Social Identities in the New South Africa
After Apartheid – Volume One
Edited by Abebe Zegeye

Culture in the New South Africa
After Apartheid – Volume Two
Edited by Robert Kriger and Abebe Zegeye

Kala Pani
Caste and Colour in South Africa
Rehana Ebr-Vally

Coloured by History, Shaped by Place
New Perspectives on Coloured Identities in Cape Town
Edited by Zimitri Erasmus

The I of the Beholder
Identity formation in the art and writing of Breyten Breytenbach
Marilet Sienaert

Contents

List of contributors

- Nombuso S. Dlamini
  Education, Mount Saint Vincent University, Canada
- Rehana Ebr.-Vally
  Department of Social Anthropology, University of Witwatersrand,
  South Africa
- Janis Grobbelaar
  Department of Sociology, University of South Africa, South Africa
- Hjalte Tin
  Centre for Cultural research, University of Aarhus, Denmark
- Franco Frescura
  Development consultant, SADC region, South Africa
- Ian Liebenberg
  Department of Sociology, University of South Africa, South Africa
- Abebe Zegeye
  Department of Sociology, University of South Africa, South Africa
- Fran Buntman
  Department of Political Science, University of Akron (Ohio),
  United States of America
- John Higginson
  Department of History, University of Massachusetts, United States of America
- John Comaroff
  Department of Anthropology, University of Chicago, United States of America
- Charmaine McEachern
  Department of Anthropology, University of Adelaide, Australia
- Denis-Constant Martin
  Centre d'etudes et de recherches internationales, France

Acknowledgements

We are grateful to Prem Naidoo, formerly of the National Research Foundation (NRF) who was instrumental in getting the Social Identities South Africa (SISA) programme off the ground. Some of the papers in this volume are updated versions of papers published in *Cultural Link, Special Issue 1998–'99*.

Charl Schutte, Julia Maxted and Beth le Roux are thanked for their attention to the details of content and language editing. We are also thankful to Omar Badsha and Liam Lynch for their able technical assistance.

Introduction

Abebe Zegeye and Robert Kriger

This collection includes a myriad of themes and views on the dynamic role of culture in the post apartheid society. As one reads the papers presented, it becomes clear that any review of cultural discourse, space and activity in South Africa would have to reflect upon the duality of cultural production within the former repressive state. While black and white cultures were expressed largely in isolation from each other, they now provide the basis for intercultural dialogue, experimentation and the search for new forms with which to express a new social and cultural identity.

The duality of culture in South Africa arose as a result of one of the premises of apartheid, i.e. that the various racial groups were so inherently different that co-existence or even close proximity would inevitably lead to conflict. Accordingly, these groups had to be kept apart, to practise their cultural traditions and exercise their political rights in isolation. A cultural pattern similar to that found in other areas colonised by Europe followed. On the one hand, artistic forms such as ballet, opera, classical music and theatre were developed and paid for by taxpayers' money to entertain the white minority, while on the other hand the cultural traditions and aesthetic practices of the majority were dismissed as inferior or, at best, encouraged as tourist attractions, and ghettoised as a result.

Most dominant within the 'white' society were the mainly eurocentric productions and products of the various cultural 'factories' such as the provincial arts councils which were heavily subsidised by the state in the interest of 'satisfaction' and ideological domestication. In their attempts to prop up the minority regime, these institutions, such as the Performing Arts Council of the Transvaal (PACT), the Cape Performing Arts Board (CAPAB) and the Natal Performing Arts Council (NAPAC), or the Federasie van Afrikaanse Kultuurorganisasies (Federation of Afrikaans Cultural Organisations, FAK), the Afrikaanse Taal- en Kultuurvereniging (Afrikaans Language and Culture Association, ATKV) and the National Monuments Council, served the purpose of propagating the ideal of white supremacy and superiority and above all, sought to maintain the supposed cultural umbilical linkages to the mythical 'European fatherlands'. At the same time, English and Afrikaans were imposed as the official languages of the country. However, even this propagation was tightly controlled by the rigorous (political) censorship laws and regulation. It was, to use a German phrase, *gleichgeschaltet*, i.e. forced into the service of an ideological framework, namely Apartheid.

To illustrate this point: when the film version of Bernard Malamud's celebrated novel *The Fixer* was released onto the South African circuit, it was initially celebrated as a clear indictment of a 'cruel, barbaric and repressive communistic [sic] system'. However, as soon as it became apparent that many blacks were flocking to the cinemas to see the film and making clear analogies with the apartheid state and its fascist tendencies, it was promptly removed from the circuit and banned for black audiences. White audiences, it would appear, were not as susceptible to the implied message and analogies. Although blacks were, by and large, excluded from participating in or attending 'mainstream' cultural events – through the segregation of cinemas, theatres, galleries, museums and so on – these restrictions generally led to a spate of cultural activities in the townships, usually conducted in church halls or at events held in sports facilities. Most of these cultural events had an overtly 'political' message of either resistance to the system and/or served as a platform for boosting (black) self-awareness, especially against the backdrop of the black consciousness movement of the seventies and eighties.

Another major effect – although unintentional – of the restrictive nature of the former government's cultural policies and practices, was to encourage the flourishing of cultural innovation and practice. 'Cultural practitioners' were actively engaged in a new discourse, pre-empting, as it were, the contours, policies and practices of culture in a post-apartheid society. Milestone events, such as CASA [1] or meetings between exiled and internal cultural representatives, served to hone the outlines, issues and concerns of this debate.

Diverse forms of cultural artefacts and practices emerged during this period, especially in literature, theatre and performance, the plastic arts and the revival of traditional modes of dance (including orature, movement, performance). The development of this counter-hegemonic discourse and practice, welded as it usually was to the political resistance movement ('the struggle'), did not go unnoticed by the authorities: works and authors were censored or banned as it was realised that culture was playing a role as a shield for political struggle. Artists were also not issued with passports which denied them the possibility of taking up international invitations, for instance.

However, despite this 'total onslaught' by the apartheid state on liberatory culture and its proponents, many cultural activists simply changed their strategy: instead of expecting visitors to attend their performances at, for example, theatres or central venues, the artists came to their audiences, to political funerals, mass rallies, church halls in the townships, and so on. Many of these artists were members of collectives, small non-governmental organisations or associations – which in turn became part of a national cultural initiative. Such organisations also advised the then-banned African National Congress (ANC) on the implementation of the cultural boycott, and generally assisted in promoting the anti-apartheid message abroad through exhibitions, plays and festivals focusing on South Africa. In a sense, these organisations were the precursor of the present National Arts Council.

One could, therefore, assume that the progressive, cultural practitioners of the apartheid era would feel very comfortable and satisfied under the present dispensation. That this is (currently) not so, could be explained as follows:

> After the unbanning of the ANC, the umbrella cultural organisations mentioned above asserted their political independence by launching the first national, non-racial, non-partisan arts lobby – the National Arts Coalition – to lobby for new arts and culture policies. This led to some tensions with their former partner – the ANC's Department of Arts and Culture – which believed that it should be at the vanguard of transformation in the country, including that of cultural transformation.

By the time the elections were held in April 1994, the National Arts Coalition had developed a strong national presence and formulated a comprehensive set of new policy recommendations. Based on public nominations, the new Minister of Arts, Culture, Science and Technology appointed a 23-person Arts and Culture Task Group (ACTAG) – representing all disciplines, regions and forms of art – to solicit and present recommendations for new policies with the support of the arts community. The ACTAG process culminated in 1995 with the adoption of its proposals by a national conference representing a broad cross-section of artists and cultural institutions. Government published its White Paper on Arts, Culture and Heritage in 1996, which reflected many of the ACTAG recommendations.

Several cultural activists of that period took up senior positions in government and provincial departments responsible for arts and culture and it was hoped that this would bring about speedy implementation of the policy recommendations. However, the momentum and enthusiasm generated through the ACTAG process has largely been dissipated through the slow process of establishing new government structures, and the equally slow process of preparing and adopting legislation.

Major arts and culture-related bills passed in 1998 include the National Arts Council Act and the National Film and Video Foundation Act which were to become bodies to channel funds to support the development and dissemination of the arts. The process of transforming cultural institutions which were the main recipients of public funds during the apartheid era and which largely reflected apartheid's interests in their structures, content and aesthetics, has also taken place largely in accordance with policy recommendations. The National Arts Council receives an annual grant from government to support the creation, development and distribution of music, dance, theatre, visual art, craft, literature and community art and it does this through a system of peer review with discipline-based panels reviewing and making recommendations on applications for funding. Much of the R7.5 million (less than one million pounds) of the R10 million government grant distributed by the Council at its first allocations in February 1998, were funds which had been cut from establishment cultural institutions such as the performing arts councils.

In terms of government policy, the councils are to be downsized to serve as metropolitan theatres, with the companies and orchestras attached to them receiving declining susbsidies over three years, while diversifying their funding bases. However, the theory of the White Paper - that orchestras, ballet and opera companies could apply to the National Arts Council and its provincial equivalents like any other creative project – is not matched by the reality, characterised by an absence of such mechanisms, and a dire lack of funding. There has been some concern that the small size of the Council's budget will destroy its credibility. (The Council received applications in excess of fifteen times the amount it was able to allocate with its first grant).

Accordingly, questions are being raised about the capacity of government officials to implement the vision and recommendations of the arts community as articulated in the ACTAG Report. While the Department of Arts, Culture, Science and Technology has control over policy and resources, it appears to lack the managerial expertise, political will and vision to effect its own policies.

The National Arts Council is required to serve the arts nationally, but there is concern about its capacity to do this. The rationale for the Council was to ensure the equitable distribution of resources throughout the country, particularly to those areas which had been neglected in the past. They appear to continue to be neglected, at least in the decision-making forums of the Council. It has become increasingly clear though, that the implementation of policy now equally requires a strong watchdog lobby from within the arts community. In this context, the '1% Campaign' is being launched to lobby for increased public funding for the arts, monitor government arts expenditure, and generally represent the interests of the arts community in this phase of policy implementation and review. The independence of the Council will also probably be closely monitored by the arts community, as it is crucial to the freedom of creative expression.

Of particular note and interest is the fact that there has been an exciting resurgence of cultural activity throughout the country. Annual festivals fulfil an important function in providing a platform for newcomers and new work: traditional and experimental dance, music and drama festivals, literary events and exhibitions all seem engaged in celebrating the vibrant opportunities and possibilities of this multi-cultural and multilingual society which is the 'new' South Africa. Although most of these events are financed with shoestring budgets, it is noteworthy that corporate (financial) support for these domains of creativity and production has shown a steady growth over the past few years. This collection of articles seeks to reflect such changes as have occurred within the cultural space(s) of the 'new' South Africa. The authors were tasked with reflecting on the changes which may have occurred within their particular domain. The brief issued by the co-editors was succint. It stated the following:

> The article/paper should ideally reflect your perceptions of changes of cultural values and cultural identity (identities) in contemporary South Africa, i.e. what is happening currently in South African culture in terms of institutional, policy and value changes?

Although the 'field' was known to be broad and varied, it was our decision to restrict contributions to such areas that were clearly linked to or tangential to that of cultural practice. As such, we were pleasantly surprised by the responses received. Authors, photographers, 'cultural practitioners', reviewers, literary critics all expressed their excitement at being allowed an opportunity to reflect on such changes as may have occurred during the past five years of the 'new' South Africa as this impacted upon the life of our 'cultural practitioners'.

The most critical issues raised are nationalism, the degree and success of institutional transition, creating new historiographies of cultural production, validating the work of artists that were excluded during apartheid and expanding access to government subsidies for artistic and literary work.

There are a number of themes and questions reiterated across several chapters:

— What counts as legitimate cultural practice must be expanded without appeals to cultural nationalism. This is a concern which must be connected to every artistic renaissance. It is our hope that acknowledging 'group identity' does not mean fostering militarism or nationalism, but may also cultivate communalism and 'reciprocity, care and affect' (Sitas).
— How does South African cultural practice confront the debates on modernity/post modernity and colonialism/post colonialism?
— What are the consequences of institutional transition, namely redistribution of state funding in the arts as well as new mission statements and visions for arts agencies?
— Can arts policy remain a medium which can make up the shortfalls in government revenues and party conflicts?
— How can the arts contribute to economic revitalisation without being subjected to naked market commodification?

- What choices have cultural activists and liberation organisations made in choosing their own cultural policies and what new directions can be suggested for them?
- How can discussion of gender be made part of the debate on cultural dynamism? And how can discussion of South African cultural dynamism inform global debates on the meaning of gender?
- How can media create greater access to practitioners, artists and activists yet still consider the conditions of people previously overlooked by apartheid segregation such as the white working class and rural female artists?

It is to such issues that the chapters turn. Alexander and Heugh argue that in post-colonial Africa the hierarchical relations characterising the different languages and varieties of language have been perpetuated *de facto* in spite of legislation and constitutional arrangements providing for equality. In South Africa, English and Afrikaans determined the wealth and status available in the past. Moreover, language continues to be intricately linked to economic exploitation and desires for social mobility. The authors caution that unless a multilingual national language and economic policy is applied, the country will not be able to overcome the economic segregation of apartheid. The democratisation of language must affirm that African languages are valid media for the cultural, scientific, technological, economic and political domains and practice. Political leaders as yet appear not to understand language beyond its connections to cultural identities, histories and discrimination.

Shepperson and Tomaselli attempt to reclaim culture that has been simultaneously trounced by apartheid radicalisation and by the static record-keeping of modernity that results when people are exposed to strictly limited aspects of culture. They suggest that South Africa's media sector has a duty to contribute to the development of the wider regional networking functions of the whole range of governmental, civil and economic sectors. Culture, they argue, is something which people *do*, an action forged in struggle, pluralism and migrating theories and practices. The authors suggest that since culture orients people towards their responsibilities and identities in their communities, a dynamic media must speak to the whole range of people's interests and priorities across generations. The chapter provides an informative view of what can go wrong when people are officially limited in their access to interpreted views of their culture.

Frescura's work on rural female architects rejects the notion that the iconography used by woman designers should be relegated to the natural history of the past. He takes into account patterns of migration, movement and attempts at incorporation into more powerful groups. Their work is contemporary and resonates with our emphasis on dynamic responses to the current situation, especially the creation of new communities and regions. Like others in this collection, Frescura emphasises that these designs persist despite and in concert with Westernisation and cross-cultural pollination. Frescura states that southern Africa's rural architecture has long been associated with a tradition in wall decoration which predates the arrival of white colonialists to the region's interior. These designs are generally acknowledged to be the product of women and have remained their preserve in rural areas right up to the present. The work is a statement made by women in respect of their fertility, political status, religious cosmology and in certain instances, their family lineage.

Regarding the future of the wall painting tradition in South Africa, it is not easy to make predictions. Because the social and economic inequalities which historically gave rise to the tradition are the subject of revision and redress under the country's new constitution, it appears likely that the motivation for continuing the tradition has either already been lost or is likely to be dissipated once a viable housing programme for rural areas is put in place. One factor that can play a role in resolving the issue is the growth of tourism. The tradition should be treated as a non-renewable resource.

Fleishman's study discusses institutional and administrative change *vis-à-vis* the redistribution of theatre funding and agency subsidies from the Johannesburg Performing Arts Council to the newly established National Arts Council. Since apartheid created racial requirements for access to funds for producers, directors, playwrights and dramatists, the new arts councils advocate increased regional representation to be more inclusive. Fleishman argues that since greater democratisation came about with the elections in 1994, the fabric of the theatre in South Africa is no longer woven from one master thread, but from multiple smaller threads. It is a theatre which focuses more on the many small narratives of the margins than on any single grand narrative of the centre. In so doing, it reflects a new freedom to articulate personal identities and subjectivities. In this respect, Fleishman points out a need for greater support among local authorities for cultural expression.

Teer-Tomaselli's contribution situates public broadcasting in the context of attempts by the South African Broadcasting Corporation (SABC) to meet the requirements initiated of the Independent Broadcasting Association Act. Technological advancement and deregulation have made it possible and desirable for the SABC to include more local content in its public broadcasting. Although the 're-launch' of the SABC in 1996 was aimed at delivering more public broadcasting through the eleven official languages, this was offset by the wide and inexpensive availability of English-language programming on the international market and the premise that English was the second-language choice of most South Africans. Accordingly, English remains the dominant language of the SABC.

Within this context, the author's main concern is how the SABC can promote the production of local and diverse programming (the self-image of society, if you will) without reinforcing nationalism, since a majority of local content programming is provided by news programmes. The SABC has, within the limits of financial constraints, attempted to fulfil its mandate of 'protecting and nurturing South African culture and creativity reflecting the reality of South Africa and itself to the world, South Africa from a distinctly South African perspective'. Although not expressing a view on the merits of this way of rekindling nationhood, the author claims that the SABC has, in attempting to fulfil this mandate, consciously aligned itself with the 'African Renaissance'.

Smit and Van Wyk use the context of the Centre for the Study of Southern African Literature and Languages to discuss the transformation of segregationist literary studies to an integrated approach to the historical complexity of South African literature. The expanding curricula of the post-apartheid era lend themselves to a fresh analysis of class, cultural encounters and an expanded notion of what counts as literature. In the context of intolerance existing in South Africa under the apartheid regime's segregationist practices, the ownership of land, industry, power and knowledge was usually perceived in racial or class terms as white, upper-class or bourgeois ownership. Through its practices, the Centre nurtures collective ownership in that the knowledge produced there is continuously shared and contributors are recognised.

The empowerment of students and their communities through creative engagement with life, culture, economy, education and work through literature is summarised in terms of Foucault's notion of the 'specific intellectual'. Such intellectuals have a more immediate and concrete awareness of struggles. They also often - especially in the case of the researchers of the Centre - come from previously disadvantaged or oppressed minority cultures. The activities at the Centre empower them to function in society as critical but also facilitating, constructive and responsible intellectuals. Although Smit and Van Wyk do not discuss this, the relation between 'specific' and 'universal' intellectuals in South Africa appears to be a relevant cultural debating point under the new dispensation in this country.

Wicomb continues the literary theme with an analysis that questions the use of black female suffering as a figure of speech that simultaneously objectifies black women and reinforces the dubious connection between whiteness and leisure and ease. Her logic in discussing familial ties and family breakdown among the white working class reveals the complexity of the betrayals of apartheid. There is now a 'scramble' for 'alterity', by which she means the otherness of the native of Africa. The practice of conjugating a new Afrikaner identity with the ready-made category of black-as-other is not a felicitous one from a black point of view that would question the very category. The scramble for alterity also does not guarantee the rehabilitation of Afrikaner identity.

Commitment to the demise of apartheid does not mean an abandonment of ethnic tags, but it does, according to the texts Wicomb analyses, at least require disaffiliation from whiteness. Whilst 'Afrikaner' has become a disgraced category, the struggle for rehabilitation crucially implicates the binary opposition of relations with Englishness. And whilst English in fact assumes national language status, cultural and linguistic space is necessarily one where whiteness will continue to reside in silence and anonymity. However, this is not the whole story. In the world beyond texts, where whiteness remains bound up with privilege and economic power, it cannot simply be written off, not least because those who benefit most from its demise are not able to read of such well-meaning resolutions to the narrative of apartheid.

Parker discusses contemporary South African women's writing in Afrikaans, particularly as produced by white women. Long overlooked, this body of work has quickly become the new avant garde of South African writing, reflecting upon and presaging dramatic transformations in the South African social fabric. Mapping the contributions of this writing in Afrikaans, Parker contrasts them with the absence of engagement in South African writing in English with narrative techniques concerned with the nuances and ironies, the boundary and border transgression of women's writing in Afrikaans. In other words, a lack of engagement with traditional styles and themes, standard subjects and narrative technologies of the gendered formation of language itself.

Parker argues that Afrikaans has been perceived as the language of oppression of black people by white people. He refers to the battle between 'Boer' (Afrikaner) and 'Brit' (British people) over who would best be able to dominate black people. He suggests that the lines in this respect be redrawn, away from conventional demarcations along the lines of language usage with affinities between a dominant liberal-humanist and residual black consciousness. Rather, the demarcation should be between an aligned black consciousness and new developments in Afrikaans writing as complementary responses to that dominant tradition. A possible explanation for the processes and outcomes of political alignments currently being negotiated by the main protagonists may be the triumph of the descendants of indigenous communities as well as those of Dutch settlers who speak about land and people and language and nation in terms in which the descendants of British settlers have never done. Parker's analysis may well prove to be correct.

In his appreciation of Thelma Gutsche, Masilela writes that in a real sense the theme of Gutsche's book *The History and Social Significance of Motion Pictures in South Africa* is the intrusion of the USA and Europe into South Africa. Gutsche examines the effects of film-making on the cultural fabric of South Africa; thus the book is not really about South African cinema, but about the entrance of European modernity into South Africa through films. Although possibly dismissive of South African films through its silence on them, it may be the best book on South African film, an extraordinary archival retrieval, according to Masilela.

Gutsche was in general not really concerned with films made by South Africans, being contemptuous of films by whites made for whites. She saw Afrikaner nationalists, with the connivance of English-speaking white South Africans, as responsible for the destruction of South Africa's cinematic visual imagination. This extracted a heavy price: in almost a century of the encounter between the South African visual imagination and cinematography not a single masterpiece has been produced by a South African film-maker. Masilela's analysis, although it appears to underestimate the influence of sheer economic inequality in the etiology of South African film culture, succeeds in focusing the reader's attention on some hitherto unknown dynamics of the cinematic culture of South Africa.

Impey, in perceptively describing one cultural response to the horro of apartheid and its attendant migrant labour system, writes that the Beatrice Street YMCA in Central Durban is a modest establishment. The upstairs hall is unadorned except for a few scattered rows of plastic chairs and several strips of flickering lights precariously fastened to warped and rotten ceiling boards.

At the far end of the hall there is a low wooden platform in front of which is a wooden table and a single chair. Every Saturday night the YMCA is a hive of activity. Zulu migrant workers begin to congregate in tight circles, hands behind backs, facing inwards towards one another and begin to sing softly in close four-part harmony, a cappella. They are preparing for the competition they call *isicathamiya*, which, literally translated, means 'in stalking approach', descriptive of the soft, tiptoed dancing styles, crouching actions and songs they perform.

Each choir is immaculately dressed in matching suits and bow-ties, two-tone shoes, white gloves, pocket handkerchiefs and shining costume jewellery. Each choir is made up of "homeboys", men who share kinship or regional ties from rural KwaZulu-Natal, a province in the northeast of South Africa. The songs are defiant and describe suffering. They represent a hybrid musical style, having originated in American mistrelsy and ragtime. They have also achieved some commercial success. Their explorations are as much an excercise in post-aprtheid self-discovery as it is a statement to the world of an emerging national identity. *Isicathamiya* is as significant for the female supporters of it as to the men. the preformance would be incomplete without the women. They play an essential role and are emotional benefactors of the genre. Their dedication and zeal has made meaningful the weekly moments of glory to male choristers whose status as migrants rendered them otherwise invisible and socially impotent.

Sitas' autobiography of the trade union movement in KwaZulu-Natal in recent times emphasises the experiences, research findings and narratives of trade unionists themselves. His findings demonstrate the methodological possibility of multiple-author narration and oral history. Sitas made use of a creative workshop involving sixteen writers and cultural activists in COSATU (Congress of South African Trade Unions). What was brought into the workshop was a simple uncontroversial point that movements in general are challenges to the social or class orders of society and not mere responses to objective stimuli. All the participants stated that that black workers joined trade unions in the 1970s and 1980s because of 'terrible wages', because they were 'treated like dogs' and because they needed a 'shield'. Racial discrimination and apartheid was a constitutive experience. Although bounded by racial oppression, racial oppression does not express the central project in their narrations, namely that they are building a nation. This slippage from race to nation and back and its co-existence with a class perspective has made for a volatile challenge to any *status quo*.

The moral core of the movement is analysed as a new solidarity which was learnt through *umzabalazo*, struggle. The word *umzabalazo* seems to be the qualifying authority for comradeship. This, according to Sitas, points to some profound conclusions, highlighting a class and racial distinctiveness among the participants, who represent over 200 000 members. The chapter is thus an imaginative undertaking backed by a sound theoretical understanding of the issues involved. It also highlights some of the operations of culture in that crucial institutional complex in South Africa – the maze of trade unions.

Vally, in a fascinating and revelatory chapter, shows how car registration numbers have become a visible new expression of cultural identity in Gauteng, a province of South Africa, as well as a source of additional revenue for the Gautneg provincial government. The point she makes is that in these circumstances, the motorist can, at a (sometimes very high) price, have almost any number he/she desires as long as it does not offend citizens of South Africa. The Gauteng provincial traffic authorities, in order to achieve this, block out ceratin combinations of numbers and letters, which can then be bought at higher than normal prices for motor car registration. For private Internet-based companies specialise in finding the numbers for motorists who want them.

The Personalised Registration Numbers can cost anything between 38 to 5 000 times the cost of an ordinary registration number (R50-00). In the Western Province, there is a R50 000-00 catergory for sought-after numbers. In Gauteng there is no such catergory. It appears that the reason for this is that the Department of Transport have the intention of auctioning off ceratin names in great demand. In South Africa, a mid-level state employee earns R50 000-00 per annum. Vally concludes that the phenomenon of identity and its various expressions to fixed sites and places.

Duncan, in her study of the Johannesburg Biennale project, claims that new South African policies are creating rather than reducing inequality. This reversal is evident in many areas of life, including the visual arts, where a growing emphasis on promoting the country's international competitiveness is marginalising key development needs in that sector. The 'competitiveness logic' requires governments to 'crowd in' resources to industries and areas capable of meeting the challenge. Cities have been identified as the productive engines of the world economy. In Johannesburg the race is on to establish the city as South Africa's first truly global city. But biennales remain blind to class questions regarding the organisation of cultural resources. There is no space for national questions in 'global' mega-exhibitions. However, a fundamental aim of emancipatory theory and practice is to realise a society where all people can live as whole human beings. A possibly effective approach for achieving this goal is encapsulated by Samir Amin's concept of 'delinking' which recognises that neo-liberal development strategies applied universally result in increasing wealth gaps between and within countries.

Local government cannot be allowed to disintegrate under the weight of global fiscal austerity. Support for arts and culture should be included in an integrated vision of local government. Such support would also promote the creative capacities of all residents, not just those considered to be 'artists'. At the same time it would be parochial: given the realities of globalisation, the vision should be both local and internationalist. Attempting to save the country money by slashing such services will have such an enormous social price that the short-term benefits will soon be swept away. Costing the implications of increasing marginalisation, inequality and alienation of large sections of South African society will be difficult, but the country needs to rise to the challenge.

Duncan's chapter can be interpreted as a remarkable and timely warning to anyone doubting the value of culture freely expressed in building a new nation, a project well underway in South Africa at present. The chapter also points to the crucial role that local government has in this endeavour, warning that any signs of deterioration at that level of government should be immediately countered.

In their concluding chapter, Zegeye and Liebenberg state that change in South Africa has resulted in both good and bad. The good is largely that an authoritatrian and racist minority regime known for its brutality has departed from the political scene and that South African citizens have become free to choose their own destiny. The bad is what might be termed 'the burden of the present'. The country and its people tend to suffer from the legacy of different colonialisms, apartheid and separation, a lack of development and potential economic stagnation and high levels of crime. The latter is due to many factors, including a recent past of armed protest politics, the militarisation of the youth and sub-optimum economic conditions. Widespread poverty is one phenomenon responsible for widespread crime and violence.

Apartheid relied on the consequences of material scarcity and the apartheid government easily imposed "nationhood" and sub-nationhood "from above". Added to this were supremacist philosophies such as ethnocentrism and eurocentrism that concretised differences between categories of people. People socialised within one entity were encouraged to fear the culture and manifestations of the culture of 'others'.

Though apartheid failed to create viable, self-sufficient nations for the majority of the people in South Africa, it did create the cultural ethos associated with defending those nations and groups. Both the resistance to inequities and the justification for the inequities came to revolve around a basic belief in political hegemony and culturally exclusive groups. In view of this, the new culture being developed in South Africa should be a culture of consensus, adaptation, process and dynamism and reflect the complexity of human relationships. The authors in this volume according to Zegeye and Liebenberg aimed to reclaim both the cultures developed "from above" and "from below" and have attempted to make them speak to each other. The volume unmasks the static nature of apartheid and reminds the reader that the struggle against apartheid has had a long history of cultural interaction. The care and affection required to hear multiple voices explain the meaning of a shared experience is the same care that individuals, families and organisations must use to protect the vitality of a democratic South Africa. The South African struggle has generated enormous creativity and inspiration for people world wide. At some point, the legacy of the present must become a celebration of what the transition to democratic rule means for South Africans themselves. That is, the dynamic new cultural process must involve an emphasis on intergenerational communication. The process must somehow pass on the dignity, elegence, innovation and aesthetic character of the persistent struggle for liberation. In these profound interactions the hopes, follies, foibles, negotiations, collaborations and triumphs an honest legacy can be the rich, living history of the present and the future.

Notes

- The editors express their gratitude to Mr Mike van Graan for valuable insights in regard to the ACTAG-NAC debates and process. The editors also wish to thank Ms Elizabeth le Roux, Omar Badsha, Liam Lynch, Willow Vercueil and Julia Maxted for their assistance.
1 *Culture in Another South Africa*: a conference hosted in Amsterdam in December 1987 which brought together South African cultural practitioners from 'home' and those in exile.

CHAPTER ONE

Language policy in the New South Africa

Neville Alexander and Kathleen Heugh

Language policy and planning can assist efforts to change a state and society in radical ways: changing identities, replacing one elite by another in the state apparatus, and altering patterns of access to reflect the replacement of a dominant class or ethnic group. In short, language planning is an important instrument of revolutionary change.

Brian Weinstein (1990, p. 14)

Some general remarks on language policy

As a general rule, language policy in any country derives from the intersection of the fundamental political principles and objectives of the ruling elites or classes and the historically evolved and inherited language situation on the ground. The language situation includes features such as the number of mutually intelligible and mutually unintelligible languages in the political entity, the number of varieties of the different acknowledged 'languages', the degree of standardisation, whether or not the different languages and varieties have been reduced to writing, the degree of literacy in each of the relevant varieties, the prevalence of a reading culture in the different languages or varieties of languages, the existence or not of a language infrastructure comprising language planning and development agencies, publishing and printing enterprises, translation and interpreting facilities, lexicographic projects and many other essential language services.

In a multilingual country, two exceptionally important features of the language situation are the hierarchical relations between the language groups or linguistic communities and the prevailing language attitudes of the speakers of the different languages. In a largely monolingual country (the minority of modern states, by any definition), the same issues are relevant but they are described in terms of 'dialectal' and not 'language', variation. Language is an instrument of communication, among other things. As such it is a necessary element of all social intercourse. A fundamental social domain is that of the economy, in which control of the resources on which the survival of the population as a whole depends is competed for. Often, this contest takes on conflictual and even violent forms.

Be that as it may, it is axiomatic that the dominant language or languages in the economy of any society is or are the language(s) of power. This power derives from the fact that in the economic domain, language is a necessary condition of production by virtue of its crucial function as an instrument of communication. Hence, citizens and others who have to engage in economic activities in the country concerned are empowered to the extent that they know the standard form of the language(s) of power.

In post-colonial Africa, generally speaking, the hierarchical relations that characterise the status of the different languages and varieties of languages during the colonial era have been perpetuated de facto, even when constitutional and other legislative provision has been made for equality of status of the main, or even *all* the, languages used in the independent state. Pierre Alexandre (1972, p. 86) has accurately described the way in which the peculiarities of colonial conquest and administration have given rise to a class structure in the independent states based to a large extent on linguistic competencies. Referring to the new elites in the post-colonial situation, he writes that:

> Power, it is true, is in the hands of this minority. Herein lies one of the most remarkable sociological aspects of contemporary Africa: that the kind of class structure which seems to be emerging is based on linguistic factors. On the one hand is the majority of the population, often compartmentalised by linguistic borders which do not correspond to political frontiers; this majority uses only African tools of linguistic communication and must, consequently, irrespective of its actual participation in the economic sectors of the modern world, have recourse to the mediation of the minority to communicate with this modern world. This minority, although socially and ethnically as heterogeneous as the majority, is separated from the latter by that monopoly which gives it its class specificity: the use of a means of universal communication, French or English, whose acquisition represents truly a form of capital accumulation. But this is a very special kind of capital, since it is an instrument of communication and not one of production. It is nevertheless this instrument, and generally this instrument alone, which makes possible the organisation of the entire modern sector of production and distribution of goods.

Weinstein (1990, p. 10) makes the same point in connection with the contest between English and French on the African continent. He shows that the French colonial regime was afraid that independence would lead to a weakening of the French language and to opening the floodgates to British and American influences which, in turn, would threaten the economic interests of French business. He adds significantly that:

> Weakening of French would also threaten the status of elites whose French education has been one of their tickets of admission to high state and private sector jobs ... They saw a direct link between the status of the French language and the nature of their state and society.

This orientation continues to inform the language policies of the global power elites, including those of international organisations such as the World Bank and the Overseas Development Agency. In spite of all protestations to the contrary, these institutions tend to promote the interests of those who function through the medium of English or some other dominant language at the expense of indigenous languages on the continent and elsewhere (see, for example, Mazrui 1997).

Another issue that should be spotlighted is the well known discrepancy between policy formulation and policy implementation. As intimated above, what is provided for in the constitution, the laws and regulations of the state and what actually happens in the day-to-day practice are usually quite different and often even quite opposite things. In the sphere of language policy, this tendency is as strong as in any other policy sphere. In spite of these reservations, however, the study of language policy and planning does give one a certain measure of insight into the economic, political and broadly social objectives of the ruling groups in any society. To quote Weinstein (1990, p. 1) once more:

> If it is true that institutional language choices can influence identity and participation, which are basic political concepts, then the study of the choices should help us understand more about states and public policies: what values underlie the policies; how a state is being maintained or reformed; how the state is trying to transform the society living within its boundaries; who will benefit, and who will lose; what groups, individuals, and elites have the most influence over public policy. In short, a study of language choice or policy and its implementation or planning can shed light on important political processes and political change. It is by no means peripheral to politics or to general public policy making.

Policy positions of the dominant group

A detailed history of language policy in the Union and subsequent Republic of South Africa has yet to be written. The most satisfying – albeit statistically dated – study is still the work by Dunjwa-Blajberg (1980). More recent, but partial, studies include those by Heugh (1987), Hirson (1981), Reagan (1987), Alexander (1989) and by various authors in Mesthrie (1995).

During the colonial period, the Dutch as well as the British pursued policies that promoted the learning and status of their respective languages by the conquered peoples. A few choice statements emanating from representatives of the colonial-imperial powers will serve to give some sense of their general orientation. The Dutch East India Company, for example, decreed, among other things, that 'the natives should learn our language, rather than we theirs' (cited in Alexander 1989, pp. 12-13). From a narrow language point of view, the main product of Dutch colonial rule in South Africa was the emergence of the creolised form of Dutch which we now know as Afrikaans. The final occupation of the Cape by Britain in 1806 inaugurated a radically different language dispensation. Under Lord Charles Somerset especially, a single-minded policy of Anglicisation was carried out. Indeed, it can be said that a whole century of Anglicisation (of the white colonists) marks the period between the rule of Somerset at the beginning of the 19th century and that of Lord Milner at the end of the century after the defeat of the Boers in 1902. So successful was this policy that by the 1870s, one of the most illustrious of the Anglo-Afrikaner clans of the Cape, Chief Justice J.H. de Villiers, could tell an audience that although the time was still far distant when the inhabitants of the Cape Colony would speak and acknowledge one common mother tongue, that time would come and 'when it does come, the language of Great Britain will also be the language of South Africa' (Alexander 1989, p. 16). Like all such grand predictions, this one, too, would turn out to be only partially correct. By the time the Act of Union was passed in 1909, both English and Dutch (after 1925, Afrikaans) were declared the official languages of the territory. This provision of the constitution of the white supremacist dominion corresponded to the linguistic composition of the social base of the ruling group.

Throughout the colonial period, the languages of the indigenous peoples of the country were treated as necessary evils that had to be harnessed in order to serve the designs of empire. The Dutch did nothing to transliterate, or even understand, the languages of the Khoi and San peoples, most of whom they pushed northwards into the arid interior and across the Garieb into what is now Namibia and Botswana. As for the slaves, they were compelled by the circumstances of their bondage, like slaves throughout the awful history of 'civilisation', to take on the language of the slave master.

This fact explains why the descendants of the slaves, most of whom came to constitute a component of the people labelled 'Coloured', are Afrikaans-speaking today. During the period of British rule, it was the Christian missionaries who were mainly concerned with the taming of the languages of the African people to serve the ends of empire.

In brief, their main concern was to reduce the Nguni and Sotho languages to writing in order to accelerate the conversion of the 'heathen'. By so doing, they unintentionally segmented the speech continua on the east coast and in the interior respectively and standardised specific varieties used by the inhabitants of the region. This proselytising drive, together with administrative and commercial-economic imperatives, was, paradoxically, the reason for the emergence of many of the 'tribes' (today we speak of ethnic groups or ethnic communities) of South Africa. Terence Ranger (1991), in a path-finding article, traced the processes by which this, on the face of it highly improbable, result was achieved in Zimbabwe, and Leroy Vail (1991) in an anthology of significant scholarly contributions, documented the process for southern Africa as a whole. The other thrust of missionary endeavour in the sphere of language policy was to teach what came to be called the 'mission elite' of black collaborators the English language and culture. These people, who were, of course, competent in one or other of their mother tongues, were an invaluable instrument of British colonial policy.

> In practice ... British colonial policy was one of tolerating basic (primary-level) schooling in the relevant indigenous languages (i.e. for the small percentage of black children who actually went to school) and promoting English-medium instruction in a classically Anglocentric curriculum for the tiny mission elite. For the colonised people themselves, this meant that English language and English cultural traits acquired an economic and social value that was treasured above all else while their own languages and many of their cultural traits were devalued and often despised. A typical colonised mind or slave mentality became one of the most potent weapons of colonial policy, a programme built into the consciousness of black people (and of many whites) that ensured that the status quo was, by and large, accepted as good and just. All that one had to do was to climb up the socio-economic ladder which stood ready for every competent, abstinent and disciplined person to mount. If one had these attributes and was able to communicate in English, then – in the mythology of colour-blind individual rights – the sky was the limit!"
>
> Alexander (1989, p. 20)

This policy remained in force, by and large, until the accession to power of the Afrikaner National Party in 1948. As is now well known, this event led to a complete change in all domains of social life. Apartheid language policy, like apartheid policy generally, was calculated to bring about and entrench division among black people and their total subjugation to the white supremacist blueprints of the Broederbond and other think-tanks of the new political class. In most respects, this could be attained by means of the intensification of colonial and neo-colonial policies, but in others it was necessary to initiate quite different approaches. This was the case especially in education and

cultural life generally. The new rulers cunningly tried to make it appear that their policies in these spheres were in synchrony with the post-war British, French and Belgian
policy of decolonisation and with the movements for independence that were beginning to get momentum on the continent of Africa. Essentially, the apartheid policies
were directed towards the reinforcement of caste-like social structures which would
prevent social intercourse between different 'ethnic' and 'racial' groups while permit-
ting all essential mixing of the same groups in the economic sphere as long as this
buttressed the inherited system of super-exploitation and racial oppression.

In the sphere of language policy, the diktat of Dr Verwoerd says it all: 'Africans
who speak different languages must live in separate quarters ...' (cited in Alexander
1989, p. 21). The most notorious and also most profound historic effects of this policy
were to become manifest in education where it culminated in the massacres of young
students and workers associated with the Soweto uprising of 1976. One of the most
poignant ironies of South African history is the fact that a policy which set out to
Afrikanerise all of South Africa and to make Afrikaans the dominant language of
South African education saw its political source, the National Party, presiding over the
installation of a mainly English system of education from about 1977 onwards, as the
direct result of the mass action of the intended subjects of the engineering exercise of
the apartheid ideologues. For other reasons, we shall have to return to this subject
presently.

At all other levels of society, a policy of colonial (Afrikaans-English) bilingualism
was put into practice, one which in effect was an affirmative action programme for
Afrikaans-speaking whites for most of the apartheid period. During the forty years
that the policy lasted more or less intact, the Afrikaans language was promoted assidu-
ously until it became possible to use it in any of the high-status functions which had
previously been the exclusive preserve of English. This very fact, incidentally, is of the
utmost importance since it represents clear evidence of the possibility of successful
planning and at the same time indicates the existence of essential expertise in South
Africa for any future language planning initiatives.

The African languages were deliberately developed as *Ausbau*-languages, i.e. even
where it was possible in linguistic and political terms to allow the varieties of a particular language cluster or sub-group, such as the 'Nguni' group, to converge into a more
embracing standard written form, they were systematically kept separate through lexical
and other corpus-planning manoeuvres (for a definition and explanation of this concept, see Fishman, in Alexander 1992). The languages concerned were, moreover, starved
of essential resources in such a way that they could not be used in contexts that implied
or demonstrated real power. General social and political policies ensured throughout
the era of high apartheid that the African languages remained languages of low status.
The apartheid governments gave the impression that they were doing their best to
develop and modernise the African languages when in fact they were underdeveloping

them quite deliberately. With utmost cynicism, a mere sense of social progress (like special language boards for each of the African languages!) was given in order to impress 'the international community' which was under the spell of the movement for African independence and liberation from colonial rule at the time.

Language policy orientations of the oppressed and of the liberation movement

As we approach the late eighties and early nineties, which were to become the years of transition to democratic rule, the policy orientations of the oppressed people and of their representative organisations suddenly assume an importance and significance which they themselves had only dreamt of. The jump from theory (and often from mere rhetoric) to implementation was to prove in many spheres to be a perilous venture, the successful completion of which is in many cases hanging in the air.

To understand what the collective wisdom of the victims of racial oppression in regard to language issues in South Africa was, we will summarise here the effects on the consciousness of the dominated groups of the rulers' policies and of their own resistance to these policies. By the time the transition begins, we shall demonstrate, some people in the NGO sector had managed to integrate this wisdom with the results of comparative research on language policy and were thus able to make a significant contribution to the ensuing debates on language policy in the new South Africa.

Besides the virtual extinction of the languages of the Khoi and San peoples as a result of colonial and apartheid language policies, the most important result of this policy for the dominated classes at the level of social psychology was the relegation of the indigenous African languages to that of low-status instruments of communication in all spheres of life. The systematic, indeed systemic, neglect and underdevelopment of the African languages – especially in the economic sphere – engendered language attitudes among the black people of the country that have become the main obstacle to the formulation and implementation of a democratic language policy in the new South Africa. In a nutshell, the attitude took root that all that is worthwhile in life was (and is) accessible only through knowledge of English. (For all practical purposes, with the exception of the Western Cape, where a definite sentimental allegiance to the language exists, Afrikaans was never considered by black people to be anything more than a necessary but burdensome tool which might help to deal with the harsh realities of life in the land of apartheid). The African languages were taken to be good only for domestic and community purposes, languages of the heart but not really of the stomach. Let it be said as clearly as possible that these attitudes are perfectly understandable and are no different from those assumed by other peoples in similar situations in other countries and at other times. The source of the tragedy of the situation is to be sought elsewhere. We refer to the fact that none of the representative organisations of the oppressed people or of their leadership was able to transcend the limits of the dominant paradigm within which the language policy of the Union and of the Republic of South Africa was conceived and formulated. With two notable exceptions before the mid-eighties, the question of the status and functions of the African languages was never posed as part of a practical programme of political and cultural-political action. The following vacuous pontifications of a Dr Abdurahman on this vital question were, by and large, typical of three successive generations of black leaders:

> The question naturally arises which is to be the national language. Shall it be the degraded forms of a literary language, a vulgar patois; or shall it be that language which Macaulay says is 'In force, in richness, in aptitude for all the highest purposes of the poet, the philosopher, and the orator inferior to the tongue of Greece alone?' Shall it be the language of the 'Kombuis' (kitchen) or the language of Tennyson? That is, shall it be the Taal (Afrikaans) or English?
>
> Alexander (1989, p. 29)

With virtually no exceptions, the 'Taal' could be replaced in this quotation by any of the varieties of the indigenous African languages. Tragically, the anglocentrism of the political, and to some extent of the cultural, leadership of the oppressed people in effect, if not in intention, ensured the predictable outcome of the rulers' policies. For it is a sad fact that the African (or black) nationalist movement did not react to cultural oppression in a manner similar to that of the Afrikaner (or white) nationalists. At the critical time when Bantu education was being imposed on the black people, the leadership of the liberation movement across the board made a de facto decision to oppose Afrikaans in favour of English. The option of promoting the African languages while also ensuring as wide and as deep a knowledge as possible of the English language was never considered seriously for reasons connected with the class aspirations of that leadership. In effect, therefore, the hegemony of English, its unassailable position – as Chinua Achebe calls it – became entrenched among black people. Because it was the only other language that could compete with Afrikaans as a means to power (jobs and status) and as the only means to international communication and world culture at the disposal of South Africa's elites, it became, as in other African countries, the 'language of liberation'.

The important point, however, is that because of the attitudes referred to and the lack of foresight on the part of the leadership, the resistance to the cultural-political policies of the National Party did not result in the kind of cultural movement for the development of the African languages which, potentially at least, was completely possible. Unlike the resistance manifested by the *Afrikaanse taalbewegings* (Afrikaans language movements) in response to the cultural-imperialist policies of Lord Milner at the beginning of the 20th century, the even cruder Milnerist policies of Dr Verwoerd and his brothers merely gave rise to a middle-class strategy of convenience and evasion, namely, the strategy of promoting or tolerating the sole value of English. While there was no policy of actually denigrating the African languages, there was also no deliberate and systematic attempt to develop, modernise and spread the knowledge of the indigenous languages both for the intrinsic empowering value of such an exercise and as an explicit strategy of cultural-political resistance.

The crisis of language policy

It is our view, therefore, that what can be called the crisis of language policy is to some extent a crisis of our own making, i.e. the leadership of the liberation movement has to take some responsibility for reducing the political struggle to not much more than a struggle for the franchise. Their failure to do what leaders such as Amilcar Cabral did in Guinea Bissau by neglecting careful cultural analysis is now beginning to tell. It is as well to describe the nature of the crisis at this stage of this article since all progressive resistance attempts at grappling with 'the language question' were (and are) ultimately attempts to address this crisis.

In a nutshell, the crisis is characterised by the fact that the vast majority of our people do not at present have sufficient command of the high status languages (English and Afrikaans) to compete for well paid jobs and prestigious career options on a basis of equality with the 20% of the population who do have the requisite language skills. On the other hand, the language resources that the majority do have (most of the metropolitan and urban population can speak with high proficiency at least two – often radically different – African languages), are not validated in the market place. In other words, the indigenous languages are not accorded a status such that knowing them is of material or social benefit to the speaker outside the relevant speech community itself. This situation is made a thousand times worse by the fact that in South Africa, language and colour (or 'race') coincide to a very large extent because of the peculiar historical development of the labour market. Because of Bantu education specifically, a general semi-lingualism prevails and most of our youth have been handicapped in the merciless race for power, position and individual progress in the very competitive society in which we live.

Because the link between language, culture, science and technology has not been explored in depth in regard to the indigenous languages, we are faced with a situation where our children have to acquire the concepts in this vital area almost entirely via what is in most respects a foreign language (usually English) for them. Since they do not live in an English environment normally, there is no spontaneous reinforcement of that which they learn (by rote) in their classrooms. Add to this the fact that their general environment is devoid of print stimuli and of a natural-science culture, and it becomes crystal clear why it is that despite millions of Rands of investment in English second-language (ESL) programmes, progress in these fields is so slow.

Another derivative element of the crisis is the lack of confidence in the value of their first or home language (mother- or father tongue) that the total situation under apartheid produced. Most people have come to believe, for example, that the African languages 'do not have the words' for most modern objects and scientific concepts. As a result, speakers of the African languages tend to believe that it is essential that they learn English so that they can overcome this 'deficit' of their languages. There can be no more devastating self-inflicted wound than this. The loss of self esteem and of a dignifying self image is fatal. Without oversimplifying the matter, it can be said that this issue constitutes the greatest challenge to language planners and policy people in South Africa. It is at base a matter of cultural policy which is integrally related to the political and economic future of the society.

Language planning from below

Developments in the early eighties led to the establishment of the Education Co-ordinating Council of South Africa (ECCSA). Organisations such as the South African Committee on Higher Education, the Teachers' Action Committee, the Education Opportunities Council, the Trust for Christian Outreach and Education and the South African Council of Churches came together because of the increasing disruptions of the educational process through the tactics of 'ungovernability' to consider what should be done. ECCSA was the result and it was given the task of identifying the main obstacles to effective learning in the schools and universities. It spawned a number of educational initiatives, one of which was the National Language Project (NLP) which was established in 1986 as a community-based project, under the directorship of Neville Alexander. The NLP's purpose was to popularise language policy issues and raise awareness about the importance of African languages in education, especially in relation to literacy and accessible second language programmes in these languages. The focus of the NLP's work was towards rehabilitating the status of African languages and giving voice to proposals 'from below'. Consequently it piloted a number of language teaching and training programmes and a small newsletter which gradually grew into a quarterly magazine, *Language Projects' Review*, which after mid-1993 became known as *Bua!*

In addition to the promotion of African languages, the project staff believed that English would function as a lingua franca or linking language if everyone had adequate access to English Second Language (ESL) programmes. Consequently, ESL courses were designed to suit adult and child learners from community organisations, trade unions and co-operatives. Initiatives in schools only became feasible after resistance organisations had been unbanned in 1990.[1] The need for translation and interpreter training programmes and services was also identified and the NLP took the initiative to set up pilot service projects. One of the most important of these initiatives was a micro-study of interpreting needs in the health care sector, the first of its kind in the country (Crawford, 1994).

Language policy and planning research was pursued through building up a network of contacts on the continent and in other specific areas, particularly in India, Australia, North America and Northern Europe and a close examination of developments in these areas. The proposals between 1986 and 1990 were essentially three-fold:

- to promote the rehabilitation of the status of African languages in order to alter the unequal relationship amongst languages of the country
- to develop strategies to ensure that each South African could access adequately the English language for purposes of educational, economic and social empowerment and to insist that civil society has the right to make policy and planning proposals from below as it were

Alexander (1989, p. 63; 1992a)

In 1991 the NLP hosted an international conference, the focus of which was to examine issues pertinent to the standardisation and harmonisation of varieties of closely related languages as part of democratic language planning processes.[2] In particular, there was under discussion a revisitation of an earlier debate initiated from within the ANC, by Jacob Nhlapo in 1944. In the context of rehabilitating the functional status of African languages in South Africa, Alexander proposed that the standardisation of the written (not spoken) varieties within a cluster of languages, should proceed along a convergent path. In particular he proposed that future terminological and orthographic development within the Nguni and the Sotho cluster, respectively, should converge where possible and acceptable, in order to avoid further and unnecessary division amongst varieties of the same language cluster (Alexander 1989; 1992b). The convergent approach is a logical correction of an historical and aberrant segregationist language planning process. The existing differences between languages within the respective clusters, are partly an accident of history in that missionaries from different religious orientations and with differing levels of linguistic expertise were responsible for transliterating different segments of the Nguni and Sotho speech continua respectively, thereby creating what became 'standard' languages with different centres of autonomy. In this way, for example, isiZulu and isiXhosa came to be seen as distinct languages. By 1948, when the National Party came to power, these differences were not yet so consolidated as to be irreversible. The pro-apartheid government seized upon the evolving language situation and deliberately fostered further division within these language clusters in order to give linguistic effect to its policy of divide and rule.

Harmonisation offers an economically feasible opportunity for the maintenance of African languages in schools and in higher education. Thus, this proposal is in part a step to reversing – by means of continuing – the process of standardisation of the African languages. The proposal is to a large extent driven by the educational and economic benefits which harmonisation would contribute to the democratisation of South African society. The issues which it embraces have been hotly contested by two interest groups: those who have benefited from linguistic division and those who fear that this would result in the loss of some spoken varieties of African languages (see Msimang 1996; Alexander 1998). The proposal is in line with similar processes in other parts of Africa; notable examples are Standard Shona in Zimbabwe and Standard Igbo in Nigeria.

By 1992 the NLP's approach to ESL had changed. Information based on linguistic audits on the continent was revealing that exoglossic languages on the continent were not effectively utilised beyond a small middle class. Democratisation in Africa was not advancing, partly because the failure of the majority of people to become proficient in English, French or Portuguese effectively left them on the margins – outside main-stream economic activity and power (Heine 1992). The failure of ESL programmes in South Africa, including the ones initiated by the NLP, was assessed against findings elsewhere on the continent.

The NLP looked also to the work of Jim Cummins (1984; 1988), Skutnabb-Kangas (1988) and their colleagues and readjusted its position. Whilst it had always promoted the use of first language for literacy and as a language of learning throughout the early years of schooling, the project had also been persuaded of the sense of a gradual transition to English. Further research on language policy and planning paradigms and the critiques of James Tollefson (1991), Phillipson (1988) and Mullard (1988) about the international failure of ELT resulted in the consolidation of a proposal that education in South Africa should ensure that additive bilingualism become the focus of language in education policy (Heugh 1992). In essence this means home language maintenance throughout schooling in addition to a language of wider communication (English for most students) or an African language for speakers of Afrikaans and English.

During the period leading up to the finalisation of the interim Constitution (September 1993) the Project for the Study of Alternative Education (PRAESA) under the directorship of Alexander, and in co-operation with the NLP, developed more detailed proposals for multilingual schooling and in particular a new language in education policy (Heugh, Siegrühn and Plüddemann, 1995). PRAESA and the NLP, arguing in favour of a language-as-resource orientation toward language policy and planning, made joint submissions to the multi-party constitutional negotiations. One of their suggestions was that an independent body, a National Institute or Council of Languages, be established for the purpose of developing language policy, planning and development programmes in the country. Such a body would include the 'voices from below' in order that it might be able to reflect more accurately the language needs and preferences of the majority, as well as avoid the paralysis of centralised control and the potential this has for undemocratic practices.

The ANC

During 1990, immediately after the unbanning of the liberation organisations, the ANC revived its own internal debates about language policy, beginning with a Language Workshop in Harare. This was followed by the establishment of a Language Commission during 1991 whose role was both to inform and consult with the public on language matters (Crawhall 1993, pp. 20–23). The Commission as a sub-structure of the ANC's Department of Arts and Culture, released a document, 'African National Congress Policy Considerations' (1992) which includes the following:

> (T)he ANC supports the deliberate fostering of multilingualism in schools, adult education programmes, in the workplace and in all sectors of public life ...Though language experts argue that initial education is best conducted through the 'mother tongue'... large sections of black urban communities have already pressurised primary schools into beginning with English as the medium of instruction from day one ... Any language policy must reflect the voice of the people and this voice is more important than any model which emerges.

The ambiguities here were a reflection of those current in the broader context of South African society with regard to the weight given to the role of English *vis-à-vis* African languages. A significant contribution from within the ANC, but independently of the Language Commission, was made via a submission to the constitutional committee by Zubeida Desai and Robin Trew (1992).

They made a distinction between passive and positive rights where, by adopting a strong position on effecting rights (positive rights), citizens could be protected from 'exclusion from effective participation in public debate and to inequitable enjoyment of public services, justice, education, power and economic advancement'. Crawhall (1993, p. 21), in analysing this contribution, draws attention to the importance of a comment included in Desai and Trew's document:

> Language rights need to deal both with what Chinua Achebe has called the unassailable position of English, and with the fact that African languages are the primary linguistic resource of most South Africans.

This signalled a shift from an entirely rights based position within the ANC to a stronger, more vigorous approach to rights which acknowledges the view of language as a resource. However, the position of the more powerful forces within the ANC lay with the ambivalent position captured by the ANC's 'Language Policy Considerations'.

During 1992 the National Education Policy Investigation (NEPI), undertook a large scale study of education and policy alternatives for a transforming society on behalf of the ANC. A NEPI researcher, Kathy Luckett, after liaison with Alexander and the NLP, amongst others, formulated a bold proposal for 'national additive bilingualism' (Luckett 1992).

During 1993 a working group, under the auspices of the Centre for Education Policy Development (CEPD) at the University of the Witwatersrand, was commissioned by the ANC's Education Desk to arrive at a new language in education model. The recommendations which emerged from this group and those from the NLP and PRAESA were entirely compatible.

Negotiations between the ANC and the National Party

Whilst the language issue continued to be debated with vigour amongst sociolinguists in the country during 1993, the multi-party negotiations were really being conducted between the two strongest political forces, the National Party (NP) and the African National Congress (ANC). The significance of language did not hold equal weight for the two groupings. Afrikaner Nationalism was rooted in the 19th century European notion that language and 'national' (ethnic) identity are synonymous. The fear of losing political power was exacerbated by the fear that the identity of the Afrikaner people would be lost if the status of their language was diminished.

Thus the official status of Afrikaans could not, for the National Party and its supporters, be compromised. In contrast, the ANC did not attach a similar importance to language issues. Much greater significance was attached to removing or diluting a wide range of symbols of apartheid, of which language policy was only one. The official policy of the ANC was that all languages would be regarded as equal, but that none should be accorded official status. The unofficial conviction, however, was that English, for pragmatic reasons, would function as the official language of government. This view of English had its origins in the early history of the ANC when English had been regarded as a language of liberation and a language through which opposition to the Afrikaans-speaking government would be mediated.

Additionally, many senior members of the ANC had been exiled in English-speaking countries for many years prior to 1990 and had come to believe that English functioned as the *lingua franca* in the country. The National Party and lobbyists for the Afrikaans language began to reassess the position of Afrikaans *vis-à-vis* English. English remained and still is the greatest threat to the status of Afrikaans as a language of vertical use. Apartheid language policy, fuelled by a fear of the supremacy of English internationally, had failed. The privileged position of Afrikaans could certainly not continue if African languages remained weak whilst the position of English gained ground, by default and with the added impetus from African language speakers who had lost confidence in the wider functionality of their languages.

Ironically, the Afrikaans language lobbyists began to see that the future of the Afrikaans language would lie within a multilingual paradigm and a strengthening of the functional use of African languages. The idea that languages could be viewed as resources rather than as problems became increasingly attractive, and the Afrikaans language lobby shifted from the segregationist position to language as a right, in order to protect its inevitable minority situation in the future and a tentative commitment to language as a resource. The *Stigting vir Afrikaans* saw the strategic value that resources built up in the Afrikaans language, in lexicography and other areas of language development, might be shared with African language development agencies.

By early December 1993, as the multi-party constitutional negotiations were reaching closure, an eleventh hour compromise was that there would be 11 official languages. Afrikaans would not lose its official status and the equal status of 11 languages would be enshrined in the constitution. Additional protection for Afrikaans was built into the Interim Constitution with what has come to be known as the non-diminution clause:

> 3.(2) Rights relating to language and the status of languages existing at the commencement of this Constitution shall not be diminished, and provision shall be made by an Act of Parliament for rights relating to language and the status of languages existing only at regional level, to be extended nationally...
>
> Constitution of the Republic of South Africa 1993

In essence this clause was intended to provide a psychological guarantee to the white Afrikaans speaking community and to ease the passage of accepting change. Not only was Afrikaans to keep its status at national level, but in those former 'bantustans'/ homelands which had jettisoned Afrikaans as an official language, its status would be restored.

However, no such act of parliament was ever effected and the rights based principle enshrined here was not or could not be implemented. The other clauses in the constitution according official and equal status to eleven languages perhaps were never intended during the early hours of the morning on which they were drafted, to take real effect.

However, they set up a series of expectations which were bolstered by provisions for the establishment of an independent Pan South African Language Board

(PANSALB) whose responsibility it would be to promote multilingualism, further the development of languages and protect the rights of each linguistic community to use its language.

Developments after the elections of 1994

The interim Constitution took language from a segregationist perspective and a view of it as a problem to that of language as a right, in synchrony with the entire thrust of constitutional discourse. The powerful private sector had in the meantime shifted its thinking from segregation only as far as assimilation which assumes that the best answer to linguistic diversity is to leave ajar the door to English, for the speakers of languages other than English. This, in combination with the more widespread mono-lingual habitus of the western world and its impact on South Africa, was likely to neutralise the rights based approach to language in the constitution. What was ex-pected though from those language groups who had believed in the word of the constitution, was that government would make unequivocal statements of a commit-ment to multilingualism.

This has not happened, with the exception of a few public statements of the Minister of Arts, Culture, Science and Technology, Ben Ngubane, during the two and a half year period of his office (May 1994–end of 1996). On the contrary, the de facto use of English has become apparent in virtually all government work both in its internal and external communication. In general, the official bilingual practice of the past and steadfast use of two languages both in the public and private sectors was replaced with a practice of monolingualism, despite the constitution's 'non-diminu-tion' clause and the official status of eleven languages.

Language policy and planning developments, in the meantime, had been set in motion by the 1993 constitution. The most significant of these were:

- responsibility for language was brought under the newly structured Minis-try and Department of Arts, Culture, Science and Technology of the Gov-ernment of National Unity (GNU)
- the Senate, as custodian of the Pan South African Language Board, initiated legislation for its establishment
- the new Department of Education began interpreting the implications for a new schools' language policy
- the Department of Defence began a lengthy process of defining a language policy for itself

  (The first three of these will be discussed in more detail below.)

What was missing, however, was the clarification of an unambiguous national language policy which could guide all government and parastatal institutions. Thus, a haphazard approach was taken in many quarters, and in most instances the previous practice of official bilingualism gave way to a new monolingual practice of using English mainly, even in the national parliament. Ideally, a national language policy should have been integrated with the development of a strategic vision for the national economic development plan. This did not happen and the Reconstruction and Development Programme (RDP) of 1994, as well as its successor, the Growth, Employment and Redistribution: A Macro-Economic Strategy (GEAR) of 1996 have neither integrated nor included language policy and planning.

Arts, Culture, Science and Technology

The Minister of Arts, Culture, Science and Technology commissioned a Language Plan Task Group (LANGTAG) during the second half of 1995. The group included a wide range of language workers and experts, largely outside of government and these consulted as widely as possible over a six-month period January to June 1996. The task was to define the outline of a language plan, but it was not tasked with explicating policy and thus delineated only the principles upon which such policy ought to be based. The spectrum of domains covered by this group was broader than any other national planning activity undertaken either here or elsewhere and credit needs to be given to Ngubane for both the insight he demonstrated and the capacity to decentralise control of this activity. This initiative provided precisely what had been called for across Africa, namely the opportunity for voices from below to inform decision-making. The final LANGTAG Report, *Towards A National Language Plan for South Africa,* was submitted to the minister on 8 August 1996. Unfortunately, within a few months and before this initiative could be taken further the minister was replaced. The Department of Arts, Culture, Science and Technology is now, two years later, recasting the LANGTAG Report into a language plan of the department.

Nevertheless, the significance of the LANGTAG Report is undoubted. Language workers, planners and implementers accepted without reservation that the direction of language policy and planning developments in South Africa would be viewed from the perspective of language as a resource and a broadly empowering view of functional multilingualism. There was agreement that the LANGTAG process was to provide 'an enabling framework rather than to put forward a prescriptive blueprint' (LANGTAG Report 1996: 8). Attention was focused on the following areas: language equity; language development; language as an economic resource; language in education; literacy; language in the public service; heritage languages, sign language and augmentative and alternative communicative systems; and equitable and widespread language services.

Of special note is the prominence given to South African Sign Language in the Report. Whilst the sociolinguistic work with Sign Language is probably most advanced in Kenya, nowhere else has the natural language of the Deaf been included in a national language planning process.

Other initiatives specific to the work of DACST in relation to extending language services, notably in the attempt to establish a trial Telephone Interpreting Service for South Africa (TISSA), signal important changes. The significance of a telephone interpreting service, particularly in order to increase access to emergency services for persons who speak languages other than English and Afrikaans, needs to be acknowledged. Once established, this would provide a pivotal service upon which DACST could build additional services and effect an equitable language plan.[3] DACST has also taken the initiative, through its State Language Services, now National Language Services, to focus on the role of language in the economy and has encouraged exploratory research in this area (DACST 1996b; 1996c). Particularly useful have been their explorations into the role of languages and trade for South Africa with the rest of the continent (see for example DACST 1997).

The establishment of PANSALB

Delays in establishing the Pan South African Language Board after the election of 1994 resulted in an intervention by the Minister of Provincial Affairs and Constitutional Development, Roelf Meyer. Legislation for its establishment was enacted in September 1995 and the members appointed in April 1996. The terms and references of PANSALB include the language clauses of the 1993 Constitution and as mentioned above, include the notion of language as a resource. PANSALB's establishment was accompanied by many expectations from civil society as well as government. The constitutional provision for this body promised, in theory, that government would effect the promotion of multilingualism and development of African languages. The structural conditions, however, under which its legislation places it, have rendered the body instrumentally weak. The regulations under which the Board is required to operate have resulted in an organisational paralysis.

At the time of writing the Board has only just been given the licence to occupy its own offices, employ full-time operational staff, acquire standard office equipment and have control of its own funds. The Senate was replaced by the National Council of Provinces under the 1996 Constitution and this organ of government became the new custodian of the board. The funding, however, was channelled through DACST and the operationalisation was to be effected by the Department of Public Works. Each of these three parties, in turn, has refused to accept responsibility for unravelling the blockages. This has led to frustration both within the Board and without.

An unforeseen effect of the establishment of the Board was that many agencies from civil society assumed that the Board would take over, better co-ordinate or fund many of their initiatives. However, this has not happened and in the interim, these initiatives have either been put on hold or small organisations have ceased to make proposals. Thus the voices from below have been effectively silenced in the process. Other provisions in the legislation have taken PANSALB in the direction of establishing subsidiary structures, some of which are consistent with the overarching goal of achieving multilingualism in the country through complementary strategies, such as the establishment of advisory Provincial Language Committees comprising representatives from each of the languages/clusters of languages in the respective provinces. Other structures, namely Language Bodies specific for 14 languages or categories of languages, could be undermined by lingering separatist interests, which are not in synchrony with an interdependent approach to language development. Finally, because the 1996 Constitution substantively altered the language clauses, the legislation under which PANSALB exists has to be amended. Currently, DACST is driving a process to amend the PANSALB Act, without negotiating this with the NCOP, and in disregard of PANSALB's views. This particular issue compromises the autonomy of the Board and for this reason, the deputy-chairperson of PANSALB, Neville Alexander, resigned from the Board in March 1998. Thus a promising beginning for the impartial monitoring and nurturing of multilingualism in South Africa has met with early disappointment.

Department of Education

During the second half of 1995 the Department of Education commissioned a working group from the NGO sector to draft a working document for a new language in education policy and this draft was circulated for comment towards the end of that year. This department, as had DACST in its early years, drew on voices other than its own and the earlier language in education proposals of PRAESA formed the basis for this policy. The Minister announced the Language in Education Policy, based on the principle of additive bilingualism, in July 1997. South African Sign Language is treated as a twelfth official language which is a development of international significance. In essence, the policy promotes the use of the home language in addition to a second language (which for most students will mean English). An implementation plan for establishing this is only in its early stages of development, whilst a parallel but almost separate process of implementing a new curriculum, undergirded by the premise that English would be the main language of education is underway. Only in the final stages of drafting the new curriculum, *Curriculum 2005,* was an unfinished draft of the new language in education policy tacked on. Language in education issues were confined for the most part to a single area of learning during the curriculum planning process. That the role of the home language in the learning process, across the entire spectrum of education, was overlooked, despite a 90 year history of commissions and reports on education in Africa attesting to this, is almost inconceivable. The prospects of success-fully implementing a new curriculum and language in education policy which are not fundamentally integrated are slim. Furthermore, given the examples of language policy in other African countries, it is clear that unless the language in education policy is supported beyond education, particularly in a national economic development plan, a policy which promotes African languages will be undermined by the monolingual habitus and drive toward English.

Constitution of the Republic of South Africa 1996: implications

Shortly after the 1994 election, a new round of constitutional negotiations began within a structure known as the Constitutional Assembly. The final constitution was eventually adopted in May 1996 and amended on 11 October of that year. Again the language clauses could not be agreed on until the final days of negotiations in October. The 1996 constitution substantively altered the language clauses and scaled down many of the earlier provisions. On the one hand the expansive commitment to achieving the equal status of 11 languages was de-emphasised, while on the other hand, the lan-guage clauses were tightened to give greater guidance for the development of an ex-plicit national language policy as well as for a division of responsibility between gov-ernment and PANSALB (Constitution of the Republic of South Africa 1996, Clauses 6.(1)–(5)). These are summarised as follows:

> Principles which are the responsibility of government:
> – there are now 11 official languages in the country
> – the state has a responsibility to elevate the status and practical usage of those official languages which did not previously enjoy official status
> – national and provincial governments must use at least two official languages
> – national and provincial governments must regulate and monitor their equi-table use of official languages.
>
> Principles which are the responsibility of PANSALB:
> – PANSALB must promote, and create conditions for, the development and use of all official languages, the Khoi and San languages, and South African Sign Language and
> – PANSALB must promote and ensure respect for all other languages used in the country.

At this point it is necessary to return to the current impasse between DACST and PANSALB. The Board's position is that government must accept its constitutional responsibility to effect the official status of the 11 languages. The proposed amendments from DACST to the PANSALB Act, however, signal a shift of this responsibility from government to the Board. In particular, under the previous government a lexicography unit had been established for Afrikaans, *Die Woordeboek van die Afrikaanse Taal (WAT)*. This had been part of a complex array of language planning activities to elevate the status of and develop the language. Advisors to the new government have indicated that it is necessary to use the apartheid logic of establishing lexicography units for each of the official languages in order to give effect to their equal official status. Furthermore, advisors to the Minister of ACST have convinced him that all the lexicography units should be placed under PANSALB. The Board's view, however, is that it cannot be both an active participant in language development and an impartial monitor and advisor of such procedures. It also believes that this activity falls directly under government's own responsibility.

It is the view of the authors that in addition to these arguments, 11 separate lexicographic units are a logical extension of separate development, not of a process which is attempting to knit together a fractured society. Furthermore, separate lexicography units do not assist in the process of maximising interlinguistic communication. Whereas there is an excellent case, in our situation, for an inclusive and comprehensive dictionary of Nguni varieties and similarly one for Sotho varieties, 11 separate dictionary units seem neither economically viable nor helpful to communities attempting to bridge barriers in communication. Should government push ahead and insist that PANSALB take on the responsibility of 11 lexicography units, then it will become clear that the path chosen for language development is one which will not succeed in promoting multilingualism. At best it would create a veneer of an elevated status for African languages. At worst it will feed separatist and ethnic division.

The Commission

The 1996 Constitution also makes provision for the establishment of a Commission for the Promotion and Protection of the Rights of Cultural, Religious and Linguistic Communities. From a structural perspective this may present a number of difficulties. Firstly, if PANSALB is to survive, an overlap of functions between PANSALB and the Commission would have to be resolved. More problematic, however, is that the commission might undermine the work of the PANSALB precisely because its point of departure is from within a different paradigm. Skutnabb-Kangas and Cummins (1988, p. 394) astutely remark that: 'Social justice is not a question of "equality of opportunity" – which is the liberal view – but of "equality of outcome", and beyond.' The *raison d'être* of the commission is to support ethnic or separatist tendencies which would give ethnic groups the opportunity to set themselves up in conflictual relationships in competition for resources and privileges. Skutnabb-Kangas and Cummins crystallise the purposes behind language policy choice in the following: 'An emphasis on ... mother tongues can thus be for "exclusion", "pacification" or "empowerment".'

The Commission is only able to promise pacification, although several analysts fear that in the long term the Commission will feed ethnic ferment and competition for scarce resources. Alexander (1998, p. 3) alludes to the danger of tiny splinter groups emerging, each claiming a separatist identity and claiming rights to resources. Since the interdependence of languages and their communities receives scant recognition within the rights paradigm, the potential for conflict and adversarial relationships to thrive amongst linguistic groups is considerable. Hence any developmental activity initiated by PANSALB or any other agencies, based on the promotion of multilingualism rather than languages in isolation from one another, would be undermined. The provision made in the new constitution for this commission is symptomatic, however, of an environment in which political leaders do not understand language beyond its connections to cultural identities, histories and discrimination.

Notes

-   The first half of this chapter was composed largely by Alexander, the second half by Heugh.
1   The success of the literacy and language learning programmes was largely limited to creating a favourable environment for other, more successful ones to flourish. All the same the NLP successes and more often its failures, contributed to the adaptation or development of other proposals for language learning programmes and language services. Probably the most successful programmes emanated from another NGO, the English Language Teachers' Information Centre (ELTIC), located in Johannesburg.
2   The International Conference on Democratic Approaches to Language Planning and Standardisation, held by the National Language Project, at the University of Cape Town, 12-14 September 1991.
3   Internal difficulties within DACST have delayed the establishment of TISSA.

References

Alexander, N. (1998). *The Political Economy of the Harmonisation of the Nguni and the Sotho Languages,* Lexicos 8, AFRILEX series 8.

Alexander, N. (1989). *Language Policy and National Unity in South Africa/Azania,* Cape Town: Buchu Books.

Alexander, N. (1992a). 'Language Planning from Below', in R.K. Herbert (ed.) *Language and Society in Africa,* Johannesburg: Witwatersrand University Press.

Alexander, N. (1992b). 'Harmonising Nguni and Sotho', in N. Crawhall (ed.) *Democratically Speaking: International Perspectives on Language Planning,* Cape Town: National Language Project.

Alexandre, P. (1972). *An Introduction to Languages and Language in Africa,* London: Heinemann.

ANC (1992). *ANC Language Policy Considerations,* Department of Arts and Culture, Johannesburg: African National Congress.

Crawford, A. (1994). 'Black Patients/White Doctors: Stories Lost in Translation', paper presented at the First World Congress of African Linguistics, Kwaluseni, Swaziland.

Crawhall, N.T. (1993). *Negotiations and Language Policy Options in South Africa,* Cape Town: National Language Project.

Cummins, J. (1984). *Bilingualism and Special Education: Issues in Assessment and Pedagogy,* Clevedon: Multilingual Matters.

Cummins, J. (1988). 'From Multicultural to Anti-Racist Education: An Analysis of Programmes and Policies in Ontario', in T. Skutnabb-Kangas and J. Cummins (eds) *Minority Education: From Shame to Struggle,* Clevedon: Multilingual Matters.

Cummins, J. and Skutnabb-Kangas, T. (1988). 'Introduction', in T. Skutnabb-Kangas and J. Cummins (eds) *Minority Education: From Shame to Struggle,* Clevedon: Multilingual Matters Ltd.

Department of Arts, Culture, Science and Technology (1996a). *Towards a National Language Plan for South Africa,* Final Report of the Language Plan Task Group (LANGTAG), Pretoria: DACST.

Department of Arts, Culture, Science and Technology (1996b). *Language as an Economic Resource,* Language Planning Report No 5.1, Pretoria: DACST.

Department of Arts, Culture, Science and Technology (1996c). *The Economics of Language,* Language Planning Report No 5.2, Pretoria: DACST.

Department of Arts, Culture, Science and Technology (1997). *Trading with Francophone Africa: The Language Issue,* Language Planning Report No 5.6, Pretoria: DACST.

Department of Education (1997a). *Curriculum 2005,* Pretoria: Department of Education.

Department of Education (1997b). *Language in Education Policy,* Pretoria: Department of Education.

Desai, Z. and Trew, R. (1992). 'Language Rights in the Draft Bill of Rights: Protection from Linguistic Disenfranchisement' and 'Language Rights: Textual Suggestions'. Submissions to the ANC Constitutional Committee.

Dunjwa-Blajberg, J. (1980). *Sprache und Politik in Südafrika: Stellung und Funktion der*

Sprachen unter dem Apartheidsystem, Bonn: Informationsstelle Südliches Afrika.

Heine, B. (1992). 'Language policies in Africa', in R.K. Herbert (ed.) *Language and Society in Africa*, Johannesburg: Witwatersrand University Press.

Heugh, K. (1987). 'Trends in Language Medium Policy for a Post-Apartheid South Africa', in D. Young (ed.) *Language: Planning and Medium*, Cape Town: University of Cape Town.

Heugh, K. (1992). 'Enshrining Elitism: The English Connection', *Language Projects' Review*, 7 (3).

Heugh, K., Siegrühn, A. and Plüddemann, P. (1995). *Multilingual Education for South Africa*, Johannesburg: Heinemann.

Hirson, B. (1981). 'Language in Control and Resistance in South Africa', *Journal of African Affairs*, 80.

Luckett, K. (1992). 'National Additive Bilingualism', Working paper/report to NEPI. NEPI (1992) *Language*, Cape Town: National Education Co-ordinating Committee and Oxford University Press.

Mazrui, A. (1997). 'The World Bank, the Language Question and the Future of African Education', *Race and Class*, 38 (3).

Mesthrie, R. (ed.) (1995). *Language and Social History. Studies in South African Sociolinguistics*, Cape Town: David Philip.

Minister of Constitutional Development (1993). *Constitution of the Republic of South Africa Bill [B 212 - 93]*, Cape Town: Ministry of Constitutional Development.

Minister of Finance (1996). *Growth, Employment and Redistribution. A Macro-Economic Strategy*, Pretoria: Ministry of Finance.

Minister in the Office of the President (1994). *The Reconstruction and Development Programme (RDP)*, Pretoria: Government Printers.

Msimang, C.T. (1994). 'Language Attitudes and the Harmonisation of Nguni and Sotho', paper Delivered at the 1st World Congress of African Linguistics, 18-22 July, Kwaluseni, Swaziland.

Msimang, C.T. (1996). 'The Nature and History of Harmonisation of South African Languages', paper delivered at the Colloquium on Harmonising and Standardising African Languages for Education and Development, 11-14 July, University of Cape Town, Cape Town.

Mullard, C. (1988). 'Racism, Ethnicism and Etharchy or Not? The Principles of Progressive Control and Transformative Change', in T. Skutnabb-Kangas and J. Cummins (eds) *Minority Education: From Shame to Struggle*, Clevedon: Multilingual Matters.

Phillipson, R. (1988). 'Linguicism: Structures and Ideologies in Linguistic Imperialism', in T. Skutnabb-Kangas and J. Cummins (eds) *Minority Education: From Shame to Struggle*, Clevedon: Multilingual Matters.

Ranger, T. (1991). 'Missionaries, Migrants and the Manyika: The Invention of Ethnicity in Zimbabwe', in L. Vail (ed.) *The Creation of Tribalism in Southern Africa*, Berkeley and Los Angeles: University of California Press.

Reagan, T. (1987). 'Ideology and Language policy in Education: The Case of Afrikaans', in H. du Plessis and L. du Plessis (eds) *Afrikaans en Taalpolitiek: 15 Opstelle,* Pretoria: HAUM.

Republic of South Africa (1996). *The Constitution of the Republic of South Africa,* Act 108 of 1996, Pretoria: Government Printers.

Skutnabb-Kangas, T. (1988). 'Multilingualism and the Education of Minority Children', in T. Skutnabb-Kangas and J. Cummins (eds) *Minority Education: From Shame to Struggle,* Clevedon: Multilingual Matters.

Tollefson, J. (1991). *Planning Language, Planning Inequality,* Longman, London.

Vail, L. (ed.) (1991). *The Creation of Tribalism in Southern Africa,* Berkeley and Los Angeles: University of California Press.

Weinstein, B. (ed.) (1990). *Language Policy and Political Development,* Norwood: Ablex Publishing Corporation.

CHAPTER TWO

Culture, media and the intellectual climate: apartheid and beyond

Arnold Shepperson and Keyan Tomaselli

Cultural debate in South Africa has tended to coalesce around the contradictions between two traditional lines of cultural discourse. On the one side, 'culture' has been the target of Leftist intellectuals because of its *anthropological* meanings. In other words, there has been great awareness of the way the apartheid state used 'culture' as a means to bolster arguments for racial separation. Indeed, anthropologist John Sharp noted that government had actually 'created greater scope for ideological manoeuvre' by replacing the idea of 'race' with that of 'culture'. However, the approach remains authoritative, and even after 1994 issues of 'cultural medicine' and 'law as cultural expression' still recuperate the sense that cultures are somehow bounded and partially incommensurable wholes.

The other line of debate followed the 'High/Low/Popular' Culture polemic, which can be approached from the point of view of the political economy of symbolic production. This basically involves confronting conceptions of 'taste' followed by various media producers and then seeing how big business and other large economic stakeholders benefited from policies based on these conceptions. On the basis of whatever findings we might have made from these studies, then, we can see how to encourage those excluded by existing ownership or subsidy systems to go about producing 'culture' for themselves. Generally, the early reputation of the Centre for Cultural and Media Studies is most commonly associated with its work in media (print and electronic) and performance, based on critical interventions using this second line of thought.

However, these two lines of analysis raise the question of whether there is any specifically 'cultural' issue that somehow unifies them. On the one hand, too enthusiastic an anthropological approach leaves the researcher with an overarching study of 'the whole way of life' (Brill 1995; Williams 1958). In this case, cultural studies takes on an imperialistic character, colonising not only anthropology, but also sociology, psychology, political studies and geography. On the other hand, too close a focus on the taste paradigm drives the researcher into an ever-expanding textualization of the topic. In this case cultural studies becomes a kind of neo-positivist practice which reduces the complexity of the world into literary-linguistic 'structures'. In either case, it becomes difficult to place the issues which may be at stake. Interpretation becomes the sole methodological strategy, at the expense of accurate description, rigorous analysis and the formation and testing of situationally-relevant hypotheses.

The Theoretical Genesis of CCMS

Early cultural studies in Natal redeveloped Raymond Williams's and Richard Hoggart's original Marxist reworkings of literary criticism, through the work of the Birmingham Centre, to elaborate a broader and less economically dogmatic form of social and political criticism. Originally, English cultural studies did this by examining different kinds of expression as if they were texts having a similar status to those in the canons of intellectual literature. Forms of expression like radio and TV soap operas, workplace practices, sport reporting and broadcasting, youth fashion and pop music, for example, were studied in relation to wider trends in education, the economy, and English class values. This provided new ways of dealing with trends in the United Kingdom and later in America and Australia.

However, research in South Africa showed that the conditions here were rooted in a much more violent history of dispossession and exploitation than existing cultural studies approaches were able to explain. In England, Australia and America, for example, people of colour are minorities who are not formally excluded from the generally accepted system of civil rights. They have long had recourse to law and the courts when they found themselves subjected to discrimination at work, in their studies, or when they are looking for a place to stay.

South Africans had to deal with a situation where a minority had almost complete power and where this power was exercised in every sphere of life. There was also, however, a long tradition of radical resistance to this situation. The Contemporary Cultural Studies Unit therefore drew its students from among activists in the labour, education and development fields. The Unit's work used the Birmingham Centre for Contemporary Cultural Studies' critical approach to expand existing lines of resistance in trade unions, schools and community organisations, and to develop a situationally African approach.

The Unit opened up a cultural studies which synthesised the rigour of British cultural studies and meshed this with strategies developed by Latin American academic activists like Armand Mattelart and Paulo Freire, and later, Jesus Martin-Barbiero, amongst others. African philosophers like Paulin Hountondji and Abiola Irele, to name just a few, provided a fertile ground for recontextualising cultural and media studies within the Southern African socio-political environment. However, this development did not depend on the emerging 'disciplinisation' of cultural studies in the USA, Australia and elsewhere. So far, South African cultural and media studies has avoided becoming the contested 'property' of communications studies, literary criticism or anthropology (Hardt 1992; Brill 1995; Marcus and Myers 1996).

Historical background

The Centre for Cultural and Media Studies began life in 1985 as the Contemporary Cultural Studies Unit, within the Faculty of Humanities at the University of Natal, Durban. The name change occurred at the end of 1989. From the start, the Unit sought to provide a location for those who were confronting cultural issues from within their disciplinary trajectories. A crucial dimension of the Unit's mission was also to provide a theoretical home for anti-apartheid cultural activists. Initially, the Unit developed its theoretical position from that of the Birmingham Centre for Contemporary Cultural Studies, with additions based in oppositional film theory, political economy and Peircean semiotics. The general thrust of this early phase is reflected in contributions to *Rethinking Culture*.

Rethinking Culture became something of a *cause célèbre*, which collated into a single volume seminar papers which had previously been individually distributed. Both reprintings of the books and the individual papers sold nearly ten thousand copies not only to academics, but also to communities of struggle, especially in the Eastern and Western Cape. Other books (Tomaselli 1988b; Tomaselli and Louw 1991; Louw 1993; Mpofu, Manhando and Tomaselli 1996) both critique and extend the First-World wisdom of cultural studies by drawing on experiences of both resistance and government.

Tomaselli and Louw's exhaustive survey of departmental communication and media studies emphases during the 1980s argues at length that the Mass Democratic Movement mobilised cultural studies in its development of communication, media and mobilisation strategies.

Work on broadcasting and cultural identity by Ruth Teer-Tomaselli and her co-authored work in political economies of the South African press and broadcasting, have informed MA and PhD theses around the world. Like the Centre's community-aligned praxis, Teer-Tomaselli brought to the SABC a pragmatic form of cultural studies which impacted on the life and thought of the nation at large at its most crucial historical moment. This was not the sort of post-LitCrit as cultural studies has largely become within literary studies.

Other vectors incorporating domestic cultural studies include the work of Ian Steadman and Belinda Bozzoli at the University of the Witwatersrand, Johan Muller at the University of Cape Town, Lynn Dalrymple at the University of Zululand, and Les Switzer at Rhodes, among others. Aside from individual articles, books and chapters in books, there are more than enough South African cultural studies-influenced journals like *Critical Arts*, which initiated the field in South Africa in 1980 with regard to media and cultural studies, later followed by disciplinarily oriented journals like *South African Theatre Journal*, *Agenda* and *Pretexts*.

All of these post-dated the culturalist strand of cultural studies popularised by the Wits History Workshop and work by Ari Sitas and the Junction Avenue Theatre Group on African performance, not to mention the seminal social humanist historical writings of Charles van Onselen. Cultural studies has been occurring in South Africa for over 20 years; it is not in the future imperfect as some recent collections seem to have suggested (Van Staden 1996; Cooper and Steyn 1996).

The existing work reconstitutes European theories into local contexts, rigorously redefining the field in terms of local discourses, values and heritages. Indeed, some, like Sitas, pioneeringly tried to start from scratch, to start from Africans and Africa. Indeed, even the early BCCCS-derived and culturalist approaches were criticised for not sufficiently acknowledging African gnoses (Masilela 1988).

But conservative cultural theory as mobilised by Afrikaner Nationalists in South Africa actually has its origins in the 1930s. It was this Khuyperian and neo-Fichtean strand which was later contested by the Unit in its research, community struggles and teaching. Handel Wright also notes that the topics and issues which contemporary US and other cultural studies schools claim in direct lineage from British scholarship, actually engaged people over a much longer time-span and geographical spread. The problems aired in the name of the Harlem Renaissance of the 1920s; the work of Russian 'Culturology' in the 1930s; and Ngugi wa Thi'ongo's indigenous performance group of the 1970s, all add to a wider record that is finally gaining acknowledgement as media and cultural work deserving recognition and respect.

The experience of cultural studies at CCMS and other centres is not the record of a discipline becoming settled amongst other disciplines. All the practitioners and publications cited above follow the 'tradition', if you like, in which cultural studies is a *field* within which disciplines may plant various seeds. Thus many of the South African interventions in the field came about through dramatic theory and popular performance (Steadman 1989; Dalrymple 1987; 1997).

Further work in education has seen cultural studies eliciting responses from South African scholars who want to make interventions developed from local experience in local conditions, making recommendations which are applicable to local practitioners in a variety of contexts. Since its inception the South African sector of the field has also featured a visual anthropological orientation.

Travelling Theory and Getting Back to Basics

CCMS's position is that cultural studies does not study some object or text or interpretive community called (a) culture. There is no such *thing* as (a) culture. Rather, there is a set of related forms of behaviour, conduct and action which constitute the *project of culture*. What this means is that the first step in any cultural studies research has to focus on how the topic relates to the practical business of culture. This is only circular if 'culture' is considered as a common noun. Following Charles Sanders Peirce, however, we take any common noun to actually contain some verb, some core reference to something which somebody *does*.

'Culture' is derived from the Latin *colo, colere*, which means among other things to 'tend, to look after, to live in a place'. The actual word, 'culture', comes from the past perfect participle of *colo* and thus might be said to refer to the accomplishment to date of some business of tending, looking after and living in a place (Shepperson 1995). Now the primary problem is that somehow cultural studies has to keep track of how this original sense, which would have been quite obvious to thinkers like Coleridge and Herder, remains sedimented in the kinds of interpretive mayhem that passes for the concept of culture today.

The concept of culture is a very European one. As a key term, it originated in the environment of specifically European problems which in turn were the result of the emerging modern age. The export of the concept followed the export of so much other baggage of the Modern Age: democracy, human rights, preventive medicine, social health and so on. Other less valued baggage includes imperialism, the division of misery characterised by global poverty, and media imperialism among others. In short, every claim to cultural independence, the democratisation of culture and similar issues, is derived from the export of a very specifically modern context of meaning.

Thus taking recourse to American and European experience does not necessarily mean seeking answers from there. Today people can draw on this work because the uneven, frequently brutal, spread of modernity makes it relevant by helping to see the concept of culture as problematic on a global scale.

To retain the original cultural studies link with the tradition of radical critical work, and since the traditional political-economic discourse of this tradition has become incoherent, one programme focuses on relating this Peircean-pragmatic phenomenology of the concept to the post-marxist radical discourse. Thus certain interventions in the fields of cultural policy, health media and communications, intercultural media, and the ethical dimension of multiculturalism draws on typical representatives of the post-Marxist tendency like Agnes Heller and Hannah Arendt. Obviously, it could be argued that this approach simply replicates the curse of cultural studies, by borrowing theories out of context. However, this accusation must take into account just what happens in an intellectual climate. Theory is a special case of language, and is proper to the realm of specialised intellectual discourse. What theory tends to confront therefore is other theories about something. When contesting theories enter the discourse we variously begin to talk of Paradigm Incommensurabilities, Paradigm Shifts, Conceptual Aporiae, Category Mistakes and the Indeterminacy of Radical Translation.

In much contemporary cultural theory this only leads to the indefinite expansion of writing, raising the quite valid observation that meaning is never fixed into a dogma. Any question about semantic stability, then, becomes another irrelevant example of the questioner's contextually-challenged consciousness. Seeking grounds for action is to be treated with pity by postmodernists because there no longer is any 'ground'. There is supposedly only the shifting play of signifiers.

This kind of interchange actually carries within it a special kind of truth, one in which the current trendy discourse actually partakes. This is the interpretation of *modernity* as the condition applicable to an age when the human world is expanded by its own *Record*. Theories are in a double sense both a kind of meta-record, and indistinguishable from the wider record itself. What modernity came to recognise as its distinguishing characteristic is that what is written *and printed* will remain constant from one generation to the next – though interpretations will differ.

Modernity does not have a single epistemic, theological, cosmological or other kind of *tradition*. Authority resides in the Record for a good reason: if Immanuel Kant or Wilhelm Meister or WEB Du Bois or EW Blyden or Sol Plaatjie or Paulin Hountondji printed a representation of some sort, we can consult *that* representation in the form *they* recorded it. In modernity, in short, authority is preserved and transmitted by the representation of its originator. What thus distinguishes modernity is the always-present capacity for Records to present the representations of those whom we cannot consult directly. Taking someone else's word about how our predecessors represented themselves is not necessary. Records of the contexts in which they were/are working, and which shaped their theories, are always open to debate. We can retrieve the representation and judge for ourselves the relevance or otherwise of what *they* wanted to argue.

The qualities of an *intellectual climate* in the modern world are a function of the kinds of selection that people can, ought, or need to make from the record. Our experiences as cultural studies practitioners in the media field show that there are several such climates present in the South African environment. The latest strategic project to promote an 'African Renaissance' is actually a serious attempt to define the meta-climatic intellectual environment for transformation in the wider regional and continental context. When people speak of 'Renaissance' there is a broad and inevitably contradictory record of what the term represents. This is not just a sort of lexicographic relation between the term and its correlates or 'meanings', but the actual Record of the Renaissance *and the Record of representations which in fact constructs the period as a Record in its own right.*

Montaigne, Machiavelli, Raphael, Michelangelo, Leonardo Da Vinci and all the others did not invent the term 'Renaissance'. But the Record shows that subsequent representations *constituted* their representations as 'The Renaissance'. Other representations exist also: the Borgias, the Avignon Papacy, the Council of Trent, and so on, which tell us more. What we may want to think of as a kind of general spiritual movement was nothing of the sort. People were also pretty brutal, and nobody from the period represents a single 'paradigm figure' or 'founding father' (Heller 1978). It's all very well to recall the glories of the Sistine Chapel ceiling; in the same period Giordano Bruno was burned at the stake. Women demonised as witches were tortured and immolated. There *ought to be* a lesson in this when we choose our terminologies!

Modernity and Postcoloniality

It is not a question of 'what is' modernity, as if one can by virtue of an existential identity 'locate' or 'reify' modernity. Instead, the concept covers a multiplicity of contested and contestable breaks with inherited conditions. It is 'contested' precisely because modernity is *political* in its origins with the representations of Machiavelli, Locke, Hobbes, Hooker and Grotius, among others. The notion is also 'contestable' precisely because it is *historical* in its locations and trajectories, since the work of Vico, Gibbon, Hegel, Marx and others. Together, these characteristics account for the *normativity* of the concept of Modernity.

Modernity is not 'centred' either: its origins and developments span generations and continents, and did not always occur in sync. 'The troubles' of Northern Ireland and the former Yugoslavia may seem to stem from the 'same' modern delinking of religion and politics. However, each situation comes from very different trajectories, in terms of religious and political struggle, attempted solutions (and related failures), and breakdowns of trust. The conditions which people in each context sought to address in order to improve their respective lots were never the same. Completely different hopes and frustrations are evident in each case. However, this does not exempt either situation from the stress of modernity. These situations indicate that modernity itself is pluralistic in character.

In the colonial and post-colonial context, every unit of oppression and resistance (dominions, crown colonies, empires, and so on) had conditions which imperialism impacted upon and from within which the units of liberation emerged. Each post-colonial position is uniquely liberated, although also generally related to other contexts of oppression and liberation. We need some way to assess the *stance towards modernity* inherited in each context of struggle and liberation. Elaborating a norm for judging a standpoint towards another normative concept is inappropriate. This is more than the fallacy of the many questions, or the potential regress to infinity of norms that we might determine as each judgement is made. Rather, the issue comes to a practical closure when such norms enable us to confront the question 'what is to be done in the here and now?' Because the origins of the post-colonial condition are as pluralistic as the many different ways imperialism impacted on the liberation project, there is little in common between the ways people in different contexts act in response to this question.

The Record has grown since the Renaissance. *Nobody can claim to know the entire record.* Modernity, no matter how 'constructed' a term, throws up a record too vast for any individual to scan and know. Raymond Williams identified as one dimension of culture, the 'recorded culture' of a period, from which people elaborate a 'culture of the selective tradition' (Williams 1965, pp. 66–68). In this light, the real question is therefore not 'what do we need to do to kick-start the African Renaissance?' Instead, the programme based on post-Marxist political theory and pragmatic cultural analysis demands that we ask 'what is the best judgement we can make of Africa's position in, and stance towards, modernity?'. Addressing the latter will perhaps clarify what we will not find when we try to answer the former.

Migrating theories are as much sweepings from the record as they are a kind of metalinguistic morphological transformation of some 'original' theories. We *choose* from the record we know. The 'migration' of theory is therefore the transfer of individuals' or collectives' familiarity with a selection of the record, from one context to the other. This is not to say that people can't say anything new. Rather, every selective record can contain validly new representations generated on the grounds of peoples' familiarity with the selection. Taking representations from a context in which the selected record is acceptable, into another context, carries the risk of marginalising that original representation. This is because the new context contains more or less radically different selections of the total record. When theories travel, they must adapt from their origins within one stance toward the record of modernity, to the conditions proper to a possibly very different stance to another selection from the same grand record of modernity.

Media in societies in transition

It is decisive that the business of developing or raising endowments into talents is one that takes place *between generations*. In general, the upshot of the modern age has been the proliferation of historically-defined generations. This came about because in modernity the classical environment of generations, the household, has been effaced into the Social Realm (Arendt 1958, pp. 8–9). Natural generations are continually born as strangers into the realm of the intimate, and culture essentially refers to the project of raising people so that they become not-strangers in the social realms of modernity.

When a large-scale change in circumstances comes about, for whatever reason, then the cultural affect is generally different across both the natural and the social generations which are present when that transformation is affected. In general, as Raymond Williams (1963, p. 101) noted, there are at least three generations present in a situation subject to these kinds of transformations.

Thus it is possible to see the whole 'post-modern' phenomenon as a generational-cultural rather than an epistemological or ontological condition (Heller and Fehér 1988). The idea of a democratically diverse media sphere is still new enough as an institution for at least one generation of people to remember the 'good old days' when they could be educated, informed and entertained in a comfortable, if limited, national environment. At the same time there is second set of generations, whose lives could hardly be said to have been well-ordered in the recent past, for whom such media represent another introduction into a changing order of life. Finally, there is a generation which is growing up into a world in which media of this nature will conceivably be part of the overall media background, a factor which will simply *be* there as they grow. Within these three broad generational groupings, there are several possible sub-generations, based on the outcomes of apartheid's ethnic-cultural institutional divisions.

These broader generations and their relevant sub-groups live together in the same world, both formally and informally. Formally, they now inhabit a socio-political environment in which the interests and need of all are of equal concern at the level of government. Informally, though, their worlds remain both culturally and structurally differentiated from each other *as a hangover from the excesses of apartheid*. At a crude level, the cultural differences between these 'media generations' correspond to the very different ways in which people develop their endowments into the kinds of talents with which they can meet their needs.

In all three of these generations, and particularly the first and second, people view the achievement of some higher standard of education and standard of living as the ideal accomplishment for those who will grow up into the new socio-political environment. From a media point of view, then, one can anticipate that – whatever the form of media control which emerges – these constituencies will be most aware of potential educational shortcomings of media in relation to their (grand)children. In other words, no matter how media - whether print, digital or broadcast - are controlled, these constituencies will react according to what kinds of effects they perceive on their children's educational possibilities.

The point is actually quite plain once this generational clarification has been made: in a context of transformation in which *equity* is one of the driving principles of change the perceptions of those who have the most to gain and the least to lose cannot be forgotten. If politics is indeed the realm of activity in which the new (that is, *unexpected*) is possible, then continued marginalisation of those who are presently the most marginal could have some uncomfortable socio-cultural outcomes in the future.

Media and the intellectual climate in transition

The political nature of transition must impinge on the ways different generations encounter the changes of circumstance in which the transition takes place. The point is not that ideas *determine* material conditions or vice versa. Instead, *changing ideas* must accompany the ways people in the various generations encounter their worlds in the time over which the transition occurs. Crucially, the cultural dimension of this process affects each generation differently. Each must discern and ponder the different sets of options which transition brings to their specific experiences, needs and desires.

Thus someone who is a member of the generation least familiar with democratic media may well find that the plurality of voices unleashed constitutes threat to the identity she or he desires for the growing generation. In another context, a member of the same generation may well consider the new media as a challenge which they may not be able to meet but which nonetheless offers greater opportunities for their children. In either case, the generation conscious of transition will draw on its familiar discourses and values to judge the situation and on the basis of these judgements *influence younger generations* to develop their talents accordingly.

The issue here is that in order for a new media environment to emerge, practitioners must recognise that there is a plurality of such generational relationships in place. There is very little information upon which to predict how people are going to respond to the transition: the development of growing generations' interpretations of media is a political question precisely because every response is likely to contain some unexpected elements in it.

It is thus conceivable that dividing media strategies along generational lines will reproduce previous political divisions in new guises. However, we believe that when viewed in relation to the 'post-modern' condition and its stress on cultural diversity and identity discourses, the generational analysis can help to define a new way of looking at the relation between the nation, culture and media.

Such a definition is beyond the scope of a presentation as brief as this, but there are some pointers as to how such analysis might work. These relate to the form of the state, the function of government and the changing nature of political interaction:

1   The State in a world of globalising economic and cultural production remains tied to the territorial reach of infrastructures, and the administration, maintenance and establishment of these (Mann 1988). In a country like South Africa, therefore, existing infrastructures will form the basis upon which new media structures will develop. This does not just mean using the broadcast, cinema, press, and telecommunications infrastructures. The point here is that not *every* person in each generation will have comparable needs for using the full range of new media. State, public service, community and

commercial media policies therefore need to include the thoroughly non-media but demographically decisive business of an efficient population census which can provide data identifying where potential audience needs may emerge. In other words, media infrastructures have to be effectively targeted to reach the audiences most likely to need them.

2 The Government of countries is becoming less and less identifiable with the administration of functions of the state. This has to do with the ways populations accost institutions when problems need to be addressed. In the developed world, the emergence of 'posted' generations divided along regional, educational and class lines means that in many cases the present generations don't encounter the problems government was designed to solve. Put differently, many public media institutions in the developed world reflect needs and interests of people two or more generations ago and are not constituted to deal with the issues that plague the generations present and maturing in the world now. In South Africa, a public medium like the South African Broadcasting Corporation (SABC) has the advantage of being capable of making demographically precise determinations of just who, how many and where these constituencies are. Government thus doesn't have the luxury of administering uniform institutions: it must provide means to facilitate communication between diverse government and civil society institutions in general. As a factor in public service broadcasting, for example, government must add its emerging *communications* function to the capacity available to the service provider, without itself doing the broadcasting.

3 Finally, politics in the era of a multiplicity of community identities would seem to revolve around networking more than any other activity. Sectors in the public realm, the non-governmental institutions, economic institutions and so on to mention just some of the fields of activity, all have different agendas on the face of it. However, the well-being of all these sectors can be understood to have a collective aspect within the geographical limits of the and in relation to the communicative networks of government. The issue therefore is whether the plurality of South Africa's generational constituencies' needs and interests can be met by these sectors. It is here that media provide the breadth of record from which people in their various generational, cultural and social surroundings can choose to break out of intellectual climates defined by narrowly sectional or sectarian interests.

Clearing out the Greenhouse Gasses

We suggest that South Africa's media sector has as its primary role a duty to contribute to the development of the wider regional networking functions of the whole range of governmental, civil and economic sectors. This is only an outline task, however. The media sector must therefore strive to *account* for the diversity of generational cultural experiences present and which define, however much by default if not actively, the 'media public' at large. These issues don't define the limits of media practice. Our analysis, obviously, doesn't provide any conclusive solution to the problem of funding, but it can serve to define the limits of the constituencies the different media providers must strive to reach. Once this is known, then the numbers make it possible to generate real production and distribution costs.

Our analysis clarifies the first strategic thread of any 'Renaissance': Africa's representations must be added to the record. However, our analysis shows that there is a broad record which already defines many voices present in the environment. Thus the objective is to nurture a readiness to explore the record as widely as people's conditions allow. Where conditions hamper this, the focus must be on the conditions and not on the people (Guambe and Shepperson 1997). The reason for this lies in a subtle difference in the ways people encounter the record. On the one hand, they encounter a limit of the record defined by that which they are *told not* to read. This states that the record consists of that which one ought to read, and that which one ought not. Conversely, people encounter the openness of the record as conditions encourage or discourage them from reading that which they *have not been told* to read.

The post-colonial world in general – this means much more than 'Africa' – must recover the globally declining talent for reading as an end in itself. One way of looking at previous development is to see these programmes as introducing a canon, a fixed and limited record that purportedly contains all the answers to whatever is needed to get from here to there. Under these conditions, reading is an institutionally instrumentalised activity that people need to do. One reads to pass an examination, upgrade one's qualifications, or to familiarise oneself with the latest technology. This reproduces the notion that education in general means demonstrating an ability to reproduce the selection from the record that constitutes a syllabus. In the context of development, this means a travelling curriculum that will reproduce a population which is a copy of some or other original context in which the curriculum worked. It does not include the library from which teachers selected the texts from the record to develop the syllabus in the first place.

However, the openness of the record demands the whole library. Indeed, development demands an entire network of libraries which spreads the record across the widest range of conditions. It is only in this way that people can become aware that there is plenty that they will not be told to read. The political imperative of the Renaissance, therefore, is to nurture and encourage people's curiosity to test and transgress the limits of the record they encounter. Conversely, the political risk of the Renaissance is that reading of this nature necessarily gives rise to original interpretations that contradict the limited record of the curriculum. Whatever we set up today, therefore, must accommodate the new and unexpected representations that reading as an end in itself will engender. In the light of this, what does the present media situation in South Africa hold out as a basis upon which to move forward? Or is the situation one in which somebody has to start from scratch?

The media landscape I: print media before 1996

Throughout the late 1980s, there were two national newspapers aimed at South African black readership, the *Sowetan* and the *New Nation*. The final edition of *New Nation* appeared in 1997. Battered by falling readership, a lack of finance and the absence of experienced editorial staff after 1994, the paper barely survived the installation of the democratic dispensation it had fought to install. On the other hand, *Sowetan* steadily maintained market share and after 1994 was one of very few print media to increase circulation. *Sowetan* focused on a specific market based on race, whereas *New Nation* followed the policy of non-racialism espoused by movements like the United Democratic Front (UDF) and African National Congress (ANC). Ideologically, therefore, the *Sowetan* took a somewhat different stance from that of *New Nation*, espousing a Black Consciousness (BC) position.

These developments apparently reinforced two trends which emerged after the 1980s: first, the apparent entrenchment of a global market-driven political economy; and, secondly, a renewed (or revived) stress on ethnic, racial and cultural politics of identity. There has been a general collapse of local economic security with the end of the ideological tensions of the Cold War. Prior to 1988 people could make a clearly intelligible choice between State and Market systems of socio-political organisation. It is arguable that the state paradigm collapsed because centrally-planned systems are too slow to adapt to changes in means and forces of production. This means that workers and others placed at a disadvantage within market economies no longer need to be protected, as a means to prevent them rebelling as a class. Indeed, it is arguable that there is no working class anywhere which can even command a majority vote for a representative parliament, let alone unite into a revolutionary force (Hirst 1990, pp. 151–152).

In South Africa, apartheid created the local situation where a small minority controlled a relatively large unrepresented majority of unskilled labourers. This made it possible to deploy proletarian organisational strategies quite successfully, based on a selection of the State paradigm record. But the change of representative status among the country's majority in 1994 introduced rural people, women previously denied residential status in urban areas, the peri-urban population, among others, into the broader 'media public'. After 1994 such people all enjoy formally equal representation and the classical working class is now a distinctly privileged minority in the broader South African context.

This impacted *New Nation's* circulation because its community of readers had shifted dramatically after 1994 in terms of ideology, aspiration and power relations. *New Nation* was part of the vibrant 'alternative media' sector under apartheid, which not only challenged conventional journalism practices, but were organically connected to community-based religious, civic, student and women's organisations and trade unions (Tomaselli and Louw 1991, pp. 8–9). The wide-range of alternative publications attempted to fill the structured absences of the state and corporate media. As such they contested the dominant ideology through developing a critical awareness of the history and context of the struggles of marginalised communities (Patel 1985, p. 14). No single publication could therefore be said to duplicate the role of another. *New Nation* fulfilled a unique role, not only when compared with other ecumenical newspapers but in relation to the progressive press as a whole. It was the only nationally circulated newspaper which provided a vehicle for the expression of the aspirations of the urban working class.

As a corporate entity, *Sowetan* responded to the growing awareness that black South Africans, no matter how economically oppressed, constituted a market worth penetrating. In 1979, a marketing counsellor for the McCann-Erikson advertising agency, for example, noted that blacks accounted for 75% of the country's soft drink consumption, 60% of beer, 54% of tobacco, 50% of detergents, 40% of clothing and footwear and 40% of expenditure on food.[1] *The Sowetan* was launched in February 1981. It was initially distributed mainly in the Pretoria-Witwatersrand-Vereeniging area and by 1987 had a circulation of 160 000.[2]

According to the 1987 All Media Products Survey, the readers of the *Sowetan* were almost all black and belonged to the two highest income groups among blacks. Some studies have suggested that the ideological role of corporate and state media in the 1970s and 1980s was to promote the emergence of a middle class of black consumers.[3] At that time, both English and Afrikaner capital used product advertising as an ingredient of just such an overall strategy (Holt 1988, p. 3).

On the other hand, the *Sowetan* and other comparable titles from time to time functioned as vehicles of vociferous opposition to apartheid. For example, *Drum* magazine is famous for its exposés in the 1950s and 1960s on a number of contentious issues such as the use of prison labour on farms, the brutality of prison conditions for blacks, and the repressive measures of apartheid from a black point of view. It is arguable that *New Nation* followed the kind of advocacy journalism encouraged by Michael Traber, William Biernatzki, Robert White, and others. *Sowetan*, in turn, followed conventional commercial reporting procedures. As a bi-weekly naturally *Sowetan* would have had to operate to deadlines, and as a commercial medium would also have made good use of wire services. As a weekly, however, *New Nation*'s staffers had the advantage of being in a position to interrogate issues from a wider perspective, by being able to contact and interview a broader range of commentators, for example.

The contraction of the left-alternative media, in the first instance, came about primarily because after 1994 funding agencies had to accommodate the shift from activism against the state to a policy of affirmation of the new representative state. The constitutional transformation of 1990 to 1996 removed the grounds for many organisations' *raison d'être*. The developmental problems bequeathed to the new and legitimate state by the old could be confronted. As a result, funding agencies channelled their support into government initiatives aimed at redress. *New Nation* was bought by the *Sowetan* in 1995 and survived for only another two years (see Mpofu 1996). This came about because its readership and editorial staff had failed to grasp the underlying struggle which both led to and ultimately destroyed apartheid. After looking in the next section at alternative cinema provision, we will discuss the ways that a cultural and media studies approach can overcome this lack of alternatives.

The media landscape II: cinema before and after apartheid

In South Africa it is reasonable to suggest that many people are conscious of cinema. But they do not experience it as a need. Cinema is part of the equipment people may or may not encounter (Heidegger 1962, p. 98). Developing a new cinema culture depends equally on both giving existing generations what they want, and developing new generations' ability to identify democratically valid options within which some may elect to have their endowments raised into cinematic talents.

A variety of studies have presented a damning critique of the ways in which successive South African film policies reproduced the racial and class divides of that unhappy country (Tomaselli 1988a; Blignaut and Botha 1992). One of Tomaselli's methodological approaches was the use of political-economic analysis to demonstrate the control over production and distribution under apartheid to keep black and white separate culturally.

Between 1910 and the late 1980s South African cinema was fairly active, producing films ranging from the seminal *De Voortrekkers/Building a Nation* of 1916 to Jamie Uys's internationally popular series of *The Gods Must Be Crazy* films. From 1913 on, the industry was controlled by I.W. Schlesinger's entertainment monopoly (Gutsche 1972). Apart from theatre and for a short while in the 1930s, radio, this covered production (African Film Productions), distribution (African Consolidated Films) and exhibition (African Consolidated Theatres). Originally, American interests had con-

tracted to distribute their wares through African Consolidated Films (AFP) for showing in African Consolidated Theatres (ACT) venues (Gutsche 1972).

The industry rapidly fragmented along racial and linguistic lines as the implementation of the National Party's apartheid strategy went ahead after 1948. An example of
the effect of these policies is the Avalon Theatres Group, established in 1939 and
owned by Natal-based South African Indians. Avalon lost heavily after 1948 as white-
owned companies edged them out of white group areas. Under normal competitive
conditions its 18 screens could have grown to about 60 by 1990 (Moosa 1994). In 1969,
a major shift in the political economy of SA film distribution occurred when Afrikaner
capital's life assurance giant SANLAM (SA National Life Assurance Mutual) formed a
shell called SATBEL (Suid-Afrikaanse Teaterbelange Beperk – SA Theatre Interests
Ltd.).

SATBEL took over the operations of independent drive-in and indoor group Ster
(Star) Films. As Fox's management style and capitalisation policies became unwieldy in
the face of emerging trends in cinema viewing, SATBEL bought out Fox and renamed
its operations Kinekor. MGM joined forces with Cinema International Corporation
(CIC) to form MGM Film Trust and continued marketing in SA through the newly
developed CIC-Metro theatre and distribution chain (Tomaselli 1988a, pp. 161–163). The
introduction of broadcast television in 1976 saw a two year lull in cinema attendance,
during which time SATBEL merged its cinema holdings into the giant Ster-Kinekor
group. Eventually, no less than 43% of prime exhibition venues were directly owned
by SATBEL (Tomaselli 1988a: 164-165). Television viewership stabilised around 1978
and by 1979 the cinema-going public had increased to levels greater than before 1976
(Tomaselli and Tomaselli 1987).

As various events unfolded during the 1980s, and the cultural boycott bit deeper,
developments slowed down in terms of international distribution linkages with South
Africa. Cinema production more or less collapsed but for the ongoing work of anti-
apartheid independents like Anant Singh (*Place of Weeping, City of Blood, Tenth of a
Second, Quest for Love*), and a quite astonishing number of subsidy-driven international
co-productions of appalling quality (e.g. *Gold!, Shout at the Devil, King Solomon's Mines*
and a series of Ninja films) (Taylor 1992).

After 1990, when the liberation movements were unbanned, and especially since
the election of 1994, things began to change. The cinema of apartheid had defined
cinema culture as something 'owned' by complete and autonomous ethico-political
groups. Post-apartheid cinema culture, however, opened the way for a sort of socio-
political division between some kind of 'high' culture and a 'low' or 'popular' or
'working class' film culture. A settled 'popular' culture commercial circuit was already in
place, profitably controlled by the big groups (Shepperson and Tomaselli 1998). At the
same time, an alternative 'art cinema' circuit based at film festivals and certain big city
suburban cinemas had emerged after 1990.

However, several small outfits survived which managed to produce and distribute oppositional cinema forms. Many of the importers and distributors of 'alternative' commercial films (Ninja films from Hong Kong, for example) provided them to exhibitors who fell outside the major chains. Over the years people in disadvantaged communities indeed struggled to make available some minimal provision of exhibition space. In community halls, illegal drinking places, garages and other spaces, video players and 16mm projectors were obtained by whatever means to show whatever could be found from the alternative importers' catalogues. In these same spaces, documentary material produced by trade unions and civic organisations was also shown for educational purposes or to inform communities (Steenveld 1992). This activity led to the formation of alternative film producers like the Film Resource Unit (FRU), which continues to operate from Johannesburg.

In 1996, FRU established its African Feature Film collection which makes films produced in Africa by Africans available in 35mm, 16mm and video formats. Student bodies at several institutions of higher education, especially in the main urban region of Gauteng Province (Johannesburg, Pretoria and the various cities around these), created African cinema appreciation societies. These groups either hired titles from FRU, or arranged outings to attend showings arranged by FRU. The latter option was made possible through a sponsorship arrangement with the Newtown Cultural Precinct in Johannesburg's central business district, whereby FRU premiered films on a weekly basis on Friday evenings.

A lot of attention is also directed at facilitating new production. Thus the Electronic Media Network (M-Net), a South Africa based multinational pay television corporation, initiated the annual New Directions competition for directors and scriptwriters. In the first half of each calendar year, the company solicits proposals from first-time cinema directors and writers. Proposals are scrutinised by a panel of experienced professionals, and through a process of mentored refinement six proposals are selected for production. The final products emerge from a further refinement session, in the form of 30-minute dramas broadcast on selected M-Net channels. Another initiative is the M-Net All Africa Film Awards, an annual event first held in October 1995.

The net result is that the opportunity for African cinema to get exposure as demonstration of an alternative field of talent gets diffused into a group of exhibitors and distributors who are likely to reach more than just middle-class college cineastes. Even more decisive is the potential for dedicated organisations to provide the context within which to identify those who possess suitable endowments. Thereafter, it is open for other organisations to develop these endowments in ways which encourage precisely the 'wild card' characteristics that set aside the talented from the competent. Finally, the co-existence of both development and exhibition activities means that even those who do not demonstrate the endowments needed for *making* film will be growing up in an environment where they can learn to *view* film differently.

The potential for critical viewing is the ground upon which a more democratic kind of cinema culture can evolve. A government cannot tell people what to watch, or what kind of movies are or will be 'good for' them. But our research suggests that it can provide a context within which audiences can learn to watch more than just Hollywood genres. The environment now exists within which these post-apartheid generations can begin to learn for themselves how to go about deciding film quality. For a viable cinema culture to emerge, such strategies can contribute to audience development. Much as encouraging a culture of reading as an end in itself will enrich the intellectual environment, so audience development can enhance the wider aesthetic climate which adds spice to the intellectual realm.

Conclusion: cultural studies beyond the media.

Referring to the enormous gap between the much-too-rich and the much-too-poor in the present global dispensation, Ted Honderich (1989, p. 5) observes that these differences are sufficiently great for one to propose that 'if one knew only the average life-times of these two groups of beings, one would suppose they were two different species.' Using life-expectancy as a criterion for making this 'pedagogic' assessment reinforces how contemporary conditions assault the sensibility of people who take the radical project seriously. Yet there is potentially a quite serious tendency among extreme cultural relativists to argue that concern over living conditions in the non-metropolitan world is an example of 'cultural imperialism'.

On the basis of the kind of work we have outlined above, cultural studies *can* stand the situation back on its feet. Research and teaching which is critically supportive of policy and constructively critical when the situation demands, is beginning to show up. Thus recent projects do not simply beg the question of government policy, but seek to develop innovative approaches to the concrete business of addressing Honderich's 'two species' conditions in South Africa. In 1995, the enormous parastatal Human Sciences Research Council (HSRC) initiated a series of innovative projects in Cultural Reconstruction and Development (CURED), followed by the Development, Culture and Communication Programme (DECCO). These integrate Non-Governmental Organisations, telecommunications provision, arts and performance, museums, environmental groups and development agencies into a growing Internet database aimed at facilitating the cultural dimension of development across sub-Saharan Africa and beyond (see Guambe and Shepperson 1997).

On another level, the Centre for Cultural and Media Studies (CCMS) responded to the new state's early attempt to create AIDS awareness media, which had taken the form of a lavish theatrical extravaganza. Although expensive and produced by an internationally renowned playwright, the extravaganza was never going to reach the people whose poverty placed them at the greatest risk in the AIDS pandemic. As an alternative approach, CCMS developed a government communications strategy designed to draw in the plurality of media players, social marketing bodies, primary health organisations and others confronting the AIDS phenomenon.

This 'Beyond Awareness' approach (Parker 1997), formally launched in 1998, not only aimed to increase the effectiveness of media-related activity, but also to set up a governmental network which linked the players in civil society with relevant state agencies. Social welfare departments are also drawn into the process, to assist with people affected by the death of parents, breadwinners, or others. A variety of other state sectors also tap into a cabinet-level co-ordination body that helps to bring best-practice methods to the attention of implementing agencies, though some commentators were less than sanguine about government's abilities to listen (Tomaselli 1997), or communities to learn (Kerr 1997). Finally, the strategy draws on the generational analysis to set up medium-term and long-term action frameworks which will hopefully accommodate unexpected developments.

The process takes place in a cultural-generational dynamic that is simultaneously political transformation, intellectual renaissance, and untreatable pandemic. The use of cultural-studies based generational analysis assists those managing the business of confronting the social and cultural side of the AIDS phenomenon at all levels. As a general strategic instrument, for use at the level of international, national or regional co-ordination, the approach generates methods that parallel those of Intelligence agencies: information is enriched through the broader understanding of the relations peculiar to the context in which events or processes occur. Yet at the local level, the approach can help NGO volunteers, local government health workers, and even sex-workers' organisations identify ways to meet immediate challenges that particular local constituencies might pose.

Finally, however, the application of cultural studies to the questions of AIDS policy should not be seen as another example of 'Cultural and Policy Studies'. What CCMS did in the Beyond Awareness instance was to take a specific approach to the conceptual analysis and logical discourse of the idea of culture, and apply it to the media and cultural situation specific to South Africa. Although the AIDS strategy was designed for a specific political and intellectual situation defined within the structures of (and the structural change from) apartheid, the conceptual basis as a ground for method has attracted NGO interest in neighbouring countries like Zimbabwe. The point as we saw it was that cultural studies must continue to test the conceptual relations between not only the concept and expression of 'culture', but also the social and (especially) political environment. And the political, the realm of beginnings (Arendt, 1970), is always the defining factor in laying the foundation for the selections from the record that are the intellectual climate within which the development of endowments into talents is determined.

Notes

1   *Work in Progress*, August 1979, p. 57.
2   CCSU 1987.
3   *Work in Progress* 1979; Tomaselli *et al.* 1989.

References

Arendt, H. (1958). *The Human Condition*, Chicago: University of Chicago Press.
Arendt, H. (1970). *On Violence*, New York: Harcourt, Brace and World.
Bertelsen, E. (1991). 'The Unspeakable in Pursuit of the Unbeatable: The Press, UCT and the O'Brien Affair', *Critical Arts*, 5 (4).
Biernatzki, W.E. (n.d.). *Catholic Communication Research: topics and a rationale*, London: Research Facilitator Unit for Social Communication,.
Blignaut, J. and Botha, M. (eds) (1992). *Movies - Moguls - Mavericks. South African Cinema, 1979-1991*, Cape Town: Showdata.
Bozzoli, B. (1981). *Capital and Ideology in South Africa 1890-1933. The Political Nature of a Ruling Class*, London: Routledge and Kegan Paul.
Brill, S. (1995). *Wittgenstein and Critical Theory: Beyond Postmodernism and Towards Descriptive Investigations*, Athens: Ohio University Press.
Callinicos, L. (1986). 'The People's Past: Towards Transforming the Present', *Critical Arts*, 4 (2), pp. 21-40.
Cooper, B. and Steyn, A. (eds) (1996). *Transgressing Boundaries: New directions in the study of culture in Africa*, Cape Town: University of Cape Town Press.
Dalrymple, L. (1987). 'Explorations in Drama, Theatre and Education: a Critique of Theatre Studies in South Africa', PhDthesis, University of Natal.
Dalrymple, L. (1997). 'The Use of Traditional Cultural Forms in Community Education', *Africa Media Review*, 11(1).
Guambe, D. and Shepperson, A. (1997). 'Developing Cultural Development Policy Research Programmes: A focus on the material communities of cultural practice', *Africa Media Review*, 11(1).
Gutsche, T. (1972). *The History and Social Significance of Motion Pictures in South Africa, 1895-1940*, Cape Town: Howard Timmins.
Hardt, H. (1992). *Critical Communication Studies: Communication, History and Theory in America*, London: Routledge.
Heller, A. (1978). *Renaissance Man*, London: Routledge and Kegan Paul.
Heller, A. (1985). *A Radical Philosophy*, Oxford: Basil Blackwell.
Heller, A. (1987). *Beyond Justice*, Oxford: Basil Blackwell.
Hirst, Paul (1990). 'Democracy: Socialism's Best Reply to the Right', in B. Hindess (ed)

Reactions to the Right, London: Routledge.

Hoggart, R. (1957). *The Uses of Literacy*, Harmondsworth: Penguin.

Hoggart, R. (1973). *Speaking to Each Other*, vol. 2, Harmondsworth: Pelican.

Holt, A.R. (1988). 'Advertising and Reform: Some Questions', CCSU seminar paper, University of Natal, Durban.

Honderich, T. (1989). *Violence for Equality: Inquiries in Political Philosophy*, London: Routledge.

Hountondji, P. (1983). *African Philosophy: Myth and Reality*, Bloomington: Indiana University Press.

Irele, A. (1983). 'Introduction', in Hountondji (1983) *African Philosophy: Myth and Reality*, Bloomington: Indiana University Press.

Kerr, David (1997). 'Cultural Engineering and Development', *Africa Media Review*, 11(1).

Louw, P.E. (ed) (1993). *South African Media Policy: Debates of the 1990s*, Anthropos, Johannesburg.

Lungwangwa, G. (1988/9). 'The Rationale for Basic Education in Developing Countries: A Critique of the Ideology of Reform in Education', *Critical Arts*, 4 (4), 5 (1).

Mann, M. (1988). *States, War and Capitalism: Studies in Political Sociology*, Oxford: Basil Blackwell.

Marcus, G. and Myers, F. (eds) (1995). *The Traffic in Cultures: Refiguring art and Anthropology*, Berkeley: University of California Press.

Masilela, N. (1988). 'Preface: Establishing an Intellectual Bridgehead', in K. Tomaselli (ed) *Rethinking Culture*, Bellville: Anthropos.

Moosa, M. (1994). Submission to the Government of National Unity's Arts and Culture Action Group (ACTAG).

Mpofu, A., Manhando, S. and Tomaselli, K. (eds) (1995). *Public Service Broadcasting in South Africa: Directions Towards 2000*, Johannesburg: Anthropos.

Mpofu, B. (1996). 'Corporate Monopoly in the South African Print Media: Implications for the Alternative Press with Particular Reference to *New Nation*', MA dissertation, University of Natal, Durban.

Muller, J. (1986). 'The White Hands: Academic Social Scientists and Forms of Popular Knowledge and Production', *Critical Arts*, 4 (2).

Muller, J. and Tomaselli, K. (1990). 'Becoming Appropriately Modern: Towards a Genealogy of Cultural Studies in South Africa', in J. Mouton and D. Joubert (eds), *Knowledge and Method in the Human Sciences*, Pretoria: HSRC.

Parker, W. (1997). 'Action Media: Consultation, Collaboration and Empowerment in Health Promotion', *Africa Media Review*, 11(1).

Patel, L. (1985). 'How Small Media can Organise Communities', *Media Development*, 32.

Peirce, C.S. (1965). *The Collected Papers of Charles Sanders Peirce*, vols 1–6, C. Harteshorne and P. Weiss (eds), Cambridge: Harvard University Press.

Peirce, C.S. (1966). *The Collected Papers of Charles Sanders Peirce*, vols 7-8, A.W. Burks (ed), Cambridge: Harvard University Press.

Scott, C. (1994). *The Lesotho Video Herders Project: Explorations in Visual Anthropology*, Hojbjerg: Intervention Press.

Sharp, J. (n.d.). *South African Keywords*, Cape Town: David Philip.

Shepperson, A. (1995). 'On the social Interpretation of Cultural Experience: Reflections on Raymond Williams's Early Cultural Writings (1958-1963)', MA dissertation, University of Natal, Durban.

Shepperson, A. and Tomaselli, K. 'South African Cinema: Before and Beyond Apartheid', in G. Kindem (ed), *The International Movie Industry*, Southern Illinois University Press, Carbondale (forthcoming).

Sitas, A. (1986). 'The Contradictions of Working Class Theatre in South Africa', *Africa Perspective*, 1 (2).

Steadman, I. (1989). 'Drama and Social Consciousness: Themes in Black Theatre on the Witwatersrand until 1984', PhD thesis, University of Witwatersrand, Johannesburg.

Steenveld, L. (1992). 'Reclaiming History: Anti-Apartheid Documentaries', in J. Blignaut and M. Botha (eds), *Movies - Moguls - Mavericks. South African Cinema 1979-1991*, Cape Town, Showdata.

Steyn, M. and Motshabi, K.B. (1996). *Cultural Synergy in South Africa: Weaving Strands of Africa and Europe*, Randburg: Knowledge Resources.

Teer-Tomaselli, R.E. (1994). 'The Mediazation of Culture: John Thompson and the Vision of Public Service Broadcasting', *South African Journal of Philosophy*, 13 (3).

Teer-Tomaselli, R.E. (1995). 'Moving Towards Democracy: The South African Broadcasting Corporation and the 1994 Election', *Media, Culture and Society*, 17 (4).

Teer-Tomaselli, R.E. (1996). 'DEBI Does Democracy: Recollecting Democratic Voter Education in the Electronic Media Prior to the South African Elections', in G.E. Marcus (ed), *Connected: Engagements with the Media*, Chicago: Chicago University Press.

Tomaselli, K.G. (1986). 'A Contested Terrain: Struggle Through Culture', *Communicatio*, 13 (2).

Tomaselli, K.G. (ed) (1988a). *Rethinking Culture*, Bellville: Anthropos.

Tomaselli, K.G. (1988b). *The Cinema of Apartheid: Race and Class in South African Film*, Chicago: Lake View Press.

Tomaselli, K.G. (1996). *Appropriating Images: The Semiotics of Visual Representation*, Hojbjerg: Intervention Press.

Tomaselli, K.G. (1997). 'Action Research, Participatory Communication: Why Governments Don't Listen', *Africa Media Review*, 11(1).

Tomaselli, K.G. (1998). 'Recovering Praxis: Cultural Studies in Africa', *European Journal of Cultural Studies*, 1(3) (forthcoming).

Tomaselli, K.G. and Louw, P.E. (eds) (1991). *The Alternative Press in South Africa*, Bellville: Anthropos.

Tomaselli, K.G. and Louw, P.E. (1993). 'Shifts Within Communication Studies: From Idealism and Functionalism to Praxis – South Africa in the 1980s', in B. Dervin and U. Hariharan (eds), *Progress in Communication Sciences*, vol. 6, New Jersey: Ablex.

Tomaselli, K.G., Williams, A., Steenveld, L. and Tomaselli, R. (1986). *Myth, Race and Power: South Africans Imaged on Film and TV*, Bellville: Anthropos.

Tomaselli, K.G. and Tomaselli, R.E. (1987). 'Before and After Television: The South African Audience', in B. Austin (ed), *Current research in Film: Audiences, Economics and the Law*, New Jersey: Ablex.

Tomaselli, R.E., Tomaselli, K.G. and Muller, J. (1989). *Currents of Power: Hegemony and State Broadcasting in South Africa*, Bellville: Anthropos.

Traber, M. (1985). 'Alternative Journalism, Alternative Media', *Communication Resource*, 7.

Van Staden, C. (1996). 'Claiming the African Mind: Postcoloniality and Cultural Studies', *Communicatio*, 22 (2).

White R.A. (1983). 'Community Radio as an Alternative to Traditional Broadcasting', *Media Development*, 30 (3).

White R.A. (1984). *Democratisation of Communication: The need for new research strategies*, London: Centre for the Study of Communication and Culture.

White R.A. (1986a). 'The New Communications Emerging in the Church', *Way Supplement*, 57.

White R.A. (1986b). 'Mass Media and the Culture of Contemporary Catholicism: The Significance of the Second Vatican Council', London: Centre for the Study of Culture and Communication.

Williams, R. (1958). *Culture and Society*, Harmondsworth: Pelican.

Williams, R. (1963). *The Long Revolution*, Harmondsworth: Pelican.

CHAPTER THREE

Rural art and rural resistance: the rise of a wall decorating tradition in rural Southern Africa

Franco Frescura

Introduction

Southern Africa's rural architecture has long been associated with a tradition in wall decoration which predates the arrival of white colonialists to the region's interior. These designs are generally acknowledged to be the product of women and have remained their preserve in rural areas right up to present times. Given its context, forms and symbolism, it is not difficult to show that this work is a statement made by rural women in respect to their fertility, political status, religious cosmology and in certain instances, their family lineage. Within this interplay of social patterns, however, the choice and meaning of pictorial matter plays a different and somewhat ambiguous role. Originally the rural artist derived much of her inspiration from natural or geometric designs and rendered them in monochromatic earth colours. In more recent times however and particularly since the 1940s, their scope has been widened to encompass a wide range of colours and subjects. Many western observers have chosen to interpret this as an obvious manifestation of 'cultural cross-pollination' and 'westernisation', thus denying it its social and historical context. Writing of the South Ndebele, for example, Betty Spence and Barrie Biermann speak of 'the coming of civilisation' and say that:

> It is curious that these two types of design reflect so clearly the two influences to which the M'Pogga have been subjected, that of the European and the Sotho,
>
> Spence and Biermann 1954

while others have called them 'foreign innovations' which 'herald the destruction of the genuine Mapogga style' (Battiss, Junod et al 1958, p. 103).

A survey of those areas where wall decoration is still practised today however, reveals that although many such designs are undoubtedly polychromatic and inspired by urban themes, these may, nonetheless, be linked to a wider concept of land control and the economic domination of a rural community on the part of another competing for the same resources. Thus what may outwardly appear to be an act of assimilation and perhaps even appeasement may, in another context, be interpreted as an act of protest and open defiance, visible only to those privy to its codification.

This paper seeks to analyse the social processes which give rise to rural wall art in South Africa and contends that, in the final analysis, this activity is the result of black resistance to outside political domination and land alienation.

Functional nature of wall decoration

It was found during the course of current field work that the decoration of rural architecture tended to fall into two major camps: the structural and the manipulative.

Structural decorative patterns arise from the fact that vernacular architecture in general derives much of its stylistic character from its functional use of found materials. Thus the natural textures, details and forms which are achieved in the process of construction are important, at a primary level, in determining the aesthetic nature of such buildings.

This does not mean to say that structural elements may not, in themselves, be manipulated (Illustration 1). It is possible to achieve, within the bounds of any one particular technology, a number of different resolutions to the same problem. It is often the case, however, that one particular solution will tend to gain predominance in

Illustration 1
Grass rope cross-bracing and decoration, Mpembe, Kwa Zulu Natal (Frescura).

a geographical location or region and thus, with time, may become identified with the material culture of its builders. At the same time it may also be incorporated into their system of cognitive symbolism. The Zulu term 'inkatha', for example, refers to a timber ring or collar which binds together the apex of a conical roof structure and gives it stability. The symbolism conferred by this building element in the current political context is therefore self-evident.

Similarly the attachment shown by the Matabele during the last century to a hemispherical grass-covered dwelling form, more commonly found in northern KwaZulu, long after it ceased to make structural or environmental sense in the mopane veld of eastern Zimbabwe, is indicative of the cultural and political identity attached to it by its builders (Frescura 1985).

It is therefore possible to conclude that, where a group living under one set of conditions develops a strong attachment to a particular style of architecture, it will, under different conditions, attempt to reproduce its more obvious and visual components by manipulative and artificial means. This is equally true in those cases where an architecture is not their own but the acquisition of its aesthetics is deemed to be either desirable or advantageous to the group's interests.

On the other hand manipulative decoration may be seen to be an imposition of textures, colours and forms upon the built habitat for reasons which bear little functional relationship to its structural performance (Illustration 2). The motivation behind such an activity may be of a social, religious, mystical, political or symbolic nature, although it is probable that, in reality, a combination of two or more of these elements will be involved at any one time. Unlike structural decorative patterns which arise as the

Illustration 2
Venda Homestead, Hamutele, Northern Venda (Frescura).

result of the combined efforts of both men and women, most if not all southern African rural groups consider the application of painted motifs to be the work of women.

Historical background

The earliest evidence of a tradition in woman's wall art was probably recorded by Burchell, who visited the Tlhaping homestead of 'Serrakutu' at Dithakong in 1812 where this man's younger wife:

> exhibited her paintings in a manner which evinced that she was well satisfied with her own performance. They were the figures of several animals, rudely drawn, with a paint of white earth, against the front-wall of the house.
>
> Burchell 1953, pp. 321–322

A year later Campbell visited the same homestead and 'found them very rough representations of the camel leopard (giraffe), rhinoceros, elephant, lion, tiger and steinbuck, which Salakootoo's wife had drawn on the clay wall with white and black paint' (1815, p. 194).

Neither traveller included pictorial graphics of these patterns with their accounts and it was left for Campbell (1822, p. 269) to rectify this omission seven years later when he depicted the interior of a chief's dwelling at Kaditshwene, a Hurutshe town located immediately to the north of present-day Zeerust (Illustration 3). This he found to be:

Illustration 3
Hurutse chief's dwelling, Kaditshwene, May 1820 (after Campbell, 1822).

neatly finished ... The wall was painted yellow and ornamented with figures of shields, elephants, cameleopards, etc. It was also adorned with a neat cornice or border painted of a red colour.

1822, pp. 227–228

Despite being relatively brief, these three reports, taken as a whole, reveal a number of significant factors :

- that decoration then, as now, was woman's work
- that lime-whites and charcoal or soot-blacks were available to the rural artist thus giving her palette of earth colours a wide range of shades
- that decorative patterns could be either geometrical and abstract or figurative and representational.

Despite what has been written in the past by such authors as Walton (1956) and Battiss (1958), wall art was not limited to any one particular area in southern Africa but can be considered to have been general practice, in one form or another, among most of its agricultural pastoralist groups. Baines (1961; 1964), who visited a Xhosa dwelling near the Kabousie river in 1848 told that:

In the mud with which the interior of the hut was plastered, pumpkin seeds had been stuck in various patterns, one somewhat resembling a snake, and then picked out, leaving their glossy scale attached to the surface of the wall.

Baines 1961, p. 162

This must have created a pattern very similar in nature to the 'dotted' drawings recorded by Matthews (1971) in this same area nearly 130 years later, a style of decoration which, in the interim, has since largely disappeared.

Kropf, who visited the same region between 1846 and 1889, struck a more contemporary note when he described how the Xhosa woman 'smooths the walls and paints them with yellow, red or white clay or uses all three colours at the same time and paints designs on them' (Shaw and Van Warmelo 1972).

Campbell's report of 1820 is also important for it reveals that a series of 'I' (or 'sideways-H') designs had been painted on the interior perimeter of the dwelling wall in a graphic representation of the Tswana shield. In view of the fact that rural communities in South Africa often refer to their chief as 'the shield of the people', a concept also used more recently in ANC symbology, it may be safely assumed that this design was used by the artist to designate the dwelling as the residence of a chief.

This means that even at this early stage rural artists were reducing material objects to their basic forms and were using them as icons, a concept which was not to be incorporated into modern European art until nearly a century later. Therefore the existence of a body of cognitive symbols perceived to exist in current Sotho, Ndebele and Tsonga wall art must be seen to have its roots in a rural society which precedes the development of industrialisation in southern Africa.

Some case studies

It is possible, in theory, for wall decoration to accommodate as many variations, based upon theme and style, as there are artists to paint them. In reality, however, the functions of rural art are governed by the same social, economic and environmental processes as those which generate rural architecture. Therefore, in art as in architecture, there

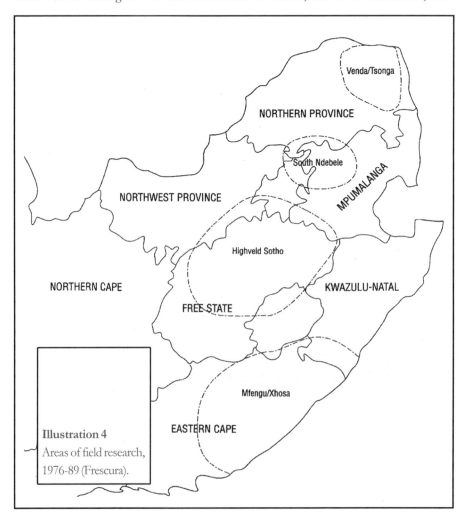

Illustration 4

Areas of field research, 1976-89 (Frescura).

are also stylistic preferences which have become established on a regional or group basis. In each instance a series of broad aesthetic principles have emerged within which the rural artist is able to create her own individual statement in terms of colour and subject matter. For the purposes of this paper we are only interested in four such regional manifestations documented in recent southern Africa history (Illustration 4).

1 The Xhosa-Mfengu case study

The eastern region of the Cape, more recently designated under apartheid as the Ciskei and Transkei, has long been an area of conflict between indigenous blacks and immigrant whites. Not only was it the stage, between 1811 and 1879, of nine separate land wars but, from 1822 to 1835 it also became the home of Mfengu refugees from the Mfecane. These conflicts, combined with the activities of missionaries, government agents and labour recruitment officers, have left a legacy of bitterness which manifests itself in the region to the present day in the form of a deep and uncompromising political radicalism. Although the boundaries of black-white settlement were formalised as long ago as 1913, these are still a matter of heated dispute (Davenport and Hunt 1974, pp. 71–72).

This region also has long historical associations with grass building technology and at one time, the grass-thatched hemispherical dwelling was ubiquitous. Although it has been recorded in some areas as recently as three generations ago, from the 1870s onwards it began to be supplanted by other architectural forms and today it survives only in a vestigial form as an initiation hut. At first the region's builders began to raise the grass dome upon a wattle and daub drum wall (Illustration 5) but from the 1920s

Illustration 5
Xhosa dwelling
Grahamstown c.1908 (Frescura).

onwards this type of roof construction began to be supplanted by a conical structure and today this has become the region's predominant form of rural dwelling (Frescura 1981). Although its introduction has been attributed by some chroniclers to the work of missionaries among the Mpondo during the 1850s (Hunter 1936), this point has yet to be confirmed by current research.

The form taken by decoration in this region tends to follow a set pattern: a white-washed panel covers the front third of the dwelling's circumference, framing the door and spanning in height from eaves' level down to a splashband some 500 mm high at the base; the surrounds to both door and window openings are expressed in white-wash; and sometimes a whitewashed band some 600 mm high runs the length of the remaining wall perimeter beneath the eaves. Further decorative patterns of an individual nature may be applied to the door and window surrounds and, in some recorded examples, the rear of the hut was rendered in a darker clay, presumably to encourage heat absorption during the late afternoon (Illustration 6).

This is a pattern of decoration which appears to have its origins in the era prior to the mid-1920s (Duggan-Cronin 1939) but could have arisen as early as the 1900s (Illustration 7), and may be perceived to bear a close resemblance to the treatment of the exterior facades of domestic structures built by immigrant whites during the Victorian era. The conclusion that this style of design arose as a response on the part of the indigenous population to the influx of missionaries and other white settlers to the region during the last century is therefore inescapable. This is supported by informants in the southern Transkei who have attributed its introduction to the Mfengu, also referred to locally as 'school people' who, as refugees from the Mfecane, were among the first in the region to gravitate into the social and economic sphere of missionary influence. At one time the use of whitewash was associated with a Mfengu and a Christian identity, a supposition supported by the fact that painting and renewal takes

Illustration 6
Xhosa dwelling,
Mount Fletcher, 1982 (Frescura).

place shortly before the Christmas festivities. However, for the past three generations the painting of walls has become a commonplace occurrence in the region, and today little popular significance is attached to it other than the fact that both the decoration and the cone on cylinder form have become incorporated into the local architectural identity.

An interesting connection was made by some informants in the southern Transkei who remarked upon the similarity perceived to exist locally between the white-washing of a hut facade and the fact that it is customary in this region for young mothers to smear white clay on their faces after the birth of a child. The domestic architecture of this region may be perceived to have strong physiognomic characteristics, with the doorway acting as a nose or mouth and the windows on either side as eyes. This parallel has not escaped the local inhabitants, leading to the question whether the two practices are not in fact part of the same process. The young mother smears her face with white clay in order to ward off evil from herself and her baby at a time when they are both vulnerable to such influences. The dwelling is perceived to be the domain of the woman and the task of painting or decorating its walls is also hers. It is conceivable therefore that the twin practices of wall decoration and facial smearing are seen to fulfil the same medical and mystical functions.

2 The Highveld Sotho case study

The highveld region of the northern Free State and Gauteng was inhabited historically by Sotho and, to a lesser degree, Tswana-speaking groups. During the Mfecane the local population was decimated by both famine and warfare and many survivors sought refuge in the mountains of Lesotho. There, under the leadership of Moshweshwe,

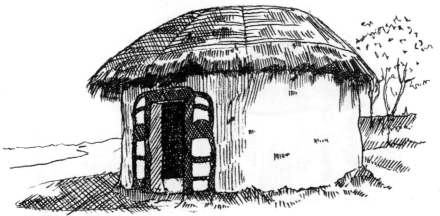

Illustration 7
Xhosa dwelling, near Keiskammahoek, c.1903 (Frescura).

Sotho, Tswana and Nguni elements coalesced into a political entity which survives to the present day as Lesotho. Their former home is now part of the South Africa where it remains under the control of a white and predominantly Afrikaner farming community. Some Sotho have since returned to these areas as migrant workers having no legal land ownership rights or tenure. Until recently many were allowed to live with their families on white farms where they were given a small plot of land to plant crops and build their homes. However since 1992 they have been denied even this small access to land as white farmers, fearful of being dispossessed by an ANC government, forced them to relocate to nearby urban areas from where they now commute.

Their residences were almost invariably built in the form of a parapet or 'highveld' dwelling, a domestic form which was introduced into Cape Town by Malay slaves during the eighteenth century and subsequently spread inland after 1837 by immigrant Dutch farmers. It usually consisted of a simple, elongated, single-cell rectangular unit topped by a flat corrugated iron roof sloping to the rear. Kitchens were usually built as separate units having a thatched roof which allowed smoke from the cooking fire to percolate upwards. Door and window openings were located on the front elevation which normally faced to the north or north-east. The facade was slightly asymmetrical, the door being placed fractionally off-centre, with small, square windows on either side, thus implying a division of the internal space into two rooms which was seldom made. The basic pattern of decoration was subject to some simple guidelines : the parapet at the top and a low splash board at the base were expressed as long horizontal bands; the two corners on either side were rendered as vertical elements; a broad surround was created about both the door and the windows which was often allowed to run into the parapet above; the parapet band was often decorated and its top profile sculpted in order to create small pediments and acroterions over the doorway and the corners respectively (Illustration 8). Within this basic framework the Sotho artist could exercise considerable choice as to colour, graphic pattern and texture.

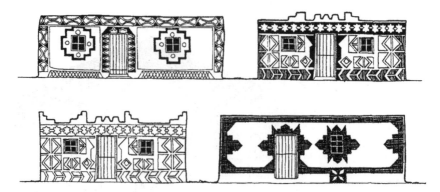

Illustration 8
South Sotho dwellings, northern Free State, 1982 (Frescura).

As in the case of the Xhosa, it will be perceived that the basic elements of this decorative style have strong links with the facade renderings of a late nineteenth century immigrant domestic architecture. In the interior too, the women often recreated, in clay, crockery display shelves which were a stylised rendering of late nineteenth century, English middle-class kitchen fittings, complete down to the presence of linoleum shelf linings rendered in paper cut-outs. The frills of these doilies was often reflected externally in the rendering on the parapet band, thus emphasising the essentially female nature of this dwelling decoration.

Significantly during the course of this research very few examples of decoration were recorded on the dwellings of family members living within Lesotho, although their kinfolk inhabiting ancestral lands, presently in white holding, do so with a great deal of vigour and vivacity.

3   The South Ndebele case study

The South Ndebele are a Nguni-speaking group who migrated into the South African highveld during the fifteenth or early sixteenth centuries (Van Warmelo 1930). They comprise two major branches, the Manala and the Ndzundza. The latter, generally regarded as being the junior of the two, is the subject of this brief study. When the Dutch first encountered them in 1847, they inhabited the area about Namashaxelo, situated near Roossenekal in the Northern Province (Kuper 1978, pp. 107–123). Today most reside on white-owned farms in the Bronkhorstspruit, Groblersdal and Middelburg districts, although in the 1980s an attempt was made by South Africa's previous Apartheid government to establish a homeland on their behalf in the Dennilton area.

On 14 August 1882 the Pedi chief Sekhukhune II was killed alongside fourteen of his advisors. The blame for this deed was laid at the door of Mampuru, Sekhukhune's

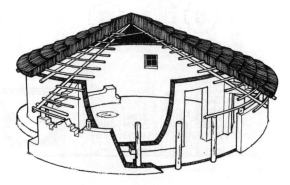

Illustration 9
Cut-away section of South Ndebele dwelling, 1979 (Frescura).

younger brother (Bruce 1976). Kruger's South African Republic (ZAR), which at the time had been endeavouring to establish a suzerainty over the Pedi, attempted to arrest Mampuru, who fled to the Ndzundza. The latter, under the leadership of Nyabele, in their turn not only refused to hand the refugee over, but also declined to pay their hut-tax, thus symbolically rejecting the overlordship which the ZAR had unilaterally imposed over them recently. As a result a Boer commando of between 1000 and 2000 men invaded the Ndzundza's mountain stronghold in October 1882. Nine months later Nyabele capitulated and handed himself and Mampuru over to the Dutch (Bruce 1976). The Ndzundza, starved and bombed into submission, were deprived of their lands, divided and indentured to the farmers who had taken part in the ZAR commando. They were thus effectively scattered in a deliberate attempt to break their political power as a group.

Up to 1883, the South Ndebele as a whole are reputed to have built their dwellings in the form of grass beehive domes (Van Warmelo 1930), a structure historically common to most Nguni speaking groups in southern Africa. Following the defeat of the Ndzundza at the hands of the ZAR, their architecture underwent a measure of change.

Illustration 10
South Ndebele polychromatic wall decoration, Kwa Msiza, Northern Province (Frescura).
Above: Msiza design, c.1952.
Below: Msiza design, c.1981.

The cone on cylinder structure, prevalent among their Pedi neighbours, was adopted with a few modifications. These include the retention of the 'umsamo', a typically Nguni feature of domestic architecture located to the rear of the hut, but acting as a seat for the men, and the partial enclosure of the hut's front circumference with a projecting veranda (Illustration 9). It is also possible that this was the stage when they adopted the Pedi manner of building courtyard walls and defining homestead perimeters. This new style of construction however, does not appear to have lasted more than three or four generations for, by the 1940s, the cone on cylinder was already being replaced by flat-roofed 'parapet' or 'highveld' dwellings.

It was also during this latter period that the South Ndebele began to paint the walls of their dwellings and courtyards using a variety of decorative patterns. Some decorations were of a textural nature; some adopted a simple geometrical motif and repeated it in various ways on a wall; some began to pick out and highlight various structural elements of their architecture; and some took a familiar object, most often a flower or a tree, and reproduced it in a stylised manner. Consequently South Ndebele decoration can be seen, on the one hand to draw deeply from a textural and geometric Sotho/Tswana tradition and, on the other, to develop a series of rules of facade decoration which break down the various structural components of the dwelling in a manner similar to that evolved by Sotho residents of the Free State highveld. Most important however, it also began to develop a series of patterns and images based largely upon the Victorian nature of southern African small-town architecture as well as the graphics of an urban consumer and industrial society further afield (Illustration 10). These were then reproduced not only on the courtyard walls and house facades of the homestead but became part of a more complex system of symbology, being transferred from mother to daughter during the course of the marriage ceremony in the form of a beaded apron. A graphic language has also been allowed to develop, similar in many ways to the Zulu bead love letter (Twala 1951), which, in some cases, has been noticed to advertise the home dweller's profession as a midwife, the husband's sexual potency or just the presence of a certain type of motor vehicle in the vicinity.

4   The Venda-Tsonga case study

The region of land immediately south of the Soutpansberg, in the Northern Province, has long been the home to a number of Venda and Tsonga groups. Although the former have laid historical claim to its control for at least two centuries, since the Mfecane of 1822 to 1837, succeeding waves of Tsonga refugees fleeing the travails of war in the east have made their way into this region. As a result the two cultures were allowed to intermingle, the Venda residing on the hill-tops, and the Tsonga settling on the plains, reputedly with little conflict of interest over land. These patterns were maintained in many cases through to the present day, despite attempts by the previous Apartheid government to enforce its peculiar ideology of ethnic separatism. Because of intermarriage between the two groups, recent times have witnessed the rise of a hybrid culture which, strictly speaking, belongs to neither but draws deeply from both.

The mechanics of this process are interesting to trace. The Venda have, in many cases, retained their historical hold on this land and although the Tsonga have been allowed to develop their own political structures, their leadership has remained largely in the hands of Venda appointees. Also many aspects of Tsonga life are still controlled by the Venda, such as the important process of initiating teenagers into local social polity. As a result the Tsonga have remained, for many years, a socially and economically underprivileged group, a status which only began to be redressed in more recent times. During this period there occurred a major shift in Tsonga architecture which took it away from the more historical models recorded by Junod (1912) as late as the 1900s towards the aesthetics (but not the structural formats) of Venda settlements (Frescura 1985). Today Tsonga homesteads in this region not only display a barely masked approximation of their Venda neighbours but, through a process of cultural borrowing and intermarriage, the decorations of the one have begun to ornament the dwellings of the other.

Nonetheless some tensions began to develop between the two groups in the mid-1970s when, as part of Apartheid's balkanisation process, a large part of Venda territory was excised and handed over to the newly-formed Gazankulu Territorial Authority. Despite the realisation on both sides that these tensions were owed to outside forces, in time and under the paternal guidance of Pretoria bureaucrats, Gazankulu began to develop an element of 'ethnicity' in its make-up which was in keeping with its Apartheid roots.

Thus, although at first the decorations painted by Tsonga women followed in demure emulation of the leaf-and-plant patterns rendered in sombre earth colours by their Venda sisters (Illustration 11), during the mid-1970s they began to diverge, introducing to their repertoire a rich variety of forms and colours which, although still noticeably related to their Venda origins, have nonetheless developed a regional identity of their own (Illustration 12).

Some common trends

An analysis of the case studies above reveals a number of strong threads which link them into a larger pattern of social behaviour:

a) **Gender identity:** like their historical counterparts documented by Burchell, Campbell and Baines, the decorations described above are all the outcome

Illustration 11
Venda wall decorations,
1989 (Frescura).

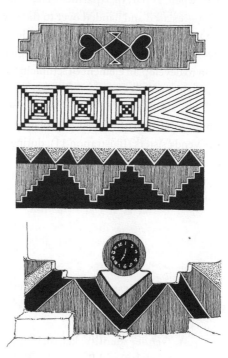

Illustration 12
Tsonga wall decorations,
1989 (Frescura).

of women's work. As such, they represent a statement which identifies rural women as the de facto heads of their homesteads.

b) **Fertility:** the walls of the South Ndebele, Venda and Tsonga homestead are only painted by the wife some two years after she has given birth to her first child. Thus, amongst these groups at least, wall decoration is a symbol of women's fertility and serves to indicate her status in the community as a mother, the head of a homestead, and a responsible adult.

c) **Family political rights:** by giving birth to her first child a woman also gains for her husband the right to participate fully in the deliberations of the group's council of men, both as the head of a family and as a responsible member of the community. Her work therefore is a public statement to the fact that her fertility has given a voice to her family in the public affairs of the community. This factor is contrasted by the status of bachelors in rural society who, for a number of reasons, are treated as 'young children' whose voice carries little weight in group gatherings, regardless of their age. Although a rare occurrence, the homestead of a bachelor in rural life is never decorated nor is it given perimeter walls.

d) **Rites of passage:** although wall decoration may, in principle, be applied at any time during the course of the year, in practice it will be seen that such activity is generally limited to two main periods :

— times of slow economic activity, generally winter or early spring, which also coincides with the dry season of the southern African interior

— times of transition in rural life, such as the initiation of teenagers into adulthood, which theoretically takes place in winter, or a marriage, which may take place at any time.

Either activity must be seen to be primarily connected with the existence of women within the rural life cycle, thus reinforcing the symbolism of wall decoration as a reflection of women and their ritual.

e) **Territoriality:** among those southern African groups who define their exterior living spaces by means of perimeter or courtyard walls, decoration plays a strong symbolic role in the creation of living areas. Recent studies conducted among Pedi groups in the Northern Province have indicated that painting has direct links to a cosmological belief which perceives women to be inherently 'hot'. Homestead boundaries are seen to be similarly 'hot', most particularly where two women in a polygamous marriage share in the same division wall (Vogel 1983). These then need to be 'cooled' by a process of wall smearing and decoration which, presumably, also implies that in the process a degree of co-operation will be engendered between the two parties concerned. Thus wall decoration not only serves to create statements of territorial control but, by implication, suggests that women are more than just passive partners to their menfolk in the control of rural household space and food resources.

f) Heraldry: all of the case studies quoted above have tended to show, almost without exception, that a measure of heraldry is implied in the designs of rural wall art. A survey conducted in the village of Madakamba in the Eastern Cape, for example, revealed that

- in virtually all cases, the dwellings in the same homestead grouping, usually numbering no more than three or four, had the same pattern applied to all the units
- where a daughter married and settled near her mother, she usually painted the same patterns upon her dwelling as those found in her parents' home
- where a son married and settled near his mother, his wife painted the same patterns upon her dwelling as those found on her mother-in-law's home
- in one notable instance, where a daughter had married and settled near her mother, after a family quarrel the former had changed her own wall decorations to a completely new pattern. However she indicated that, should reconciliation take place, she was willing to revert back to her mother's designs as a token of respect.

When questioned further on this point local informants admitted to there being a degree of identity implied in wall patterns but did not give it undue significance. As one young woman phrased it, 'I could see a drawing from the bus and take it home in my head'. Therefore, although these results are not in themselves conclusive, other notable cases of implied heraldry were also recorded among other groups. Among the South Ndebele, for example, the work of wall decoration is conducted either by the mother or her daughters under her direct guidance. The complex patterns which are thus part of a young woman's training are reinforced when, as part of the procedures of marriage, she is presented by her mother with a partly-finished beaded apron bearing the essential elements of this same design. The daughter is then expected to complete the apron and although it may be argued that this represents a handing over of family skills, it should also be seen as a tacit contract between the two parties that the symbols of the older generation will be carried on by the next. Thus, although in theory the young mother will have a wide choice of decorative patterns, in reality, her first designs seldom stray far from those she learnt at home as a child and which she carried away with her, in a shorthand form, as part of her wedding dowry. Among this same group it is also possible to extend the symbolism of female rights and fertility to the homestead plan as a whole. Historically the South Ndebele used to build their homes in the same manner as the Nguni-speaking groups of northern KwaZulu, and although during the latter part of the last century they began to adopt the dwelling forms of their Pedi neighbours, some vestigial elements of their Nguni past persist. One is their use of the 'umsamo', a low shelf at the back of the dwelling used by Zulu women to house food, beer pots and various household utensils, but which the South Ndebele have pragmatically translated into a seat without losing any of its more spiritual significance. Another is the concept of the parent's dwelling as the 'womb' from which the children and the wealth of the family originate, something borne out by Nguni etiquette which decrees hat a dwelling should not be exited backwards, as if in a breach-birth. Given the existence of this kind of symbolism, then the front walls, which are normally the most elaborately decorated areas, become the equivalent of the wedding apron through which the family's designs are transmitted; these shield the front courtyard or the lap of the woman; while the rear quarters which house the children and the cooking areas are the breasts where all nourishment resides. Although not specifically identified as such by informants during the course of fieldwork, the implied physiog-nomy of the South Ndebele homestead was reinforced by the decorative links between the front walls and the beaded apron, as well as the use of the front courtyard as a private area reserved for the women of the household. When one considers the practice of wall painting in the larger socio-eco-nomic and political context of a pre-democratic southern Africa, this activity could also be interpreted as being an indication of the changing status of rural women. From the 1930s onwards the widespread practice of using migrant labour in our urban areas effectively removed a large proportion of the rural male population from their families for protracted periods of time. During this time the control of resources was left largely in the hands of their women, and although their society was both patrilineal and patrilo-cal, the absence of the menfolk began to meet at least some of the criteria for the establishment of a matrilocal and even matrilineal society (Fox 1981).

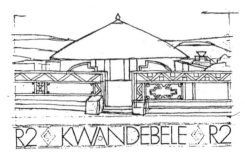

Illustration 13
Essay for proposed definitive stamp issue for Kwa Ndebele, 1986
(A. Barratt).

It may therefore be suggested that rural wall decoration is the outward manifestation of such a development and although South Ndebele society has remained firmly male orientated, the transmittance of decorative patterns through beadwork and wall decoration has been documented through at least three generations and is now probably entering a fourth.

g) **Regional identity:** although it can be shown that the indigenous architecture of rural southern Africa falls into two major settlement types not unrelated to the cosmologies of their builders (Frescura 1985), it is equally true that within this larger framework a number of smaller regional identities have also developed. Their nature has often been dependent upon the creation of aesthetic stereotypes based upon building technology, dwelling form and decorative motif. However, whilst the first two may be found to be common to a number of geographical areas, there is no doubt that in each of the case studies quoted above the women concerned have created a style of wall decoration unique to their region. Thus the work of women can be seen as a major factor in the creation of smaller social polities in this country, a fact which did not go unnoticed by the creators of apartheid. Original separatist thinking made allowance for only nine so-called 'ethnic homelands', but one can only imagine the glee of apartheid officials when, during the early 1980s, a South Ndebele tribal elite came forward and demanded recognition as a tenth 'state'. Plans for their 'independence' had been advanced to the point that its stamps had been designed and printed, when popular indignation led by the UDF forced them to be abandoned. In this regard it is ironic to note that the stamps featuring South Ndebele architecture were drawn from buildings found at the Open Air Museum at Botshabelo, which are the not the work of local builders, but of a white anthropologist from Pretoria (Illustration 13). This is not to doubt their validity as reconstructions (Frescura 1988b), merely to point out how South Ndebele identity was hijacked by Apartheid to meet its own 'ethnic' agendas.

h) **Source of decorative material:** Each of the case studies quoted above also high lights the fact that rural artists have derived their decorative motifs from the artefacts and culture of another socially, economically and politically dominant group. The Mfengu, the Xhosa, the highveld Sotho and the South Ndebele have all drawn deeply from the material culture of late nineteenth century colonial society whose artefacts they observed in white urban areas. The Tsonga, on the other hand, patterned themselves upon the aesthetics of the neighbouring Venda upon whose lands they settled some generations ago.

Political resistance and land control

A clue as to the more fundamental reasons underlying the development of a wall decorating tradition in these study areas can probably be found in the struggle for land which has taken place in southern Africa over the past two centuries, most particularly since the 1920s. Although such competition has, in the main, involved indigenous black and immigrant white groups, the Venda-Tsonga case study indicates that the control of land is also a point of contention between indigenous communities.

Despite the claims of white propagandists, it may be shown that the arrival of European settlers in southern Africa did not bring about a pax abaLunga over the region. On the contrary it is recorded that, since 1811, we have seen 24 major conflicts and over two score smaller localised conflagrations. This means that, on average, one major rebellion, war or uprising has taken place in this country every third year for the past 187 years (Frescura 1988a).

An analysis of these conflagrations also makes for interesting reading. Only two were the result of internal black-on-black schisms, although seven others were affairs to which only whites were invited. Their chronology also reveals that, in almost every case, they coincide with the spread of white settlement throughout the region, beginning in the Eastern Cape, fanning out onto the highveld and eventually engulfing the entire coastal belt. The reasons recorded for these conflicts are many and varied. The majority however were the result of competition for land between white and black rural groups. The single most important source of friction between the two therefore must be seen to lie in the control, or lack thereof, that each exercises over agricultural land.

The relationship between the rural activity of wall decoration and the land conflict which has taken place between indigenous black and immigrant white is not one which may be easily quantified. For one thing, it is doubtful that any one person or body took the conscious decision that walls should be painted as an act of popular protest against the process of land dispossession. For another, the nature of the subject matter renders it highly unlikely that it would be openly discussed with strangers, particularly if they were white. Also, the possibility of stumbling across the fountainhead – if indeed she may even be considered to exist! – is so remote as to make such empirical research virtually impossible. However all circumstantial evidence on the subject seems to indi-

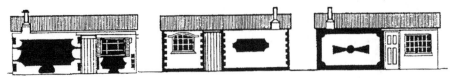

Illustration 14
Decorated dwellings, Western Native Township, Johannesburg (Beinard 1965).

cate that such a hypothesis is indeed correct.

In every case study quoted thus far the aesthetics of wall decoration have played an important role in reinforcing a unique regional identity for the groups concerned. The Mfengu began whitewashing their walls at the urgings of white missionaries upon whose stations they had settled as landless refugees. The practice spread to other Mfengu occupying Xhosa land outside the mission as a statement of their identity but, as the differences between 'school people' (Mfengu) and 'red blanket people' (Xhosa) began to be reconciled through social interaction and marriage, wall art gained undertones of Christian religious affiliation. Ultimately, during the 1940s and 1950s the practice became identified with a wider Xhosa-speaking identity. Significantly current research has shown that a notable reduction in wall decorating activity took place in the Eastern Cape once that region gained a measure of governmental autonomy in 1976.

Similar patterns may be established for the Tsonga whose precarious land tenure led them to adopt the architectural aesthetics of the neighbouring Venda and for the highveld Sotho and the South Ndebele whose land is currently in the holding of the very white farmers whose colonial architecture they emulate in their decoration. It is again important to note that Sotho residing in Lesotho seldom decorate their walls, whilst a marked reduction in wall decoration was noted amongst the South Ndebele with the establishment in the 1980s of an autonomous South Ndebele Tribal Authority immediately north-east of Pretoria. Since the onset of democratic government in South Africa in 1994 this activity has virtually disappeared.

The connection between wall art and black political protest was also made in 1975 by Julian Beinard during the course of research set in the Johannesburg suburb of Western Native Township. In it he described how the first decorations, consisting of basic patterns and animals scratched in the mud plaster, were applied between 1918 and 1930 by baKwena (Tswana-speaking) residents. The practice reached its peak between 1950 and 1962 during which time 'decorations on plaster walls (became) very popular with many variations on a limited number of themes' (Beinart 1965, pp. 184–193).

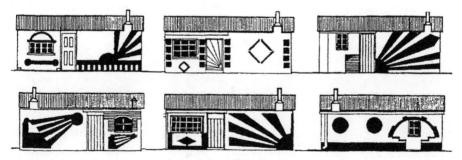

Illustration 15
Decorated dwellings, Western Native Township, Johannesburg (Beinard 1965).

At that time two major decorative themes began to emerge. The first and probably most common, laid particular emphasis on the corners, opening surrounds and base of the house facade. Often, the remainder of the wall surface was filled with square, diamond and 'razor blade' designs (Illustration 14). These are patterns so similar to the South Ndebele and highveld Sotho case studies described above as to warrant no further comment. The second used the sun in a number of variants, either as a set of bold radiating lines reminiscent of the Japanese flag, or simply in a stylised format (Illustration 15). At the time white observers attributed this design to the aesthetic influence of a peculiar brand of floor polish, an insulting inference that black people were all employed as servants and therefore derived artistic inspiration from their servitude. It also denies the importance of the sun as a symbol of rural cosmology and black nationalism, something that was not ignored by the Pan Africanist Congress in the early 1960s when it incorporated a set of bold radiating rays overlaid on a map of Africa into its own battle flag. A third design that was recorded but not specifically remarked upon at the time was the creation of painted quoins about an arch which some houses had over their veranda openings. Depending upon the social perspective used, the result could be interpreted as a wheel of industry, one of the symbols used by the ANC to signify progress (Beinart 1989). Given the oppressive nature of South African society during that time, one cannot blame Beinard for having suppressed such details in his publications.

Ultimately, in 1962, the black residents of Western Native Township were forcibly resettled from their homes into the newly established suburb of Moroka, in Soweto. The new inhabitants of the suburb, now renamed Western Coloured Township, did not have the same political links and did not bother to maintain these decorations. As a result, within a short time these had all disappeared (Beinart 1977, pp. 160–182).

The chronology of rural wall decoration

There is little doubt that, like the women of the Eastern Cape who whiten their faces in propitiation of ancestral spirits, there is an element of appeasement in the practice of wall decoration. The use of western building technologies and house aesthetics may well be attributable to pragmatic reasons such as economics and ease of construction, but the use of decorative patterns acquired from another group stretches beyond this into the field of symbolism and social practice. However one needs to question whether such a message of overt appeasement is not, in reality, an act of subvert resistance. Generally speaking, the use of borrowed wall designs is limited to the outside facade of the dwelling or the homestead concerned. Internal walls are normally rendered in a simpler monochromatic style linked to the decorative motifs of earlier generations which stand in sharp contrast to the complex polychromatic work of recent times. The latter's chronology of development places it firmly into a time when formal resistance to white political dominance was at a low ebb; when the effects of the rural land acts were beginning to become evident; when rural poverty was beginning to spread; when rural women began to find their men being channelled in increasing numbers into a system of migrant labour; when whites across the spectrum of political opinion saw blacks as being voteless, dispossessed and landless in perpetuity and at a time when formal black resistance was limited to an ANC which had but recently adopted a more confrontational stance.

It was during this time that rural women took up the cudgels of their people's struggle and began to decorate their homestead walls, making statements about their social conditions and creating images of regional and political identity.

This chronology tends to vary considerably from region to region. Among the highveld Sotho, for example, it is certain that the basic elements were present in a rudimentary form before the 1930s, but the practice did not begin to gain momentum until the decades before and during the Second World War. Certainly the use of industrial pigments did not begin before the 1950s. In the Eastern Cape, on the other hand, the practice pre-dates the onset of apartheid and is linked to both the land wars and the work of missionaries. Consequently it probably began in the early 1900s and reached its peak during the rural Poqo rebellion of the 1960s.

The South Ndebele are recorded to have used a basic pattern not dissimilar from their Sotho-Tswana neighbours at a relatively early stage, but little if any decoration of import was taking place when Duggan-Cronin visited their region in 1937. It is doubtful that he, of all people, could have failed to record its existence had it been present in any way. On the other hand, by the time Barrie Biermann, Betty Spence, Margaret Stewart-Larraby, AL Meiring and Alexis Preller had begun their documentation of Ndebele architecture in the early 1950s, their art had already reached a highly qualitative level of development (Biermann 1989).

Finally, there is no doubt that the emergence of a polychromatic tradition of wall decoration among the Tsonga coincides with the excision of Gazankulu from Venda and its establishment as a separate Territorial Authority. Its links to a recent ideology of ethnic separation are therefore inescapable.

The future of rural decorative art

It is not easy to make projections regarding the future of a wall painting tradition in southern Africa. Given the fact that many of the social and economic inequalities which historically gave rise to it are the subject of revision and redress under the country's new constitution, it now appears likely that the motivation for such activity has either already been lost, or is likely to be dissipated once a viable housing programme for rural areas is put in place. One of the first victims of such a move would undoubtedly be the more obvious and visible elements of rural material culture, such as local decorative patterns, building textures, dwelling forms and ultimately, regional architecture as a whole. The choice, quite obviously, remains in the hands of the builders as well as the artists themselves. If, for example, the practice can be reduced to a manifestation, in aesthetic terms, of the status and role of women in rural society, then its survival can be safely predicted for as long as it continues to fulfil a pragmatic and functional role in their daily lives. The concepts of marking the times of transition the family, or even creating a sense of continuity and gender identity for the women themselves may be sufficient reason for this to happen. Many parallel examples may be quoted from other cultures to support this generic assertion.

On the other hand, if the symbolism of wall decoration is connected entirely to a wider concept of political resistance and land tenure, then the question becomes more difficult to answer. We do not know, for example, to what degree the new South African constitution is going to supersede regional ethnicity and relegate it to the same closet as apartheid and other ghosts of separatist ideology. The obvious intention of the Government is to redress the economic inequalities of the past on a more equitable regional basis, but to date the various regions have responded to these plans in different ways. Also, the full effects of dismantling the powers traditionally accorded by rural society to their chiefs and other tribal authorities must still be felt, and the degree of support that these enjoy amongst a normally conservative constituency must still be assessed. All of these factors, taken singly or as a whole, could either reinforce or remove the reasons for its survival and bring about its demise.

One factor which has yet to be taken fully into account, but which can play a leading role in resolving this issue, is the growth of tourism as a lead sector in our economy. The impact that the disappearance of rural architecture and its decorative textures from our national landscape will have upon this industry is potentially disastrous. Rural society is a storehouse for the decorative motifs and traditional craftwork which gives our nation its unique African flavour and unless it is treated as a non-renewable resource, the time could well come when airport tourist shops and other commercial concerns become the custodians of our national heritage. In view of the fact that most of these artists and crafters are self-employed, the impact that this will have on our economy is predictably negative.

References

Baines, T. (1961 and 1964). *Journal of Residence in Africa, 1842–1853*, Cape Town: Van Riebeeck Society.

Battiss, Junod, Franz and Grossert. (1958). *The Art of Africa*, Pietermaritzburg: Shuter and Shooter.

Beinart, J. (1965). '2000 Two-Faced Houses by the Violent Playground', in J. Donat (ed.), *World Architecture 2*, London: Studio Vista.

Beinart, J. (1977). 'Patterns of Change in an African Housing Environment', in Oliver, P. (ed.) *Shelter, sign and symbol*, New York: The Overlook Press.

Bruce, H.J. (1976). 'The Arts and Crafts of the Transvaal Ndebele', in A.H. Smith (ed.), *Africana Byways*, Johannesburg: AD Donker.

Burchell, W.J. (1953). 'Travels in the interior of Southern Africa', in I. Schapera (ed.), *Travels in the Interior of Southern Africa*, London: Batchworth Press.

Campbell, J. (1815). *Travels in South Africa*, London: Black and Parry.

Campbell, J. (1822). *Travels in South Africa ... Being a Narrative of a Second Journey*, London: Francis Westley.

Davenport, T.R.H. and Hunt, K.S. (1974). *The right to the land*, Cape Town: David Philip.

Duggan-Cronin, A.M. (1939). 'The Nguni – The Xhosa and Thembu', *The Bantu Tribes of South Africa*, Kimberley: Alexander McGregor Memorial Museum.

Fox, R. (1981). *Kinship and Marriage*, Harmondsworth: Penguin Books.

Frescura, F. (1981). *Rural Shelter in Southern Africa*, Johannesburg: Ravan Press.

Frescura, F. (1985). 'Major Developments in the Rural Indigenous Architecture of Southern Africa of the Post-Difaqane Period', PhD thesis, University of the Witwatersrand, Johannesburg.

Frescura, F. (1988a). 'The Freedom Charter: Land Redistribution and Social Conflict', in J.A. Polley (ed.), *The Freedom Charter and the future*, Cape Town: IDASA.

Frescura, F. (1998b). 'Open Air Museums – A Critique of Current Policies', *SA Journal of art and Cultural History*, 2(2), pp. 77–82.

Hunter, M. (1936). *Reaction to Conquest*, London: Oxford University Press.

Junod, H.A. (1912). *The Life of a South African Tribe*, Neuchatel: Imprimerie Attinger Frères.

Kuper, A. (1978). 'Fourie and the Southern Transvaal Ndebele', *African Studies*, 37(1), pp. 107–123.

Matthews, T. (1971). 'Tribal Painting in South Africa, with Particular Reference to Xhosa Painting', DLitt et Philthesis, University of South Africa, Pretoria.

Shaw, E.M. and van Warmelo, N.J. (1972, 1974 and 1981). *The Material Culture of the Cape Nguni*, Ann.S.Afr.Mus, Cape Town.

Spence, B. and Biermann, B. (1954). 'M'Pogga', *The Architectural Review*, July, pp. 34–40.

Twala, R.G. (1951). 'Beads as Regulating the Social Life of the Zulu and the Swazi', *African Studies*, 10(3), pp. 113–123.

Van Warmelo, N.J. (1930). *Transvaal Ndebele Texts*, Ethnological Pulications No 1, Department of Native Affairs, Pretoria: Government Printer.

Vogel, C.A.M. (1983). 'The Traditional Mural Art of the Pedi of Sekhukhuneland',
    MA dissertation, University of the Witwatersrand, Johannesburg.
Walton, J. (1956). *African Village*, Pretoria: Van Schaik.

CHAPTER FOUR

Unspeaking the centre: emergent trends in South African theatre in the 1990s

Mark Fleishman

In 1990, Peter Larlham, Associate Professor in the Drama Department at San Diego State University spent time travelling in South Africa and Zimbabwe viewing the work of 'contemporary indigenous playwrights' (Larlham 1991, p. 202). It was of course a time of flux as all certainties of the past were thrown into confusion by the unbanning of the African National Congress (ANC), the Pan African Congress (PAC) and the South African Communist Party (SACP) along with thirty or so other organisations; the relaxing of restrictions on freedom of expression; the release of political prisoners and the possibility that exiles could return home.

All of this created - in Larlham's words - 'new dynamics in South African culture and art' (1991, p. 200). At the end of his stay he published his observations in an article entitled Theatre in Transition: The Cultural Struggle in South Africa. In the article he proposed that definite characteristics of current South African theatre had begun to emerge. These included:

- a theatre that addresses issues of immediate relevance to South African society with a de-emphasis on producing Western works
- an eclectic, intercultural theatre that integrates performance conventions and acting styles from diverse cultures
- playmaking, rather than working from pre-existent scripts, often with a director-playwright who organises and records improvisations. The actor is regarded as a role-maker rather than an interpreter of roles
- actors' theatre with an abundance of song, dance, and music; a de-emphasising of technical theatre or lavish productions
- a theatre that records the cultural history of the people, that assists in re-education after the long period of enforced censorship and disinformation

Larlham 1991, p. 210

Almost eight years have passed since that visit and those conclusions were expressed. In that time we have passed through the negotiations of CODESA,[1] through elections for the new democratic parliament; we have seen the inauguration of the first black President; passed through the Constituent Assembly to our new constitution and the Bill of Rights. Next year we will go to the polls once more to register our collective opinion as to the successes or failures of the current government. And in all of this time what has happened to theatre? Have the characteristics highlighted by Larlham indeed continued to develop? Have new ones emerged? Have changes taken place in the institutional realm of theatre practice?

It is my intention in this paper to examine the current moment in South African theatre practice in an attempt to reveal trends that have emerged since Larlham's visit in 1990. By way of introduction I will begin by outlining what changes have been brought about at an institutional level through emerging government policy. Using this as a basis I will then go on to examine a number of productions in an attempt to reveal emergent trends. Finally I will examine various events which challenge the dominant paradigms of theatre practice itself.

Arts and culture task group

The Minister of Arts, Culture, Science and Technology appointed the Arts and Culture Task Group (ACTAG) in November 1994. ACTAG consisted of artists, arts educators and cultural administrators and was tasked with consulting as widely as possible in order to formulate a new cultural policy for the new dispensation. After months of deliberations, consultative conferences and the formation of some, but not all, provincial task groups to aid in the process, a final report was submitted to the minister in 1995. The report was then transformed into a white paper, published in 1996 which now serves as a framework within which government, in the form of the Department of Arts and Culture, should act. Since then the government has passed a number of pieces of enabling legislation, the most relevant to the performing arts being the National Arts Council Act[2].

The gist of the new policy as regards the performing arts concerns the relationship between government and the Performing Arts Councils - the main recipients of funding for the performing arts in the Apartheid years. The new policy envisaged the restructuring of the Performing Arts Councils with the appointment of new, racially inclusive boards to oversee their transformation. Coupled with this was the downsizing of the councils intended to be achieved through the gradual decrease of guaranteed funding over a period of three years. The policy envisaged that the money saved from the reduction of funding to the councils would be made available to a wider group of practitioners through the formation of a National Arts Council (NAC) which would accept and process applications for funding and disburse public funds to artists and cultural institutions and organisations. This new policy of 'arms-length funding' through the National Arts Council, coupled with guarantees of freedom of expression enshrined in the Bill of Rights of the new Constitution where 'everyone has the right to freedom of expression, which includes ... freedom of artistic creativity' has been described by critic Robert Greig as an attempt by government to create a 'benevolent atmosphere' in which the arts could prosper (1996, p. 23). However, although the new system has major advantages over past government policy towards the performing arts, there are a number of major structural problems which mitigate against the successful implementation of the new policy. Firstly, the decision by government to continue guaranteeing the funding of the Performing Arts Councils' infrastructure, their buildings and their bureaucratic and maintenance staff, and the grants made directly to the Market Theatre and the Baxter Theatre, radically reduce the amount of funding available to artists, thereby hampering the NAC from the outset in its ability to foster new work and cultural development. Secondly, certain pieces of legislation with roots in the apartheid era, such as the Censorship Act and in particular its latest incarnation as the Film and Publications Act,[3] continue to have a worrying effect on the cultural terrain. Recently a number of exhibitions in the visual arts sphere have attracted the wrath of the censors raising vigorous debate around the issue of freedom of expression and creativity and its relationship to the broader society. In the context of this debate certain statements attributed to members of the government appear to limit artistic creativity and freedom of expression in certain circumstances. For example, Baleka Kgositsile, then deputy speaker of parliament wrote in the Star newspaper:

> People's pride and dignity cannot be trampled on in the name of freedom of expression. If needs be, legislation must protect our people from degradation that's likely to continue in the name of trying to keep up with some ideals not set by the majority ...
>
> Douglas 1996, p. 21

This seems to imply that the ideal of artistic freedom of expression is not set by the majority, that the culture of rights which is a major feature of the Constitution is indeed something which can and should be legislated against in certain circumstances where the majority of 'our' people (as opposed to whose people?) decide it is okay to do so because they are being 'degraded'. Would the same apply to the death penalty issue where a majority of South Africans seem to be in favour of reinstatement?

Despite the above reservations, the policy has become reality and the NAC has disbursed its first funds. By the beginning of 1999 most guaranteed funding to the Performing Arts Councils will have dried up and the councils and their resident companies will have to join the queue along with everybody else when it comes to funding time. One of the results of the transformation of the Performing Arts Councils and their boards and the formation of the NAC has been the rise of a new theatre elite who occupy numerous positions of power in the industry. The tendency for a few prominent individuals, particularly in Gauteng,[4] to wear many different hats has caused some eyebrows to be raised. John Kani is executive trustee at the Market Theatre, and chairman of the Performing Arts Council of the Transvaal (PACT) board and of the NAC. Mannie Manim, who started the Market Theatre with Barney Simon in the mid-70s, has his own production company, works for the performing arts administration at the University of the Witwatersrand (Wits), and sits on the board of the Market Theatre and Civic Theatre, and on the National Arts Festival committee. Alan Joseph is CEO at PACT and also sits on the National Arts Festival committee. While critics such as Robert Greig (1997b, p. 12) suggest a conflict of interests, others, like arts and culture consultant Mike van Graan (1997, p. 13), counter that the situation is simply indicative of 'an historical legacy in the maldistribution of skills, the needs of an emerging and transforming cultural milieu and the demands of arts practitioners to participate directly in the structures which affect their lives and livelihood ...' He argues that it would be much more useful for journalists to point out where the 'potential [for conflict of interest] is translated into reality'. What is also clear is that most of the new elite have emerged from the Market Theatre stable, in most instances first moving to the Civic Theatre, then on into PACT and now the NAC, where the Market has two executive members in John Kani and Vanessa Cooke. In Johannesburg it is only the Windybrow Theatre which bucks the trend, run as it is by Walter Chakela and showcasing work by directors such as Duma Ka-Ndlovu, neither of whom were Market Theatre stalwarts in the past. It is not my intention here to point accusing fingers at any of the individuals named above, but to indicate the nature of the institutional changes that have taken place over the past five years and the new power structures that are emerging.

So how have these institutional changes translated into theatre practice itself? Each year the festival committee of the National Festival of the Arts in Grahamstown assembles a programme of theatre events which many consider to be the premiere showcase of South African theatre. Although it is clearly the choice of a small group of individuals it seems to me to be a good place to start the search for emerging trends in South African theatre.

An analysis of the programmes at the last four festivals reveals that of 49 productions mounted, 28 have been South African texts and 4 more have been South African adaptations of foreign texts. Five productions were brought to the festival from abroad, leaving only 12 productions mounted of texts written elsewhere. On the surface at least the number of new works showcased by the festival is impressive and given that we are not here considering the fringe festival or other major festivals such as the Klein Karoo Nasionale Kunstefees, or the indigenous output of established theatres such as the Market Theatre, it indicates that South African theatre is alive and kicking. Many of the characteristics observed by Larlham in 1990 are present in these plays, including an emphasis on local content over western texts; the continued popularity of playmaking alongside new writing; an intercultural focus; and a mixture of performance forms in a single production.

However, further analysis of the productions mounted reveals that whereas there is a good racial and gender spread of actors used the same cannot be said of directors. 32 directors were used of whom 24 were white and only 8 were black; 25 were men and only 7 women. This seems to indicate that although the South African content is well established, so too are the power structures, in terms of race and gender, which were established during the apartheid era.

It can be argued that things have been changing steadily over the four years and that the situation in 1998 is much better than the situation in 1995. Certainly the ratio of black to white directors in the 1998 festival programme - 4 black to 6 white - is an improvement on 1 black to 12 white in 1995. However the position of women directors has not substantially improved over the same period. In fact the position of women in South African theatre practice continues to be embattled and reflects a general post-colonial malaise. As Anne McClintock (1994, p. 260) comments in another context:

> The term 'post-colonialism' is prematurely celebratory and obfuscatory in more ways than one. The term becomes especially unstable with respect to women. In a world where women do two-thirds of the world's work, earn 10 per cent of the world's income and own less than 1 per cent of the world's property, the promise of 'post-colonialism' has been a history of hopes postponed. It has generally gone unremarked that the national bourgeoises and kleptocracies that stepped into the shoes of 'post-colonial' 'progress' and industrial 'modernisation' have been overwhelmingly and violently male.

Furthermore, a breakdown of provincial representation in the festival programmes reveals that 26 productions emanated from Gauteng, 11 from the Western Cape, 3 from the Eastern Cape, 2 from Kwazulu Natal and 2 from the North West Province. This indicates the strong central position Gauteng occupies in theatre practice and the marginal position of the other provinces with the Western Cape being the only other province to feature prominently.

One of the central debates around the performing arts in the ACTAG process concerned the question of whether national companies should be established in each art form to operate as flagship institutions for the performing arts. These national companies would, it was argued, become the pinnacle of achievement in each art form and be entrusted with the task of developing a national cultural identity in the new South Africa. The counter-argument was that such institutions would not only suck up huge amounts of funding and hamper cultural development but that the idea of a national cultural identity was mythical and that a multiplicity of small companies based at local level in the provinces would, in their diversity, better reflect the identity of the South African population.

The support for the national company idea amongst theatre practitioners emanated mainly from Gauteng. The intention seemed to be to locate the company in Gauteng and at the Market Theatre in particular. This was seen in some circles as a reward to the Market for its years of struggle, against many obstacles, to keep South African theatre and particularly anti-apartheid theatre, alive. The proponents of this scheme argued that it would simply be a case of turning a de facto situation into an official one. The main opposition tended to be focused in the other provinces, particularly the Western Cape where the provincial task group argued vigorously against national companies and interpreted the proposal as an ongoing attempt by Gauteng to consolidate its central power position in South African theatre practice.

ACTAG in its final recommendations to the minister agreed not to push for national companies although they opened the way for a possible revisiting of the subject in the future. The department accepted the ACTAG position and no national theatre or performing arts companies were suggested in the white paper. However, the tension between a push for 'central' and 'national' on the one hand, and 'dispersal' and 'local' on the other, continues to be present in the theatre industry. Although no national companies exist, in practice Gauteng operates as a kind of national centre for theatre activity in the country, enjoying better infrastructure, attracting more funding, having greater access to international contacts and often being mistaken for the totality of South African theatre by journalists, administrators and practitioners alike.

However, in the last two years both the North West Province and the Eastern Cape have had productions included in the festival programme and if this indicates a trend towards the widening of the regional representation then it is indeed worthy of note.

One of the interesting aspects of Larlham's article is that almost all the examples he chooses to quote are located in Kwazulu-Natal, whereas his conclusions indicate characteristics of South African theatre as a whole. On the one hand this could be interpreted as a weakness confusing a part for the whole in a country as diverse as this one. On the other hand however it could be seen as a move to de-centre the power structures inherent in theatre practice; a strategy designed to redefine the margins as multiple new centres from which perspectives the old centre becomes marginal. It seems to me that such a strategy is appropriate to a country such as South Africa which, in its diversity, reflects the impossibility of any idea of stable centre or homogeneity, geographically or socio-politically. It seems to me that the centre in South Africa, and by extension South African theatre practice, is constantly shifting and the relation between centre and periphery is constantly being redefined, despite the strong centralising tendency located in Gauteng as the economic power base of the country.

I would therefore suggest that what we have in theatre practice in South Africa at present is a tension which can be defined in spatial terms. On the one hand there is a desire of the centre - Gauteng - to maintain and preserve a clearly demarcated binary of centre/margin in order to keep the old power relation, inherited from the past, intact. On the other hand there is a push from the margins, geographical and socio-political, to displace the very notion of centre and margin, to deny the existence of any 'master-territories' (Minh-ha 1991, p. 9), and to refuse its place as 'Other'. Instead what is proposed is a series of spaces which are simultaneously marginal and central, and neither; in-between spaces which are fragmentary and incomplete, precarious but filled with possibility.

In the light of the above and with this spatial tension in the forefront, I would like to move on to a more detailed analysis of a number of productions in an attempt to begin to piece together emergent trends within the practice of theatre in the 1990s.

Theatre into the 1990s

> ... the barricade strikes me as an appropriate and valuable metaphor for the two linked voices which might structure all cultures of the oppressed and define the dialectics of cultural liberation. There is the public, strident and rhetorical voice of protest and accusation, shouting over the barricade to break the silence of censorship and demand justice; and there is the intimate poetic voice of reflection, exploring the contradictions within which often undermine our cause and even reinforce our oppression. The rhetorical voice must be given priority in times of extreme vulnerability and need. But that quiet voice of 'argument with ourselves' is the voice which might be heard whispering in the safety behind the barricade, in the silence which follows the cease-fire.
>
> Baron Cohen 1996, p. 62

The 1980s in South Africa were the years of protest theatre. The 'rhetorical voice' boomed loud over the barricades. Subjects were unambiguously and loudly defined as clear binaries: white/black, oppressor/oppressed. Difference and contradiction were smoothed over or hidden away as we sought to project an image of unity in the face of tyranny. With the political changes of the 1990s and the apparent passing of the master-narrative: apartheid (at least in an official sense), came the demise of the protest voice leaving something of a vacuum as theatre practitioners groped around in search of a new voice.

One of the features of the 'rhetorical voice' is that it drowns out all other possible voices while it is booming over the barricades. When it stops booming, other 'quieter' voices begin to be heard. These voices, which sound from the edge, are signs of presence which break the darkness behind the 'barricades' and become the co-ordinates by which new spaces begin to be defined for theatre. Now, from our current perspective near the end of the decade, we can begin to discern not a singular 'new voice', but a collection of multiple voices, reflecting multiple subjects constructing many, changeable identities, located in new and varying locations. These new locations are both material and metaphorical spaces that reflect actual, imagined and produced geographical and socio-political positions. With this in mind, and in order to take this discussion further, let us examine a number of specific examples from theatre practice in the 1990s.

On the one hand there have been those productions which continue to focus on the grand narratives: apartheid and colonialism. Here I have in mind productions such as Deon Opperman's Donkerland, Handspring's Faustus in Africa and Ubu and the Truth Commission, Paul Herzberg's The Dead Wait, as well as Jazzart/Magnet Theatre's Medea. These represent attempts to rewrite the colonial/apartheid narrative from the post-colonial/post-apartheid perspective. However, despite being productions of great note, like all such attempts they remain anchored to the grand narrative, one foot tied to the past, struggling to move on.

On the other hand more recent trends seem to point towards a theatre of smaller narratives which is more personal, more introspective, more reflective of the ambiguities and contradictions which are at the heart of our new society. It is also a theatre which is more localised, tuning into its environment and its specific community, being more content with being a fragment, making fewer claims to representing the whole, the national identity/culture.

By choosing to focus on these 'smaller' narratives I do not mean to suggest that apartheid and colonialism have somehow been finally or completely spoken for, but rather that the strategies of their speaking or unspeaking have changed to a more dispersed and plural utterance. And the speakers are travellers too. In a country where so much space has been off limits to so many in the past, in which travel and migration have been either restricted or enforced, there is something essentially liberatory about the idea of free travel, of exploration, of a willingness to move on from fixed positions.

The performers of these narratives are travellers, explorers, cartographers who traverse the uncharted, previously silenced spaces, mapping the landscape of the new society, revealing through their performances the changing cultural and personal identities that are emerging. Most of them locate themselves on the extreme edges of the landscape geographically and socially in spaces which are relatively free of the controls of the political and geographical centres, yet they are not averse to travelling through the centres themselves, redefining them in the process.

Dawn Langdown is an actress, dancer, choreographer, storyteller and teacher. She is also a nomad, continuously travelling like the hunter-gatherers before her, who form one part of her complex origins. She was born in Cape Town to teacher parents who themselves originated from the Eastern Cape coastal region but were constantly moving from post to post. At the age of three she moved to Loeriesfontein; at ten further north to Okiep in Namaqualand, the barren, rain-starved desert area of the Northern Cape which once a year for a short moment bursts into life with the blooming of spring flowers. She was sent back to Cape Town to attend high school making frequent trips back to visit her parents in Okiep and spending holidays with her grandparents in Plettenberg Bay. After school and university she returned to Namaqualand, began to dance, and then moved back to Cape Town with a stop in Windhoek on the way.

In Cape Town she established herself as a performer and teacher over a number of years in which her range of skills continued to develop as she explored other forms of live performance. In 1997 she returned to Namaqualand where she now runs a performing arts school for young children. Her life has been a constant shuttling between the centre and the periphery, a seeming inability to settle in one place or the other, or on one or other identity for too long.

Centre, in the above context, is to be understood in one sense geographically, as in the relation between Cape Town as regional centre and Namaqualand and Plettenberg Bay as regional peripheries; and as in the relation between the city of Cape Town and the townships of the Cape Flats as its peripheries. In another sense the centre is also understood to be the centre of theatre practice (very white) located in Cape Town, a place where Langdown can access infrastructure, visibility, critical acclaim, and the chance to participate in opera, contemporary dance, straight and avant-garde theatre and film. But in a more personal sense, the centre of Langdown herself is probably located out on the periphery in Namaqualand, living in her mother's house – the 'homeplace' of bel hooks (hooks 1990: 47). From that perspective Cape Town is very much on the periphery. The act of shuttling between these centres and these peripheries is in fact an act of displacement and of disordering, a refusal of the hierarchy of the binary: centre/periphery. By refusing to make any one place a stable and consistent home, she and her performance exist in an in-between space, in what Gloria Anzaldúa (1987) describes as the 'borderlands':

> ... Borderlands are physically present whenever two or more cultures edge each other, where people of different races occupy the same territory, where under, lower, middle and upper classes touch, where the space between two people shrinks with intimacy ... It's not a comfortable territory to live in, this place of contradictions. Hatred, anger and exploitation are the prominent features of this landscape ... Living on borders and in margins, keeping intact one's shifting and multiple identity and integrity, is like trying to swim in a new element, an 'alien' element ... [that] has become familiar ... No, not comfortable but home.

Different communities; different, shifting, multiple identities; different languages from one place to another. Her solo performance 'Soe Loep Ons ... Nou Nog!'[5] is a personal reflection on these communities the so-called 'coloured'[6] communities of what was the Cape Province but is now Western, Eastern and Northern Cape. In the production which uses storytelling, song and dance, she trawls her own biography for characters who reveal intimate, often painful aspects of her communities. The stories she tells map out the journey of her life from Namaqualand to Cape Town and on to Plettenberg Bay. In the first story set in Namaqualand, a group of women is attempting to stage a nativity play. One of the women, auntie Sophie, is not allocated a part even when there is nobody to play the role of the 'angel of the Lord'. Sophie attributes this to the fact that she is too black and her hair is not straight. When the rehearsal ends Sophie sets off for home, but while trying to catch a stray dog, she is knocked over by a truck and dies. Weeks later when the women stage the nativity play, Sophie returns to haunt them when she appears on the stage as a real angel. Unwilling to forgive her former tormentors, she is bent on revenge, and she takes the ringleaders off on a ride to hell and back via the 'whites only' public swimming pool. When she finally returns them to the church hall stage and disappears, the women are unrepentant refusing to accept that Sophie could have become an angel, instead they put their experience down to a dream which prompts Sophie to send down a thunderbolt blowing the women back to the fires of hell.

The second story reveals Uncle Abie, a man who has worked for the army for many years without being accorded any respect or receiving any promotion. Excessive drinking and a sense of powerlessness outside of the home has turned Abie into a monster inside the home who verbally abuses his wife and his three daughters. Falling asleep one day after a bout of drinking and abusing he enters a nightmare world from which he cannot escape. Here he is pursued by marching rifles, a floating teapot which refuses to come close enough to help him quench his thirst, and a sergeant-major who calls him a 'klonkie' and a 'hotnot'[7] and forces him to drill aimlessly on the spot. Finally he is caught in a net from which there seems no escape. Suddenly he sees the doors of heaven opening and three angels appear whom he recognises as his daughters. The angels release him from the net and begin to show him the way out of the dream, but at a crucial moment Abie explodes and begins to abuse the angels, refusing to accept orders from children and ending with a final curse directed at their mother, Abie's long-suffering wife. The angels immediately drop Abie and fly away leaving him stranded forever in his own wilderness, somewhere at the bottom of a brandy bottle.

The final story takes the form of a dramatised interview between Oom George Langdown, a seventy-six year old plumber from Plettenberg Bay, and a reporter from the Sunday Times newspaper at a time when Plettenberg Bay was beginning its transformation from fishing village to leisure resort. In the interview, with his wife Mathilda at death's door in the room behind him, Oom George reveals the history of a community in the process of destruction. He has lived his entire life overlooking the sea, with the view from his stoep[8] his most precious possession, and now the land is being taken away and he and his family are being moved to a new location without any view. It is a story of the effect of the Group Areas Act on a small community outside the major centres and the major spotlight. Ultimately his complaints are in vain and by the end of the narrative the bulldozers are flattening his home.

The three stories are framed by various song and dance numbers which present the decaying image of the laughing, happy-go-lucky 'coloured' who is caught in the middle space between black and white, fighting to find an identity in a new reality, seemingly locked in a self-perpetuating cycle of abuse and victimisation. What starts off as the predominant image of the smiling, laughing 'coon'[9] gradually decays and develops into a bitter and angry image of marginalisation.

Throughout the performance Langdown is alone on stage. She alone peoples her stories rapidly transforming from character to character often jumping backwards and forwards from one character to another from line to line. Langdown's characters are men and women and she tackles all with a seemingly never-ending supply of energy. The physical body is at the heart of the storytelling and operates as a text in its own right not simply as a means of illustrating the spoken text. The spoken text itself is a Bakhtinian heteroglossia combining Afrikaans, English and the patois of the streets and the taxis. The text refuses to settle into one or other language, setting up at one moment what seems to be a sort of consistency, only to undermine it the next moment by infiltrating other languages and dialects. From another perspective the use of Afrikaans as a language of representation in the process of identity formation can be seen as a reclaiming of the language - or at least a version of the language - from its status as the language of the oppressor to a new status as a language of the people.

In many ways the piece is Langdown's response to the dominant representation of the 'coloured' community in performance: the smiling, happy faces, the songs and dances which are able to wipe away pain with apparent ease, the constant sense of 'party' above all else. Langdown acknowledges the tension between the 'party' and the 'pain' but is intent on balancing the two, on drawing out the 'pain' and allowing it to feed the 'party' in a much more dynamic way than is usually the case. This repositioning allows her to express the residues of anger which are still prominent in the community, particularly among those women who do not or will not allow themselves to be subjected to the patterns of abuse and victimisation that are all too common. Langdown will not allow the ambiguities, the contradictions to be laid to rest. She is intent on hauling them out into the spotlight and using them as building blocks in the construction of her identity, for this is not an uncovering of some essential 'colouredness' but a painstaking building up, from fragments, of a splintered, changeable identity in process. This is not a strategy designed to attract mainstream acceptance and large paying crowds. In fact Langdown's apparent belligerence, as well as the fact that she is a woman with 'attitude', situates her on the periphery even within her already marginal community. But it is a marginality which is also chosen by her in a conscious attempt to create new and clear spaces from which resistance can begin, from which the speaking back can start. This is not a comfortable place, but one which can be extremely dynamic as bel hooks (1990, pp. 145–149) makes clear:

> As a radical standpoint, perspective, position, 'the politics of location' necessarily calls those of us who would participate in the formation of counter-hegemonic cultural practice to identify the spaces where we begin the process of re-vision ... for me this space of radical openness is a margin – a profound edge. Locating oneself there is difficult yet necessary. It is not a 'safe' place. One is always at risk. One needs a community of resistance.

The choice of performance space is relevant here too. Langdown chose not to perform in a mainstream venue although such a choice was possible. Instead she chose to perform at the Jazzart Studio, a rehearsal venue by day hastily transformed into a makeshift performance venue by night. In the '80s the studio became one of the few alternative performance venues in Cape Town, regularly attracting large crowds from the townships. During the '90s, as previously marginalised performance groups began to claim the spaces of the centre, venues like the studio fell out of use as performance spaces. By choosing to locate her performance in such a space, Langdown consciously invited in her admittedly small, but selected community (essentially but not completely composed of politically committed 'coloured' men and women) who might not have been ready, able or willing to enter hegemonic spaces. At the same time, Langdown's reputation as a performer, and the dearth of quality performance work on show in Cape Town, drew mainstream audiences out of their comfort zones and onto the periphery. This was not always the case, with at least one mainstream newspaper refusing to send a critic to review the production on the grounds that the newspaper didn't review 'studio concerts', this despite Langdown's long history of performance and her reputation as a performer and choreographer. Location here seemed to annul all value or quality in the mind of this particular arts editor.

Soe Loep Ons played in Cape Town, in Namaqualand, in Oudtshoorn at the Klein Karoo Kunstefees, and on the fringe at Grahamstown. It is interesting to note the difference of response from audiences in different locations. In Cape Town and Namaqualand where the audience shared in and related to the narratives the response was intense. Audience members were deeply moved and exhilarated and responded in an active way often speaking back to the stage in recognition and agreement. In Grahamstown, where there is no major 'coloured' presence, and to a lesser extent in Oudtshoorn where the audience is predominantly white and the local coloured community have not yet claimed/gained access, the response was far more muted and the audience seemed more alienated from the work. This raises an interesting question about productions built around 'local knowledge' in a specific context and the effects of leaving the homebase, the local community, to be performed elsewhere. What seems to happen is a kind of professionalisation of the 'local' where the skill of the performer counts for more in the eyes of the audience than the 'knowledge' being communicated and the 'knowledge' itself is simply viewed as exotic. At one particular performance in Grahamstown a group of people from the coloured communities in George and Plettenberg Bay came up to Grahamstown to watch the performance. Immediately the response of the audience was completely different and the rest of the audience on that particular occasion had a very different experience from the average audience member at the festival.

Like Langdown, Jay Pather is a traveller. Brought up in Durban, he studied at New York University with Richard Schechner. He has been a teacher in Zululand, a choreographer and dancer in Cape Town, and now runs the Siwela Sonke Dance Theatre company at the Playhouse in Durban. His stories too, map the geography of his life and through them he constructs his identity. His The Stories I Could Tell[10] is another one-person performance consisting of a collection of narratives, in which the performer transforms from character to character with great skill and apparent ease, in which the body is centrally placed in the text and in which the voices change from dialect to dialect even though here the language is all English. It is another example of a work of great intimacy and self-reflection which is more intent on revealing contradictions and difference than uncovering something essential and complete. It was also performed in Cape Town at the Jazzart Studio and was extremely well supported by an audience which was primarily local in the sense that it drew from a particular community (the gay and lesbian community) but which also drew from a wider pool as mainstream audiences were coaxed out onto the margins by the production's reputation. From Cape Town the production travelled to the Artrage Festival in Perth, Western Australia, an example of the growing connectedness between the local and the global, bypassing the central and the national altogether.

The first story opens with the tentative entrance, bathed in pink light, of Berna-Lee, a fairytale princess from Mitchell's Plain. Here Pather is adorned in a pink and white dress with a tulle skirt, high heel shoes and a blonde wig - something akin to the sugar plum fairy. The story is told in the form of a fairytale, spoken in the camp tones of Cape Town's 'coloured' gay community, as Berna-Lee pages through an oversized photograph album recounting the story of her life. Born a boy to a king and queen in Mitchell's Plain, and reborn again at the age of sixteen, 'a woman'. Thrown out of home when her mother dies by her wicked step-mother, she is left to fend for herself in the jungle outside the castle only to be saved from the marauding beasts by a handsome prince on a white charger. And here the story ends with Berna-Lee declaring that 'life is one big fairytale!' Or is it ...?

Pather removes his dress to reveal a second outfit beneath: short, black mini-skirt and elasticised black boob-tube. The light changes to a cold blue, the music-box tinkling of the first story gives way to more sultry vibes as Pather launches into the poem 'Raw Dog Night'[11]. Here the harsh reality takes over: the streetwalker, bruised and humiliated, evicted from his/her apartment, looking for the next bed. S/he meets a man – 'a prince floating by' – who picks him/her up but balks at taking him/her back to his flat. Instead they decide to go for a ride in his car but before they can go anywhere he collapses, blood gushing from his mouth. Police pull up in another car and seeing the body of the john on the pavement they throw the streetwalker into the back of their car and cut, beat and rape him/her repeatedly. Finally, she escapes and runs naked (here Pather rips the blond wig from his head), bleeding down the street 'one raw dog night when too much of my queerness was showing'.

Bright, eastern music introduces the third story told with a combination of words and Bharata Natyam mudras – set poses, movements of the head and eyes, and hand gestures. A young boy – ten years old – is celebrating his father's fortieth birthday. He decides to create a dance for his father to show the world how much he loves him. He composes a dance about Lord Shiva, the Hindu god who is also known as 'Lord of the Dance'. He prepares for weeks while his mother sings for him. He fashions bells for his ankles and ties an old sari of his mother's around his waist. The day of the party arrives and many guests come to his home. He waits quietly behind a screen for the right time to dance, wanting the dance to be 'a surprise to the world'. But just as he is about to dance his brother stops him and tells him that his father has found out about the dance and will not allow him to dance in front of the guests. Perhaps he can dance later when the guests have gone home. 'Boys,' says the brother, 'shouldn't do these things'. The young boy is confused but he waits until the guests have gone home and then he is allowed to dance for his father and a few aunts. At this point, Pather dances the dance before his father in the Bharata Natyam style. When the dance ends there is silence. The boy's father says nothing. So the boy unwinds the sari and leaves not looking at his father's face. Just as he gets to the door he looks up into his father's eyes and they are filled with anger and the boy leaves the room devastated. Once more Pather launches into a dance but the music is more soulful, more mournful now.

As Pather dances he dresses in a collar and tie, a black suit and leather shoes. When he speaks again his accent is strong Natal Indian. There is a tone of confusion in the voice and a sense of uneasiness in the body. The character tells of his marriage to a North Indian woman – he is South Indian – which lasted for five years, five happy years, he assures us. During this time, he tells us, he was honest with his wife and told her of a relationship he once had with a man. He assures us he is not gay; it was a one-off affair. He tells us that he and his wife had one child only and that they were divorced after five years with custody of the child awarded to the woman and visitation rights awarded to him. A while later, he tells us, his ex-wife wanted to change the daughter's

surname to her own and to limit his access. When he asked her why she was obstruct-
ing his right to see his daughter, his ex-wife, he tells us, told him it was a matter of
'values', their daughter needed to be brought up in an atmosphere of 'family values'.
Then she asked him whether he was seeing another woman and he asked her why she
supposed it was another woman he was seeing, at which point she exploded and told
him that his daughter didn't need him anymore because he was just the biological
father and nothing else. From that day, he tells us, he has not been able to see his
daughter but now he is fighting back and is taking his ex-wife to court. Yet he is unsure
about the court case, he says. He wants to keep things quiet. He's worried about the
effect on his daughter. He's not sure he's done the right thing. People have already
stopped talking to him, he tells us. He is being ostracised from his community. He
feels, he says, like 'a square peg in a round hole'. The story ends with Pather dancing a
dance of uncertainty with a sari draped uneasily over the character's black-suited shoul-
der.

The fifth story opens with a definite change of mood. The music is more contemporary now with a stronger beat. A slide is projected against the back wall: a picture of
Pather as a streetwise gay man bedecked in leather jacket, Levi's, steel-caps, white T-shirt
and thick, black leather belt with a large buckle. He talks back to the last character,
discarding his previous costume into the wings. 'Get out! Mr Naidoo' he says, 'a
square peg in a round hole ... find a square hole'. In upbeat poetic rhythms he describes
his new persona as 'a gay black man in the city', a traveller 'from village to city/from
township to town/from Chatsworth to Jo'burg/from Mitchell's Plain to Cape Town',
empowered, confident and politically committed. But then he launches into yet another story in which the character is picked up by a white man and taken back to his
apartment. They begin to caress each other, the black man exploring the white man's
body all over until suddenly he discovers 'a red bump' where it isn't supposed to be.
The black man stops his caressing and escapes into the kitchen for water. The white
man follows him placatingly. 'I know what you are thinking', says the white man: 'Why
didn't you tell me?' 'No', thinks the black man: 'Why did you choose me?' But the
black man doesn't voice his thoughts and they return to the other room and indulge in
safe and protected sex after which the black man flees into the night, out into the street,
and he dances his rage and his fear as an outsider in the white gay world which he
'desires' and 'seeks out' but which suffocates him. 'He is, he says, 'a stranger to my
community/ Not quite a member of your tribe/ I sometimes forget who I am!'

Once more the music changes. Now it is an African sound that fills the space and
Pather transforms once more, with the aid of leopard print leggings, a kikhoi or two
and a flat topped African hat, into a praise singer, singing a praise to Simon Nkoli..
Nkoli is a political activist, detained in the uprisings of 1976, jailed for four years in the
wake of the Delmas treason trial, who also happens to be gay. And he is a problem for
the liberation movement because he won't shut up about being gay, on the contrary he

is intent on telling the world this truth. He fights for acceptance and recognition and he gains it from mainstream leaders. He forms a new political organisation for lesbian and gay people and his efforts are rewarded because the president himself, Nelson Mandela, announces at his inauguration that there shall be no discrimination against anyone on the basis of sexual orientation. And these 'heady times', Pather tells us, require us to move on in the spirit of Simon Nkoli towards a 'new correspondence with ourselves'. And he tells of his relationship with a black man, Godfrey, whom he meets in a club and who rather than sweeping him off his feet, 'makes his feet feel firmly on the ground'. His lover does not hide their relationship but flaunts it in the open for all to see and know. So in a re-writing of a traditional Africa praise poem in which a woman praises her warrior husband, Pather launches into a description of his lover, a warrior himself whose 'hair is a forest of shrub and baobab', whose 'dreads are worn like a crown', whose 'lips are large and luscious and soft' and whose 'skin is black and pock-marked'. And he ends by dancing to a bowl of water at the front of the stage, lifting it up, swirling it around a few times and then pouring it over his head and down over his body in a ritual of cleansing as the lights go down slowly.

Through his stories and his characters, Pather refuses the monolithic interpretations of masculinity, of 'Indianness'[12] and of being black in South Africa which were shaped by apartheid in the first place and are being re-shaped once more by the developing hegemony of the democratic state. Pather is unwilling to accept the pre-conceived categorisations – Indian man; black man; gay, Indian man; gay, black man – for himself. For him it seems, we are all but fragments of stories picked up at the local stop-off points on the map of our journey through life and through these we construct, speak, dance our multiple identities which are never fixed or complete, always in process. His very presence on the stage, engaged in this process, his claim to a space, to a voice, to be seen, problematises the heterosexual/male centre's claim to all the space and what fills it.

Aubrey Sekhabi is a graduate from the University of the Witwatersrand, one of a growing number of young black performers and directors who are emerging from training programmes in universities around the country. Whereas the black practitioners in the past were mostly self-trained or passed through quasi-training with practitioners like Gibson Kente, these new graduates are attempting to put the experience gained in institutions to work in local contexts in order to tell their own stories. At first glance Sekhabi does not seem to occupy a marginal position at all. He is an educated member of the emergent black middle-class in the new South Africa and originates from Gauteng. However, Sekhabi has consciously located himself on the geographical margins, operating as he does out of Mmabatho in the North West Province, the territory which was previously the homeland of Bophutatswana. He is the artistic director of North West Drama Company, a part of the North West Arts Council which is funded by the provincial government. Here, far away from the bustle and hype of

Gauteng, he has, together with his company, created a number of new plays such as On My Birthday, Nkoyeni High and Not with My Gun. While the first two plays were created in workshop with the cast the latter was penned by Sekhabi with Mpumelelo Grootboom. In these gritty, social-realist plays Sekhabi, like the other practitioners we have looked at, veers away from the grand narrative and focuses instead on th smaller, more localised issues, particularly as they concern the emergent black middle-class and its attempts to fashion a new identity amidst the hard and often depressing realities of life in our townships and suburbs. In On My Birthday he tackles the issue of domestic violence. Nkoyeni High deals with problems in education, particularly in predomi-nantly black schools. His most recent work, Not with My Gun, presents a group of male friends at a stag party celebrating one of their number's final night of singlehood. In the midst of their celebrations they discover a burglar, who happens to be white, in the act of burgling the house. This leads them into the dilemma of what to do with the intruding 'whitey'. Should they act violently against the intruder thereby replicating the behaviour of whites in similar situations in the past or can they behave differently? The play refuses the niceties and conciliations of our 'simunye'[13] culture in favour of presenting the attitudes of people, particularly in this case, young, black, middle-class men, when they are alone behind closed doors, attitudes which are sometimes hard for outsiders to swallow.

The fact that Sekhabi locates his work outside the centre allows him the space to develop in a way that other young aspiring directors have not been able to. He is not at the mercy of nervous managements caught between a desire to present local content and promote young black talent, and a need to watch revenue as attendances fall. Instead he is in a position of power in his own small pond where he makes the choices and is therefore able to claim the space which he might have been denied elsewhere. Sekhabi and his company have worked hard to cultivate an audience from the local community. They constantly tour around the province, staging performances and run-ning acting workshops. A percentage of all moneys taken at the door is ploughed back into local community groups. In Mmabatho the company lays on a bus to transport students from the university and colleges to the theatre. The result is a growing and loyal audience who support the company and its work. This supportive environment and the space to create, free from excessive commercial pressures, have allowed Sekhabi to develop and mature as a director/writer so that he is now able to approach the centre with greater confidence and the ability to command support and space. Currently, Not with My Gun is being performed on the main stage at the Market Theatre in Johannes-burg which is a major achievement for Sekhabi, but raises many interesting questions about the relationship between margin and centre as well. Can Sekhabi maintain his sense of independence and loyalty to the local community in Mmabatho or will the allure of the big stages and bright lights finally appropriate his energy and vision? Is the move to the periphery an active political, counter-hegemonic move or is it simply a stepping stone towards bigger things? The fact that Sekhabi has been able in the past to tour with his productions to international festivals and theatres whilst still retaining his local focus, might be an indication of his commitment but the lure of the city of gold has long been a powerful one. Can Gauteng ever be simply another place to travel through or will it always remain the centre, bent on incorporation?

It is of course important to recognise that there are margins in the centre as well and that activities in these margins challenge the stability of the centre itself, threatening to redefine its certainties. Although I do not have the space in this article to examine this in detail it would be nevertheless useful at this point to mention a few of these counter-hegemonic activities.

Other young black playmakers in Gauteng have struggled to claim the same space at the Market Theatre that their white counterparts achieved in the past and which Sekhabi now seems to be enjoying. This can, in part, be attributed to what Robert Greig (1997a, p. 15) describes as 'an egg-dance challenge'. How to 'retain loyal, existing and often affluent audiences and reach audiences and artists who have not had opportunities in the past'. This leads to a nervous management who are not too keen to rush into major changes or take big risks with new, unknown directors and writers. However, there have recently been indications that some previously marginalised black playmakers are beginning to gain access to space at the centre in which to produce a range of new and exciting works, the content of which concerns marginal subject positions such as the mass of unemployed youth in Gauteng and their inevitable drift towards crime. These playmakers include Sello Maake-KaNcube (Koze Kuse Bash); Pule Hlatshwayo (Gomorrah!); the members of the Positive Arts Society (Hola Majita); and Obed Baloyi, whose Ga-Mchangani caused a stir when it was performed at the Market because it was entirely in the Shangaan language, raising issues of language usage on South African stages and questioning the dominant position of English in black theatre work.

It is also of interest to note the development of the Windybrow Theatre on the border between Hillbrow and Joubert Park. Windybrow is a theatre located in an old Victorian mansion in what was once an upmarket suburb but has now become an inner city slum. Windybrow has grown out of PACT and still, for the remainder of this year, receives a subsidy through that organisation. However, from next year it will become an independent theatre. It is run by Walter Chakela and a dynamic young team including Ali Hlongwane, Nomsa Manaka and Thabiso Leshoai. Located within and speaking to a specific, local community, it aims to foster the development of black theatre and to produce African plays. It has forged ahead presenting new and developing playwrights and directors for new local audiences without the need to consider the tastes and sensibilities of 'loyal, existing and often affluent audiences' from the past.

Robert Colman has produced two productions recently which utilise non-specialist actors from particular communities to articulate narratives based on personal testimonies which originate in marginal social positions: victims of human rights abuses who appeared before the Truth Commission (Indaba Engizoyixoxa - The story I am about to tell) and black lesbian women (After Nines). These productions were not performed at mainstream venues but at community venues and engage with different, particular, situated audiences in their local contexts. This final example leads us on to widen our examination by looking at theatre events which challenge the dominant paradigms of theatre production: where it is performed, by whom and with what ultimate aim.

Moving out of the mainstream

Although the content of theatre productions in South Africa has over the past few years continued to explore issues relevant to the lives of South Africans, and although the casts on stage have continued to grow more representative of the South African population, the same cannot be said for theatre audiences. Statistics on theatre attendance are hard to come by but it is generally accepted by theatre practitioners that attendance at theatre productions is very low and that there has been very little growth in attendance figures over the past few years. In fact, the audience attending productions in established theatre spaces is declining. The reasons suggested for this apparent decline are numerous. They include the fact that theatres have traditionally been built in the centre of major cities and that the move over the past few years has been away from the cities and into a more sheltered and self-contained life in the suburbs and townships, particularly at night. People simply do not travel into the city at night for recreational purposes. In fact people don't like to travel anywhere at night if possible because of a general fear of crime. It is also argued that with the declining economy and rising inflation there is little surplus income to spend on recreation. Theatre tickets have risen in price while cinema has become more accessible to the broader community. However, in my opinion, the single most important problem with regard to theatre audiences is the fact that the composition of the audience has not changed significantly since 1994. Theatres have not managed to make theatre-going an attractive and relevant activity for the majority of the population and rely too heavily on white middle class patrons who have a history of consistent theatre-going. Part of the problem facing theatre managers is the dominance of 'televisual' culture in which 'the televisual is an intrinsic and determining element of our cultural formation' and '... it is indeed no longer a question of thinking about television in various cultural contexts but of seeing it as the cultural context' (Auslander 1997, p. 50). Television, which has the capacity to reach out to a potentially infinite number of viewers, has been able to multiply its spectators over the past number of years as television sets have sprung up all over our townships. Theatre, which can only ever tolerate a limited audience and one which must move out of the domestic space into the public arena in order to watch, has been unable to compete and is increasingly embattled as a result. From my particular perspective as a teacher in a university drama department who encounters a large number of young people seeking access to training, I can attest to the fact that most young people in South Africa today find it difficult to distinguish between live theatre and television drama. A large number of applicants for a theatre training have never seen a live theatre production but are very knowledgeable about local television drama and the soapies. It is important to point out that when Gibson Kente was drawing large audiences in the townships for his live musical theatre performances in the late sixties and early seventies there was no television in South Africa.

However, despite the general mood of gloom amongst theatre managers in the established theatres of the major cities, progress is evident in some areas. I have already argued at some length for the recognition of localised performance out of the mainstream. Such companies, as we have seen, target audiences better as a result of their continued presence in and around their communities, their visibility and availability to the community and through the construction of narratives which the audience shares. Furthermore, it must be recognised that an increasing number of South Africans are experiencing theatre outside of traditional theatre spaces in events which challenge the basic paradigms of theatrical production in terms of space, what constitutes a performer, and the relationship between performers and audience. For the remainder of this article I will focus on a number of these manifestations.

One particular growth area has been in community-based arts education and site-specific performance projects. In the past community theatre was often a code for black theatre and it was often a label used pejoratively by white critics and practitioners. Today as black theatre practitioners begin to occupy positions in the mainstream of theatre practice the term has begun to free itself from these associations and has taken on a more nuanced and developed meaning. Here the community are both participant/ performers and audience and the experience of the process is as important as the product. One such project is Project Phakama.

Phakama is a participant-centred, community-based performance and educational project for young people. It was started by the London International Festival of Theatre (LIFT) and Sibikwa Community Theatre in 1996. Since then it has facilitated projects and performances in Benoni (Bulang Dikgoro - Open the Gates), Seshego in the Northern Province (Ka Mor Walo Ka Seatleng - With a Suitcase in My Hand) and most recently on the Cape Flats (Met 'n Sak Onner die Blad - With a Suitcase in My Hand), In the latter project young people and arts workers from Cape Town's suburbs and townships were joined by similar groups from Seshego, Mmabatho and Benoni and from Deptford in London for a two week residential process of skills development which culminated in an outdoor site-specific performance at a local scout camp.

The performance, which was attended by the local community of Grassy Park and friends and family of the performers, explored stories of journeys, migrations and forced removals. Once more we encounter the motif of the traveller, with suitcase under the arm, filled with stories which have been picked up at various stop-off points (the participants' own histories), stories that are used to construct new, emerging identities. Phakama is on one hand an extremely localised project but on the other hand it has a strong cross-national dimension and is able to explore commonalities of experience in communities as diverse as the ones mentioned above.

Another interesting dynamic is playing itself out at the centre of theatre practice in the new South Africa, the Market Theatre. When the Market Laboratory[14] was started in 1990 it consciously chose a peripheral position in relation to the Market Theatre itself. In order to encourage community theatre groups to use the Laboratory as a resource, a separation was actively established between the activities in the Laboratory and at the theatre. This was done in order to allay fears that the Laboratory was simply a way for the theatre to appropriate ideas and stories from local communities. Today the Laboratory is beginning more and more to redefine the centre of the Market itself. The sense of focus and the apparent success of Laboratory activities, and the contrasting struggle for audiences and generally perceived lack of direction in the theatres, have begun to shift attention and power to the Laboratory. As Greig (1997a, p. 15) reports:

> The Lab costs the Market complex a mere 11 percent of the Market's overall budget. But this is no indication of the energy behind its projects and their long-term value. In fact, the Lab is securing the Market's future. These are some of the results:
> — workers ran 50 fieldwork projects in Gauteng
> — the Lab held three large festivals for emergent drama groups and children that attracted attendances of 78 percent capacity. About 38 groups were showcased
> — regular Saturday afternoon showcases were held, with 65 new plays or works by unknown groups
> — the Lab devised and toured a schools production of Julius Caesar to 30 schools – reaching a total of 10 000 Matric pupils
> — it held fieldwork workshops in Botswana and Zimbabwe and five two-month projects, mainly dealing with text development, at the Lab
> — it toured a primary school Aids and child abuse play to 12 500 scholars at 52 schools ...

This record of activity not only indicates the success and importance of Laboratory activities to the Market and its right to claim a more central place in the Market Theatre as a whole. It also indicates the extent of community interest in and involvement with theatre and drama in the Gauteng region. And this is only one theatre; others, such as Windybrow, are engaged in similar activities themselves.

A further interesting example which shows the virility of the centre: its ability to fight back, and the overall complexity of the relationship between centre and margins, is the case of Industrial Theatre. In the 1980s one of the most significant areas of theatre practice was in the context of the labour movement in the form of Workers Theatre. This was theatre which originated with workers, dealt with their problems and issues, was performed by workers for other workers and which embodied a strong counter-hegemonic thrust. It operated from the theatrical and political margins as a site of resistance to the hegemony of the centre. However, there seems to have been little significant development in this form of practice during the 1990s. Instead, management has co-opted the theatre as a tool placing it at the 'capitalist' centre in the form of what is now known as Industrial Theatre: the use of theatrical performance or theatre-based workshops in corporate situations. Now performances given in the corporate environment originate with management, deal with issues defined by management and are performed by professional actors for worker audiences who remain essentially passive throughout the experience. A slight variation on this is the workshop situation where performer-facilitators use theatre exercises as a means of initiating and provoking discussion on particular themes or issues again defined by management. In such workshops it is possible that workers might be asked to participate actively as performers. In my opinion, this is an excellent example of the risks which face activities on the margins, the way in which they can be completely absorbed and refashioned at the centre.

Large numbers of performers, directors and writers have abandoned the traditional theatres in favour of working in this area. Clare Stopford, a past associate artistic director of the Market Theatre is now permanently employed as a director for the Blue Moon Company, the largest Industrial Theatre company in the country. She estimates that in some instances between thirty and forty thousand workers might be exposed to a theatrical performance mounted by Blue Moon in one of the major corporations. There is no doubt that industrial theatre is a major growth point for the theatre industry in South Africa and that it has become very attractive to practitioners because it is where the money is located with fees being significantly higher than in the traditional theatre context. Detailed analysis of its political dimensions on the other hand has yet to take place within the realm of theatre research.

Conclusions

I have tried in this article to present some sense of the fabric of theatre in South Africa in the 1990s particularly in the period since the democratic elections of 1994. I have argued that this fabric is no longer woven from one master-thread but from multiple smaller threads. In other words that it is a theatre which focuses more on the many small narratives of the margins than on any single grand narrative of the centre and by so doing it reflects a new freedom to articulate personal identities and subjectivities. In those multiple spaces - material and metaphorical - which have traditionally been peripheral in South Africa and South African theatre practice we find the emergence of localised, situated stories, histories and identities being spoken, invented and constructed within theatre performances. Here there is no attempt to find the imaginary sense of unification at the heart of a 'national identity' but rather the sense of diffusion and fragmentation of multiple personal and cultural identities that is so much more a part of the way in which reality in South Africa is perceived today. And it is not only on the level of content but at the level of production too: where the plays are presented, who performs them, and their relationship to their particular audiences which is significant.

What I am suggesting here is that these smaller narratives constitute co-ordinates of a new radical theatre geography which challenges the binary of centre and margin itself, replacing it with a new, fuller map which charts more diverse practices across multiple, shifting, local centres.

This is not however to say that these small narratives simply stand by themselves, hermetically sealed off from one another, a multiplicity of diverse and separate and competitively fragmented stories, devoid of political activism or radicalism, easily ignored and silenced by the emergent hegemony at the centre of the new state. For it is important to note along with Stuart Hall that 'the politics of absolute dispersal is no politics at all'. What is required is the recognition that these narratives and their performers constitute in the words of Edward Soja (1996, p. 84) 'multiple communities of resistance, polyvocal political movements capable of linking together many radical subjectivities and creating new "meeting places" and real-and-imagined "spaces" for diverse oppositional practices'.

It remains to be seen whether the theatre will continue to develop in this way or whether the centre, always suspicious of multiplicity and intolerant of fragmentation and openness despite its own rhetoric to the contrary, will find ways to enforce the hierarchy of centre and margins. However, if these links between 'radical subjectivities' can be made and these 'communities of resistance' formed, both locally and globally, then there is no reason why the margins should not continue their unspeaking of the centre.

Notes

1   Convention for a Democratic South Africa, the multi-party forum in which the settlement was negotiated which lead to the democratic elections of 1994.
2   Act 56 of 1997.
3   The original act falling under the heading 'Censorship' in the statute books was the

Publications Act number 42 of 1974. The new Film and Publications Act is number 65 of 1996.

4   Gauteng is the name of the province previously known as the Transvaal. Although it is not the largest province it contain the largest city, Johannesburg, with its huge township of Soweto, and the city of Pretoria with its townships including Mamelodi and Shoshanguve. Johannesburg is the economic centre of the country while Pretoria is the capital and therefore the political centre despite the fact that parliament sits in Cape Town. There are concerted moves afoot to move parliament from Cape Town to Gauteng which is loated almost in the centre of the country geographically.

5   Soe Loep Ons ... Nou Nog! (literally: 'This is the way we walk ... still!') was produced by the Jazzart Dance Theatre and Magnet Theatre, and directed by Mark Fleishman with movement direction by Jennie Reznek. Additional choreography ws by Alfred Hinkel. The text was composed by Dawn Langdown with Mark Fleishman.

6   The term 'coloured' was one o the apartheid racial classifications. It referred to people of mixed descent, as well as those descended from Malay slaves, and from the Khoisan peoples. The main concentration ofso-called 'cooured' peole is in the three Cape Provinces.

7   The words 'klonkie' and 'hotnot' are terms of derision particularly when used by white people in referring to 'coloured' people. The first term has the sense of small boy and the second is a shortened version of hottentot.

8   A veranda or balcony.

9   The annual festival in which the Klopse, troops of minstrels with white painted faces, march through the city of Cape Town on the day after New Year, playing music and dancing is often referred to as the 'coon carnival'.

10   The Stories I Could Tell was produced by the Hearts and Eyes Theatre Collective and directed by Peter Hayes. The text was composed by Jay Pather with Peter Hayes.

11   'Raw Dog Night' is a long dramatic poem by the American poet Assoto Sant and is the only piece of writing in the production not written by Pather or director Peter Hayes.

12   'Indian' is another apartheid racial classification which refers to people who originated from India, Pakistan and Sri Lanka. This category includes a number of religions and a number of languages. According to apartheid classification people of Indian descent were not 'black' although many might have considered themselves to be, particularly after the Black Consciousness Movement highlighted the unity of all the oppressed people of South Africa who were not white.

13   'Simunye', meaning 'we are one', is the catch phrase of the South African Broadcasting Corporation's first television channel. It is meant to signify the idea of unity in diversity but has become something of a joke in South Africa.

14 The Market Laboratory was started in 1990 by Barney Simon and John Kani as the development and outreach arm of the Market Theatre Foundation. The original funding was secured from the Rockefeller Foundation.

References

Anzaldúa, G. (1987). *Borderlands/La Frontera: The New Mestiza*, San Francisco: Spinsters/Aunt Lute.

Auslander, P. (1997). 'Against Ontology: Making Distinctions Between the Live and the Mediatized', *Performance Research*, 2(3), pp. 50–55.

Baron Cohen, D. (1996). 'Resistance to Liberation: Decolonizing the Mindful-Body', *Performance Research*, 1(2), pp. 60–74.

Douglas, C. (1996). 'If the Censorship chAnges seem Dangerous, the Secrecy Surrounding Them is Even Worse', *Sunday Independent*, 18 August.

Greig, R. (1996). *Sunday Independent*, 9 June.

Greig, R. (1997a). 'Funding Stethoscope Reveals Market's Health', *The Star Tonight!*, 12 February.

Greig, R. (1997b). 'New Roles in Management of the Arts would Make you Wonder Who's Wearing What Hat', *Sunday Independent*, 13 April.

Hooks, B. (1990). *Yearnings: Race, Gender, and Cultural Politics*, Boston: South End Press.

Larlham, P. (1991). 'Theatre in Transition: The Cultural Struggle in South Africa', *The Drama Review*, 35(1), Spring, pp. 200–211.

McClintock, A. (1994). 'The angel of progress', in F. Barker, P. Hulme and M. Iversen (eds), *Colonial Discourse/ Postcolonial Theory*, Manchester: Manchester University Press.

Minh-ha, T. (1991). *When the Moon Waxes Red: Representation, Gender and Cultural Politics*, New York: Routledge.

Soja, E. (1996). *Thirdspace: Journeys to Los Angeles and other real-and-imagined places*, Cambridge: Blackwell.

Van Graan, M. (1997). 'If the Fishbowl's Too Small, Don't Blame the Poor Fish', *Sunday Independent*, 27 April.

CHAPTER FIVE

Nation building, social identity and television in a changing media landscape

Ruth Teer-Tomaselli

Historically, the South African Broadcasting Corporation (SABC) played an important role in both constructing and supporting the apartheid structures of pre-1991 South Africa. In the 1980s the SABC explicitly supported the then government in its effort to combat the 'Total Onslaught' of revolutionary forces, seen to be spearheaded by the ANC in exile (Teer-Tomaselli and Tomaselli 1996). With the general transformation of South African political imperatives, being the voice of the government was no longer an option – it was a liability. From January 1991 began a process of restructuring, in which pragmatism, rather than propaganda, became the dominant ethos.

The structural change was in part a result of a prolonged campaign to 'free the airwaves', which culminated in the establishment of the Independent Broadcasting Authority (IBA). This statutory body was a council established to operate independently of government and commercial influences, with the mandate of regulating broadcasting activities in the public interest.

It was charged with promoting diversity in a range of sound and television broadcasting services on national, regional and local levels. Of particular note in this regard, the IBA was charged with ensuring that broadcasting services, when viewed collectively, should 'develop and protect a national and regional identity, culture and character' (IBA Act, October 1993, Section 2(c)).

One of the first tasks of the IBA was to carry out a 'Triple Enquiry', which would cover the protection and viability of the public broadcast services, cross-media control of broadcasting services, and locally-produced television content. The Report was released in September 1995.

After an extensive process of public nominations and hearings, the election of the new Board of Directors of the SABC, announced in May 1993, can be seen as the point heralding the 'new' broadcast environment. In line with the social, economic and political changes taking place within the country as a whole, the SABC was in the vanguard of visible change. To this end, much creative energy was expended on negotiating a new 'Vision and Values' framework which would act as the blueprint for the task of transforming a former *state* broadcaster into a fully fledged *public* broadcaster. Summarised briefly, this vision was:

> a commitment to deliver full-spectrum services to all South Africans, in all parts of the country, and in each of the eleven official languages. Their programme content is aimed at protecting and nurturing South African culture and creativity, and reflecting the reality of South Africa to itself, and to the world, South Africa from a distinctly South African perspective.
>
> SABC 1996, p. 2

The most visible evidence of the SABC's new approach has been the reconfiguration of television channels. Prior to this repositioning, television in South Africa served the interests of the middle classes only: predominantly, white, 'coloured' and Indian, with an increasingly large percentage of black[1] people falling into this category.

The aim of the 're-launch', which took place in February 1996, was precisely to move closer to delivering public broadcasting by providing more of the country's eleven official languages, as well as ensuring that the seven which were already broadcast, did so with greater equity. The SABC television service has three channels at its disposal: SABC1, with the largest footprint, or signal distribution network, broadcasts programming in the Nguni family of languages, that is isiXhosa, isiZulu, isiNdebele and isiSwati, during peak hours, filling in the morning and afternoon schedules in a mixture of these languages interspersed with English. Similarly, SABC2, with a strong signal network in the northern part of the country, uses the Sotho language family, that is SeTswana and SeSotho, during peak viewing time; while SABC3, the smallest signal footprint covering predominantly urban areas, broadcasts only in English. Smaller language communities, for example, Tsivenda and Xitsonga, are provided for only sporadically through windows of breakaway programming.

The various languages are scheduled in blocks in order to provide a continuity for viewers: for example, on SABC2, the main News bulletin on a Tuesday evening will be in Zulu, preceded by a Zulu-language game show, and followed by a Zulu-language drama. The predominance of English in the schedules is premised on the notion of English as a core language, understood as the second language choice of most South Africans, and more practically, on the wide and inexpensive availability of English-language programming on the international market.

While much of the transformation work was aimed at television, in radio too, substantial changes needed to be implemented, most notably the upgrading of the African language channels, and the extension and improvement of the news division. In order to put into effect such an ambitious plan, the mandate of the SABC was stretched considerably. Among other projects, the following targets were aimed for:

- extension of language services towards full equity on television
- increase in local content programming
- extension of TV footprint to reach all potential viewers
- introduction of regional television slots in all provinces
- equity and universal access to religious programming
- provision of curriculum based education on both radio and television
- upgrading of the African language radio services.

The Broadcasting Bill 1998

The Green Paper[2] identified a number of alternative models for the structuring of the SABC. The most crucial finding of the consultative process surrounding the Green Paper was the realisation that any restructuring of the SABC would have to take account of the realities of the commercial market place in which the SABC found itself. Two issues were foremost in the collective mind of the drafters:

- the SABC should maintain its financial viability
- in doing so, the commercial activities of the SABC should not threaten other commercial broadcasters through the massive advantage of belonging to a national corporation with a huge economy of scale, particularly in the marketing of advertising time.

The Broadcast Bill presented to Parliament for enactment on 3 November 1998[3] replaced the Broadcast Act of 1976. This is the first South African broadcasting legislation explicitly to take account of three separate arms of the broadcasting: public service; commercial and community, across various means of signal distribution: radio and television, both terrestrial and satellite. In doing so, the Bill took account of the provisions of the IBA Act of 1993.

In some respects the Bill also curtails the powers of the IBA, since it was the government's position that the IBA's powers should be curtailed. As a regulatory, rather than a legislative body, the IBA should be responsible for the monitoring and enforcement of broadcast policy within the industry, rather than its formulation.

In terms of public service broadcasting per se, the Bill's most important contribution is to set up a Charter for the SABC, another first in South African broadcasting legislation, bringing it into line with other public services, particularly those in the commonwealth countries, such as Britain (BBC); Australia (ABC) and Canada (CBC).

Structurally, the Bill makes provision for the division, or corporatization, of the SABC into two arms: the 'public commercial arm' and the 'public service arm'. It is anticipated that there will be four radio stations and one television channel presently operated by the SABC, along with merchandising, programme sales and other commercial activities relating to those services. The thinking behind the legislation has been in keeping with the world-wide trend towards deregulation, which has seen the opening up and liberalisation of public service enterprises, from power provision through to national airlines.

Funding for the public service arm will still come from licence fees, grants, advertising and sponsorship. The public broadcasting arm of the SABC will be required to report to the Minister from time to time on the profile of its revenues. The purpose of separation is to ensure that the commercial activities of the SABC do not enjoy an unfair advantage over other commercial broadcasters – a fear that had been vociferously expressed by some broadcasters prior to the passing of the act, in the consultation stage of the legislation process.

It is envisaged that the commercial arm of the SABC will become a Section 21 company, which will allow it to trade on the stock exchange, undertake the acquisitions, co-productions and sales necessary to be a fully-fledged commercial enterprise. Profits from this arm will be used to cross subsidise the public service mandate. The predominant form of revenue for the commercial arm of the SABC will be sourced from the sale of audiences to advertisers. The commercial arm of the SABC will be expected to conduct itself in a fully commercial fashion and provide dividend payments to the portfolio Minister (of Broadcasting and Telecommunications).

Reallocation of these dividends to the public arm of the SABC will be in the hands of the Minister. Any surplus will be paid into the Nation Revenue Fund (the general Fiscus), This provision is a cause for concern among some critics, who counter that apart from the fact that under this scheme, the identified revenue mix is too unstable, making it difficult for the public service sector to plan ahead, the corporatization arrangement seriously compromises autonomy.

If the commercial arm is to return a dividend to the Fiscus, there is no guarantee that the money will find its way back into the public service arm: in fact, given current budgetary constraints, especially for the social services, it may well not ... open the door for political manipulation of the PBS arm through financial control.[4]

This criticism hits not only at the business objectives of the business of broadcasting, but takes seriously the compromising possibilities of interlocking between financial vulnerability and political interference. Independence from the government of the day is a vital component of the legitimacy of any broadcaster, a theme I will return to at the end of this paper. In this respect, the London-based campaigners for human rights in the media sector, *Article 19*, conclude in their research on the organisation and funding of public broadcasters that 'it remains our view that adequate public funding should remain the rule for public broadcasting'.[5]

Challenges facing public service broadcasting

The now classic version of public service broadcasting is an essentially modernist one. It incorporates all the optimistic hope of rational discourse and the firm belief in the edifying and uplifting potentials of broadcasting as a conveyer of 'culture'. It is also indicative of colonial belief in upliftment. This is despite the very limited view of who constitutes 'the people' broadcasting was to serve, an understanding which in the South African case was confined to white, English speakers, and only grudgingly extended to white Afrikaans speakers.

Public broadcasting was premised on the understanding that the broadcasting spectrum is limited, and belongs to the nation. The government, while it may act as the guardian of the nation-state, should be kept at arm's length from the day to day operations of the broadcaster. Broadcasting, in this view, is a public good belonging to the whole nation, not to be exploited for private or sectarian gain of either a monetary or ideological kind. Conceptually the appropriate place for the broadcaster is the public sphere (Habermas 1989; Calhoun 1992; Garnham 1993; Thompson 1993).

From its inception, politically and commercially powerful sectors of society expected public service broadcasting to accomplish an important democratic and cultural mission. It was given the task of providing the entire population with information, education and quality entertainment. For both economic and ideological reasons, the tasks implied in this mandate could only be performed by a state-regulated monopoly – i.e. public broadcasting services. This was the rationale which governed public service broadcasting until the early 1980s. From that period, the global media landscape underwent fundamental changes. National broadcasting systems were deregulated, or rather re-regulated, private providers were admitted to the market and the state facilitated and promoted the development of the technological infrastructure, and was occasionally involved in its operation. All these developments jeopardised, or at least undermined, the economic and political system under which public broadcasting presently operates. In the South African situation, the main issues we can identify here can be summarised under three strands:

- the end of the monopolisation of the media environment by the SABC, through the largescale introduction of competition and deregulation
- the developmental imperative for the provision of information, education and entertainment to those sectors of society which are economically non-profitable
- the economic decline of the pre-eminence of the nation-state as the primary economic structure, with the concomitant issues involved in the rise in nationalism and cultural identity.

In this paper, I will survey these trends briefly, paying particular attention to the broadcaster's implication in the rise of a South African nationalism through the promotion of the 'African Renaissance' and inclusion of local content programming on television.

Recent trends in media industries

Throughout the world, media industries are undergoing major changes both at the level of technology as well as at the level of political economy. Most obvious have been the twin processes of technological advancement – explosion would not be an exaggeration – together with the trend towards deregulation and corporatisation. New technological opportunities imply a nearly limitless spectrum capacity. Since the original notion of broadcasting as a national asset was premised, in part, on the argument of the scarcity of the spectrum, the new spectrum abundance brings into question the right of the nation-state to continue to regulate broadcasting as tightly as previously, and makes the idea of the monopolistic public service broadcaster a total anachronism. The advances in digital transmission, satellite technologies and broadcasting through the Internet have changed the face of broadcasting forever.

The international movement towards *deregulation*, or rather *re-regulation*, through the opening of opportunities to new market entrants, which has characterised the ideological perspective of the post-cold war era, has impacted on South Africa to a notable extent. In 1996, the SABC was close to a monopoly, with three television channels, twenty-two domestic radio services, and the effective control of *Channel Africa*, the external broadcast channel of the Department of Foreign Affairs. Only M-Net, the encrypted subscription television channel (which includes a two hour unencrypted 'open window') provided television competition. Two regional commercial radio stations – Capital Radio in Durban, and Radio 702 in the Witwatersrand (now Gauteng) area, broadcast on medium wave as opposed to the SABC's stronger and clearer FM services.

In 1998, the position is vastly different. As a consequence of the Triple Enquiry undertaken by the Independent Broadcasting Authority (IBA), a recommendation was made to Parliament that the SABC divest itself of its regional commercial radio stations in order to hasten the establishment of a competitive broadcasting environment in the country. The move was seen as the first round of privatisation of state assets in the New South Africa. Six of the most lucrative regional radio stations were sold at the behest of the IBA in 1996, and the money transferred directly to state coffers.[6] A further eight 'greenfields licences' (i.e. licences without existing stations attached to them) are in the process of being allocated by the IBA. M-Net developed *Supersport*, a second channel dedicated to sports programming; satellite broadcasting is a reality under the auspices of DSTV, another subsidiary of the M-Net stable; and in

October 1998 the first free-to-air television channel began broadcasting. Monopoly is a thing of the past. The growth of *media technologies* and *convergence* which threaten the pre-eminence of the public broadcaster as the chief articulator of the nation-state must be seen in conjunction with a growing *concentration* of resources within media industries, which occurs at the same time as the contrary process of fracturing and *diversification*. Industries based in one sector of the economy spread their investments, and their risks, not only into horizontally and vertically integrated activities, thereby expanding into areas which are traditionally outside their core business. At the same time, there is evidence of a dialectical process of decentralisation and de-diversification, as huge conglomerates disentangle their various components in the understanding that economic efficiency demands meticulous attention to specific tasks. All the above takes place against a tendency towards *globalisation*, set against the antithetical processes of localisation and the rise of the politics of identity.

Public Service Broadcasting and the universal provision of programming

What purpose does public service broadcasting serve? This simple question has been the subject of a great deal of argument, debate and deliberation over the past six years in South Africa, and indeed in every country in which there has been a strong tradition of public broadcasting. As a point of departure, I take the purpose of public service broadcasting to be the provision of a universal service of excellent programming, while maintaining public legitimacy through an editorial independence from both the government of the day and rampant commercial interests.

By 'universal' I mean programming which covers a full range of genres, from information through to education and entertainment, for the widest possible audiences, over the greatest possible geographical coverage. The early McBride reports on the New World Information Order stressed the understanding of cultural rights as human rights. Culture, education and the provision of information were seen as basic human rights, alongside and equal to, the material rights of food, water, health and housing. These informational 'needs' have to be provided as social goods – and not simply as commercial commodities. This debate has been revived by the recent publication of the UNESCO report 'Our Cultural Diversity', which stresses the intimate connection between culture and development (UNESCO 1996, p. 24).

One of the most important indicators of the difficulties inherent in fulfilling the public service mandate has been in the provision of *universal service*. Both in terms of complete geographic coverage of the country, as well as in terms of programme type and language, universal service largely has been a myth. In the case of South Africa, for instance, the issue of language on radio must serve as exemplary.

Reith's understanding of 'the people' was confined to those people who spoke

English, and in this vein, initially only English language radio was set up. By the late 1930s, an hour of Afrikaans was introduced, becoming a separate, but not equal station in the 1940s, aptly labelled the 'B service'. In similar fashion, 'Bantu language' radio programmes were introduced in the 1950s. With the technical advances made possible by the introduction of FM, the now infamous 'Radio Bantu' became a set of fully-fledged array of stations mirroring and contributing to the apartheid grand narrative of separate nations, speaking separate languages, and living in separate areas of the country.

Arguing for the protection of cultural educational and social value broadcasting, or what Jay Blumer (1992) has eloquently referred to as 'vulnerable values', is not the same as distinguishing between needs and wants. Put in those terms, 'wants' are thought of as the legitimate desires of the audiences, signalled through the two mechanisms of *audience research* - that is, ratings which signal audience preferences and appreciation indices, and measure off the intensity of those preferences – and *the market* – that is, consumer support for encrypted or encoded channels. In the same framework, 'needs' are envisaged as the paternalistic response of whose who know best - a top-down approach compared with the more participatory approach of 'wants' (White 1984).

There is enormous competition to provide information goods to those who can pay for them, or those whose economic status defines them as attractive audiences to advertisers. This affects the ability of the public broadcaster to provide some categories of programming which may be seen to be in the public interest. The issues of programming for the very young; curriculum-based education; the elderly and disabled, including close-caption broadcasting or sign-language inserts for the deaf; as well as minority language and cultural groups; readily come to mind here. But broadcasting is big business commanding big capital outlay, and nowhere is this more evident than in the question of sports rights. When these rights involve national teams, they are seen by many as national assets and not only as a right of the privileged few.

Nationalism and nation building

Social solidarity is reinforced when consumers share the same cultural and informational environment. John Reith, the first Director General of the BBC and the father of public service broadcasting, opined in 1925 that 'public service broadcasting should act as a national service. It should act as a powerful means of social unity, binding together groups, regions and classes through the live relaying of national events' (cited in Keane 1996, p. 33). He argued that this is best achieved when audiences share common cultural resources, and are subjected to a monopoly provider of a single service.

Although the ideal of a universal single-channel environmental is now an anachronism, nation-building continues to be an over-riding consideration with many public service broadcasters, not least the SABC, as is evidenced by the Corporation's *Guidelines for Programme Content*:

> In a multi-cultural society, the SABC needs to ensure not only that the diversity is reflected, but that it is reflected positively ... Programmes should contribute to a sense of nation building and should not in any way disparage the lifestyle or belief systems of any specific cultural group or in any way attack the integrity of such a group, unless it is established to be in the public interest. However, the news and beliefs of different groups are obviously open to honest, thoughtful scrutiny in programmes like documentaries.
>
> SABC 1996b, p. 10

These sentiments are repeated so frequently, and have become so entirely self-evident, that they have now become a canon of common sense assumptions. Therefore, it is worth critically reconsidering the concept of 'nation building', and the part that television, and especially programming broadcasts by the SABC, plays in this process.

'A powerful means of social unity'

In *Imagined Communities*, Benedict Anderson (1983) reminds us that 'the Nation' is an abstraction , a construct of the imagination. It is a community which is imagined as both sovereign and limited. In his view, 'the nation' emerges when the realm of the church and dynasty recede, and no longer seem to answer to mankind's craving for immortality. The nation, with its promise of identification with history, enables people to surpass the finality of death and eradication. The need to create a view of the nation arises most profoundly in periods of distinct social stress: when new developments within, or pressures from outside, undermine a sense of continuity, then most strikingly, is there a 'need for "ethnic revival"' (Smith 1986, p. 17).

The need for the consolidation of national identity is keenly felt in developing countries, and the role of the mass media rightly has been foregrounded in this debate. Media provides the self-image of a society. In their exposition of 'bardic television', John Fiske and John Hartley (1978, p. 86) note that

> the bardic mediator occupies the centre of its culture: television is one of the most highly centralised institutions in modern society. This is not only the result of commercial monopoly or government control, it is also a response to the culture's felt need for a common centre, to which the television message always refers. It's centralisation speaks to all members of a highly fragmented society.

In somewhat more colourful language, Colin Morris (cited in Tusa 1992), one-time documentary commissioner for the BBC, makes a similar point:

> In the Book of Genesis, it is God who brings order out of chaos; in the modern world, television journalists have to make a stab at doing it. They subdue into harmony a mountain of telex printouts, miles of video tape and a pandemonium of ringing telephones. They organise into a coherent picture, a riot of impressions, a chaos of events, a bedlam of attitudes and opinions that would otherwise send us scurrying to the hills in panic. And they have to construct this world view at lightning speed, in a welter of instant judgements. Not for them the luxury afforded to philosophers of earlier ages who could reflect at leisure on the fitness of things. Aristotle had no six o'clock deadline to meet.

Nations are created in the historical and sociological imagination through identification with generalised communal heroes set in equally generalised, but dramatised, locations and times. Eric Hobshawm (1983, pp. 13–14) regards 'that comparative recent historical innovation, the "nation" with its associated phenomena: nationalism, the nation-state, national symbols, histories and the rest' as closely bound up with 'invented traditions' which are 'exercises in social engineering ... often deliberate and always innovative'.

Anthony Smith (1992, p. 68) points to the 'instrumentalist' conception of nation-construction, in which nationalism is 'an instrument of legitimation and mobilisation, through which leaders and elites stir up mass support for their competitive power struggle. Elsewhere, he notes that central to all modern ethnic mythology is the idea of linear development:

> Communities exist in nature, as it were, and obey the same laws of birth, growth, maturation and decline - and rebirth. The development is linear rather than cyclical, because the period of decline is regarded as 'unnatural', a matter of 'betrayal' from within, or 'subjugation' and decay from without.
>
> Smith 1986, p. 191

Smith suggests that in recounting the history of nations, both historicist intellectuals and political commentators fail to conform to later canons of historiography and scientific method; indeed, objectivity is not their main concern. Their aim is to retain the 'past', in such a way as to 'explain' the lot of their community and prescribe remedies for its ills.

Typically, such national mythologies devolve into a series of motifs or elements and commonly follow a set pattern:

1   A myth of origins in time; i.e. When the community was 'born'.

2   A myth of origins in space; i.e. Where the community was 'born'.

3   A myth of ancestry; i.e. Who bore us, and how we descended from him/her

4   A myth of migration; i.e. Wither we wandered.

5   A myth of liberation; i.e. How we were freed.

6   A myth of the golden age; i.e. How we became great and heroic.

7   A myth of decline; i.e. How we decayed and were conquered/exiled.

8   A myth of rebirth; i.e. How we shall be restored to our former glory.

Apart from the second and perhaps the fourth motif, all these elements require the mediation and inspiration of superhuman agents, or 'heroes' to be either present or to have been taken forcibly out of the narrative. Although ostensibly the story of a 'community', the narrative requires human and superhuman agency to bring it to fruition. The legends are to be personalised: they are the stuff of drama. These dramas, in turn, are often elaborate 'reconstructions of the communal past, mixing genuine scholarship with fantasy ... legend with objectively recorded data, in the service of an ethic of regeneration' (Smith 1986: 191).

Nations learn to 'know' these people, these events and myths, through what Anderson (1983, p. 49) calls the 'technology of print capitalism'. The rise of printed literature and the press made it possible to 'narrate' the nation and to imaginatively 'construct' it. All the more powerful is the rise of radio and television culture, which has allowed national leaders unimpeded access to their constituencies, while at the same time providing a fertile ground for the re-articulation of stories, mythologies and romances of the past. Nostalgia for the past, especially the ethnic past of 'one's own' people has indeed been a feature of society in all ages and continents. As Walker Connor (1992, p. 50) reminds us, 'nationalism is a mass phenomenon' and what exemplifies the phenomenon of massification better than the electronic media?

'In dying we are born again'

In one of the clearest examples of the remembering of a golden age, and rebirth and restoration to former glory, come the mythologies which make up the 'African Renaissance'. The SABC has taken it upon itself, as part of its Vision and Values, to promote the African Renaissance with missionary zeal. In fact, they have gone beyond the narrow ambition of nation building, and in the spirit of global (or at least supra-regional) enterprises, have taken on the challenge of spiritually revitalising the entire continent: 'As a nation builder, the SABC is committed not only to our country, but to the rebirth of the whole continent'. This disclaimer echoes the words of an SABC spokesperson:

> The SABC has a major role as nation builder in our own country, and being the 'pulse of Africa's Creative Spirit' we have a responsibility to spread the African Renaissance message to all corners of the continent.[7]

The occasion of the statement was the pre-publicity for a banquet hosted by the SABC at which Deputy President Thabo Mbeki delivered his 'African Renaissance' address. The event was televised lived on SABC2 for the full period of 2 hours, and by satellite to the rest of the continent. Similarly, a theatrical production entitled, tellingly, *An African Dream*, 'examines Africa, past and present historical epochs, in a quest to find those values and experiences that imperatively facilitate a smooth transcendence into the Renaissance'. The communiqué goes on to tell us that 'the play illustrates the history of the values embroidered in Africa's quest to realise a vision that will usher in a new beginning and rebirth of the African soul.'

Thus, in the most unambiguous terms, the SABC has associated itself with the process of mythology-building. Not only in its celebrations and the provision of a platform on which national leaders are able to articulate their vision of the African Renaissance, but also through the everyday programming. Most notable, in this regard, is both the sheer amount, as well as the thematic content, of local drama productions. In the following section, I look at the *context* of local content production, examine the amount and patterning of local productions, both drama and news, and finally, end with some remarks on the themes carried in local television series.

Local is lekker[8]

The Triple Enquiry Report of the IBA laid a considerable emphasis on local content programming in South Africa, and imposed significant quotas on the public broadcaster.

> Through local music, and through locally produced, entertaining, informative and educational programming, produced by a wide range of South African producers, television and radio will make a vital contribution to democracy, nation-building and development in South Africa.
>
> Local quotas will protect and develop our national culture, character and identity, and will address needs and extend choice for the public and will enable growth and development in the South African industry.
>
> IBA 1995

The regulations seem to address two separate, but interlinking goals:

- the ideological, directed towards the purposes of building a nation and an identity
- the economic, direct towards the development of a film, television and recording industry.

Simons 1998, p. 22

In this paper, I will interrogate only the first, leaving the second for another occasion. The IBA argue that South Africa, as a nation with diverse cultures and languages, has not sufficiently seen itself reflected on the country's television screens (IBA 1995, p. 134). Fears of imported foreign programming over-running the national culture and identity of nations are commonly expressed, and even more so in a deregulated, multi-channel environment of satellite and cable, which is able to offer a myriad of programmes simultaneously. This, of course, is the case throughout the world, where the great bulk of television programming is procured from the cheapest possible source – mostly in English, and typically from the United States. The latter country has enjoyed a 'first mover advantage', allowing it to dominate the global audio-visual market. In the United States, the domestic broadcasting sector is structured on a private basis, with networks related to a tangle of stations and affiliates. This allows for great economies of scale, since the cost of production is recovered in the primary, domestic market, and copies can be sold into the foreign market at a far lower price than the original. Michael Ward (1997) reflects that in the audio-visual industry, unlike almost any other industry, it is far more expensive to produce a television or radio programme, a compact disk or film than it is to copy it. Thus, it is always cheaper – indeed up to thirty times cheaper – for a broadcaster to buy a programme than to produce it for themselves.

Local content programming, particularly when it includes a high proportion of drama, documentary and sport, is an enormously expensive enterprise, as any national broadcaster world-wide will testify. Nevertheless, it is essential to the project of protecting national identity and national culture, as well as providing for the diverse language needs of the audience. It is worth noting that a locally produced drama could cost as much as R15 000 a minute (the norm is R8 000) while a drama of the same standard produced abroad, in English, could sell for as little as R600 a minute. Audiences used to exogenous programming, in which the quality is typically very professional, are not prepared to settle for inferior productions, simply on the grounds that they are 'local'. One way around this dilemma is the large-scale use of dubbing into a local language. An added advantage of dubbing is that the original imported soundtrack can be 'simulcast' on another audio channel – either through the television set, or synchronised on radio.

As a means of achieving its policy goals, the IBA was able to prescribe specific conditions regarding programming, including the broadcasting of local programming both during the daily schedules and at prime time. Different quotas were set for the commercial channels, since it was argued that the SABC had to carry higher local content obligations to meet its specific mandate as a public broadcaster. A median of 50% of local content was set for the SABC, to be complied with over three years.[9] In subsequent modifications the level was adjusted to 30%, to be complied with over five years.

The IBA reports to Parliament through the Department of Broadcasting, Posts and Telecommunication. But that is not the only government department with an interest in broadcasting, and more specifically, with the broadcasting of local content. The Department of Arts, Culture, Science and Technology hosted a two day seminar in 1997 in order to explore the question. Its interest in local content stems from its responsibility for ensuring that all South Africa agencies, including the broadcasters, consider the cultural implications of their policies (Mtshali 1995, p. 5).

In this regard, the Department has been active in developing its own position on local content, a position which is unequivocally ideological in its orientation. According to Minister Mtshali, the cultural policy of the department is based on the concept of the African Renaissance referred to above. Within the broader concept of the African Renaissance, suggests Mtshali, lies a notion of what can be called a South African Renaissance; the emergence of a new consciousness and a sense of shared heritage, culture and history, and according to him, local content on television is a prime contributor to this.

The SABC's position towards local content is best reflected in its submission on the question to the IBA (SABC 1994). In 1994, the SABC was prepared to comply with a requirement of 50% broadcast time, or 70% of programme origination budget, whichever was the greater, on local content. A revised submission put the figure at 30%. This commitment was to be phased in over five years. In reality, these levels have not been met to any substantial degree so far. While different sources of statistics differ widely, indications are that the figures are still below the envisaged 30%.[10] The Department of Arts, Culture, Science and Technology quote figures for the years 1992-1997 which vary from 26% to close to 33%.

Yet Media Monitoring Project research done during the year 1994 indicates up to 44% local programming. Figures from the SABC Broadcasting Research Unit (1997) indicate that while the total proportion of local content fell from 40% to 25% directly after the publication of the McKinsey Report, a management audit which advised the considerable down-scaling of production expenditure. While the proportion of local content is climbing slowly, it is still far from the promised 50% optimistically suggested to the IBA in the SABC's 1994 submission.

Table 1   SABC Local Content levels for October 1997 in percentage of broadcast
                 minutes

	Local	Imported
SABC1	29,34%	70,66%
SABC2	53,64%	46,38%
SABC3	28,80%	71,20%
TOTAL	37,26%	62,74%

Source: SABC Broadcasting Research Unit 1997.

Not only do figures from different sources tell a slighly different story, but more
importantly, local content across the three channels differs widely. From 1994 on, TV1,
relaunched as SABC2, popularised with the catch-phrase 'Come Alive with Us', had the
highest levels of local television content, and met the revised quota of 30% within the
first two years of implementation. However, neither SABC1, branded with the slogan
'Simunye – we are one', which broadcasts predominantly in English and the Nguni
Languages (isiZulu and isiXhosa), nor SABC3, an all-English channel catering for a
more upwardly mobile audience, and branded as 'Quality Shows', have reached the
30% goal.

News, views and legitimacy

A more intriguing anomaly is the situation in prime time, that is, the hours between
18:00 and 21:30, during which the greatest numbers of viewers are attracted to television, and broadcasters are thus able to charge premium rates on advertising space, is
the reverse of normal schedules. During these precious hours, local content is above
the 30% mark for all channels. SABC3, with its notoriously low levels of local content
overall, is particularly striking. The explanation for this anomaly appears to lie in the
amount of news and current affairs programming put out on SABC3 during this time,
which raises the local content level substantially.

Table 2   SABC Local Content levels for October 1997 Prime-Time
                 (18:00–21:30) in % of broadcast minutes

	Local	Imported
SABC1	59,18%	40,82%
SABC2	68,76%	31,24%
SABC3	24,15%	75,85%
TOTAL	50,70%	49,30%

Source: SABC Broadcasting Research Unit 1997.

The English language *News* of SABC3 features significantly among the top ten most highly rated programmes broadcast during prime time. However, there is a 'double value' in these news programmes: not only are they very popular, and therefore, in a semi-deregulated market very profit programme genres, but they are also prime carriers of legitimacy. The trinity of the public service mandate is to educate, entertain and inform, and as broadcasters internationally have learnt over the past sixty years, information is a highly powerful, as well as profitable, enterprise. Indeed, it can be asserted that *News* is the most important part of the public service mandate. John Fiske (1987, p. 281) notes:

> News is a high-status television genre. Its claimed objectivity and independence from political or government agencies is argued to be essential for the workings of a democracy. Television companies applying for renewal of their licences turn to their news and current affairs programs as evidence of their social responsibility.

In line with this, the SABC increased its daily news bulletins from September 1998 from four to seven a day.[11] However, even if news conveys legitimacy onto the public service broadcaster, this is always measured in terms of its editorial independence. The SABC, particularly, remembering its historically close connections with previous political dispensations, is aware that one of the most significant threats to the ethos of public service broadcasting is the international phenomenon of the loss of legitimacy and credibility in the face of pandering to governments. With the heavy emphasis on nation building, there is always the danger that unbridled Nationalism may disintegrate into unashamed apologies for sectarian interests. Traditionally, public service broadcasters have looked to the legislation to protect them, and maintain a degree of independence from the government of the day. This is a theme to which I will return at the end of this paper.

Television drama and national cultural reconciliation

Although the popular media are frequently commercially driven, there has been an increase in the use of television to promote social change in many parts of the world (Brown 1992). Local content programming not only transfers legitimacy onto the broadcaster, it is popular and attractive to audiences. In the first quarter of 1998, the two most popular programmes in South Africa were the local production, *Suburban Bliss,* which heads the audience appreciation index for adults, and with the international soap opera *The Bold and the Beautiful*.[12] In a recent ethnographic reception study, Dorothy Roome (1997, p. 17) investigated audience's responses to two locally produced drama/

sitcom programmes, *Going Up* and *Suburban Bliss*. Her purpose was to evaluate the SABC's success in using humour as a catalyst to transcend the aftermath of apartheid, and in addressing sensitive social and cultural issues which has arisen in the transition to a more inclusive democracy.

Going Up was produced by Penguin Productions, an independent production company with a long history of programme production for the SABC. Set in a law firm in Johannesburg, the series depends on the inversion of a number of well-recognised stereotypical characters, whose good humour, tolerance and teasing illustrate the changes faced by all races and socio-economic groups in the New South Africa. The main characters include Jabulani Cebekulu, a colonial style general factotum; Reginald Cluver, an elderly liberal white lawyer; Edward Tsaba, the black law associate, representing the new black elite in South Africa; and Mrs Jakobs, the 'coloured' secretary, always helpful, always politically correct (she answers the telephone in four languages) and just a little ditzy. Secondary characters include Squeeza, an ex-jazz queen and owner of the black shebeen (informal pub) and Klein Piet Gouws, a lower-working class white Afrikaans-speaking security guard in the foyer of the building. The narrative of each episode is motivated by the introduction of new clients. The producer wanted to produce a series representing a microcosm of the whole of South African society in a series which would bring together music of the 1950s and 1960 rendering the colonial/ apartheid era, and also be reminiscent of what it was like in the days of prohibition, when blacks were not allowed to be served liquor. This harkening back to a golden age of township jazz, shebeens and the whole ambience of the freehold culture of the 1940s and 1950s, is typical of Anthony Smith's typology of mythological national building.

The programme ran for three seasons, and the differences in the direction and ethos over the three years is telling. In the first series, the producers described their aim as one of creating 'a vehicle for a multi-cultural/multi-lingual "melting pot"' to an attempt in the third-year season 'to make people speak and respond to events the way they occur in South Africa'.[13]

Suburban Bliss exploits the situations which arise between a black and white family who are in business together, but fortuitously end up living next door to each other. The characters in *Suburban Bliss* are portrayed in the process of cultural integration. Their ultimate goal is to achieve social mobility (Roome 1996: 2). The concept behind the *Going Up* series was to reach a white viewership, to cross over the divide between different cultural (read 'racial') groups, to provide a greater understanding of the differences and commonalities of all South Africans in the post-election milieu. Since most whites could not understand Zulu, the programme made extensive use of subtitles. Most of the dialogue – nearly two thirds – was in English.

Such programmes would not have been possible even a few years ago. During the apartheid era the SABC had been completely under the control of the government, spreading the ideology of apartheid through both news and narrative. The extent of the of the SABC control is illustrated by the fate of the forerunner to *Suburban Bliss*, which was refused permission for broadcast. The story involved a coloured doctor living in a white neighbourhood, and hearsay suggests the decision not to air was made at the highest level of government, since in 1987 the Group Areas Act made it illegal for coloureds to live in white neighbourhoods.[14] Similarly, the producers of *Going Up* tried from 1989-90 to persuade the SABC programmers to air the pilot production before the programme was commissioned.

Simunye – we are one

At the outset of this paper, it was pointed out that the mission statement of the SABC included the sentiment that programming content was 'aimed at protecting and nurturing South African culture and creativity, and reflecting the reality of South Africa to itself, and to the world, South Africa from a distinctly South African perspective' (SABC 1996a, p. 2). I have endeavoured to show how, through restructuring and reconfiguration, as well as the increased amount of local content – a process not without its financial and logistical contradictions - the SABC attempted to fulfil this mandate. In doing so, it has consciously aligned itself with the process of the African Renaissance, in attempt to re-find the spirit and values of 'Africanness' through harking back to a past Golden Age with the objective of creating a sense of national solidarity and oneness.

Notes

1 Racial categories are used in this paper not to imply any pejorative distinctions, but to indicate the manner in which the broadcast sector was historically segmented.

2 Ministry of Posts, Telecommunications and Broadcasting: 'Green Paper for Public Discussion on Broadcasting Policy', 6 November 1997.

3 Republic of South Africa: 'Broadcasting Bill', introduced to National Assembly in November 1998.

4 FXI *Response to the Broadcast Bill*, September 1998, p. 4.

5 FXI *Response to the Broadcast Bill*, September 1998, p. 2.

6 Radio Oranje in the Free State was sold for R11 million, and East Coast Radio in KwaZulu Natal for R45 million to the New Radio Consortium. Radio Algoa in the Eastern Cape went to Umoya communication for just over R10 million. Highveld Stereo in Gauteng was sold to Newshelf 63, while a sister consortium, Newshelf 71, bought Jacaranda Stereo in the Pretoria region for R70 million. KFM Stereo in the Western Cape was acquired by Crescent Consortium at a price of R65 million.

7 Enoch Sithole, Senior General Manager: Audience Service, in a press release on the African Renaissance Dinner hosted by the SABC, 12 August 1998.

8 A colloquial expression which translates literally as 'local is nice'.

9 In meeting the 50% quota, the IBA established specific minimum quotas for different programme categories, as follows:

Drama	20%
Current Affairs	80%
Documentary and Informal knowledge building	50%
Education Programming	60%
Children's programming	50%

10 The Department of Arts, Culture, Science and Technology quote the following average figures for the years 1992-1997:

1992	32,6%
1993	30,2%
1994	32,8%
1995	29,4%
1996	30,3%
1997	26,3%

Source: Cited by Newman 1997.

The Media Monitoring Project conducted research on local content performance of the SABC, based on two months of programming schedules during 1994. Their findings show a ratio of time devoted to local content versus time devoted to foreign programming as 1:1,28, or 44% local to 56% foreign.

11 Up until September 1998, there were television news bulletins at 07:00, a short headline bulletin at 13:00, a national news bulletin at 18:00, the main news bulletin at 20:00 followed by news headlines at 22:30. Under the new arrangement, short bulletins were added at 10:00 and 16:00, while the lunchtime bulletin was extended to a full service, including live business reportage, together with information and stock prices direct from the Johannesburg Stock Exchange.

12 According to an SABC Press Release, 17 April 1998, the ten most popular television programmes in South Africa were:

1	*The Bold and the Beautiful*	SABC1	12.7
2	**Suburban Bliss (English)*	SABC2	12.7
3	**Emzini Weziniswa (Zulu)*	SABC1	12.4
4	**Generations (English/ Multi-lingual)*	SABC1	12.4
5	**Xhosa News (Thursdays)*	SABC1	11.9
6	**Footprints (English)*	SABC1	10.9
7	**Xhosa News (Tuesdays)*	SABC1	10.2
8	**Jam Alley (English)*	SABC1	9.8
9	**Kelebone (Multi-lingual)*	SABC2	9.6

10   *Pacific Blue*   SABC2   9.3

13 Personal interviews with Roberta Durrant, 1995, and Richard Benyon 1996, cited by Roome 1997, p. 69.

14 Personal interview with Carl Fisher, cited in Roome 1996, p. 2.

References

Benedict, A. (1983). *Imagined Communities: Reflection on the Origin and Spread of Nationalism*, London: Verso.

Blumer, J. (ed.) (1992). *Television and the Public Interest: Vulnerable Values in West European Broadcasting*, London: Sage.

Brown, W.J. (1992). 'Socio-Cultural Influences of Pro-Development Soap Operas', *Journal of Popular Film and Television*, 2, pp. 157–171.

Calhoun, C . (ed.) (1992). *Habermas and the Public Sphere*, Cambridge: MIT Press.

Connor, W. (1992). 'The Nation and its Myth', in A. Smith (ed.), *Ethnicity and Nationalism*, Leiden and New York: EJ Brill.

Fiske, J. (1987). *Television Culture*, London: Methuen.

Fiske, J. and Hartley, J. (1978). *Reading Television*, London: Methuen.

FXI (1998). Freedom of Expression Institution Response to Broadcasting Bill, September.

Garnham, N. (1990). *Capitalism and Communication: Global Culture and the Economics of Information*, London: Sage.

Habermas, J. (1989). *The Structural Transformation of the Public Sphere: An Inquiry into a Category of Bourgeois Society*, trans. T. Burger and F. Lawrence, Cambridge: Polity Press.

Hobshawm, E. (1983). 'Introduction', in E. Hobshawm and T. Ranger, *The Invention of Tradition*, Cambridge: Cambridge University Press.

Independent Broadcasting Authority (1995). *Report on the Protection and Viability of Public Broadcasting Services, Cross Media Control of Broadcasting Services and Local Television Content and South African Music*, Johannesburg: Independent Broadcasting Authority.

Keane, J. (1996). 'Structural Transformation in the Public Sphere', in M. Brun-Andersen, *Media and Democracy*, University of Oslo, Oslo.

Mtshali, L.P.H.M. (1997). 'Address to the Conference on Local Content', Paper presented at a Conference on Local Content, Department of Arts, Culture, Science and Technology, Durban.

Newman, N. (1997). 'Local Contempt', Paper presented at a Conference on Local Content, Department of Arts, Culture, Science and Technology, Durban.

Roome, D. (1996). 'Humour as Cultural Reconciliation: *Suburban Bliss* and Multicultural

Female Viewers', Paper presented at IAMCR Conference, August 1996, Sydney.

Roome, D. (1997). 'Transformation and Reconciliation: *Simunye*, a Flexible Model', *Critical Arts*, 11(1&2), pp. 66–94.

Simons, C. (1998). 'Made in South Africa: Local Content and Public Service Broadcasting in a Global Era', MA research project, University of Amsterdam.

Smith, A. (1986). *The Ethnic Origins of Nations*, Oxford: Basil Blackwell. South African Broadcasting Corporation (1995). *SABC Annual Report*, Johannesburg: SABC.

South African Broadcasting Corporation (1996a). *Launch SABC Television: Commemorative Publication on the Relaunch of the SABC's Television Channels,* Johannesburg: SABC.

South African Broadcasting Corporation (1996b). *Guidelines for Programme Content*, Johannesburg: SABC.

Teer-Tomaselli, R.E. and Tomaselli, K. G. (1996). 'Reconstituting Public Service Broadcasting: Media and Democracy during Transition in South Africa' in B. Anderson (ed), *op cit.*

Thompson, J.B. (1993). 'The Theory of the Public Sphere', *Theory, Culture and Society*, 10, pp. 173–189.

Tusa, J. (1992). 'Fourth Estate or Fifth Column? Media, the Government and the State', ComBroad March 1992, Commonwealth Broadcasting Association.

UNESCO (1996). *Our Creative Diversity: Report of the World Commission on Culture and Development*, Paris: UNESCO Publishing.

Ward, M. (1997). 'Address to the Conference on Local Content', Paper presented at a Conference on Local Content, Department of Arts, Culture, Science and Technology, Durban.

CHAPTER SIX

Literary studies in post-apartheid South Africa

Johannes A. Smit and Johan van Wyk

Background

With the first non-racial elections in South Africa in 1994, the period of apartheid officially came to an end. Many apartheid attitudes, institutions and structures within institutions established in the apartheid era nevertheless persist. Many South Africans anticipated the end of apartheid though. Some developed blueprints for transformation as early as the late 1970s. During the 1980s, this tendency reached a climax. This double bind of intransigence and radical transformation also affected literary studies.

Apartheid's segregationist institutionalisation of the study of literature within separate language departments was grounded in its view that South Africa consists of a number of nations that should develop as separate independent entities. The alternative view was that South Africa is an integrated society in which people of different language groups and cultures are interdependent economically, politically and socially. The assumption for this view is that South African society is a complex and diverse whole which develops its own identity and a shared culture. The aim was to transform hegemonic and segregationist values and attitudes by strengthening and extending the network of interdependencies and co-operation outside the heterogeneity which served as alibi for apartheid mentalities and segregationist institutionalised power. This, many felt, would eventually lead to a shared dominant culture.

In the period between 1910 – when the Union of South Africa came into being – and 1961 when South Africa became an independent republic, British Imperialism and Afrikaner Nationalism combined to dominate South Africa. The whites-only South African parliament determined policy. In literary studies this meant that in English Departments the focus was mainly on the literature of Britain and the United States, with hardly any attention given to South African literature. In Afrikaans Departments, Afrikaans literature was studied as that of an independent nation. African language literary studies slowly emerged, but were strongly influenced by anthropological, missionary and linguistic interests and in accordance with the 'homeland' policy of the Apartheid government. Between 1961 and 1976 the situation did not really change much. This is evident in the virtual non-existence – except for a few rare exceptions – of any literary histories of South African English literature or any histories of literatures in the black languages during this period.

In the 1970s, things started to change. The first major political crisis after the Sharpeville riots (1960) was the 1976 Soweto uprising of school children and increased international economic pressure on the apartheid government. This is the period that marks the emergence of a generation of prominent black poets such as Oswald Mtshali, Wally Serote and Sipho Sepamla, as well as the establishment of the journal Staffrider. Anti-apartheid publishing houses such as Ravan Press and Ad Donker that nurtured this new literature also came into being. Theory also came to the fore, particularly Marxism. Marxist scholars emphasised a historical approach to literature, especially in relation to South African working class culture. Scholars such as Tim Couzens and Isabel Hofmeyr made an important contribution in this regard. The interest in black working class culture also had a major impact by focusing attention on oral tradition and oral performance as an important literary form in South Africa.

In Afrikaans literature, authors unified against stricter censorship laws. After his stay in Paris in the late 1940s, the Afrikaans author Jan Rabie broke away from the literary concern with the 'poor white' problem, opening avenues to broader views of international culture and life. This, however, was not heeded by the white apartheid ideologues who won the 1948 election on an apartheid or 'separate development' platform.

Having already scrapped black and coloured voters from the roll during the 1930s and 1940s, the Afrikaner Nationalist Government systematically introduced apartheid legislation during the 1950s and 1960s. With the events around Sharpeville, the popular dissent, organisation against, and resistance to apartheid, became more vocal, visible and pronounced both locally and internationally. Within the Afrikaans writer community, the so-called 'sestigers' - Afrikaans authors from the 1960s - attempted to refract what was becoming a predominantly Afrikaner apartheid system in South Africa. During the 1970s, this changed dramatically when some Afrikaner authors started to write some militantly anti-apartheid novels and poetry, most of which were banned.

Authors such as André P. Brink and Breyten Breytenbach became intensely involved in the struggle against apartheid. When the apartheid government banned Brink's book, Kennis van die aand (the English translation, Looking on darkness, did not suffer the same fate) in 1974, he started to write his books simultaneously in English and Afrikaans. The exiled poet, Breyten Breytenbach, returned to South Africa on an underground mission, was caught and imprisoned for nine years. During the 1970s, the increased militarisation of South African society affected particularly young white male South Africans. Many became part of the End Conscription Campaign.

Events and strategies ranging from the Soweto uprising (1976) through to the development of an anti-apartheid discourse within the black and white English and Afrikaans literary community in reaction to the apartheid government's increased militarisation of society, helped to establish a sense of a common South African destiny beyond apartheid among many South Africans.

In English departments, particularly at postgraduate level, there developed an increased focus on South African English literature. The focus though was often too narrowly on what became the canon of South African writing: J.M. Coetzee, Wally Serote, Roy Campbell, Lady Anne Barnard, Ellen Kuzwayo, Breyten Breytenbach. This narrow focus can be ascribed to the absence of a solid South African English literary history[1].

The University of the Western Cape, under the rectorship of Jakes Gerwel, became the intellectual home of the left. The apartheid government established this university to cater for the 'coloured' people. It has a long history of resistance against apartheid and was an integral part of the struggle by the United Democratic Front. Jakes Gerwel, when he was head of the Afrikaans department, established a Marxist approach to the study of Afrikaans literature. This department increasingly went beyond the confines of Afrikaans literature and incorporated South African English literature on a comparative basis, while unearthing a tradition of Black Afrikaans writing.

The 1980s were a turbulent time at the Black universities in South Africa[2]. Annual boycotts, strikes and pressures for institutional transformation towards greater accountability and democracy marked these campuses. These confusing times also created an opportunity for the changing of departments, the renewal of curricula and syllabi and the establishing of new units. It is in these circumstances that the Centre for the Study of Southern African Literature and Languages was established. In this context, the aim of this article is to position the Centre and its contributions in terms of the transformation of South African literary studies.

The establishment of the CSSALL

The Centre for the Study of Southern African Literature and Languages (CSSALL) was established at the University of Durban-Westville in 1994 - the year in which South Africa became a non-racial democracy. It was established in order to contribute towards the transformation of literary studies from ethnically, culturally and institutionally segregated disciplines each with its own history, to a non-exclusionary multilingual, comparative, intertextual and hybrid discourse. This move was made possible by South Africa's new political reality.

During the apartheid era, there were separate departments for the study of the literature produced in different languages. Afrikaans literary studies were generally housed in departments of 'Afrikaans en Nederlands' (Dutch). South African English literature was studied as a sub-section of a broader English literature (British, American, Australian, African and West-Indian). Literature in African languages was studied in departments of African languages or in a department carrying the nomenclature of the dominant African language of a region - such as a Zulu department.

The establishment of the Centre was aimed at displacing this institutionalised segregationist mentality. The assumption is that South Africans, although linguistically, ethnically and culturally diverse, belong to one nation with a shared and complex history of exploitation, conflict and (often ironic) co-operation. Although fraught with difference, the Centre contributes to South Africa's always to be constructed unity in the areas of literature and language studies.

The Centre thus researches South African literature from an interlingual, comparative and intertextual point of view. For example, Johan van Wyk, Pieter Conradie and Nik Constandaras compiled an 800 page anthology of South African poetry, doggerel and verse, SA in poësie/ SA in poetry (1988). This volume contains representative poems from different South African languages. Translations accompany the poems in Zulu, Sotho, Tswana and Xhosa. The aim of the anthology was not to collect the most aesthetically pleasing poems in South Africa, but to illustrate through poetry the development of different ideological formations over the last century or more.

After much consultation and planning, the Centre for the Study of Southern African Literature and Languages was at last established. The aim of developing interdisciplinary and intertextual research into South African literature was achieved through close co-operation with various departments in the Arts Faculty at the University of Durban-Westville, as well as with departments at other Universities. It was recognised that the concept 'South Africa' is arbitrary, having at various times in history had different signifieds. Participants in the planning process also did not want to promote a new South African nationalism. Even so, many of the people participating in the projects of the CSSALL are from a Marxist background and have been involved in various projects deconstructing racist nationalist ideology and the economic exploitation it fostered. The decision to retain the designation, South Africa, is due to the fact that South Africans (despite class, culture and language differences) share a history: a history of conflicts and differences that occurred in one geographical area around what increasingly became a shared, if exploitative, economy.

Postcolonial studies

Postcolonial studies have come into focus in nearly every English and Afrikaans department in South Africa. Studies on autobiography, travel writing and gender in colonial texts are abundant. Studies of colonial literature such as Es'kia Mphahlele's

The Non-European Character in South African English Fiction (later published as The African Image, 1962) date from 1956 and could possibly be identified today as one of the early landmarks of postcolonial studies.

From its inception, the Centre has thus had to deal with questions which were already raised within postcolonial studies. In the early 1990s postcolonial studies came into vogue in South Africa - particularly through texts such as Marie Louise Pratt's (1992) Imperial Eyes: Travel Writing and Transculturation, Benedict Anderson's (1983) Imagined Communities and Homi Bhabha's (1990) Nation and Narration. These texts deal with theoretical questions such as:

- the relationship between nationalism and literature
- the definition of literature away from imaginative fictional works to include travel writing, biographies and autobiographies, historical and anthropological texts, and specifically African forms such as oral traditions, rock painting, and ritual
- the impact of writings produced in the frontier societies or contact zones on the systems of western knowledge.

Shared with Anderson and Bhabha is the assumption that nation is a shifting signifier with no essential referent[3]. It is a construct of a newly literate native middle-class or of settlers gone native. The ideological uses of literature by these classes make for interesting analysis from Marxist, poststructuralist and psychoanalytic points of view. This is the case particularly in texts which elaborate a national identity through the use of selective and manipulated historical memory and texts that betray their resistance to and mimicry of the Imperial Centre. A stimulating exploration of these approaches and themes can be found in Isabel Hofmeyr's 'Building a nation of words: Afrikaans language, literature and ethnic identity, 1902–1924'[4] in Marks and Trapido's (1987) The politics of race, class & nationalism in twentieth century South Africa.

From a focus on nationalism there is a shift to a focus on colonialism and its discursive formations around concepts such as reason, civilisation and progress. The discourses around these concepts informed racial prejudice from the nineteenth century onwards and were essential to the marginalising practices inherent in colonial ideology and western empire discourses.

The CSSALL's multilingual approach to colonial literature is an important element of its research. Participating scholars try as far as possible to relate texts in the various African languages to the context of the whole. The consequence is that heroic[5] and African discursive formations have become more important than they have been in other colonial and postcolonial studies.

In Hesiod's (1979) Works and days, the term 'heroic' refers to one of the stages of history dominated by war and migrations instigated by kings and princes. The early nineteenth century in South Africa was such a heroic period. It is characterised by the wars of dispersal, or the difaqane, which emanated from the Zulu kingdom, particularly around the figure of Shaka. This period more or less coincided with the Napoleonic wars in Europe which also affected South Africa. When the French revolutionary forces invaded Holland in 1795, the Prince of Orange fled to Britain and the Cape went to British control. This happened after some skirmishes in the Cape between supporters of the French republicanism of the newly established Batavian Republic and the invading British fleet. In 1803 the Cape became part of the Batavian republic but reverted back to British control in 1806 after again being invaded by Britain as part of the war between France and Britain.

Ideologically, the French revolution inspired republicanism particularly amongst the white farming community in South Africa. This eventually became a strong motif behind the Great Trek of frontier farmers into the African interior in 1838. The Napoleonic wars also meant the emigration of large numbers of Europeans to the Cape Colony. The British settlers of 1822 are an example of one such migration.

There is therefore a strong sense of overlap and continuity between the heroic and the colonial. In both formations, war and mass migrations are central. It is the CSSALL's mission to explore this overlap, but also the subtle differences. These differences came about with the disciplining institutions and mapping practices which the Colonial powers brought to the region: the institutions include Christianity (which implied a radical new way of looking at the world when compared to the heroic outlook of the precolonial peoples), education, writing and print, the monogamous family unit, hospitals (a whole new way of conceiving health and illness), labour, the law, prisons and the notion of representational politics. These institutions affected particularly those who sought refuge from the difaqane at the mission stations. These refugees became the first converts, the first literate Africans in the South African region. They were also the first to promote a transtribal panafricanist nationalism based on Western party political organisation. This crystallised with the establishment of the South African Native National Congress in 1912.

The study of boundaries and borders in South African literature, on the other hand, is a fascinating area for postcolonial analysis. The border is a notion introduced by colonialism, particularly as colonial forces tried to demarcate the frontier between what was seen as areas under 'civilised' administration and the Other - that which was still to be conquered, subjected to and included in the empire economy. Another colonial strategy was to map areas in such a way that tribes were split. This meant that tribal lands were geographically divided and governed from different colonial administrative centres or even from different countries. Such a state of affairs contributed to the demise of the authority and power of tribal structures. Ultimately, however, imperialism is also a movement against existing boundaries and borders.

The more recent explosion of the South African economy - since the discovery of

gold and diamonds during the late eighteen hundreds - brought about new developments. It was not only from the various South African 'homelands' that black labour
was contracted for work on the mines, on farms and in cities, e.g. Johannesburg. This
experience was shared by many – black males in particular – from Lesotho, Swaziland,
Botswana and Mozambique. As a magnet for contract workers, South Africa became to
many southern Africans a new imperial centre after the demise of colonialism. This
reality made South Africa an important theme in the literatures of these countries. It is
therefore difficult to divorce the literature of such countries from South African literature.

Apart from the fixation on boundaries and borders, there is also another tradition
concerning borders in South Africa - that of an informal borderless world. In 1915,
South African socialists interestingly developed the notion of a borderless world. S.P.
Bunting, one of the South African leaders of the Internationalist Socialist League,
propagated the idea of a socialist 'frontierless empire' (Roux 1993, p. 22). The many
South African authors living in voluntary or forced exile in the twentieth century are
further examples of modernist universalism or postmodernist globalism if you will.
This highlights the fact that the national story is one constituted by exchanges with the
rest of the world.

In his article so far, the focus has been on the context and intertexts which made the
establishment of the CSSALL possible. The next three sections treat the Centre's
various activities, emerging theoretical positions[6] and lecture/learning practices.

Projects of the CSSALL

The centre's projects include:

- the Centre's journal, 'Alternation', facilitates research and the publication of
  articles on the different Southern African literatures, colonial discourse and
  the historical conditions of these literatures and discourses. Two issues are
  published per annum
- the Centre organises an interdisciplinary conference every two years. The
  theme for the first conference (held in 1995) was 'The Dancing Dwarf in the
  Land of the Spirits'. This title refers to a hieroglyph depicting an Egyptian
  expedition to the South of the African continent, and which returned with
  a 'dancing dwarf from the land of spirits'. In ancient times the area below
  Sofala was known as Wakwak, the 'land of the shades', inhabited by the
  Khoikhoi and Khoisan. It is possible that 'the land of the spirits' indicated
  by this Egyptian hieroglyph is the same as this 'land of the shades'. The
  image of the dancing dwarf forms an interesting intertext with current

studies on the trance dances of shamans, and we used it as a metaphor for South African literature itself. The focus of the conference was on different micro-areas, or formations, which would contribute towards a South African literary history.

The second CSSALL conference was held in 1997. It focused on 'The body, identity, repression and sub-cultures in texts from Africa'. The idea was to gather papers together that would form a basis for a theory in which the body, and especially the movements of power in the body, would be central. This entailed the study of 'inspiration', trance and states of possession in the production of oral literature. The development of concepts also aimed at explaining some of these phenomena in written texts. The rationale is that such a discourse could link traditional African explanations of power to psychoanalytic models of the psyche, such as Freud's early writings in which he saw the psyche in terms of energy movement. This conforms with the traditional African view of the body in terms of power.

–   Due to its focus on South African literature and languages, a third project is the South African Literature Translation Series. This series publishes African language texts translated into English. Andreas Z. Zungu's uSukabekhuluma and the Bhambatha Rebellion is the first to have appeared. Dr. A.C.T. Mayekiso from the Department of isiZulu at the University of Durban-Westville completed the translation of this text just before her death in 1996. It is a transcription of an oral account as told to Andreas Z. Zungu by USukabekhuluma himself - the main strategist of the last great insurrection by the Zulu people. Other texts to be published in the series are two books by John Langalibele Dube, a founding father of the African National Congress. The texts, Isita Somuntu Nguye Uqobo Lwakhe (The enemy is one's self, 1928) and Ukuziphatha Kahle (Good manners, 1935), focus on self-help schemes for African upliftment and explore the customs of the Zulu and the British. These texts reflect on the transition from precolonial society to a Victorian middle-class value system.

–   The CSSALL is currently busy developing a computer database containing about 32 000 bibliographic entries of interest to South African literature research. We hope to make this database accessible to researchers on the internet soon. The development of a South African literature encyclopaedia in CD ROM and book form is closely related to the database. This project still has to be developed and will be the product of intensive co-operation with other researchers both in and outside South Africa. In order to develop such linkages, we recently set up a South African literature electronic mailing list.

- From the latter two projects, the Centre is set to develop a condensed and extensively illustrated history of South African literature aimed at scholars and students. Through this project we hope to lay the foundation for the study of South African literature as a whole.
- Various theoretical projects intersect with the projects and explanations provided above. They concentrate on problems of literary history when dealing with a multilingual and multicultural society, identity formation in a heterogeneous society such as South Africa – exemplified in the diversity of its texts and intertexts – and challenges of theorising colonial and apartheid literature and ideology.

Theoretical projects of the CSSALL

A group of South African researchers explored the feasibility of a comprehensive South African literary history at a colloquium entitled 'Re-thinking South African literary history' in 1995. A concern of many participants was the totalising tendency of such a project: the fact that many micro-areas of comparative research in South Africa would be ignored. Some participants expressed fears that it might be a new ideological narrative that glosses over the various conflicts and differences in South African literature. The shortcomings of such a totalising narrative literary history had already materialised in Michael Chapman's Southern African Literatures (1996). This is the first South African literary history to attempt to cover the literatures in the various South African languages since Manfred Nathan's South African Literature of 1925.

Chapman described his book as a 'moral narrative': a narrative that, like a soap opera. resolved itself in the political change-over of 1994. He states:

> Without diminishing 'difference', it has been important to examine the potential of a common humanism, whether in the utterance of an ancient Bushman or a contemporary metafictionalist. It has also been important, in an intellectual climate currently favouring decentered subjects, to recover an 'African' justification for the accessibility and sociability of communication as well as for the moral agency necessary to effect change.
>
> ... What the scars of the emergency have left on the study is a concern for a social contract between writer and citizen that is humanising and democratising in its obligations.

This approach, with its roots in a humanising middle-class morality, is reminiscent of Victorian pietism and didacticism. Chapman does not explore the complex relationship between 'morality' and 'literature'. To him there is no moral unconscious or dark side to the democratic, representative and 'soap opera' values that he promotes in literature. It is not strange, therefore, that he pleads for a realist form of literature. He finds it difficult to relate to modernism, or to understand it in its historical context, and particularly rejects Afrikaans modernist texts for not paying attention to the political realities of South Africa.

Modernism in Afrikaans developed in the 1920s. It developed in reaction to the narrow-minded demands for socialist realist texts in service of the nationalist politics of the time. In this, these texts were political, but in a different sense. The magic realist novels of Zakes Mda, She plays with the darkness (1995a) and Ways of dying (1995b) point to a similar reaction in black literature, against the simplicities of struggle literature.

The CSSALL's approach to South African literature is different. It is not normative or evaluative in terms of aesthetics or ideology. It rather attempts to explore why a particular literature, ideological phenomenon, or text came into existence: what type of institutions, discourses, social conflicts, economic systems and so on made its emergence possible. In this we owe much to Pierre Macherey (1978) and Michel Foucault (1967). Ultimately, the aim is to produce a new theoretical approach and develop its own terminology, using South African material. The first attempt in this regard is the book Constructs of Identity and Difference in South African Literature (van Wyk 1995), which, in its attempt to explore the relationship between Afrikaans literature, nationalism and the working class, focuses too narrowly on Afrikaans literature. The text combines Marxism, semiotics and psychoanalysis. From a semiotic point of view it uses the concepts of iconic and indexical signs to describe different kinds of identity formation.

In recent research, the focus is increasingly on how institutional changes are depicted in South African literature. Of particular interest are the changes involved in the transition from a heroic/precolonial society to one in which Western institutions became central. Important texts for this approach are transcribed oral histories such as the History of Matiwane and the Amangwane Tribe as told by Msebenzi to his Kinsman Albert Hlongwane (van Warmelo 1938). The comparative terror of precolonial oral society and society based on Western institutions (with reason as the founding principle) is of interest here. The terror of reason in its history is both genocidal and productive. It is its productive element that is enigmatic: the way in which it transforms a heroic society into a middle class one.

An interesting moment in the history of reason in South Africa is the white working class and socialist discourses around the industrial uprisings in the period 1910–1924. Ivon Jones describes the uprising in 1922 as 'the first great armed revolt of the workers on any scale in the British Empire' (Hirson 1993, p. 81). Many of these socialists described themselves as rationalists. What is interesting here are the formulations of a counter-empire. They manipulated the discourse of civilisation and barbarism in such a way that the capitalist system became equal to the so-called barbarism of heroic societies. The appropriation of Darwinist evolution theory combined with historical materialism features strongly in these discourses. In a completely different context, the first Zulu author, Magema M. Fuze, in his The Black People and Whence They Came (1979) combined genealogy, a prominent feature of praise poetry, with evolutionary theory and genetics. Through this he hoped to challenge the beliefs of his Christian and colonial masters.

The notion of civilisation (which is a product of a history of terror) is inseparable from its opposite, namely regression. To the white socialists this was evident in the First World War. Fuze also uses an image of regression in his text, an anecdote about the Thusi clan who became baboons living in the veld after becoming weary of cultivating crops. These are variations of a theme that were globally prevalent at the time in texts such as Freud's Civilisation and its Discontents (1985)[7]. More recent and relevant is Foucault's Madness and Civilisation (1967)[8]. It is relevant as a deconstruction of Reason and its institutions.

As part of colonial ideology, Reason was instrumental in genocidal projects against the colonised. But this genocidal drive of Reason also turned into a death drive against itself. This death drive is evident in the many intrigues of the Communist Party of South Africa during the early Stalinist period. The texts dealing with this issue make for interesting discursive analyses. Civilisation, reason and progress are discursive objects which are of central deconstructive concern to the CSSALL.

The CSSALL's focus on history is in many ways absurd. As one of the nineteenth century informants of Callaway (1970, p. 18) in the book The Religious System of the Amazulu declares: 'there (is) no going back to the beginning'. There is in the African explanations of the world a concern with the immediacy of visible things and the present. The past is no longer part of the visible and is therefore irrelevant. Yet there are very old visible records in the form of the rock paintings of hunter-gatherers. These form the oldest 'writing' in the region. Similarly, archaeological finds raise the question of humanity's transition to the semiotic realm: when did human beings become aware of death, when did a rock or something from the natural environment become a tool, and is this metamorphoses or shapeshifting not poetry? Is poetry (an opaque sign system) not older than language? The conception of language as a transparent sign system was an invention of the Enlightenment.

The African turn against history and the embracing of the abundance of the immediate is reminiscent of Nietzsche's notion of tragedy from his early The Birth of Tragedy (1967). This text is of central importance to the study of South African literature. Nietzsche wrote this text in order to deconstruct the programs of Naturalism in the literature of the late nineteenth century. Naturalism was an attempt to bring the newly emergent science forms of reasoning into literature: it wanted to portray the effects of poverty and heredity in the world. It wanted to illustrate science. As such it inspired many movements in literature concerned with development and upliftment programs. Tragedy on the other hand does not see poverty, but rather the omnipotence of the satyr. The satyr is that figure behind all the constructs of civilisation and represents the counter-civilisation, the futility of civilisation. It stands against all blueprints and programs which want people to conform to the image of Reason. The satyr and tragedy express the abundance of nature. Callaway's (1970, p. 24) Zulu informant who says: 'Just as we married many wives saying, 'Hau! we cannot deny ourselves as regards the abundance which uNkulunkulu has given us: let us do what we like' expresses the philosophy of Nietzsche and the world outlook of the satyr. Similarly, the African king embodies a heroic consciousness: a psychology which expresses omnipotence. The death of the king with the tribe as satyric chorus are images of tragedy – of the interaction of individual and group psychology, of the interplay of consciousness, abundance, power and death.

Nietzsche's chorus of satyrs is another version of Bakhtin's (1984) carnival. And South Africa, like many a postcolonial country, is one in which carnival plays a central role. It is a country of mass processions, marches, toyi-toyi, public oratory and mass-gatherings. This is not only part of recent black culture. The 1922 worker uprisings on the Witwatersrand and the Voortrekker Centenary of 1938, amongst others, point to white carnival culture, to continuity between white and black cultures in this regard, and the need for comparative analysis. This is a society in which different carnival formations, different formations of lawlessness, contest with one another. Moreover, '[c]arnival is not a spectacle seen by the people; they live in it, and everyone participates .... it is a special condition of the entire world, of the world's revival and renewal, in which all take part'. Its parody of extracarnival life through folk humour 'denies, but it reviews and renews at the same time. Bare negation is completely alien to folk culture'. In addition, the grotesque 'liberates man from all the forms of inhuman necessity that direct the prevailing concept of the world' (Bakhtin 1984, pp. 7, 11, 49).

Postcolonialism, although recognising hybridity, has been hampered by a narrow focus on the European language literatures from the colonies - also the European language of Reason. We believe that a renaissance could come about through the study of First Peoples' languages and traditions, not as something anthropologically different, but as something continuous with and relevant to our post-modern industrial existences. In the magic realism of Zakes Mda, the return to a rural and traditional past is a rediscovery of spirituality against the materialism of contemporary life.

The Centre's lecture/learning practices

Five elements form part of the Centre's lecture/learning practices: 1) respecting and expanding the resources each student brings into the Centre's programmes; 2) the intertextual, dialogic and interactive nature of lecture hall practices; 3) the challenging nature of the student or learner-lecturer interface; 4) the fostering of a culture of collective ownership and interactive tolerance; and 5) the empowerment of students and their communities through the creative engagement of life, culture, economy, education and work through literature.

The resources and skills students bring into the lecture hall are respected but also expanded - in terms of challenges to expand the existing knowledges of each, i.e. interactively, intertextually and dialogically. Due to the multicultural backgrounds of students, the resources they bring range from home language, culture, religion, knowledge(s) developed in undergraduate studies to their own personalities. Research topics and programmes are formulated in line with the interests of the student and the Centre's stated area of specialisation – Southern African Literature and Languages. Whereas there are many culture studies, African studies and African Languages centres and departments in South Africa, this focus is informed by broad interdisciplinary studies including historical, cultural, literary, social, economic, political and discursive approaches[9]. This makes for the recognition that all forms of identity – ranging from culture and group identity to that of the self – are different manifestations of distinct but also overlapping hybridities[10].

Further, research and the production of knowledge encourage the intertextual and comparative study of what Foucault (1980, p. 81) calls 'subjugated knowledges' – knowledges which are central to the majority of the people of South Africa but which have been marginalised and subjugated by the savage systems of the past. The resources students and researchers bring to the Centre are not only part and parcel of their own lives - these knowledges are also expanded in similar approaches in their own work as teachers, lecturers or community leaders in various professions.

The intertextual, dialogic and interactive nature of lecture hall practices is informed by Bakhtin's notion of 'dialogism', as developed by Kristeva into 'intertextuality', and Freire's 'dialogic cultural action'. The focus on dialogism means that all forms of human knowledge and existence are dialogical to various degrees - existence itself, language, aesthetic expression, history, poetics and the authoring act itself (Holquist 1990). Kristeva's developing of this perception into 'intertextuality' implies that all literary or aesthetic expressions are systems and structures which are not folded into themselves but infinitely dispersed into surrounding texts and environments. 'Intertextuality' therefore indicates the transposition or transformation or multiple intersections of systems of signs with others. This means that systems which have previously been viewed as homogeneous, or disciplines separated into discursive enclaves, are unpacked in their refractedness but also studied in terms of their productive effects. In terms of 'dialogism', the lecture situation itself becomes an intertextual and dialogic space where students, lecturers and researchers interact creatively and learn from one another. As such, intertexts exist and are continuously created and unravelled at the times of production as well as consumption, reading, listening or communication. This means that all present at a 'lecture', are 'learners' or 'partners' in the production and consumption of knowledge (Freire 1970).

It is for this reason that lecturers foster curiosity by positively challenging students to find out, read, research and develop their thinking and writing. Problems or questions which arise in lectures and during the student's research are further problematised, possible approaches and resources suggested and the student challenged to become and remain a learner - or in common parlance, to be a lifelong-learner. Central to this practice of problematising and challenging while simultaneously enabling research is the fostering of personal responsibility and dignity.

These three processes foster a culture of collective ownership and interactive tolerance. In the context of existing intolerances in South Africa - which were fostered by the apartheid government's segregationist practices - the ownership of land, industry, power and knowledge was usually perceived in racial and class terms as white, upper-class or bourgeois ownership. Through its practices, the Centre nurtures collective ownership in that knowledge produced are continuously shared and contributors recognised. Research topics focused on Southern African realities make for knowledge which is first and foremost to be appreciated by the local market. Where students and researchers engage in cross-cultural research projects or where they participate in lecture situations where they interact cross-culturally, the Other is continuously recognised, thereby facilitating cross-cultural understanding, appreciation and tolerance but also the empowerment of people(s) previously exploited.

The last point, the empowerment of students and their communities through the creative engagement of life, culture, economy, education and work through literature can be best summarised in terms of Foucault's notion of the 'specific intellectual'. Contrary to hegemonic discourse which hypostatised the 'universal intellectual' - notably in his left or liberal guise as having 'the right of speaking in the capacity of master of truth and justice', 'the spokesman of the universal', 'the consciousness/conscience of us all' operating in 'the modality of the "universal", the "exemplary", the "just-and-true-for-all"' - Foucault postulates the specific intellectual. Specific intellectuals work in 'specific sectors, at the precise points where their own conditions of life or work situate them (housing, the hospital, the asylum, the laboratory, the university, family and sexual relations). The specific intellectual has a 'much more immediate and concrete awareness of struggles'. Since s/he also - especially in the case of students and researchers at the Centre - often comes from previously disadvantaged or oppressed minority cultures or generally speaking the masses and black proletariat, the activities at the centre empower them to function in society as critical but also facilitating, constructive and responsible intellectuals. Not the image and role of the 'writer of genius' but that of the 'absolute savant', is fostered (Foucault 1980, pp. 126, 129). As intellectuals coming from and functioning in their communities, not only are they as individuals empowered, but the communities – through their work – are empowered – i.e. in fostering independent thinking and action[11]. This also articulates with Freire's (1972a: 54) 'problem-posing education' which 'involves a constant unveiling of reality' and which 'strives for the emergence of consciousness and critical intervention in reality'.

Gramsci once used the image of the fortress to picture the process of struggle, liberation and the taking of control. This image may lead one to think that, after independence, the only challenge for new powers is to clear out the fortress and its trenches and fill them with new powers. This is not the Centre's approach. Its various practices – as e have attempted to explicate briefly above – are, through its dialogic and intertextual approach to Southern African literature and languages, enabling, challenging, collective, interactive, and empowering.

Conclusion

The CSSALL is not the only place in South Africa researching the complexes outlined in this article or following similar practices; nor is it the intention of this article to devalue the work of other South African scholars in the field. Rather, the purpose is to position the Centre and its contributions in terms of the transformation of South African literary studies. And we think that, in terms of the exciting possibilities South Africa's new dispensation has opened up for the developing of the quality of the life of all its people, the Centre makes an important contribution and may in future continue to develop what is nothing more nor less than a crucial intervention in the refracted South African literary landscape.

Notes

1   Stephen Gray's (1979) *Southern African Literature: An Introduction*, worked in this direction and was followed a decade later by Malvern van Wyk Smith's (1990) *Grounds of Contest*.

2   Under 'black' is included the University of Durban-Westville established for the Indian community and the University of the Western Cape established for the coloured community.

3   To capture the complexities of this understanding of 'nation', Bhabha introduced the notion of 'cultural difference'. 'Cultural difference' does not fall into the trap of retaining and entrenching homologous identities as captured with notions such as 'cultural diversity' or even 'multiculturalism'. Rather, it 'marks the establishment of new forms of meaning, and strategies of identification, through processes of negotiation where no discursive authority can be established without revealing the

difference of itself'. It also 'articulates the difference between representations of social life without surmounting the space of incommensurable meanings and judgements that are produced within the process of transcultural negotiation' (1990, p. 312).

4   Hofmeyr traces the manufacturing 'of an Afrikaans literary culture which was an important terrain in which nationalist ideologies were elaborated' through the 'contours of a broader political, economic and social geography' (1987, p. 95). Similar studies sensitise the reader to the complexities of society and pre-empt homogenising tendencies in scholarly discourse.

5   'Heroic' literature is the term the Centre has adopted for what is elsewhere referred to as precolonial literature. This came about in accordance with the use of the term 'heroic' by H. Munro and N. Kershaw Chadwick (1932–1940) in their volume, *The growth of literature* and because DP Kunene (1971) adopted it to describe the praise poetry traditions of Lesotho in The Heroic Poetry of the Basotho.

6   The assumption is that this might be of interest to other postcolonial societies, which share experiences similar to South Africa's. Like South Africa, other postcolonial countries may have a multilingual society - including two or more European languages - with a variety of minority indigenous languages. Also like South Africa, these countries were frontier societies with a history of conflict and assimilation. Unlike South Africa, they may not have such a strong tradition of nationalism and republicanism, or the variety of precolonial political formations. They also may not have a visible history of institutionalised racism still influencing society, such as Apartheid. In studying the literatures of these societies, the issues which can be explored intertextually are those of multilingual literary heritage, existing anthologies, literary histories and theories that attempt to represent this multilingual literary heritage. The issue of the need for such studies may itself be an important enterprise.

7   Departing from his thesis that the purpose of life is dictated by the pleasure principle, Freud contends that humanity's hostility towards Civilization (which he uses as synonym for culture) is precisely due to the conflict between the pleasure principle and the continuous development of culture. Since the moment someone made a tool to skin an animal, all culture developed to 'control our instinctual life'. Not being able to provide an answer to this conundrum himself, he writes that 'one day someone will venture to embark upon a pathology of cultural communities' (1985, pp. 263, 266, 339).

8   Throughout his career, Foucault aimed to develop a method for the analysis of the ways through which Reason developed discourse (with particular objects, strategies and the establishing of institutions which controlled subjects in particular subject positions). It is precisely the limits which Reason draws within disciplinary discourse which include and exclude. At first focusing mainly on an archaeology of

knowledge(s) and later developing it into a genealogy of power, both these systems of analysis focus on the developing of ways and means which would allow for the analysis of a history which advocates and sustains current west-European modernist practices (1967; 1972; 1973; 1977; 1982).

9   Contrary to the 'implicit generalisation of knowledge' or the 'implicit homogenization of experience' - the two 'major strategies of containment and closure in modern bourgeois ideology' according to Claude Lefort - interdisciplinary studies recognises that one must 'always keep open a supplementary space for the articulation of cultural knowledges that are adjacent and adjunct but not necessarily accumulative, teleological or dialectical' (Bhabha 1994, p. 163).

10 Closely associated with Bhabha's notions of 'cultural difference' and 'interdisciplinarity', is that of 'hybridity'. Hybridity denotes 'the perplexity of the living as it interrupts the representation of the fullness of life; it is an instance of iteration, in the minority discourse, of the time of the arbitrary sign - 'the minus in the origin' - through which all forms of cultural meaning are open to translation because their enunciation resists totalisation' (1990, p. 314; 1994, pp. 162–164).

11 Since the various communities in South Africa are – despite their largely racial and class segregations on the basis of previously demarcated group or racial geographical demarcations – extremely hybrid, calling for cross-cultural interaction in many events virtually every day, empowerment at the Centre aims at an informed interaction between people. It addresses local realities in their past and present complexities and challenges.

References

Anderson, B. (1983). *Imagined Communities. Reflections on the Origin and Spread of Nationalism*, London & New York: Verso.

Bakhtin, M. (1984). *Rabelais and his World*, trans. H. Iswolsky, Bloomington: Indiana University Press.

Bhabha, H.K. (ed) (1990). *Nation and Narration*, London: Routledge.

– (1994). *The Location of Culture*, London & New York: Routledge.

Callaway, H. (1970). *The Religious System of the Amazulu*, Cape Town: Struik.

Chadwick, H. and Kershaw, N. (1940). *The Growth of Literature*, Cambridge: CUP.

Chapman, M. (1996). *Southern African Literatures*, London & New York: Longman.

Dhlomo, H.I.E. (1985). 'Dingane', in *Collected Works*, Johannesburg: Ravan Press.

Dube, J.L. (1928). *Isita Somuntu Nguye Uqobo Lwakhe*, trans. N.N. Dhlomo as *The Enemy is One's Self*, (forthcoming), Durban: CSSALL.

Dube, J.L. (1935). *Ukuziphatha Kahle*, Trans. N.N. Dhlomo as *Good Manners*, (fortchoming), Durban: CSSALL.

Foucault, M. (1963). *The Birth of the Clinic: An Archaeology of Medical Perception*, trans. M. Sheridan-Smith, London: Tavistock.

– (n.d.). *The Archaeology of Knowledge and the Discourse on Language*, New York: Pantheon.

– (1967). *Madness and Civilisation: A History of Insanity in the Age of Reason*, Trans. R. Howard, London: Tavistock.

– (1970). *The Order of Things: An Archaeology of the Human Sciences*, London: Tavistock.

– (1977). *Discipline and Punish: The Birth of the Prison*, Trans. A. Sheridan, London: Allan Lane.

– (1980). *Power/Knowledge: Selected Interviews & Other Writings*, 1972-1977, C. Gordon (ed), trans. C. Gordon, L. Marshall, J. Mepham & K. Soper, New York: Pantheon.

Freire, P. (1972a). *Pedagogy of the Oppressed*, London: Penguin.

– (1972b). *Cultural Action for Freedom*, London: Penguin.

Freud, S. (1929). *Civilization, Society and Religion: Group Psychology, Civilisation and its Discontents and Other Works*, trans. J. Strachey, Harmondsworth: Penguin.

Fuze, M.M. (1922). *The Black People and Whence They Came*.

Gray, S. (1979). *Southern African Literature: An Introduction*, Cape Town & London: David Philip & Rex Collings.

Hirson, B. (1986). *The Making of the African Working Class on the Witwatersrand: Class and Community Struggles in an Urban Setting*, 1932-1947, MA thesis, Middlesex Polytechnic.

Hesiod (1966). *Works and Days*, T.A. Sinclair (ed), New York: Arno Press.

Hofmeyr, I. (1987). 'Building a Nation of Words: Afrikaans Language, Literature and Ethnic Identity, 1902-1924', in Marks, Shula & Trapido (eds), *The Politics of Race, Class & Nationalism in Twentieth Century South Africa*, New York: Longman.

Holquist, M. (1990). *Dialogism. Bakhtin and His World*, London: Routledge.

Kristeva, J. (1970). *Le Texte du Roman*, The Hague: Mouton.

– (1974). *La Révolution du Langage Poétique*, Paris: Editions du Seuil.

Kunene, D.P. (1971). *Heroic Poetry of the Basotho*, Oxford: Clarendon Press.

Macherey, P. (1978). *The Theory of Literary Production*, Trans. G. Wall, London & New York: Routledge.

Mda, Z. (1995a). *She Plays With the Darkness: A Novel*, Florida: Vivlia.

Mda, Z. (1995b). *Ways of Dying*, Cape Town: Oxford University Press.

Mphahlele, E. (1962). 'The Non-European Character in South African English Fiction,' published as *The African Image*, New York: Praeger.

Nathan, M. (1925). *South African Literature: A General Survey*, Cape Town: Juta.

Nietzsche, F. (1872). *The Birth of Tragedy and the Case of Wagner*, Trans. W. Kaufmann, New York: Vintage Books.

Roux, E. (1993). S.P. *Bunting: A Political Biography*, B. Bunting (ed), Bellville: Mayibuye Books.

Pratt, M.L. (1992). *Imperial Eyes: Travel Writing and Transculturation*, London & New York: Routledge.

Van Warmelo, N.J. (ed.) (1938). *History of Matiwane and the Amangwane Tribe as Told by Msebenzi to his Kinsman Albert Hlongwane*, Pretoria: Government Printer.

Van Wyk Louw, N.P. (1942). *Die Dieper Reg*, Kaapstad: Nasionale Pers.

Van Wyk, J. (1995). *Constructs of Identity and Difference in South African Literature*, Durban: CSSALL.

Van Wyk, J., Conradie, P. and Constandaras, N. (1988). *SA in Poësie/SA in Poetry*, Pinetown: Owen Burgess Publications.

Van Wyk Smith, M. (1990). *Grounds of Contest. A Survey of South African English Literature*, Kenwyn: Jutalit.

Zungu, A.Z. (1997). *uSukabekhuluma and the Bhambatha Rebellion*, Trans. A.C.T. Mayekiso, Durban: CSSALL.

CHAPTER SEVEN

Five Afrikaner texts and the rehabilitation of whiteness

Zoë Wicomb

One of the more refreshing qualities of Apartheid was the abandon with which we all talked about and identified ourselves in terms of race, a situation that compares rather favourably with European cultures where official 'anti-racism', notwithstanding avowed awareness of the constructedness of race, stifles its own discourse with a fastidious reluctance to speak of white or black. It is, I fear, in such advanced societies, where whiteness as a category is masked, that Apartheid (with which Afrikaner has become synonymous) will be sorely missed as ready-made Other whose aggressive naming of white and black has come to define racism. In South Africa where the material effects of institutionalised racism linger, ethnicity as a contrastive system ensures that not every-one wishes to abandon racial naming: black groups jealously guard their blackness, coloureds cling to the colouredness of a mythologized District Six, the more-memorious-than-thou AWB howl for a white Homeland, and only 'English' liberals are puzzled by the persistence of their perceived whiteness.

Whiteness, the condition once assumed by diverse European settler communities, is no longer one to be cherished. Indeed, it is no longer a nice word. Whiteness does not collocate with the key words of our narrative of freedom and thus there is no potential for discursive appropriations or refiguration of its general field of meaning. As a construct, whiteness cannot be fully addressed; indeed, it appears to be only from within and bound up with the meaning of a specific ethnic group that a revision can emerge; in other words, it must literally be deconstructed. It is not surprising that Afrikaners, the group most in need of rehabilitation, are engaged in such a discursive struggle. In this paper I examine a number of contemporary texts concerned with Afrikaner identity and focus on the textual strategies for refiguring Afrikanerhood in relation to whiteness.

An article on the Truth and Reconciliation Commission in the London newspaper, *The Guardian*, is a convenient point of departure precisely because investigation and disclosure appear to be common tropes in the literary discourses of a revised

Afrikanerness. An entire page of the broadsheet of 18 January 1997 is devoted to the issue and more than a quarter of the page constitutes a closely cropped, larger than life photograph of the crumpled face of a black woman whose chin rests dejectedly on her right hand. Looking directly into the camera she cries with abandonment: her eyes are narrowed; a plump Tretchikoff teardrop trembles on her cheek; through parted lips we see her clenched teeth; from the tonality of her lower lip there is a suspicion of slavering. In the left-hand corner, below the injunctive headline of 'Cry, beloved country' with its evocation of Alan Paton liberalism, is a passport-size photograph of the poet, Antjie Krog, whose account as head of the team of radio reporters covering the Commission, fills the rest of the page. Besides the matter of size, there are other inversions in these photographs: Krog's smiling face is tilted; her right hand appears to lift the chin giving her a meditative air; the intelligent, penetrating look engages with that of the viewer whilst the black face is blanked with grief. The black woman's tears dissolve her subjectivity; there is no reciprocity as we are forced into an unequal, voyeuristic gaze.

The report, it turns out, is at odds with the images. There is no story of black tears. Instead, the scripto-visual text finds its cohesion in Krog's crying, her grief and breakdown as a result of the trauma of listening day after day to stories of atrocities and the horror of having to convert these into sound-bites. It is of course perfectly appropriate that Antjie Krog (whose dissident credentials are well established in the British media) should cry, but the article raises the question of why *The Guardian* should want to translate her tears into that of a black woman, or why her text should be slid under the signification of blackness. Krog states her task as follows: 'It was crucial for me to have the voices of the victims on the news bulletin. To have the sound of ordinary people dominate the news. No South African should escape the process.' And so too in *The Guardian's* report where the nature of the *process* remains unexplained but where we are given four extracts from the voices of victims. These are not racially identified, except one knows that the tea-lady in the police station who sees her grandchild falling down from the upper floor is black by virtue of being a tea-lady. Her edited story was broadcast: 'and the voice of an ordinary cleaning woman is the headline. We lift our fists triumphantly. We've done it!'

The other two texts are more difficult to identify in terms of race but the voices are not stereotypical of dispossessed blacks. The final and most detailed account is that of two families wiped out by an ANC bomb on the northern South African border – in other words, victims of liberation warfare. This gory story, told by an identified Mr van Eck in 'formal old-fashioned Afrikaans' and ending with 'I sat for days... I simply sat... I lost my business. I am reduced to a poor white', has, it turns out, been previously represented. Reporting the request for a further sound-bite, Krog tells of her instruction to a colleague to 'send the one about where he was just sitting and remember to add that the newspapers of that day said that pieces of his son's hair and eyes were found in a tree near the bakkie.' Such re-presentation of texts as I will later show is precisely what seems to be required to produce a revision of ethnic identity. Significantly these accounts of atrocities, originally reported on different occasions, are dispersed in Antjie Krog's extraordinarily moving book on the Commission.[2] But it is the particular meanings produced by the specific recycling for *The Guardian* readers that I wish to discuss.

Class has come to replace race: the text suggests an equivalence between the ordinary black cleaning woman and the once prosperous white man, and Van Eck's identification of himself as a poor-white amounts to an effacement of whiteness with its dominant meaning of privilege. Indeed the word takes us back to a deeper historical memory of British oppression of the Afrikaner that drove them into the lager, an oppression that is historically responsible for Van Eck's very geographical location on the northern border. Atrocity, memory and grief are in the liberal-humanist idiom shown to be categories that cannot admit of racial differentiation, since that would hamper the process of reconciliation. If the assertion of a white right to grief is overt, what is covert in the text where whiteness is disavowed, is the conjugation of Afrikaner ethnicity with blackness. Hence the peculiar anchoring of the linguistic message of Afrikaans tears with the visual information of a crying black woman. At the intersection of image and text a new meaning of self-other relations is produced.

Relations of alterity

One of the less predictable phenomena to develop out of the scramble for Africa is the current scramble for alterity. There is still the native other, the object of ethnography, whose difference and inferiority has been established in colonial discourse, but there is also the psychoanalytic other, closely related to the post-modern crisis of reason. The fashionable anthropological turn in critical theory as well as contemporary artistic production or struggle in the name of the cultural or ethnic other could be seen as an attempt to engage the first in defence against the nihilistic tendency of the second.[2] Otherness then comes to acquire a peculiar valency within metropolitan culture, peculiar, that is, from the point of view of the native who can only be baffled by her new symbolic status.

Hal Foster (1996, p. 173), outlining the pitfalls in the American artist-as-ethnographer paradigm where alterity is seen as the 'outside, the Archimedean point from which the dominant culture will be transformed or at least subverted', discusses such assumption of otherness as problematic and offers a solution of self-reflexivity for the artist to protect herself against over-identification. The notion of textual strategies for the management of identification is suggestive, and informs my investigation of the ways in which, with the decline of Apartheid, Afrikaner writing appeals to alterity in the process of redefining Afrikanerhood.

Nowhere is the scramble for alterity more prevalent than in post-modern theory itself which in its negation of Truth and Reason continues to idealise the other. For instance, theorists like Deleuze and Guattari may reject the term, but their aestheticised discussion of the minoritarian, located within a metaphor of territory and linked with a process of becoming, deftly blends the colonial and the psychoanalytic other. Alterity is conceived as a process of growth that is not bound to territory, indeed is deterritorialized:

> One reterritorializes, or allows oneself to be reterritorialized, on a minority as a state; but in a becoming, one is deterritorialized. Even Blacks, as the Black Panthers said, must become-black … if Jews themselves must become-Jewish, if women must become-woman, if children must become-child … it is because only a minority is capable of serving as the active medium of becoming.
>
> Deleuze and Guattari 1988, p. 291

The overarching metaphoric system of *A Thousand Plateaus* is that of the land and its mapping, a system that is continued underground where the dominant representative model of the tree and its vertical root is replaced by the horizontal rhizome with its multiple entryways. Since otherness is clearly not a desirable condition for actual minorities or for the politically colonised who actively struggle for territory itself, it would seem that such an idealised view is essentially an albocentric, metropolitan one.

However, it is the case that literary representations of identity during the establishment of Apartheid in some respects correspond to the Deleuze-Guattarian model of territorialization. Afrikaner writing rooted its identity in an aesthetics of the land whereas black writing, characterised largely by a 'becoming of blackness', was not concerned with geography or its translation into landscape – as Sipho Sepamla's poem states, 'I've never had to say/ this land is mine'. Since the demise of Apartheid, however, Afrikaners, who have constituted themselves as minoritarian, have been representing in literary texts their 'becoming', a process in which black-as-other is necessarily implicated.

The textual construction of Africa as other to Europe has in the past been well charted and the description of black-as-other enthusiastically embraced by black and white alike. For instance, much of black resistance to the term *postcolonial* centres around exclusive claims to alterity: there is no basis, it is popularly felt, for a term that posits equivalence between the black condition and that of white colonials. This view claims race as the only site of alterity, or where the other axes along which identity is constructed, such as class, gender or ideological positioning in terms of centre and periphery, are acknowledged, there would be insistence on the foregrounding of race. But without resorting to Homi Bhabha's theories of hybridity and mimicry, the homology of white:black :: self:other is clearly inadequate and simplistic. At the level of common-sense it disregards the fact that even when racism succeeds in undermining or estranging the self there remains a sense in which people cannot possibly think of themselves as other. Thus Othello's negative descriptions of himself attributed to his blackness as in the following examples, '... for I am black/ And have not those soft parts of conversation/ That chamberers have ...' (III.3.261) or 'Her name that was as fresh/ As Dian's visage is now begrimed and black/ As mine own face' (III.3.383), are for black readers, even as expressions of irrationality, not possible utterances especially by someone of Othello's social status. Such perception of his otherness is an albocentric view of the black entirely refracted through white eyes, one that fails to appreciate the double exposure effect of a subjectivity that is acutely aware of being the object of white focalisation.

I want to dwell for a moment on the word *utterance* as distinct from *writing*. Textuality has come to mean the written word and thus we have focused on the ways in which blacks have been represented in ethnographic and literary texts. We tend to overlook the popular spoken texts of the disenfranchised who demonstrate the inalienable, if residual, existence of a self in their construction of whites as other, in popular discourse, in jokes, derogatory naming and contemptuous informal accounts of their cultural practices. In South Africa such oppositional identity was not shaped purely along the racial axis of black-white, but in ethnic terms, so that it was barbaric Afrikaner behaviour which was mocked and against which blacks defined themselves. The common homology of white:black :: self:other is then clearly inappropriate as textual othering of the white oppressor is routinely practised, allowing for slippage between the sets. Such practice may not in itself overturn the undeniable power of the oppressor but rather serves as necessary rehearsal towards insurrection.

Thus the oppressed cannot fully embrace a post-modern theory of decentredness and loss of subjectivity as they cling, if periodically, to the humanist notion of a core self that is essential to the possibility of resistance. Such a sense of self readjusts and redefines itself in relation to different self-other dyads when a goal like the overthrow of Apartheid is achieved. Identity, being something always in process, constitutes a constant realignment of intra-affiliations between ethnicity, class and gender, as well as perspectival shunting between self and other. Whilst there is a real level on which blacks cannot see whites as having given up any power in South Africa – because there is no material evidence of the latter having done so – there is nevertheless a sense in which white-black/ self-other relations are manifestly in flux.

When black South Africans in the 80s reinflected the word Boer to signify something distasteful, they succeeded in making Afrikaners accept that meaning to the extent that the majority now disown the name. In spite of the fact that *Boer*, in accordance with their power, was a name proudly chosen by themselves to signal their connection with the land, the word had become infected with black distaste which culminated in the Pan African Congress's chant of 'Kill the farmer, kill the Boer' so that

Afrikaners have abandoned what they now perceive to be a racist term. Since the balance of power in the New South Africa is shifting, it is perhaps not surprising that Afrikaners should assume the condition of otherness. I examine this assumption of otherness in terms of textual representation of the land, precisely because of the geographical origins of their name, and the traditional self-definition of the Boers as white in relation to the land.

Afrikaner geography and the land

Literary representations of the land have typically relied on the ideologies of nature and space, given categories with which humans interact or which somehow reflect society. Contemporary critical geography however dismisses this model as one that separates social and physical space, and as Neil Smith (1998, p. 77) suggests, both nature and space are, in fact, produced by humans, a concept that enables geography to demonstrate, rather than simply assert, the unity of space and society. Those of us who would otherwise have been lost in high theory's cultural critique of spatiality – Jameson's spatial model of culture, Soja's post-modern geographies or Foucault's cartography of power – found ready understanding in Apartheid's crude commodification of space, the geographical division driven by economic exploitation.

The Homeland was a construct of ethnic groups that 'naturally' belonged in particular undeveloped, arid and scattered bits of land, an improbable mapping of alterity that both included and excluded it from the republic according to the use-value of its people. Its deployment of the ideologies of nature and space to boost unequal economic development is a clear example of how geographical space was produced and hierarchised.

In accordance with the project of domination the South African land was idealised and considered by settlers to underpin their history. One of the educational staples of the Apartheid years, Gie's *Geskiedenis van Suid Afrika* ('History of South Africa', 1942), has a geographical appendix of some twenty pages, *The Geographical Foundations of Our History*, by Dr P. Serton, a title that asserts the determining role of immutable nature in historical developments. In preparation for the Nationalist Party's establishment of Apartheid in 1948, Serton offers the following bizarre physical description:

> South Africa clearly forms an independent geographical unit, isolated by nature from other connected territory. Not only is the land surrounded by oceans on three sides, but in the fourth direction, to the north, it borders on tropical regions which are unhealthy for the white man and which in the past constituted a more effective line of separation than the broadest water expanse.
>
> (my translations)

Thus the South African (is)land is produced, textually severed from the African continent by the white subject who identifies the borders of his territory from within the
imagined space. Here whiteness and geography produce each other. The albocentric
logic which constructs the southern part of the continent as a separate landmass on the
basis that it accommodates the white constitution is also an appeal to nature to legitimise occupation of South Africa. But anxiety about such legitimacy finds expression in
fears of desertification. Serton refers to popular contemporary theories of diminishing
rainfall which would show that 'the white man would have settled in a land sentenced
to death' then summarily dismisses such fears. He quotes the Drought Investigation
Commission of 1922: 'No proof of significant changes in the average annual rainfall
of the Union in recent historical times has been delivered, and such change is considered to be unlikely.' Serton nevertheless comments on the problems of diminishing
water supply as follows:

> ... rivers become more irregular in their flow and the veld becomes drier in
> many regions, whilst a great number of fountains have disappeared. These
> phenomena can however be fully explained by human influences. There is no
> need here to think of climactic change.
>
> Gie 1942, p. 269

Given the fact of diminishing water, the Commission not surprisingly adopts the
passive voice to diminish responsibility for its assurances against desertification. In the
legal metaphor of a death sentence, Serton betrays his awareness of transgression
although the settlers are metonymically displaced by the land itself on which the sentence is pronounced. We are invited to infer that God, seat of divine justice, will not
turn against the settler; indeed the occupation of the land is sanctioned so that actual
instances of water scarcity are irrationally attributed to unspecified human activity.
What is, of course, suppressed in this geographical text is the Land Act of 1913 by
which black people, deprived of their ownership, were pauperised and sent into the
cities in search of labour.

The geographer's anxiety about the land's refusal to support white settlers is also to
be found in Afrikaans literature, and especially from the 1920s to the 40s, in the genre
of the *plaasroman* or narratives about the farm where drought produces crises that are
not only geographical but also moral. Here we find that land and nature are socialised
into the farm; there is no Romantic celebration of nature that is not embedded in the
ontological concerns of a boer (literally farmer) who tills the land that yields or with-
holds according to the blessing or curse of God. In the conversion of land into farm,
nature into culture, the homologous relationship with other and self is developed, so
that apart from the land's commodification, the natural claim of the savage native is
effectively countered. Awareness of such claim was, of course, repressed as the early

colonisers, both Boer and English, apparently encountered vast tracts of empty land that invited occupation, a literary construction of space that failed to include the presence of indigenous people. Such human absence allowed nature to represent freedom: expansion into the interior was after all a product of the Afrikaners' love of liberty, as they trekked away from the disciplinary social space of the Dutch colonial authority and later from British imperialism. Since they could not claim autochthony, the settlers adopted the myth of the Israelites who after trials and tribulations abroad reached the homeland assigned to them by God. This they tilled and developed as farmland, thus establishing a white ethnic identity that relied on a slippage between nature and culture.

For C.J. Langenhoven (1873–1932), author of the old national anthem, '*Die Stem van Suid Afrika*' (The Voice of South Africa), such slippage is deployed in the description of a land voicing its geography – out of the heavens, the depths of the sea, the eternal mountains, the far-flung empty plains – that merges with human echoes and the groan of Boer trekwagons. The voice of the anthropomorphised land rises through a series of parallel prepositional phrases to articulate the relationship between demanding nature and Afrikaner culture, producing a fulsome patriotism. The poem ends in a plea to God that 'the farms of our fathers remain the farms of our children', in order that they may be free against the whole world. The word '*erwe*' which I have loosely translated as farms has, in fact, the ambiguous meanings of legacy and land. Edward Said's (1983, pp. 18–20) characterisation of the shift from pre-modern biological filiation to modernity's affiliative mode (the passage from nature to culture) here finds an example as genealogy is set in the service of timeless land or farm. Thus the filiative comes to be re-presented in the larger social structure of the nation.

Langenhoven's most anthologised poem is a diptych called '*Die Onteiening*' ('The Disownment' – by nature, according to his footnote) that deals with drought and destruction of a farm which is mirrored – formally, stylistically and in terms of the narrative – by an account of rainfall and regeneration, except that the voice of the farmer in the second poem turns out, only in the last line and in italics, to be a replacement of the first owner. It is not within the scope of this chapter to consider the intimations of a split Boer subjectivity, but the implied self-other slippage performed by the mirror figures of retribution and blessing is suggestive. The speaker's belated acknowledgement of the replaced farmer in the line, 'it's other voices that I hear ...' hints at a repression of the (disowned) other within the self, a voice which to the excluded black South African has always rendered into falsetto the loudly-sung land.

Afrikanerhood and language

It is precisely this racialised geographical space that must be invoked and reinscribed in order to produce a revised non-Boer identity. In 'Cry Beloved Country', Antjie Krog, after her account of Van Eck's horrific loss, reports her own anguished escape from the studio to look out on to the veld:

> My eyes claw at the trees, the kloofs ... see, smell ... a landscape of paradise and a language from paradise: mispel, maroela, tarentaal, I whisper. The air is drowsy with jasmin and kamferolie. I sit down on the steps and everything tears out of me.

The response is a personal one, but it is also, in its references to landscape and the communality of language, as Afrikaner, with a particular time-honoured relationship with the land as paradise, that Krog reacts to the horror stories. Her breakdown is signalled by a breakdown of language and the italicised difference encodes the struggle within South Africa's definition of whiteness as English versus Afrikaans. The refusal to add the anglophone 'e' to jasmin, to turn 'kamferolie' into oil of camphor is an assertion of Afrikaner identity and the untranslatability of the land into English. The sensuousness of Krog's Africa, however, departs from Afrikaner Calvinism, and 'tarentaal', or guineafowl, carries a particular significance for such revision. In the iconography of an informal and popular anti-Apartheid movement of dissident, urban, whites in the eighties, this bird assumed a central place. Its ubiquitous image dominated design from expensive craftshops to open-air clothing markets; as design icon it signified liberation, and the very speckled black and white pattern of the bird's plumage came to represent an alternative to whiteness, a new multiracialism that chose to embrace indigenous blackness. In other words, an image of desire. In this text the iconicity is appropriated from such alternative whiteness to forge a link through suffering and victim status between black and Afrikaner. Overloaded as the icon has become, it must also carry the mechanism by which the vilified 'language of the oppressor' can be translated into a 'language from paradise'.

Thus the troubled history of the Afrikaans language comes full circle. Early white rejection of the 'kitchen language' followed by denial of its evolution as a Creole of Dutch developed initially by Indonesian, Mozambiquan and Malagasy slaves, and the subsequent standardisation of a white variety of long-vowelled *beskaafde* (civilised) Afrikaans, enters yet another phase. After the Cape Coloured adoption of the spoken variety of diglossic non-standard Afrikaans, known as Kaaps with its typical code-switching into English, came to be valorised as a literary language, post-Apartheid white translation of Afrikaans from its oppressor status takes a similar course (see Hein Willemse's 'Die Skrille Sonbesies' in Trump 1990, pp. 367–400). The non-standard, urban, spoken variety of Afrikaans previously associated with coloureds or poor-whites is used in much of the new writing, especially by women, which deflects the language from the old, discredited Boer identity. Narratives from the late eighties onwards, whether in standard or non-standard dialects, are crucially concerned with a laundered

Afrikaner ethnicity, its whiteness effaced through an association with blackness. This phenomenon can now be seen to be institutionalised at least at the University of Cape Town where the Department of Afrikaans, previously linked to Nederlands, is to be merged with African languages.

Krog's naming of fauna and flora alludes to Genesis, to desire for the prelapsarian with an Adamic language that proposes a simple correspondence between things in the world and language, a desire which at the same time invokes the old

> home-grown Calvinist myth in which the Afrikaner has his type in the Israelite, tender of flocks, seeker after a promised national homeland, member of an elect race (volk) set apart from the tribes of the idolatrous, living by simple and not-to-be-questioned commandments, afflicted by an inscrutable Godhead with trials whose purpose is to test his faith and his fitness for election.
>
> Coetzee 1988, p. 95

Not only must the subject formation of a New Afrikaner necessarily scavenge from previous liberal discourses, it must also invoke such old myths and translate them from whiteness into a new discourse of conciliation.

Effacing whiteness

Let me return to my initial question: Why is a report about Afrikaner response to the horrors of Apartheid and the inscription of the (male) Afrikaner as victim accompanied by a large photograph of a crying black woman? Contemporary theorising about whiteness would seem to have an answer: that white is an empty signifier, both everything and nothing, that being invisible to itself it cannot acknowledge its existence, that it can only articulate itself in terms of the markedness of black, the contrast which supplies the meaning of white as the norm. Its avowed transparency, its refusal to acknowledge itself as an examinable category, at the same time asserts the unthinkability of itself as object, or other.

As my earlier metaphor of focalisation would suggest, black-as-other is a white narration of the marked category of blackness; whiteness as a given, masks its existence and therefore also cannot be seen as the subject of a narrative, not least because focalisation through an other has been unthinkable.

Richard Dyer (1988, pp. 44–64; 1977) gives the following revealing account of a British experimental video that sets out to investigate whiteness as an ethnic category:

> In an attempt to get some white people to explore what being white means, the video assembles a group to talk about it and it is here that the problem of white

people's inability to see whiteness appears intractable. Subcategories of whiteness (Irishness, Jewishness, Britishness) take over, so that the particularity of
whiteness itself begins to disappear ...

Such denial was, of course, not the case in South Africa where the settler minority
unashamedly celebrated and claimed privileges on the basis of their whiteness which
has a varied history of self-representation related to particular historical stages of the
political programme. In the establishment of Apartheid in the forties, far from presenting itself as invisible, codification of whiteness as cultural and political dominant
became necessary in the face of being outnumbered by blacks.

Application to be classified as white, for instance, demanded an explicit set of
physical and cultural criteria. At this stage too the colonial terms European and native,
inappropriate to the new project, came to be replaced by white and non-white, as
whiteness assumed native status in the promised homeland. Thus came the invention
of a privileged white 'race' which ensured political and demographic domination by
constructing various black 'ethnic' groups that could be forcibly moved into far-from-
paradisiac Homelands. That a sub-group identified themselves as 'English', regardless
of the fact that it was constituted of mainly Scottish and Irish settlers as well as various
Western European nationals and Eastern European Jews, was a response, based on
preferred language, to the aggressive assertion of whiteness by Afrikaners who in-
sisted on a separate ethnic and linguistic identity bound up with a special association
with the land.

In his introduction to *White Writing: On the Culture of Letters in South Africa*, J.M.
Coetzee (1988, p. 11) offers a definition of the category white. He explains his title
which refers to the post 1948 neo-colonial period, in the following historical terms:

> the phrase white writing (does not) imply the existence of a body of writing
> different in nature from black writing. White writing is white only insofar as it
> is generated by the concerns of people no longer European, not yet African.

In other words Coetzee overturns the paradigm by giving whiteness a marked meaning, the name for something incomplete, not fully adapted to its environment, something in transition, a meaning of inbetweenness caught in a process of acculturation,
the presupposition being that the condition must inevitably be absorbed into Africa.
Coetzee's whiteness, far from being the transparent, irreducible category of Europe, is
subjected to history and so anticipates Krog's translation. Her news article, at the
intersection of image and text, engenders a new meaning of Afrikaner that is slipped
under the signification of capacious black woman.

Ethnicity translated through the *plaasroman* ('farm novel')

Derrida's commentary on the story of Babel as a central figure of deconstruction is suggestive for the story of apartheid - Babel being a trope for the built-in entropy of apartheid with its attempts at a totalizing construction, at giving whiteness and blackness proper noun status, and at replete translation of the indigenous culture. Babel, the name of the tower which means both confusion and God the Father, is as Derrida (1991, p. 251) points out, not translated and occupies a status of both common and proper nouns: 'Translation then becomes necessary and impossible, like the effect of a struggle for the appropriation of the name, necessary and forbidden in the interval between two absolutely proper names.'

In his study of the *plaasroman*, (farm novel) J.M. Coetzee (1988, p. 110) points out how the master of the genre, C.M. van den Heever, 'broadly came to integrate nature into the farm, that is to relate certain romantic commonplaces about the recovery of man's truth in nature to the thesis that the Afrikaner will lose his independence and (eventually) his identity if he loses his base in landownership.' It is this relationship between truth and the land which in post-Apartheid writing is being unravelled. Until recently, it was dissident writers in English who rewrote the genre: Coetzee's own *In the Heart of the Country* is a revision that explores elements repressed in the *plaasroman*, and Gordimer in *The Conservationist* offers a farm on which the corpse of a black man buried in a shallow grave resurfaces to challenge Afrikaner construction and appropriation of the land. Now, however, a trend in contemporary Afrikaans writing itself, concerned with re-presenting the land, is discernible. My reading below of influential texts by Etienne van Heerden, Marlene van Niekerk, Antjie Krog and Chris Barnard attempts to show how they investigate and rehabilitate Afrikaner identity through re-negotiation of the traditional affiliation with the land and particularly through the redeployment of the *plaasroman's* old tropes of drought and water. Read within the political context of the Truth Commission and the post-Apartheid programme of land redistribution and restitution, these texts would appear to establish a new non-Boer identity in terms of revised relations of alterity between white and black.

Textual construction of ethnicity is traditionally bound up with a narrative of genealogy, and the *plaasroman's* generic treatment of the family, who improve and develop the farm and so legitimise its occupation, is characteristically concerned with filiative identity established through successive generations. Etienne van Heerden's acclaimed novel, *Toorberg*, translated as *Ancestral Voices* (1993), stages its events under the sign of Babel and around the proper name of the Afrikaner family. The novel starts with a diagram of the Moolman family tree that crosses over traditional racial lines to reveal the branch of their coloured relatives, known as the *skaamfamilie* (family of shame). The Moolmans occupy a farm called Toorberg, and their coloured relations, live (improbably) on an adjacent arid territory called, according to the family paradigm, the Step-veld, a spatial division that allegorises Apartheid's geography. The original Afrikaans title is also the name of the mountain that towers over the farm, from which the coveted commodity of water fountains, but which for the current generation has dried up, the drought serving as central symbol for the demise of a corrupt culture. The word, 'toor', derives from 'tower' which means to bewitch or enchant; besides its homonymous relationship with the English word, mountain is also symbolically re-lated to tower. It is in the Toormountain that a Malay magician is consulted by genera-tions of Abel Moolmans and babbles his prophesies. The prosperous farm Toorberg is also a Babel in the sense that the Afrikaner family sets out to make a name for itself, a totalizing project that according to the narrative cannot be completed. The story tells of the Moolmans' vain attempts to replace the natural mountain source with bore holes drilled into the earth. Thus Van Heerden replaces horizontal penetration into the interior by which the trek-boer freely acquired land in the past with verticality. The puncturing of the land recasts the *plaasroman's* conversion of nature into culture as delegitimation, a process that triggers a deconstruction of the entire series of culture/ nature, self/other and white/black homologies. Toorberg, the prosperous farm, is a Babel in the sense that the Afrikaner family had set out to name the world and make a name for themselves, a totalizing project that Van Heerden shows cannot be com-pleted. Instead, the narrative traces the demise of the Afrikaner whose only form of survival is through melanisation, in other words, through assuming the condition of otherness.

The novel's intertextuality includes references to Sarah Gertrude Millin's *God's Step-children* (1924), a key text in the culture's myths about miscegenation and racial purity. The Shame-family are not only descendants of Afrikaners, but also of a Millinesque English missionary. The coloured Andries Moolman has in disgust spent his hard earned savings to have his name changed to Riet, an Afrikaans pronunciation of Reid, the name of his missionary ancestor, a gesture of disaffiliation that anticipates his son's commitment to the black revolutionary movement. It is a complex translation from the Afrikaner name to an Afrikanerisation of an English name which signifi-cantly links indigenisation with an hybridity whose mother tongue is Afrikaans. The assumption and translation of the new name, Riet, is at the same time an assumption of agency that undermines self-other relations as oppositional and constitutes the first chiasmic move in a refiguration of the racial homology: the coloured subject can no longer be viewed as purely other as he attempts to throw off an identity of shame[3] focalised through the Moolmans; indeed, the act shows the naming of the Shame-family to be white displacement of shame. Black subjectivity is also inscribed in terms of location: the Riets move between the contemporary shack in the Step-veld and the mountain cave with its historical Bushman paintings and the skeleton of their Bushman ancestor, in other words, horizontal space is crossed with the verticality of time. Their implied identity as Cain, adversary of the patriarchal Abel Moolman, replicates stereotypical portrayal of the coloured condition as marked, but it also constitutes a revision of the old Afrikaner-Israelite myth of exclusivity, for an actual physical mark of sterility is borne by both white and black members of the family. Van Heerden thus seeks to instate new affiliations that are not a re-presentation of the old filiative order.

Ancestral Voices offers an allegorical account of the hubristic story of Apartheid: the arrogant occupation of the land by generations of Abel Moolmans, and the subsequent disappearance of the water without which the farm can no longer be paradise. Afrikaners have through overweening pride, megalomania and greed forfeited the inheritance of the land whilst their coloured shame family have turned against them to support black revolutionaries. The Moolmans' majoritarian intolerance of gentleness and dreaminess, their prejudice against blacks, Catholics and English, result in an inbreeding that produces madness. Thus at the geographical margins of their estate are those they have cast out: the coloured, the poor-white and the mad relations who are excluded from the dominant definition of Afrikaner. The family is avenged when the last of the patriarchs uses water diviners and a grand machine to drill a water-hole that drives his ancestors out of their graves. Van Heerden also deploys an idiot figure, a generic character in the *plaasroman* where he represents a way of living harmoniously with the natural world, but in this case Abel's subnormal grandchild, named both Noah (denoting flood) and Trickle (denoting drought) serves as deconstructive agent. Noah/Trickle falls into one of the boreholes and is with the consent of the entire family, both coloured and white, shot by Abel who himself dies during the investigation of the child's death. The gift of water divining (yet another figuration of the vertical or subterranean as site of transformation) borne by Noah was the last hope of breaking the drought. Modernism's romantic idiot-other deployed by the *plaasroman* to access Truth is here replaced by a racialised postcolonial alterity: the remaining son, CrossAbel, is sterile, and the inheritance of the land as well as the perpetuation of the family lies in the prospective union of one of the poor-white Moolmans to his coloured second cousin, Kitty Riet. Thus the new hybridised Afrikaner, melanised through indigenous black blood.

Significantly the stories of the family, told in the voices of both the living and the dead, coloured and white, are in response to a judicial enquiry into the death of Noah/Trickle. But the magistrate can come to no conclusion: the investigation is belated, a good year after the dream-child's death; the stories refuse to translate into a coherent, transparent picture of the events of the past. As the ghost of Old Abel predicts: 'You haven't got the guts to pronounce sentence on the sons of Abel', and it seems as if the one-armed magistrate, Abraham van der Ligt (of the Light), is himself an incarnation of one of the dead Moolmans. He does in the end not produce a judgement; instead, things sort themselves out, or rather nature does, in the death of the current Abel. It is thus through an inclusive narrative, the Babelesque allegory that deconstructs an exclusive Afrikanerhood into its suppressed meanings – the poor-white relations, the coloured shame-family, the self-extermination, or in Derrida's terms the 'multiplicity of idioms' – that the old link between land and Afrikaner lineage is severed. But with it goes historicity: the story of the past cannot be reconstructed; the post-modern otherness that is being embraced denounces the old grand narratives of truth and justice.

The narrative of *Ancestral Voices*, framed as a judicial enquiry, prefigures the post-Apartheid Truth and Reconciliation Commission, although its judgement asserts the need to draw a veil over the past. Not only is the truth irrecoverable, not only are the coloureds both wronged blood relations and accomplices in the crime, not only can there be no outcome, but an insistence on Truth and Justice would amount to something vulgar, a failure to appreciate the equivocal. In 'Cry, Beloved Country'. Antjie Krog, also speaks of the crassness of Truth, the need for its deconstruction: 'I hesitate at the word ... I am not used to using the word... I prefer the word lie... Because it is there that the truth liest closest'.[4] The focus in *Ancestral Voices* is not surprisingly then on reconciliation: 'I am quite sure ... that your laws will have nothing at all to say about mercy', says the sensible Amy, last of the grand Moolmans, and the magistrate concludes that '(p)erhaps it is forgiveness, and not the chill, focused jet of judgement and sentence, that is the clearest water of all' (van Heerden 1993, p. 250). Thus the refiguration of the Afrikaner as one who investigates his crimes, who acknowledges his coloured offspring, and sheds his arrogant whiteness, is staged in the historical context of the inevitable demise of Apartheid, and the future democratic elections in which the Afrikaner's hope of political survival would be the coloured vote.

Whilst van Heerden's narrative of genealogy traces the decline of whiteness through madness and melanisation, genealogy is deployed in radically different ways by Marlene van Niekerk whose representation of Afrikaners' self-consciously refuses identification or any trading with black-as-other. *Triomf* (Triumph), the title of her award-winning novel,[5] is the actual name of a white suburb, previously the site of Sophiatown from which black people had been forcibly removed. In this unflinching account written in a scatological non-standard urban variety of Afrikaans, the hallowed rural family and the romantic idiot figure of the *plaasroman*, are replaced by the suburban horror of working-class Mol, her brothers who sexually abuse her, and Lambert, their crazy incestuous offspring who continues the practice. Focalised through Mol, it is a sympathetic representation of the dystopic 'family', two generations removed from farming the land, whilst at the same time the novel parodies the writing of ethnic identity through genealogy. The neighbours, a lesbian couple (who have not reproduced themselves) of whom the family are surprisingly tolerant, support the negative genealogy. Without the ameliorative presence of black characters, Van Niekerk's representation of Afrikaners disrupts the white/black: self/other homology; instead, alterity is explored from within the dominant meaning of Afrikaner, the Calvinistic self from which debased, landless 'poor-whites' have been excluded. The 'natural' white location of the farm is accordingly replaced by the social space produced by Apartheid, the poor-white pre-fabs, and again, as in the case of *Ancestral Voices*, verticality becomes a significant modality of space as Lambert obsessively excavates the yard to collect relics from the bulldozed black homes that Mol contemptuously refers to as 'kaffergemors' (kaffir rubbish).

In her collection of stories, *Die vrou wat haar verkyker vergeet het* (*The woman who forgot her binoculars*), Van Niekerk parodies reconstructed Afrikaners, the new dissident generation, who are shown to be marked by tension, neurosis and ambivalence in their assumption of otherness. 'Kanonbaai' rewrites the traditional Afrikaans treatment of drought in the story of a water catastrophe. The eponymous Afrikaner holiday resort is flooded on New Year's day and even the coloured plumbers who are persuaded to help, are unable to stem the flow. In Kaaps dialect they describe the catastrophe as the underground raging of a mad ostrich who should be left to wreak its full havoc so that the entire system could be repaired from scratch – again the underground as site of transformation. Gustav, the artist, whom we first see in the act of piecing together an ancient Khoi ostrich shell once used for storing water, mediates between the coloureds and the unreconstructed older Afrikaners who misread the presence of the plumbers as an act of submission and so expect them to take orders with humility. The ideological gap between old and young is described in terms of the child reproaching the father. Instead of immersing himself in political struggle for the sake of a better world, the child adopts on the one hand a position of fruitless fate-bound rebellion against the father and, on the other hand, dreams of an impossible paradise ('vrugtelose lots-verbonde opstand teen die vader en aan die ander kant in drome van 'n ontmoontlike paradys'). Thus the genealogical shift from filiation to affiliation is also cast as an ambivalence; it would seem that transformation cannot occur within the context of reproduction and the family.

Van Niekerk's trope of water offers an allegory that departs significantly from Van Heerden's: drought is converted into a plethoric flood that offers no opportunity for racial solidarity, indeed excludes the plumbers who wash their hands of the problem. This paradise gone wrong is something Afrikaners have to deal with themselves; it is invoked as an expression of their neurosis and ambivalence; and attempts at identification with the other are shown to be so much posturing. The ostrich shell that Gustav hands over to the coloured plumbers is an act of self-mockery as he invents a history of enslaved Khoi-khoi forced to produce water from a treadmill for the settlers, thus showing the gesture to be one of post-modern nostalgia. The paradise that Van Niekerk so scornfully invokes is indeed a revision of the popular Afrikaner naming of the South African countryside, its history of violence ironically encoded in the name of Kanonbaai for a holiday resort. Paradise mountain was what Van Heerden's Founder Abel at first thought of calling the farm he staked out for himself with the help of a 'tame Bushman' and a coloured bondsman, that is before the drying up of the fountain. The extraordinary naming of a largely arid land as paradise suggests an acknowledgement of the imaginary, mythologised view of the land as idealised space, an appeal to the prelapsarian, and nostalgia for pre-colonial innocence.

The land and desire

In 'Cry, beloved country' Antjie Krog's language and landscape of paradise encodes the ambivalence of the Afrikaner, desire for rebirth set against horrific accounts of Apartheid atrocities. Krog is driven out of the recording studio to respond physically to the veld ('I whisper', 'I sit down', 'see, smell', 'my eyes claw'). The image of evisceration in 'everything tears out of me' literally leaves the speaker as empty signifier, Afrikaner without connotation, and thus open to invasion by the dominant visual image of the black woman. This is surely what Krog's puzzling reference to a 'process' of listening to witnesses relates to – a process of ethnic translation. Which also goes some way towards explaining the extraordinary final paragraph in 'Cry Beloved Country' where her spirits are restored in a gesture of indulgence and ingestion: 'when in despair, bake a cake … a bowl full of glistening colourful jewels soaking in brandy. I relish the velvet of 12 eggs, butter and sugar …' Marinading, mixing and baking as an image of syncretic transformation could be read as allegory for writing the melanisation of whiteness, but the luxurious excess of its ingredients also points to the unwieldiness of the trope in an unequal society. In this discursive struggle, superordinate whiteness with its connotations of gluttony and opulence takes over so that Krog's attempt at then superimposing paucity on an image of excess – 'I... eat small fragrant slices in the blinding blue Cape summer heat' – is doubly poignant in its symbolic attempt at recuperating through ingestion an Afrikanerhood revised through blackness-in-apposition, a translation of the exploded white body into the marked category of blackness.

Krog's earlier poem, called 'land' (1996), similarly invokes the body in a relation of unbelonging to the land that in itself others the Afrikaner. Cast in the romantic tradition of a speaker's unrequited love, the land as indifferent lover is directly addressed. The poem starts with an acknowledgement of a history of inequity since the speaker's ancestors simply colonised or ordered occupation, so that land at this stage also appears to be a metonymic displacement of native, a meaning we are forced to revise towards the end of the poem. However, in spite of her love and implied disaffiliation with her ancestors, the land (or native?) rejects her:

> but me you never wanted
> no matter how I stretched to lie down
> in rustling blue gums
> ...
> me you could never endure

time and again you shook me off
you rolled me out

It is a syncretic vision gone sour. The rejection by this cruel lover robs the speaker of language and identity: 'had I language I could write for you were land my land', which perhaps accounts for the peculiar syntax and later she claims: 'I became nameless in my mouth', placing herself in the realm of the very nature that is indifferent to her desire. Desire, usually suppressed in self-other representations, is foregrounded by Krog in the dramatisation of a lover who is other to the land. The land as subject who rejects, here produces its object, an abject Afrikaner, othered by the land that she is now forced to relinquish.

However, the grammatical fronting of the object in, 'me you never wanted/ me you could never endure', suggests an ambivalence in subject-object relations that replicates an ambivalence in the representation of time. The past is invoked in references to the named waters of 'Diepvlei' that sustain cattle and to imported blue-gum trees, in other words, to land as cultivated farm. The present, in a final dystopic stanza, is described as commercially infected denaturalisation where the land is 'negotiated divided paddocked sold stolen mortgaged', an undignified situation marked by typographic gaps of disbelief. It is 'now ... fought over' as opposed to earlier (more genteel?) occupation. This is presumably a representation of the post-Apartheid programme of redistribution and restitution of the land in which the wide natural space of Afrikaner mythology is about to be replaced by social space, sullied by financial transactions, whilst colonial occupation remains romantically inflected, without the vulgarity of struggle. The speaker is appalled by the land's current 'unnatural' treatment and the poem ends with the following:

I want to go underground with you land
land that would not have me
land that never belonged to me
land that I love more fruitlessly than before

As in the case of the other texts, verticality is invoked. The distinction between surface and underground heralds the end of an historical era, of the land's accommodating horizontality, as it retreats into its own depths. An obvious inference is that such a retreat is a protest both against Afrikaner occupation and against the new dispensation that goes against nature. One might well ask how going underground *with* the land could be accomplished, unless the connotation of revolution radically redefines land so that it simply can no longer be identified by its surface. The passive construction, 'now you are fought over', not only elides a black agent but keeps land in the subject position; nature and space remain given; they most certainly are not as critical geography would have it, produced. All contemporary writing in South Africa is to some extent dystopic, even necessarily so, since the promises of a new order remain unfulfilled. Popular recoil from the epithet of the Rainbow nation is not simply a response to the notion of nation, or an inability to attach such colourful syncretism to the chaotic aftermath of Apartheid, but also an ambivalence towards relations of alterity. Krog's poem disrupts the old homological relations in so far as the unmentioned black struggle for ownership of the land allows the farm of the past to slip back into nature. Thus mutable land, or nature, prevents the native from usurping its subjectivity and so retains dominance over humans, an authority that the new mute and humbled Afrikaner abjectly acknowledges.

Melanisation and subjectivity in Chris Barnard's *Moerland*

On the face of it, Barnard's project in *Moerland* (Motherland, or in the demotic sense, Fucked-up land) appears to offer, via the emotive question of language, a direct revision of Afrikaner identity as white. In that narrative an Afrikaner patriarch who had trekked to Angola to escape British imperialism, gives his daughter to a native in exchange for land. He returns to South Africa, deserting the daughter who remains to raise her impoverished black child and grandchild as Afrikaners. Barnard then introduces a new ethnic category: Lukas van Niekerk, the grandchild, is a Black Afrikaner, suckled by his Afrikaner grandmother and raised on Afrikaans literature. When he escapes to South Africa during the Angolan war of independence, he is surprised to find himself unacceptable to Afrikaners and so spitting out 'Africa's white nipple', translates himself into a black revolutionary with the new name of Sipho Mbokani. The investigating journalist, the narrator whose research on the role of standard Afrikaans in the post-Apartheid era frames the narrative, recognises Lukas's speech as a white variety, 'a flawless Afrikaans without any accent'. Barnard's exploration of Afrikaner identity based on inaccurate folk beliefs about language such as speech without accent, lack of variation according to class as if there were no such difference amongst Afrikaners, and lack of influence from other languages where Afrikaans is spoken outside its speech community, finds its motivation in the desire to redefine Afrikaner to include blacks acculturated via the language and the improbable canonical texts that Lukas inherits from his poorly educated grandmother. Lukas's story of albescence is prevented from developing through crude Afrikaner racism; instead, amelioration is achieved through the melanisation of the Afrikaner.

Afrikaners, the novel declares, can no longer be considered in opposition to black, indeed as the frontispiece map of Africa with its inset of Angola suggests, it is a process of Africanisation that defines them. Barnard's journalist-protagonist responds angrily to an Englishman who calls him Dutch:

If you have to call us anything call us half-castes (sic), but we're no more Dutch than you are ... we're of mixed descent. We have Dutch forefathers, yes, but we also have French blood, German blood, Malay, Khoi, Portuguese, even English blood ... After ten generations in Africa we can hardly call ourselves a bunch of Europeans ...The name Afrikaner refers to a language rather than a continent.

1992, p. 52

Fear of relinquishing whiteness is expressed through the far Right to whom the journalist's son is affiliated. The boy argues with his father for an Afrikaner Homeland:

'It's we Afrikaners who have tamed and broken in this land. Now, everything, you want us to just ...'
'And the English, and the Jews, and the Portuguese, and Greeks and Germans and Dutch and ...'
'Yes alright. They too. But they all have countries to return to. All except us. If we can't get a little piece of the land for ourselves, Dad ... We are three million. What will happen to us amongst thirty million black people under a Marxist government?'

1992, p. 28

Within the apparent dissolution of whiteness, we find, however, that subject/object relations remain the same. Black can become Afrikaner through white agency, through the speech act of a white grandmother, or the journalist's acceptance of Lukas as Afrikaner via his competence in the standard variety of the language. Not surprisingly then the journalist's voice of reconciliation acknowledges only white contribution to South Africa, to the development of the land from nature to culture - hardly an invitation to partnership. And not surprisingly his syncretic vision of Afrikaner as mixed race, of negating his whiteness, has its origins in the terrifying demography expressed here by the far right. In this narrative there is no figuration of verticality; the underground is the conventional 'revolutionary' space into which the son, as member of the right wing movement, disappears and disaffiliates from the liberal father in order to engage in the struggle for (horizontal) land. Strangely, the category of other is not applied to the far right; it is instead the liberal who assumes otherness through association with the black.

Conclusion

Like any other diverse ethnic group, Afrikaners, whilst crucially concerned with a process of detoxification, rewrite themselves in a variety of ways, but what is noteworthy is the common redeployment of geographical tropes in the works discussed above. Whilst these texts do characterise deterritorialization, they depart significantly from Deleuze-Guattari's celebration of the horizontal in the figure of the rhizome, their emblem for becoming. The revised Afrikaner self is staged before a backcloth renovated from the old picturesque surface of landscape to the land in cross-section, thus privileging verticality and revealing an underground significant for its association with revised self:other white:black culture:nature homologies.

The practice of conjugating a New Afrikaner ethnicity with the ready-made category of black-as-other is, of course, not a felicitous one from a black point of view that would question the validity of the very category, neither does the scramble for alterity guarantee rehabilitation of Afrikaner identity. Van Niekerk's *Triomf* would seem to be successful precisely for releasing a suppressed alterity from within the old Calvinistic image of buttoned-up Boer respectability. More importantly, it avoids over-identification with blackness by keeping black characters on the very margins of her narrative as a category over which the poor-white can crow. If *Triomf* through its brutalised poor-whites or the madness of Lambert rewrites Afrikaner as other, such alterity hardly represents that which has the capacity to transform the dominant culture. Filiation as the foundation of identity has imploded in the perverse incestuous family, and the possibility of transformation would seem to lie instead in the novel's figuration of the excavated hole, or verticality, as an affiliative appeal to memory and history. Mol's reference to the remains of black homes constitutes a humorous Boer version of history, but Lambert's excavations do uncover the material past of Sophiatown that makes for transformed social and neighbourly relations – even if such a past gets covered over all too quickly under the new dispensation.

The peculiar coincidence of verticality can, of course, not be explained in terms of a single meaning. It seems to appeal to a humanistic depth model linked to modernity's faith in knowledge, truth and transformation with which to revise the horizontality of colonial occupation and its Apartheid connotations of surface, lies and aridity. It invokes Edward Said's shift from filiation or biological continuity to social affiliation and its implied revision of nature-culture relations. The subterranean then does present itself as site of 'becoming' which, according to the above texts, is also bound up with the destabilisation of the old homologies. In addition, the rewriting of Afrikanerhood seems to support Homi Bhabha's (1994, p. 147) argument against orthodox representations of the horizontal spatiality of the modern nation. Nationness, he argues, as a form of social and textual affiliation, requires also a temporality of representation:

> The secular language of interpretation needs to go beyond the horizontal critical gaze if we are to give the nonconsequential energy of lived historical memory and subjectivity its appropriate narrative authority. We need another time of writing that will be able to inscribe the ambivalent and chiasmatic intersections

of time and place that constitute the problematic modern experience of the Western nation.

Afrikaner texts that are overtly concerned with memory and an interrogation of history seem to replace the old dynastic filiation with geographical verticality which, as a new figuration of the land, offers a crossing over between the spatial and the temporal. Thus we have – although with varying degrees of commitment – a reconceptualisation of relations with the land as secular and non-dynastic. That this is done in the interest of survival and is marked by ambivalence is not so remarkable. What is remarkable is that whiteness itself is being addressed, that these narratives not only question the validity of the category and imply the liminality of white nationhood, but that narration itself is focalised through other marked categories such as the black-white Lukas, the disaffiliated 'shame-family', or the abused poor-white woman.

To return to my opening remarks about South Africans clinging to old identifications: what contemporary literature appears to engage with is a new meaningfulness of ethnic tags,[6] a probing of identifications that it would be dishonest to disown in a society riddled with inequities, but ones which can be divested of received meanings and can be negotiated afresh. Ethnicity, as every schoolgirl knows, is agonistically produced; we use it in our struggles of self-assertion; we abandon it only when it becomes in our interests to do so. For those black people whose material conditions have not changed in the New South Africa, racial identity remains the platform from which the fight for equality must be staged. Commitment to the demise of Apartheid does not mean an abandonment of ethnic tags, but it does at least according to the given texts require a disaffiliation from whiteness. Whilst, as Krog so poignantly outlines in *Country of my Skull*, Afrikaner has become a disgraced category, the struggle of rehabilitation crucially implicates the other old biary opposition, relations with Englishness. And whilst English in fact assumes national language status, that space of cultural and linguistic capital is necessarily one where whteness will continue to reside in silence and anonymity. But then, textuality is of course not the whole story. In the world beyond texts where whiteness remains bound up with privilege and economc power it cannot simply be written off, not least because those who ought to benefit most from its demise are unable to read of such well-meaning resolutions o the narrative of Apartheid.

Notes

1   *Country of my Skull*, 1998.
2   Pippa Skotnes's post-modern ethnographic artwork/exhibition at the South African National Gallery, called *Miscast: Negotiating the Presence of the Bushmen* – like the

accompanying publication edited by Skotnes, 1996 - is a case in point. The controversial exhibition attempted to represent and challenge colonial othering of the Bushman.

3 See my 'Shame and identity: the case of the coloured in South Africa' in Attridge and Jolly, 1998.

4 *The Guardian*, 18 January, 1997.

5 Winner of the Noma Award for Publishing in Africa.

6 See Zakes Mda's *Ways of Dying*, 1995, where the invention of new selves in opposition to received identities, a development on the black essentialism of much of 'struggle' writing, is an important departure. Mda's fiction is distinctive not only for its lack of reference to whiteness but also in its abandonment of ethnic 'authenticity'.

References

Attridge, D. & Jolly, D. (eds) (1998). *Writing South Africa*, Cambridge: Cambridge University Press.

Barnard, C. (1992). *Moerland*, Cape Town: Tafelberg.

Bhabha, H. (1994). *The Location of Culture*, London: Routledge.

Coetzee, J.M. (1988). *White Writing*, London: Yale University Press.

Deleuze, G. and Guattari, F. (1988). *A Thousand Plateaus*, London: Athlone Press.

Dyer, R. (1977). *White*, London: Routledge.

– (1988). 'White', *Screen*, 9(4).

Foster, H. (1996). *The Return of the Real*, Cambridge: MIT Press.

Gie, S.J.N. (1942). *Geskiedenis van Suid Afrika*, Stellenbosch: Pro Ecclesia.

Kamuf, P. (1991). *A Derrida Reader*, Hempstead: Harvester.

Krog, A. (1996). 'land,' *World Literature Today*, 70(1), Winter.

– (1998). *Country of my Skull*, Johannesburg: Random House.

Millin, S.G. (1924). *God's Step-Children*, London: Constable.

Said, E. (1983). *The World, the Text and the Critic*, Cambridge: Harvard University Press.

Smith, N. (1984). *Uneven Development*, Oxford: Blackwell.

Trump, M. (ed.) (1990). *Rendering Things Visible*, Johannesburg: Ravan Press.

Van Heerden, E. (1993). *Ancestral Voices*, London: Alison & Busby.

Van Niekerk, M. (1994). *Triomf*, Cape Town: Queillerie.

CHAPTER EIGHT

Gendering a language, liberating a people: women writing in Afrikaans and the 'new' South Africa

Kenneth Parker

The conferment of the prestigious Noma Award for Publishing in Africa in 1995 to Marlene van Niekerk for her novel, *Triomf* (Truimph), is a significant moment in the relatively short history of a work written in Afrikaans, the language that has been popularly (and with considerable validity) perceived as the language of oppression of blacks by whites. In winning the Noma Award, Van Niekerk joins an early winner from South Africa, the distinguished poet and political activist Wally Serote, *Third World Express* (1993), as well as others such as the Nigerian poet Niyi Osundare (1991). To account for so signal a recognition of a text written in Afrikaans by a woman writer who had previously been a university teacher of philosophy, and who now teaches the language she writes in, as well as for the central theme the novel addresses, it is needful not only to look briefly at the novel, but also to locate the event in its own historical and aesthetic contexts and, in particular, the impetus provided by writing in Afrikaans by a new generation of women writers, though, as the cone of Triomf shows, not always without acrimony.[1]

Triomf is a vast (450 page) interrogation of an event whose symbolic significance continues to resonate as a particular instance of the application of the founding tenets of 'grand apartheid', whereby (reputedly) each of the so-called 'racial groups' would be afforded 'equal freedoms' – but only in their 'own' separate areas. It was in terms of that policy that, in 1995, the multi-racial communities that made up the Johannesburg suburb of Sophiatown were brutally uprooted from their homes, and those homes thereafter razed to the ground.

Sophiatown had to go – not only because it was the last place in the country in which it was possible for black people to have freehold property rights, because it was an obvious 'black spot' (as the language of the time had it!) too close to the city center. Above all it had to go because it was here that many of the leaders of the ANC lived and organized a now well-documented history of resistance. In the bulldozed space the government proceeded to build houses for 'poor white' Afrikaners, themselves moved from their hovels in their overcrowded 'white' area, Vrededorp (City of Peace): Sophiatown, without apparent awareness of irony, was renamed Triomf.

Van Niekerk's novel is about the ways of lives and thoughts of several of these inhabitants. These are individuals no longer called 'arm blankes' (poor whites) but 'minder gegoede blankes' (less well-endowed whites). Now, forty years after the expulsion of blacks but in the year of the first elections in which all adults, irrespective of colour, will participate, they contemplate their own situations: Pop Benade and Mol, both in their seventies and apparently married to each other, Pop's sixty year old brother, Treppy, and Lambert, Mol's forty year old mentally retarded son, referred to by one of the others as a 'genetic *cul-de-sac*.'

Van Niekerk follows a long line of black writers and artists who have taken Sophiatown as text as well as theme. But whereas for black writers it was celebrated in fiction, poetry, drama, painting, music and subsequently in autobiography[2] as exemplary of resistance, of refusal to be crushed, Van Niekerk seeks to probe the effects of that same policy of apartheid on the lives of those whites in whose name the blacks were removed. The critical and cultural significance of her creation, in that regard, cannot be stressed sufficiently.

As was the case in the title story of her 1992 collection of short stories, *Die vrou wat haar verkyker vergeet het* (The Woman who Forgot her Binoculars), where a city-bred woman goes to a remote place in order to write, but discovers that in order to be able to do that she has to be stripped of all her antecedent illusions through excavation of her personal and psychological past, so here too: except that now there is a literal excavation of the past – materials scavenged from what had once been Sophiatown are now recycled endlessly in Triomf, and some objects are even hoarded as one resident's private museum.

And as with material objects, so, too, with language: the novel is the most wonderful amalgam of (on one hand) an elegantly poetic and expressive modern language of the so-called 'high culture' of those writes who sought to demonstrate a symmetry between the language and the politics of separatism, yet (on the other) the celebration of the arrival (especially in the past ten years or so) of a new language that is rumbustiously hybrid and popular. It is this ability to write in the language of the tribe, but without being condescending about that language, and how it is used, that makes the text so exciting, although that is not new since, arguably, Jeanne Goosen's 1992 *Ons is nie almal so nie* (translated as *Not All of Us*, by Andre Brink) may be regarded as a precursor.

Admittedly, some critical opinion inside the country – especially from within the ranks of the so-called higher journalism - has keen exercised about the copious use of racist epithets by poor whites about blacks, and even more so about the familial/ sexual relations of the family[3], but my sense is that it is a reaction that has more to do with recently discovered white fastidiousness manifested in the refusal to call a spade a spade. Mol, for her part, is perhaps unwittingly closer to what appears to be the current ethos of reconciliation than such guardians of political correctness when, near the end of the novel, in the aftermath of Mandela's inauguration, she states very simply that words like 'kaffers' or 'hotnots' or 'koelies' should no longer be used since 'wat verby is, is verby' (what's past, is past). Given the ideological and cultural baggage that constitutes her past, it is, for Mol, a telling triumph over that racist past. For white women who write in Afrikaans, an equally telling truimph over the thematic and textual inheritances from their literary mothers, who were as complicit in hymning the apartheid state and the racist nation as were their male counterparts.

I am bound to say that in discussion with them, several of the women writers demurred against my suggestion that their predecessors had been the victims of marginalization on the part of their male counterparts. But the evidence is readily available: when women first start to write in Afrikaans, their efforts are directed at publication in magazines like *Die Brandwag* or *Die Huisgenoot*, aimed largely at a female readership.

Indeed, the very titles of these magazines manifest a politics of confinement: *Brandwag* in the sense of 'sentry' or 'outpost', with all its associations of being constantly watchful against being infiltrated and overrun by either 'uncivilized' blacks or 'imperialist Brits, against which the only safety lies in an exclusive Afrikaans identity; *Huisgenoot* with the parallel senses of 'housemate' as well as 'inmate', with the more specifically gendered sense of not only the subordinate status of the woman in that society, but also of the specificities of her role as housebound. Nevertheless, re-reading the writing of even this first generation of women writers will show that, while on matters of race and colour they do not deviate from the Afrikaner tribal myth, when it comes to matters of gender there are, nevertheless, signs of awareness and resistance: their themes are not supportive of the 'housemate/inmate' construction.

Bear in mind, further, the conditions that led to production of these texts. In the battle between Boer and Brit about who would be best able to dominate blacks (always reputedly in the interests of those blacks), the former often established cultural organizations that might be said to have mimicked those of the latter, of which organizations the one devoted to the protection and defence of the language by means of literary competitions was particularly energetic. Henriette Roos observes that one of the first literary contests organized by that 'Suid-Afrikaanse Akademie' was won, in 1913, by a women, Chris Euvrard. Roos points out, further, that when the Afrikaans publisher, J.L. van Schaik, ten years later organized a competition to seek to out the 'best novel' in the language, the first three prizes were all won by women (Roos, 1992).

While Roes might have pointed out that the three titles (either separately, but especially taken together) – Marie Linde (a pseudonym for Elise Bosman) *Onder bevoorregte mense* (Amongst Privileged People),[4] Meg Ross (pseudonym for M.E. Grosskopf) *Oogklappe* (Blinkers), Eva Walter, *Eensaamheid* (Loneliness; Seclusion) – richly, if certainly unintentionally, evoke the real relations of Afrikaner women of the same time: skin colour that confers priviledge while imposing blinkers in dealing with those of a different colour, while simultaneously condemning to loneliness in a dominantly masculine world, Roos is right to stress that the settings as well as the themes of these texts differ from those of the (male) canon in several ways. In these novels, set in urban rather than farming communities, men have minor roles, and some women show an interest in personal careers, while others include an Afrikaans orphan employed as a servant.

For Roos the reason for the relative neglect of these founding texts is that their kind of realism was in conflict with the dominant (male-defined) version, of which J.R.L. van Bruggen was arguably the best-known exponent in the novel, and HA. Fagan and J.W.F. Grosskopf in drama. This reason is corroborated by the writer of the standard history of Afrikaans literature (Kannemeyer, 1984) who suggests that the neglect of these texts can be located in the counterfeit/spurious/inauthentic psychology (*onegte psigologie*) in Linde and an equally questionable characterization, allied to a somewhat crumbly/friable style (*brokkelrige wyse*) in Meg Ross. This (at least) presumes to offer a more critically sophisticated critique than simple male bias, though the masculinist assumptions underlie the purportedly literary critical conclusions -falling short of the mark is becscause the writers are women.

C.N. van der Merwe has added other names to those mentioned by Roos. Some of these texts, he informs us, dealt with themes like premarital sex, adultery and divorce, and Van der Merwe notes that while there was initial criticism of the publishers, Nationale Pers (the name of the publishing house itself a telling insight into the ideological pretensions of the language project) these novels, widely read in the 1930s and 1940s, "were not canonized and were therefore gradually forgotten. In the first of these three stages in Afrikaans female writing the female author it not silent, but rather unheard and ignored' (Van der Merwe, 1994, p.70).

Although I am sceptical of the rather rigid schematization of the so-called 'three stages' Van der Merwe discerns (with its implicit Hegelian encrustations of a notion of 'progress'), in which he marks the second stage as dating from the 1935 novel *Sy kom met die sekelmaan* (She Comes with the Sickle-Moon) of MER (pseudonym for M. E. Rothmann) and culminating in the work at Anna M. Louw, whose 1975 *Kroniek van Perdepoort* (Chronicle of Perdepoort) and Elsa Joubert's 1963 *Ons wag op die kaptein* (translated into English as *To Die at Sunset*) he sees as exemplary instances of women writers whose texts are still 'in complete accordance with traditional male attitudes' (p. 72). But such a reading it to succumb (at least) to the snares of an intentional fallacy. Rather (as this chapter will seek to demonstrate), women writers in Afrikaans since the 1960s have embraced not only a wholly new set of themes, but especially a variety of new ways of engaging with the business of writing. It is important to stress what it seems to me to be the project of this new generation: these women do not to seek to write the story either of white oppression of blacks, or of resistance to that oppression; rather, their project would appear to be that of writing back to their own inherited authenticities of *land en volk en taal* (land and people/nation and language). Exemplary here might be the story 'Die Vrou: Kobus Oosthuizen' (The Woman: Kobus Oosthuizen) in the 1991 collection of short stories by Riana Scheepers, entitled *Dulle Griet* after the 1563 painting of that title by Pieter Bruegel that shows the female figure, pannier with food as well as cooking utensils in the left hand, sword in the right hand, breastplated and helmeted, silhouetted against a background of violence and destruction. Destination uncertain; but prepared.

'Die Vrou' is a story about an adolescent boy's wish to write a story about the phenomenon that is of greatest interest to him, that of The Woman, 'the most wonderful of God's creations'. Kobus wants to write about the 'beauty and grace and femininity of the woman', devoting one chapter to each key characteristic he can discern, starting with the woman as Mother, based upon his recollection of experience at his mother's breast, interspersed with wrestling with himself about his conflicting desires to sleep with his girlfriend or to keep his promise to 'keep themselves pure' until their wedding night.

For this Afrikaner male adolescent the problem is stark: while his rhetoric asserts that 'Naturally it is not necessary first to sleep with a woman before you can write about The Woman', it is how to cope with the recollection of his sexual urges are aroused by the presence of a slightly older woman who is part of a walking tour in a forest. What Scheepers manages superbly here is the portrayal of that particular version of white South African masculinism stemming out of deep-rooted Calvinisms that invariably seek explanations for their own thwarted desires by means of deflections upon and blame laid at the door of the other – here Kobus learns from one of his male friends that the woman it a lesbian. Kobus has no ideas of what that means; but such ignorance will not stand in the way of what he proposes for his book: "When I write my book, I shall not even consider whether or not to devote even a paragraph to women like her. These are women whom you cannot honour with a capital W, who do not deserve a place in society. Because I know now that there are women who are capable of bringing out the worst in a man. I want to begin to write my book as soon as possible.'

This, if one impetus for the re-writing by Afrikaner women is how they have been written by their past histories, another is their keen interest in the business of writing itself. Scheepers, in the *Dulle Griet* collection, is again exemplary in the manner in which she combines stories about women who are victims of varieties of violence but who display varieties of resistance and resiliance with stories about how to write: the story entitled COMMAND: COPY DELETE FORMAT GALLERY HELP INSERT JUMP LIBRARY OPTIONS PRINT QUIT REPLACE SEARCH TRANSFER UNDO WINDOW is about the woman who bought a wordprocessor with her scholarship money, not simply in order to assist with her writing and research, but in order therewith to reorganize her life. She names her machine 'Pandora's Box' and that first night she dreams that she is a wordprocessor. Instead of waking up from the dream, she decides to apply her newly acquired wordprocessing possibilities referring to filenames for texts which appear elsewhere in the collection as stories. But when she wakes the next morning, she can remember nothing of the dream. '*Sy het vergeet om dit te save, of om 'n back-up te maak*' (she had forgotten to save it, or to make a backup).

That concern with story-telling manifested itself not only in her first collection of stories, *Die ding in die vuur* (The Thing in the Fire), but has continued into her most recent '*n Huis met drie en 'n half stories* (A House with Three and a Half Stories). Where the first collection (1990) demonstrates not only the writer's fluency in the Zulu language, what is impressive is how she deliberately seeks to adapt the tradition of Zulu oral story-telling around the night-time fire to a written version that is equally destabilising – not only about telling, but also about the tales themselves, which have their own risks: when the young Afrikaner woman lecturer asks the professor of African languages to relate one of the tales he is collecting for an anthology, his response is that, should he do so, she will develop horns. But, the story (and the Scheepers collection) concludes with the recognition that while she can understand the story he tells her in a language which she understands but in which she has a limited verbal facility, she knows it is one in which she will never be able to dream, or shed tears, or sing, or be able to tell tales. So, perhaps out of that recognition, her most recent collection, with the pun on the word 'stories' in the title – of story as tale and of storey as the number of floors in the house (three and a half, in this case) she reverts to writing about women: not only South African women, but European women, as well as women from the Bible. One recurrent theme in these stories, at least until recently, is the taboo in Afrikaans literature concerning female sexuality in several of it's manifestations. Thus, it seems to me what connects, for instance, the Scheepers version of Jael killing Barak (*Judges*, 4: 5) ('with the same contempt with which he will violate you, a man will trust you in his distress, as long as you will simply offer your body as a guarantee') with that of the arguably key story set inside South Africa of three Afrikaner males who terrorize women from a local Zulu village is that the ending is in Zulu – not now, as in some of her stories, the introduction of the odd word or phrase, but several sentences that constitute the story of the women who, instead of eating their food, stare into the fire and discuss the event. It is fascinating – though ultimately futile – to speculate on how an Afrikaner reading public responded to as alienating an account as that given to Jael, or what means they would have had to adopt to gain access to the ending of a story called 'Klipsop', literally 'stone soup', figuratively, an illusory meal (as in, for instance, the case of the prince who, in *The Arabian Nights*, fed a beggar on a succession of empty dishes in order to test his sense of humour).

Such writing back to antecedent Afrikaner nationalist and Afrikaans language authenticities has, of course, to be set in the wider context of the contribution of writers and writing to the struggle for political freedom, especially since the 1960s: a moment marked in politics by the modernization of racist practices by the Afrikaner Nationalist regime and the countervailing adoption of armed instead of constitutional forms of struggle by the African National Congress and its partner organizations.

If that history is evoked as well as symbolized by the names 'Sharpeville' (19 March 1960) and 'Soweto' (16 June 1976), when defenceless black protesters were mown down by police and military firepower, then in Afrikaans literature it is best captured by the poem 'Die kind wat doodgeskiet is deur soldate in Nyanga' ('The child who was shot dead by soldiers in Nyanga') by that fine poet Ingrid Jonker, who some years later walked into the sea to embrace her own death by suicide. It is needful to remember that the poet's father, Abraham Jonker (1905–66) had been one of the most influential makers of Nationalist literary and cultural theory in the period in which so-called 'grand apartheid' was being formulated: not only was he a novelist, an editor and anthologist, but as a member of parliament[5] and, important for our purposes, the person responsible for drawing up the legislation for the establishment of the Publications board (1963) whereby the government could censor, control, ban and prohibit the import of works of literature and art. Jonker became the first chairman of that Board.

It is this moment of extension and sophitication of the theories and practices of state violence aimed specifically at blacks, but increasingly against oppositional fractions in the white society as well, that is also the moment of renewal in Afrikaans literature; the moment of the birth of what has become known as that of the Sestigers (writers of the 1960s) – a naming that is correct with respect to the historic moment, but misleading if intended to describe a coherent group. With the exception of one black man from the cape, Adam Small, these writers are all white: Jan Rabie; Etienne Leroux; Dolf van Niekerk; Chris Barnard; Breyten Breytenbach; Andre Brink. But once again, one of the effects of popular association of the names as a coherent group rather than as a moment marking transformations in literary froms and styles has the effect of excluding the women by positioning them elsewhere – Kannemeyer, for instance, hives off Elsa Joubert with two other women writers, Anna M. Louw and Henriette Grové, into a section called *Realistise kuns op pad na die eksperimentele'* (realist style on the road to the experimental) which has (at least) the effect of misrecognizing her contribution to the moment of the Sestigers. For instance, Henriette Grové's heroine is as concerned as any of the male characters in other texts of the times about the meaning of words and the relation between the word and the truth; early on in *Die Kêrel van die Pêrel of anatomie van 'n leuenaar* (The Chap from Paarl, or, Anatomy of a Liar – Paarl (pearl) being the name of a town near Cape Town), the heroine explains that her story is about words; but also about the truth and the relation between the two:

In the nature of things, my medium consists of words. It is always a story. But words, as I have sought to demonstrate, are notorious deceivers. They constantly resist the truth, and instead of clarifying, they violate it ... That is why I say: what does it benefit to will the truth, even when it is passionate and obsessional. I am too destitute-dependent on words.

What made the Sestigers so important was not only that these writers sought their creative and critical inspiration in European modernism (several had lived on the continent before returning to the land of their birth; Breyten Breytenbach still lives there thought he now returns regularly to South Africa), but that their challenge to the state was not limited to literary practice only: for the first time, writers in Afrikaans not only renewed the language but did so quite deliberately by confronting the taboos of Afrikaner culture, especially the particularly pernicious versions of Calvinism expounded by the dominees – though again, not all of them; there was, for instance, the polemic around the publication of *Delayed Action* (undated, arguably late 1950s), a collection of essays by Dutch Reformed Church divines and academics including B.B. Keet and A.S. Geyser.

While these 'delayed actions' were still way behind the demands of the liberation movements that called for an unqualified equality, these writings were denounced by the political leaders of the tribe; indeed, in a famous case some years later, a university professor who was also a minister of religion was arraigned by his church on a charge of heresy, when in reality his 'crime' was simply that of denying the racist foundations of the doctrinal practices of that denomination.

So, when writers ceased to hymn the Afrikaner tribal myths for the first time there is a total fracture between writer and imagined community. For a community which had always venerated its writers, this was seen as the ultimate betrayal in a moment of great need. What is noteworthy here is that the animus against these writers of the 1960s was especially marked in the book review pages of Afrikaans daily newspapers and popular weeklies, with one prominent element being that critics deflect engagement with the politics of the text by rejecting the experiments with the language as 'foreign' – the irony here that a community which constructed itself as 'European' proceeded to reject precisely those modernist techniques their writers aquire, adopt and adapt as means of seeking to write at the tip of the African continent.

If the polemics caused by this new writing stayed largely within the Afrikaner community, there are two obvious reasons and a third to which hitherto little attention has been given, being largely occluded by the obvious reasons. The first obvious one is of Afrikaans as rightly being seen by the black oppressed as the language of the oppressor (even its origins as a new language made by the black dispossesed is obliterated and re-written). The second is that the relatively small local (overwhelmingly white) readership who consume what they percieve to be liberal and humanist texts are largely monoglot: to them Afrikaans is a closed book. Yet, despite their incapacity to read Afrikaans, they reject it as a language and confidently dismiss it as incapable of sustaining a literature.

For me there is a third reason, to do with the nature of the political struggle of the late 1950s and early 1960s. One of the problems Afrikaners who sought to challenge the dominant myths of their tribe were confronted by was the absence fo a political organization that ministered to their needs. The orthodoxy within the ranks of the liberation movement at that time, quite correctly, was that since different communities were affected in different ways, and by different laws, the nature of their campaigns and slogans should take that into account. So, while organizations such as the African National Congress, and the South African Coloured Peoples Congress expressed (until they were eventually banned and large numbers of their activists imprisoned) the political aspirations of the main black groups, Afrikaners simply did not see either the white umbrella organization, the South African Congress of Democrats, or its main alternative, the Liberal Party (which refused to join the alliance led by the ANC), as a congenial home. There was no organization in which Afrkaners could simply be anti-apatheid, anti-racist; always implicit was the requirement that they were expected to embrace positively either a version of English liberal humanism in South Africa that Afrikaners remember as stifling their own embryonic cultural aspirations, or a Marxism that they felt was equally alien to their way of life.

This new generation of writers in Afrikaans no longer conform to conventional representations, either within their own community or abroad: they are affluent, cultivated, well travelled (and often in places in Africa where, according to Boer tribal myths all that exists are jungles and savages). This is a generation of writers who are (above all) in tune with European literary developments and experiments - a fundamental difference that sets them apart from their white counterparts who write in English. Compare their project that seeks inspiration in Sartre, Joyce and Beckett as the basis for renewal in Afrikaans with that of the doyen of English poetry in South Africa, Guy Butler, whose collection *Stranger to Europe* (1952; enlarged 1960) is located in a binary opposition between Dionysus (European rationality) and Apollo (African instinctiveness) that is rejected by black South African intellectuals (Mphahlele, 1974).

Save for a few notable exceptions - J.M. Coetzee being the most obvious exponent, but with Stephen Gray's recent *War Child* (1991) perhaps fascinatingly signalling possiblities for renewal - South African writing in English has steadfastly continued to avoid engagement with narrative techniques aimed at disrupting habitual perceptions whereby their readers might see their world either from a different perspective or in a different light. Their practises have continued to be based upon versions of a tradition of the classic realist text, paired down to a narrow and rigid set of conventions. The argument here is not that some version of realism is, at the present time, either inapproriate or even outmoded, it is to do with the apparent lack of interest in anything else. It applies to writers in English, irrespective of colour or political affiliation. Indeed, yet another irony is how fervently influential black critics like Andries Oliphant and the late Richard Rive defend realist modes (imported from Europe) as guardians of a tradition of committed writing being challenged by the new 'Eurocentric' dangers to be found in recent literary-isms.

Even when allowance is made for the effects of isolation brought about by culural boycotts (but recalling that writers and literary critics in English were, by and large, free to travel abroad) there is, until recently, scant evidence of a shred interest on the part of the writers in English (say) that of the literary productions from Africa, or from the Caribbean, or Latin America, or to do with engagements with theories relating to post-colonialisms.

For instance, to the extent that academic critics like J.M. Coetzee or Stephen Gray or David Maughan-Brown or the late Richard Rive, or novelists who are also critics (e.g., Nadine Gordimer or Christopher Hope) or those associated with the Congress of South African Writers (notably Andries Oliphant) interrogate the nature of the South African state, they share in one objective of the post colonial project: that of writing back to their centre, white South Africa.

But notice the limited nature of their project - to seek to modernize the existing dominant tradition, inherited from Britain and modified in South Africa, by freeing of its own racist incubus. What is especially noteworthy is the virtually non-existent interest, on their part, in the matter of gender: and that despite the fact that some of the best critical work in recent years has come precisely from within the ranks of women whose engagements are located in varieties of feminist, post-structualist and post-colonial discursive practices: Dorothy Driver, Zoë Wicomb, Ingrid Fiske, Isabel Hofmeyer. It has become the commonly accepted critical view that against the dominant realist consensus is ranged a countervailing tradition usually described as Black Consciousness. In support of this assertion of difference on the part of writers who are supposedly attached to that project is their purported indifference to the narrative concerns of the white master discourses: theirs not the desire to inform the 'cross-border reader' - a catergory defined by Lewis Nkosi as someone for whom South Africa emerges 'as a country of borders, both internally and separated from the outside world by international borders', of which one consequence is that 'to a greater or lesser degree, it is possible to argue that the character and identity of South African literature is determined somewhere else, by people outside of the community in whose name the writer claims to be speaking'.

While this notion of the 'cross-border reader' needs further interrogation in order to test the validity of a categorization, one of whose consequences is to construct the reader as invariably other, one test of Nkosi's geographically-located observation is evident not only in the nature, but especially the figures, whose names recur in the shaping of critical and cultural comprehesions of readers of northern hemisphere journals of opinion: at the one end of the spectrum, hardly ever a black critic; from time to time a token Afrikaner; overwhelmingly, the interpreters continue to be from within the ranks of a dominant liberal-humanist tradition, of which the most egregious manifestation is arguably that which apparently requires the endorsement of Nadine Gordimer on the back outside cover of texts (often of autobiographies by black women writers) as 'authentically South African'.

Application of that test to Afrikaans writing will reveal that one of the consequences for writers in that language is that decisions with reference to translation of Afrikaans texts have, by and large, kept much of the new work from European and American scrutiny unless texts conformed to themes and styles - above all, positions - forged (in both senses) by writers in English. In that regard I have often wondered whether or not European and North American views of Afrikaners might have undergone modification had they been more familiar with some of the texts in translation: rather than (say) the inevitable cultural clichés of André Brink, to have access to that flawed but centrally important novel by Jan Rabie (1961) *Ons die afgod* (We the Idol), that inaugurated the Sestigers, the real counterpart and rival to that equally flawed and in many ways pernicious for its portrayal of black figures, *Cry the Beloved Country* (1958) by Alan Paton. Again, note that despite the success of the English translation of *Die swerfjare van Poppie Nongena* (1980) Elsa Joubert has not been able to find a publisher for the translation of her much-acclaimed and excellent *Missionaris*, whereas Dalene Matthee's sentimentalized evocation of racism in rurality, *Fiela's Child*, could do so with a prestigious US publishing house.

If Nkosi is correct about the role of the 'cross-border reader', and if we can go on to posit that what marks the writers in the Black Consciousness category is to seek to return to historical memory, to versions of oral forms of narration of the rural past as well as the urban present, then the postion of these Black Conciousness writers and critics might best be described as 'residual' in the sense that the late Raymond Williams defined it (Williams, 1977), as one that is:

> usually at some distance from the effective dominant culure, but some part of it, some version of it – and especially if the residue is from some major area of the past – will in most cases be incorparated if the effective dominant culture is to make sense of those areas. Moreover, at certain points the dominant culture cannot allow too much residual experience and practice outside itself, at least without risk. It is in the incorporation of the actively residual - by reinterpretation, dilution, projection, discriminating inclusion and exclusion - that the work of the selective tradition is especially evident.

One element to my analysis is therefore to stress what might be considered an ideological as well as critical absurdity – that instead of our conventional demarcation along lines of language usage (Afrikaans versus English), with affinites between a dominant liberal-humanist and residual Black Consciousness, the lines should be redrawn to show Black Conciousness and the new developments in Afrikaans writing as complimentary responsese to that dominant tradition: Boer and Black aligned against the old enemy, the Brit, the fromer by re-invention of historical memory, the latter by attachments to European modernism, both of which appear as being of marginal interest to the dominant tradition.

Is such a reading all that fanciful? Might an explanation for the processes as well as outcomes of political allignments currently being negotiated by the main protagonists not be seen as the truimph of the descendants of indigenous communities as well as those of Dutch settlers who speak about land and people and language and nation in terms in which the descendants of British settlers have never done?

But note again that this process of negotiation functions side-by-side with a continuation into the present of a history of gendered apartheid: when it suits, it is clear that we are mostly all boys together, irrespective of race and class. A classic instance of how that gendered marginalization was applied in the case of black women writers is that when the anthology, *Ten Years of Staffrider* (magazine), was published in 1988, it included only a few of the many contributions it had published by women. As the critic Boitumelo Mofokeng quite rightly observed:

> No reason can be sufficient to justify their exclusion: its effect has been to deny them not only the recognition which should belong to them as writers of our times, but their rightful place in the development of our culture.[6]

While there is no scope within the confines of this paper to illustrate my contention about class, a brief look at one recent text will corroborate my assertion about how the gender/nation relation is being handled by one of the key Afrikaner male writers of the Sestiger generation, Chris Barnard, author of *Moerland* (1992).

The resumé from the publishers accompanying the text is fascinatingly selective in its description of *Moerland* as meaning 'both wrecked land and motherland'. Such a description is coyly silent about the two dominant and closely related senses of the word 'moer': (i) to '*moer*', to beat an opponent with especial violence - a phrase most commonly used by white males in authority over black being '*ek sal jou moer!*' ('I will beat the living daylights out of you'); (ii) the expletive '*jou moer!*' (literally, as well as pejoratively: 'your mother!') as the Afrikaans equivalent for 'fuck off!'

The publishers' description is also silent about two other (admittedly more fugitive, nevertheless present in the text) meanings of the word '*moer*': (iii) as in 'grounds, dregs, lees, leftovers'; (iv) as in 'screw', whereby objects are held together. All these versions of the meaning find expression in the text.. That these meanings undermine the dominant Afrikaner construction of South Africa as 'Fatherland' is as noteworthy as the historical and ideological contexts: of white South Africans (and Afrikaners specifically) staring at the lees of Fatherland, attempting to bolt together – violently – a post-Apartheid dispensation of ways of thinking which are in their *moer*.

For an (overwhelmingly white) Afrikaans reading public the immediate popular sense of the title alone would force attention on the relationships between violence (personal, as well as political) and the making of 'motherland', the white South African state, in the process of being 'moered' in the sense of being transformed, uprooted, unbolted from conventional constructions of Afrikaner histories - with especial reference to the language, Afrikaans, that is seen as the foundation of the culture of the volk (people; nation).

A white Afrikaans reading public would almost certainly and immediately presume the title to be an ironized intertextual commentary upon well-established conventional evocations of their 'freedom struggle' as treated in (for instance) the four novels about the 'Great Trek' by F.A. Venter: *Geknelde land* (Pinched or Pained Land); *Offerland* (Sacrificial Land); *Gelofteland* (Covenanted Land); *Bedoelde land* (Intended Land), or even the more recent fiction by Karel Schoeman, *Na die geliefde land* (To the Beloved Land). The *Moerland* dust jacket excellently focuses the issue for the potential reader:

> All these years during which he had looked forward to the country in the south, the country of his origins, the land of milk and honey, there was one thing above the rest that humanized Lukas van Niekerk among the people around him: his language. Together with Moeka's milk, he acquired words in his mouth, and stories, a complete history that made him different in Angola where he had been born: he was an Afrikaner. When he eventually, in fear of his life, attempted to cross the border to the promised land, they made him into a kaffir.

Lukas van Niekerk, the black man, is devastated. Having made a most hazardous journey from the north to the south of Angola in a Henschel truck, accompanied by in invariably drunk and often theologically despairing Catholic priest (ironically?) named Bravo (who will he killed by sniper fire near the border because of that ancient theme of being in the wrong place at the right time) and for part of the time by a woman who simply prefers to be known as Buba (who will choose to remain in Angola), the South African immigration authorities provide the black man with 'a pisspot, a can of drinking water and six loaves of bread' and bundle him on a train bound for Mozambique. Since he is without the neccessary papers, that country also rejects him, which brings the realization that,

> I am nothing; I am nobody. I could not believe it. All these years and years I had wished that I could see my country. My actual country. Moeka's country. The country of Afrikaans.

Twenty years later, a while journalist visits the black township of Alexandra to conduct research about blacks who speak Afrikaans; his interest is in the future of the language in a post-apartheid South Africa. Here he encounters Lukas, now re-named Sipho Mbokani because:

> there is no place in this country for a black man with so ostentatious a name ..
> If you look like me, your name can be Lukas or Andries or Petrus – but God
> help a black Van Niekerk.

By now Lukas has changed: he is a respected figure in liberation politics in Alexandra, and his view is clear: when the journalist asks him 'Do I understand correctly (he searches for the correct word) the only sensible discussion about the future of the country is between black and black?' Lukas replies, 'That is in any case the only discussion for which I have any time. I am tired of sucking on Africa's white tit'.

It is this journalist, divorced from his wife because of his so-called 'liberal' (usually a term of abuse on the part of both 'left' and 'right') views, who will eventually write the story of Lukas' past history, as well as his escape, while at the same time dragging the black man into his own problem: that of his teenage son who has joined a far-right paramilitary organization, and who will, near the end of the text, be shot to death by white South African police in a moment in the not-to-distant future by which time the country has descended into complete political chaos.

By that stage there will have developed an understanding of more deep-seated intertwined histories - symbolized not only by Lukas' reading at classic Afrikaans poetry that directly celebrates the taming of the country (and less directly, the dispossession of its black peoples), but especially by family objects brought back from Angola and now having pride of place in Alexandra: an old Cape stinkwood bobbin-chair which his Boer great-grandfather had taken to Angola with him: a photograph of a sullen-faced white woman, his grandmother Moeka, in an oval frame; an oval brooch, identical to that worn by the woman in the photograph. It is these items which are the 'moer' in the sense of 'mother' as well as mechanism by which Lukas remains connected to his past, and which becomes the basis for his politics: he now thinks that everyone living in the country, not only the Afrikaners, are *his* people. That is the lesson derived from his *Moeka*, evidence of the success of her matriarchal authority, one that is deliberately contrasted with the skin-based racism of Deon, the journalist's son, for which much of the blame is laid at the door of the right-wing ex-wife: hers represents the failure of matriarchal authority that proposes a symmetry between skin-colour (white) and language (Afrikaans). Lukas is himself not free of that association:

> I still dream in Afrikaans. And at the moment when I manage to get it right to
> pray, then I pray in Afrikaans. I could never speak easily to the Lord in Portu-

guese. And I struggle to speak to the Lord in Zulu. That sounds pretentious. Moeka taught me that the Lord spoke Afrikaans.

It would be easy to dismiss Lukas as (at worst) naïve. But that would be to underestimate, on the one hand, the centrality of the question of the future of the Afrikaans language, and on the other of the burden of the past history of the connection of that language to the management of white oppression; so that, try as they may, white journalist as well as black taxi driver, find that their shared 'moertaal' (mother-tongue), for as long as it privileges discourses of race and nation, will be discursively inadequate for the new situation: not even the unique in Afrikaans (perhaps even in South African) literature figure of Lukas van Niekerk.

Lukas is unique for two related reasons: (i) he is not a black who happens to speak Afrikaans; he is an Afrikaner who happens to have a black skin. Once that possibility is conceded, the dominant ideology is in its 'moer'; (ii) this enables the author to probe the hitherto unthinkable: how might a Boer experience living in a black skin; how might a black rejuvenate and ensure the survival of the Afrikaans language?

It is a telling reversal of fortunes: Boers originally dismissed Afrikaans as a 'kitchen language' suitable only for communication at the simplest levels between white masters and black servants. In the process of their struggle for hegemony, dating from the turn of the present century, Boers wrestled that language from its black originators, and annexed it to their cause as the 'moer' for bolting them together as a volk. That the descendants of those originators should now, in their turn, be annexed to the task of cleaning up the language as a basis for its future existence as a 'moertaal' for people other than white-skinned Afrikaners, is one of those ineluctable ironies of the history of South Africa: perhaps no more so than that I, a black from South Africa, whose first language is Afrikaans, should seek to tell this story.

But for all the radical revisionings in Barnard's text, there is one stark and unreconstructed umbilical to the past. *Moerland* is also about mothers as representing negation: not now simply the motherland that disappoints, but the women figures in the text who do so as well, and for all the well-known reasons – that in the face of disappearing and disappointing wives and mothers, all that can be relied upon is by reconfirming fraternal links by way of applying on old Afrikaner habit to new circumstances, that of the re-drawing of borders, as well as of what happens on those borders, in order to shape new centers. It is that process, as well as those inscriptions, that some of the women write against.

To take a simple example of that endeavour. Elsa Joubert is one of the few women writers translated into English; while she is best known for her *Die swerfjare van Poppie Nongena*, a text about whose reception in South Africa Anne McClintock took as the basis for one of the most elegant essays I have read on the themes of gendered and communal identities (McClintock, 1991).[7] Two of Joubert's other novels, *Die Laaste*

Sondag and *Ons wag op die kaptein* have also been translated as, respectively, 'The Last Sunday' and 'To Die at Sunset'. For me Elsa Joubert is the link between the women of the 1960s generation, and those of the present. In her recent collection *Dansmaat* (Dancing Partner), Joubert has an opening story *'Dogters van Afrika'* (Daughters of Africa) in which an Afrikaner mother and her oh! so politically correct daughter, having braved the self-inflicted psychological fears of being encircled in their car by vast numbers of black commuters trying to catch their trains, proceed to a city-center hotel where a meeting by women in politics is followed by a fashion show.

In the crush of the reception a large number of the women, including the mother, find themselves against their will in the swimming pool. The mother's chief wish is to retain a semblance of dignity despite the fact that *'sy sluk en proe asyn of wyn of chloor of pie'* (she swallows and tastes vinegar or wine or chlorine or piss). When she eventually exits the pool from this unscripted but symbolic baptism, arm-in-arm with a (silent) black woman, her answer to the daughter's apparent worry that she might have drowned is not only that a Boer does not drown in so little water, but 'actually', she said, 'I feel great!'

If the opening story ends on a moment of one woman's euphoria and solidarity, the title story might be read as signifier for one response to Afrikaner male responses to the rhetoric of 'the new South Africa'. The wife of an Afrikaner officer is flown to a forward base to visit him, only to find that he will be away for three days. In his absence she is first forced to dance with drunken troopies, then compelled to do the same with a shackled *'terr'* (orist) who had been confined to a hole in the ground white awaiting interrogation. In her desperation, the white woman pleads with the black man to look her in the eye in the hope of finding an answer there, but even her final attempt at sympathy by kicking off her shoes and dancing until her feet, too, are bloodied, is to no avail. Alone in her hut, that night she is raped by one of the white officers, the one known as *'die doodmaker'*, a word for which the nearest English translation of 'murderer' misses out the nuances of the professionalization of methods of putting to death. All she can do the next day is to go and sit under a tree and continue knitting in order that the young troops being ferried past her might see her; she wants to wave to them but they refuse to look at her.

What has happened to these young men, black as well as white? The decade of war that was marked by South African troops violating the borders of neighbouring states produced the genre of *'grensverhaal'* (border tale) written mostly by male writers: P.J. Haasbroek, *Heupvuur* (Hipfire), 1974; Dan Roodt, *Sonneskyn en Chevrolet* (Sunshine and Chevrolet), 1980; John Miles, *Blaaskans* (Breathing Space), 1983; Louis Krüger, *'n Basis oorkant die grens* (A Base Across the Border), 1984; Etienne van Heerden, *My Kubaan* (My Cuban), 1984; Alexander Strachan, *'n Wêreld sonder grense* (A World without Borders), 1984; Koos Prinsloo, *Die hemel help ons* (Heaven Help Us!), 1987; Gawie Kellerman, *Wie de hel het jou vertel* (Who the Hell Told You!).

There were also distinguished contributions to this genre by women, notably one that (from memory) was either banned by the state, or withdrawn by the publishers; Welma Odendaal's *Keerkring* (Tropic). A more recent example is that of Erika Murray-Theron whose 1992 novel *Toubrug* (Rope Ladder) attempts to find an answer mothers seek about their disappearing sons whose choices included university politics, going abroad either to escape the draft, or to go for military training and how those choices by sons had the effect of bringing the political struggle into the homes of those sons.

If Elsa Joubert and Erika Murray-Theron are examples of women writers whose work is a bridge to the present, they are also measures of the extent to which the women writers have broken away from their literary pasts: from an inaugural moment that celebrated the Great Trek, the idyll of rural life, and the heroism of Afrikaner women in British concentration camps, via the classical moment of the 1930s, with its inscriptions of the woman as mother of the family and reproducer of its future, of the woman as the guardian of racial purity, as someone who – above all – never leaves her husband, no matter what.

It is important to stress the gulf between inherited origins and present practices that is being traversed, and not to resort to an all too easy vanguardism (as, for instance in a 1992 article by Christel Stander and Hein Willemse) which asserts that ' Although a coherent Afrikaner (and for that matter South African) feminist critique is still lacking' (as if it were immediately apparent as to what such a singularity might consist!) from which there issues the magisterial dismissal:

> Most of the critical writings by these women tend to be introspective, taking on the form of self-criticism rather than criticizing of the larger society in which they are living. In many cases, their criticism has been negative, focussing on individualistic expressions of guilt or cynical accounts of dissatisfaction
>
> Stander and Willemse, 1992

Even the most cursory interrogation of the texts published in the past fifteen years or so will deny so gross a misreading as that by Stander and Willemse. Indeed, as I shall hope to show, the outstanding feature of Afrikaans published prose by these women writers is how each one of inherited so-called traditional themes is filleted. In that process, the concern with technical experimentation, with the business of writing, is as invariably present as that of the recuperation of history. Two examples of interestingly divergent approaches: in Jeanne Goosen's novella *Louoond* (literally 'warming oven', but also a colloquialism for the womb), an interrogation of the nature of power relations, although one of the key figures is a remarkably self-possessed domestic servant, there is no attempt to seek to speak on behalf of the oppressed, instead, authorial interest becomes devoted to the process of writing. In Jeanette Ferreira's *Die mammies, die pappies, die hondjies, die katjies* (The mums, the dads, the doggies, the kittens), which takes its title from a verse that was apparently sung during one of the boycott campaigns: 'The mums, the dads, the brothers, the sisters, the doggies, the kittens, are all together in the struggle', there is not only direct identification with that struggle, but also written in the form of a documentary narrative, a type of 'faction' that would seem to be chosen form for Afrikaans women writers in more or less the same way, as well as for the same reason that their black counterparts have tended to produce autobiographies.

That resort to documentary narrative is deployed with consummate skill by Emma Huismans. While her collection *Berigte van weerstand* (Despatches Concerning Resistance) commences with the warning that 'Any agreement between these stories and reality is authentically South African', the Huismans text breaks one of the hitherto unnameable taboos – she is one of two women who openly parade their lesbian credentials; the other is the poet Joan Hambridge. (In this regard it is again noteworthy how the dominant discourses of race and colour have tended to occlude those of sexual orientation. One of the most dispiriting manifestations of the debates concerning the 'new South Africa' has been a populist rhetoric against gays and lesbians on the part of males who readily drop their differences and assert – unblushingly – that such practices are 'un-South African') – precisely at a time when yet another feature that is new in Afrikaans writing is that concerned with the politics of being a 'moffie' (a gay man), of which arguably the most talented was the late Koos Prinsloo who succumbed to AIDS, tragically young, in 1993.

While both Huismans and Ferreira are keen that their texts be seen as participating in the broader political struggle, others are more directly concerned with the impact of modernity on Afrikaner society. Thus Rachelle Greeff in her two collections of short stories *Die rugkant van die bruid* (The Back of the Bride)(1990) and *Onwaarskynlike engele* (1993), probes the banal lives of housebound and bored Afrikaner women and their invariably gross menfolk. Strikingly, Greeff's second collection not only has an epigraph from Ben Okri (a writer whose colour, as well as origin would have put him beyond the pale until recently), but the epigraph itself, 'We're very far behind ourselves' is one that clearly lends itself to the unpicking with reference to gendered and national identities in the process of being remade.

Greeff takes on an apparently recently created type – that of the young Afrikaner woman obsessed with her figure; that war is no longer against her black domestics, but against cellulite and her conversations are about the impact of dieting. Thus a group of women on a slimming diet march on parliament behind banners which announce ONS IS HONGER (We are Hungry) and STOP THE VIOLENCE OF DIETING; the chromed coffee-tables of the salons devoted to slimming to which they go are laden with magazines which blazon slogans in Afrikaans that, in the process of translation, lose much of their marvellous resonances conferred by alliteration and onomatopoeia: *'wees slank en leef lank'* (be slim and live long); *'wees woedend oor gewig'* (be violent about weight). To which their men, the self-appointed enlightened holders of power in the media, who have so readily learnt to deploy the rhetoric of the 'new South Africa', respond by recommending that the women seek psychiatric help.

Other writers whose range encompasses most of these new themes and styles include Corlia Fourie, Lettie Viljoen (pseudonym for Ingrid Gouws) and Marita van der Vywer. Fourie is, as the title of her first collection of short stories, *Liefde & geweld* (1992) implies, especially concerned with the love/violence relation – especially in that version in which violence masquerades as love, where, in the name of freedom, violence becomes not only a faceless but ever-present threat which can lead to the annihilation of whole communities – in all of which the woman figure stands centrally positioned. This theme is carried on in that most appositely-titled collection of stories by women she edited, *Vrou: mens* (1992) – literally, woman:person, but resonant with the contest of meaning, where it can be (on the one hand) an assertion of gendered identity by women, it is also (on the other) more usually an expression of male annoyance and dismissiveness. So, too, Lettie Viljoen's *Karolina Ferreira*, the eponymous heroine goes to work in a town named Voorspoed (Prosperity) where she is caught up between the antithetical pressures of public violence and private love, in which male bonding on the part of those who are charged with maintaining peace – the magistrate, the lawyers, the police, in particular – not only deny the black residents in their separate ghetto the protection they need but also force Karolina to consider her own situation in this love/violence nexus.

Van der Vywer's *Griet skryf 'n sprokie* (1992) has been published in English (*Entertaining Angels*). In these tales, the eponymous teller engages in writing in order to cope not only with the breakup of marriage and the death of her child, but especially in order to retain her sanity when she discusses her situation with her shrink – one of the new generation of svelte Afrikaner psychiatrists and psychothrapists until recently denounced as alien to the needs of Afrikaner society. In this new South Africa, with such brave men as her husband in it, while Griet acknowledges that she believes in fables, she questions whether belief itself is enough. Or shock? The therapy that she finds most beneficial is that of writing – more correctly re-writing.

Which is an appropriate moment in which to return to the woman in Marlene van Niekerk's *Die vrou wat haar verkyker vergeet het* (The Woman who Forgot her Binoculars) (1992) where the title story is about the city-bred intellectual woman who forgets to take her binoculars with her when she goes to a remote and wild place to write. If one consequence is that she is unable to write, the other is how her illusions are finally and slowly stripped from her – in order to enable her to write. That woman has her counterparts in stories like '*Andries*', or '*Honderd en vyftig jaar Spekfontein*' (One Hundred and Fifty Years of the Foundation of the Town Spekfontein), or '*Die storie van my neef*' (The Story of my Nephew) all of which dissect (at times lovingly, but always unerringly) the blighted mentalities of Boers in rural areas. While 'White noise' superbly fillets the cynicism that underpins the new generation of young professional Afrikaners who have learnt to speak in the rhetoric of 'the Struggle', the equally superb story *'Die laaste noodlottige somer van die hardlywige Minister van Wet en Orde, Pierre M. Labuschagne'* (The Final Ill-fated Summer of the Constipated Minister of Law and Order, Pierre M. Labuschagne) is perhaps final proof of irreverence towards what has, until quite recently, been so-called traditional authority in Afrikaner society whose mocking in this way would have led to sharp reprimand. Finally, the story 'Kanonbaai' (the name of a fishing village where traces of the original inhabitants can still be found), teasingly confronts the suppression of the history of those inhabitants in order to raise the question of whether or not the so-called 'New Afrikaner' will be different.

Current critical convention seems to be that when the debate reaches this stage, there is the obligatory (knee jerk?) resort to Gramsci on the evidence of the appearance of morbid symptoms because the old is dying and the new cannot be born. I am bound to say that I hope to have given you a glimpse that, when it comes to some of the projects of some of the white women who write in Afrikaans, there is scope for optimism: their project of gendering the language is crucial to that of en-gendering the new nation, the so-called 'New South Africa'.

Notes

1   Of a number of somewhat jaundiced responses in the Afrikaans press in particular to the announcement of the award is that by Joan Hambidge (*Die Burger*, Cape Town: 21 October, 1995). That Hambridge is herself a university teacher in Afrikaans and not a negligible poet, and (as a lesbian) a courageous advocate of the rights to sexual freedom in a society that in that regard remains quite remarkably unreconstructed, makes her remarks even more unworthy than the tone of a series of sentiments which, in translation, lose a great deal of the bite – hence the appeal – to crude prejudice. Starting her column with giving the names of the judges and their critical and institutional affiliations, she must be aware, will have the obvious effect of emphasizing the otherness of the judges. Confidently unaware that not all the judges were male, she nevertheless poses the question: 'Can these uncles read Afrikaans?' Since they clearly cannot, since the novel has not been translated, and since the Noma Award committee were apparently unwilling to make public the names of the advisors, readers, referees, Hambridge provides a number of hypothetical reasons for the award, of which the following: that the book is politically correct; that it was written by a woman who demonstrated the appropriate sentiments; that the text made the Afrikaner out to be not very bright; that it is a contribution to the post-colonial debate. That Hambridge is silent not only about

the fact that she knows the author well enough to know that the sentiments ascribed to her are grossly unjust; that she knows the rules by which the award
operates (it is not the first time that works in Afrikaans have been submitted; and
on at least one occasion has been commended); above all, that the international
recognition comes on top of the novel also being awarded prizes from within the
ranks of the Afrikaans cultural and critical establishment.

2　See for instance: Maggie Resha (1991) *'Mangona Tsoara Thipa Ka Bohaleng. My Life in
the Struggle,* Johannesburg: COSAW and Don Mattera (1987) *Gone with the Twighlight:
a Story of Sophiatown,* London: Zed

3　For a typically jaundiced assesment, see the review by Phillip John in *Current Writing: Text and Reception in South Africa,* 6 (2) (October 1994, pp. 199–201. Compare
that with the much more subtly measured review, 'Klipdrift and Coke', by Marion
Hattingh (1995), *Southern African Review of Books,* 38 (July/August): 5.

4　Translated by E.M. Arderne and G.A. Tomlinson (1927), London: Stanley Paul, it
is arguably on e of the first novels in Afrikaans by a women writer to be made
available to an English-reading public.

5　Jonker had a chequered political career. At sixteen already an assistant secretary of a
National Party branch and later a travelling organizer for the party, he apparently
joined the opposition United Party whose daily newspaper, *Die Suiderstem,* he edited. Having been elected to an all-white parliament on a United Party ticket (1948;
re-elected 1953), he resigned the following year to create the Conservative Party, but
then rejoined the Nationalists in 1955.

6　Some of the key texts on which the above argument depends include articles by
David Maugh-Brown, Njabulo S. Ndebele, Mbulelo Vizikhongo Mzamane and
Boitumelo Mofokeng in *Current Writing: Text and Reception in South Africa,* 1,
Durban: University of Natal (1989), and the exchange between Kelwyn Sole, Grey
Willoughby, Isabel Hofmeyr, Gareth Cornwell and Lewis Nkosi in 6 (2) (October
1994 of that same journal; Elleke Boehmer, Laura Chrisman and Kenneth Parker
(eds), *Altered State? Writing and South Africa,* Mundelstrup (Denmark): Dangaroo
(1994) for articles by Ndebele, Nkosi, Benita Parry and Graham Pechey; *The African
Past and Contemporary Culture* (ed.) Erhard Reckwitz *et al,* Essen: Die Blaue Eule
(1993) for contributions by Parker and Cornwell; Karen Press and Ingrid de Kock
(eds), *Spring is Rebellious,* Cape Town: Buchu (1990); Isabel Hofmeyr (1987), 'Building a Nation from Words: Afrikaans Language, Literature and Ethnic Identity,
1920-24', in S. Marks and S. Trapido (eds) *The Politics of Race, Class and Nationalism
in Twentieth Century Africa,* London: Longman, pp. 95–123.

7　For an indication of the debate about *Poppie* in South Africa, see especially David
Schalkwyk (1986) 'The Flight from Politics: an Analysis of the South Africa reception of *Poppie Nongena',Journal of South African Studies 12* (2), pp. 183–94 and, by the
same critic, 'Elsa Joubert: Women and Domestic Struggle in *Poppie Ngema',* in C.

Clayton (ed.) (1989) *Women and Writing in South Africa,* Johannesburg: Heinemann, pp. 254–74.

References

Kannemeyer, J.C. (1984). *Geskiedenis van die Afrikaanse literatuur,* 2 volumes. Pretoria: Academia.

McClintlock, A. (1991). 'The Very House of Difference': Race, Gender and the Politics of South African Women's Narrative in *Poppie Nongena*', in D. LaCapra (ed.) *The Bounds of Race. Perspectives on hegemony and Resistance,* Ithaca and London: Cornell.

Mphahlele, E. (1974). *The African Image,* London: Faber, and New York: Praeger.

Roos, H. (1992). 'Drie Damesromans', *Tydsrif vir letterkunde,* 30 (2), pp. 41-52.

Stander, C. and H. Willemse (1992). 'Winding through Nationalism, Patriarchy, Privilege and Concern: a Selected Overview of Afrikaans Women Writers', *Research in African Literatures,* 23 (3) Fall, pp. 5-24.

van der Merwe, C.N. (1994). *Breaking Barriers. Stereotypes and the Changing Values in Afrikaans Writing 1875-1990,* Amsterdam: Rodophi.

Williams, R. (1997). *Marxism and Literature,* Oxford: OUP.

Afrikaans novel written by women refered to in the text

Ferreira, J. (1989). *Die mammies, die pappies, die hondjies, die katjies,* Bramley: Taurus.

Fourie, C. (1992). *Liefde & geweld,* Cape Town: Tafelberg.

– (1992). *Vrou: mens. Verhale deur vroue oor vroue,* Cape Town: Human and Rosseau.

Goosen, J. (1987). *Louoond,* Pretoria: HAUM-Literêr.

– (1990). *Ons is nie almal so nie,* Pretoria: HAUM-Literêr, translated by A.P. Brink (1992). *Not All of Us,* Pretoria: Queillerie.

Greef, R. (1991). *Die rugkant van die bruid* , Cape Town: Tafelberg.

– (1992). *Onwaarskynlike engele,* Cape Town: Tafelberg.

Grové, H. (1983). *Die Kêrel van die Pêrel, of anatomie van 'n leuenaar,* Cape Town: Tafelberg.

Huismans, E. (1990). *Berigte van weerstand,* Bramley: Taurus.

Joubert, E. (1982). *Ons wag op die kaptein,* translated by K. Steytler as *To Die at Sunset,* London: Hodder and Stoughton.

– (1978). *Die swerfjare van Poppie Nongena,* translated (1990) as *Poppie,* London: Hodder and Stoughton.

– (1989). *Die laaste Sondag,* translated by A. Jonker as *The Last Sunday,* London: Hodder and Stoughton.

– (1993). *Dansmaat,* Cape Town: Tafelberg.

Louw, A.M. (1975). *Kroniek van Perdepoort*, Cape Town: Tafelberg.

Murray-Theron, E. (1992). *Die toubrug*, Cape Town: Tafelberg.

van Niekerk, M. (1992). *Die vrou wat haar verkyker vergeet het*, Cape Town: Tafelberg.

– (1994). *Triomf*, Pretoria: Queillerie.

Odendaal, W. (1997). *Keerkring*, Johannesburg: Perskor.

Scheepers, R. (1990). *Die ding in die vuur*, Pretoria: HAUM-Literêr.

– (1991). *Dulle Griet*, Cape Town: Tafelberg

– (1994). *'n Huis met drie en 'n half stories*, Cape Town: Tafelberg.

Stockenström, W. (1981). *Die kremetartekspedisie,* Cape Town: Human and Rousseau, translated by J.M Coetzee (1983). *The Expedition to the Baobab Tree*, London: Faber.

Viljoen, L. (1993). *Karolina Ferreira*, Cape Town: Human and Rousseau

Van der Vywer, M. (1992). *Griet skryf 'n sprokie*, Cape Town: Tafelberg.

CHAPTER NINE

Thelma Gutsche:
a great South African film scholar

Ntongela Masilela

While I was doing my post-doctoral studies in communication systems in West Berlin in the late 1980s, it was a marvellous joy to discover Thelma Gutsche's remarkable book, The History and Social Significance of Motion Pictures in South Africa 1895–1940 (1972) at the Staatsbibliothek (State Library), located in the magnificent building by Hans Scharoun, close to the Berlin Wall. Those of you who have seen Wim Winder's Wings of Desire (1987) know how breathtaking the sense of space is inside the building, since a long sequence of the film takes place therein. I had the book on my desk for a year just flipping through it, totally unable to read it through systematically. The liberation struggle which was traumatising and unfolding at home just made it impossible for some of us to read any kind of books at that transitional moment in our history. While I was in my imagination doing a ritual dance around this book, totally transfixed, I received a copy of SAFTTA Journal (published by the South African Film and Television Technicians Association) which had a short obituary notice on Thelma Gutsche. I do not know why, but I was profoundly shaken that the obituary was so short and did not say much, given the mythic proportions she had taken on in my imagination. I had thought and wished that the Journal would later do a special tribute by devoting a whole issue to Thelma Gutsche. This was not to be.

I think part of the significance of the book for me is that I associate it with the incredible joy and pain of the end of apartheid era. In my mind I associate The History and Social Significance of Motion Pictures in South Africa with a certain kind of sacredness. I am mystified by this for I consider myself an atheist embracing the rationalism of the European Enlightenment. It may be that my putting an aura around this book disqualifies me from commenting on it, since I might be incapable of reading it critically. I have waited for nearly a decade for someone in South Africa with greater authority – since her archives are located there – to write an appreciation of the book, or even, as is fashionable to say today, a deconstruction of it. As far as I am aware, none has been written as yet.

The thing that impresses one immediately upon encountering *The History and Social Significance of Motion Pictures in South Africa* is the extraordinary amount of archival work that went into its construction. This really impresses and should be an unforgettable lesson to all South African scholars of film culture: to construct a theoretical and conceptual edifice or an architectural structure based on archival material and/or concrete facts. This is a lesson worth re-learning in our post-modern times. It is as though Thelma Gutsche wanted to write a total history of South African cinema from the moment of its inception, interweaving the endogenous and exogenous elements of its making. Gutsche's preoccupation with these factors seems to have compelled her to develop a very peculiar thesis in the book: for her South African cinema is not constituted by the totality of films made by South Africans on aspects of South Africanness, but rather, in the early decades of its inception, by the impinging of foreign films on the imagination of South Africans as well as the cultural and social institutions that made this possible. In other words, Gutsche approaches the making of South African cinema as a historian of social and cultural institutions, rather than a film historian of artistic processes or from a concern with the aesthetics of form. To fully appreciate what she was attempting to achieve in this book – or did achieve in it – it has to be seen in the context of her other writings.

Gutsche achieved the astonishing feat of publishing six books within a six year period from 1966 to 1972: *No Ordinary Woman: The Life and Times of Florence Phillips* (1966); *Old Gold: The History of the Wanderers Club* (1966); *The Microcosm* (1968); *The Bishop's Lady* (1970); and *A Very Smart Medal: The Story of the Witwatersrand Agricultural Society* (1970). The seventh book, a biography, was published much later: *There Was A Man: The Life and Times of Sir Arnold Theiler K.C.M.G.* (1979).[2] All of these are huge books; all the more amazing that their publishing sequence clusters them together. Gutsche's book on South African cinema was the last one to be published within this series, yet it was the first to be conceptualised and written. Although the book was completed as a dissertation in 1946, it was actually begun in about 1936, yet, as far as I am aware, first published in 1972. Even though it is of later publication than the other texts in the series, the methodological approach and conceptual thesis of *The History and Significance of Motion Pictures in South Africa* underpins the epistemological framework of the other books.

I am not sure what accounts for this quarter of a century's delay in publication. I would suggest that it perhaps has to do with the peculiarity of the thesis formulated, rather than its scholarship, which is impeccable. I would also suggest that its lack of impact on later generations of South African scholars is because of its thesis: it is perhaps too revolutionary for our present day conceptions. To give a concrete instance of the lack of appreciation of the achievement of Thelma Gutsche, she is conspicuous by her absence in an imposing book of over 500 pages, *Movies-Moguls-Mavericks: South African Cinema 1979–1991*. This anthology has contributions from a stellar list of South

African scholars of South African cinema. Perhaps the argument of the editors would be that since it was about a later period – 1979 to 1991 – there was no necessity to refer to Thelma Gutsche. Yet the anthology bristles with chapters like 'Retrieving History'. The real ironic question here is: can South African film scholarship really go forward without retrieving the archival mastery and intellectual skills of Thelma Gutsche, let alone her scholarly thoroughness, or her revolutionary conception of cinema which is perhaps unhinging to many South African film scholars of later generations?

Since all of Gutsche's books are interrelated as part of a comparative system within her historical project, I would like to cite a relatively long quotation from one of them. In her last published book, *There Was A Man: The Life and Times of Sir Arnold Theiler K. C. M. G.*, she writes:

> Adaptation of living organisms to their environment and problems of sur-vival remain the basic facts of existence. The vaunted 'balance of Nature' of the past and the ecological dilemmas of the future perennially preoccupy Mankind. Since first consciousness, man has presumed to control his environment by reason and not by instinct only... When navigators found routes to new areas, the quest accelerated and travellers, hunters, traders and mere adventurers joined the dedicated botanists, zoologists and biologists in investigating the feral world. They reported many things (notably the failure of man and beast to control natural forces) and many strange and inexplicable occurrences like the mass suicide of whales and lemmings, the huge areas of land uninhabited by humans or animals because of flies, sudden pestilences and rampaging plagues, mass migrations of men and animals destroying all before them, and other 'wonders' that had no reason. Man had his place in the feral world. He might be a pastoral itinerant, moving his flocks or herds or troops of horses or yaks to better grazing when he had denuded an area or droughts or floods had done it for him... In gradually-evolving societies, there was often nowhere to move and it became imperative to control natural forces – to engage in communal action and concerted works. Uncontrolled exploitation at all times leads to disaster. The 'balance of Nature' fails to assert itself since Man himself seems no part of it. Deserts and desolations ensue on his negligence.

In this book which intersects medical history and natural history, Gutsche re-articulates a theme that unifies all her written work: the taming, control and ordering of chaos. One can extrapolate from this major theme of her work why she had an inclination for writing historical texts: she had a passion for constructing an orderly and rational process of chaotic archival material. The book *There Was A Man* is about classifying and ordering of Nature, the formation of medical institutions with the aim of making and creating space for European cultural forms in Africa: in other words, the bringing of

European civilisation into Africa. In parentheses: the book has several pages celebrating the Tiyo Soga family, especially one of his sons. Gutsche writes: 'Jotello Festiri Soga M.R.C.V.S. was the first South African to qualify as a veterinary surgeon and the first man of colour. He was more of European than Xhosa cast of countenance but had the "kroeshaar" (crinkled hair) betokening mixed blood. Good-looking and with the noble bearing of his people, he never aped the white man' (*There Was A Man*: 24).[3]

With this book in mind, it is clear what *The History and Social Significance of Motion Pictures in South Africa* is about: it is a monumental project of ordering the cultural space of the cinema, the ordering of chaotic forms into a rational order and other cohesive structures. Another book, *Old Gold: The History of the Wanderer's Club*, about the formation of a rugby organisation in Johannesburg, is also about the creation of institutions in order to harness chaos. In this book she elaborates further on the conceptual framework she had originally sketched in her text on South African cinema: the importance of cities as cultural and social spaces for the realisation of certain happenings of modernity. So, one of the central ideas that preoccupied Gutsche in *The History and Social Significance of Motion Pictures in South Africa* was the importance of cities in shaping the cultural imagination of modernity through films. This partly explains the point that it did not matter much to her whether it was actually South African films doing the shaping or foreign films. I think she was more favourable to American and European films constructing this imaginative structure than what she called 'amateurish' South African films. A point to indicate here, is that given her Anglophilia at this time, she had no patience with any form of cultural nationalism about our then incipient film culture and industry.

Old Gold reconfigures another of her central themes resonating in her book on South African cinema: the importance of Johannesburg as the hub of inventiveness and the making of the new. She was fascinated by the new things that were being invented in Johannesburg or were coming from overseas through our great city. Her book on cinema interweaves all these complex cultural intercrossings into her narrative. Part of the fascination of this book is in the interweaving, as well as in the density of its archival material. The underlying subtext of *Old Gold* is that the formation of the Wanderers Cricket Club and Rugby Football Club in a mining town like Johannesburg was a way of institutionalising order and imposing order on the chaotic space of modernity. Can one doubt that for Thelma Gutsche one of the missions of film culture in South Africa had been *the institutionalisation of visual order in our emergent modernity*? In a strange way, she had tremendous fear of the political and social chaos brought into being by the cultural dominance of modernity. For her film was serious business in the cultural sense, and not in the monetary sense. Let me add that her preoccupation with the process of consolidation of sports in this book was prefigured in her investigation of the consolidation of film companies in her book on South African cinema.

As the title of her book *Old Gold: The History of the Wanderers' Club* implies, Thelma Gutsche was well aware that what she perceived as the Manichaean struggle between chaos and order within South African modernity had been unleashed by the discovery of diamonds in Kimberley in 1867 and gold in Johannesburg in 1886. All her historical texts are circumscribed by the mining revolution as a seminal event in our national history. The first page of *The History and Social Significance of Motion Pictures in South Africa* carries the following sentences:

> The nineteenth century culminated in a wealth of scientific inventiveness which resulted in a complete and fundamental change in the social life within the following fifty years. The more widespread use of telegraphy, the expansion of the telephone service, the increased application of electricity and the invention of the motor car, the sudden appearance and phenomenal development of the cinema, and finally the invention and speedy public utilisation of the aeroplane and the wireless have combined to obliterate (except in trivial instances such as its 'naughtiness') appreciation of the atmosphere of the period in which motion pictures first appeared ... The discovery of gold on the Witwatersrand in 1886 gave further impetus to this demand [for music halls, theatre, good music, commercial development] and where previously only the country's sea port towns (Cape Town, Port Elizabeth, East London and Durban) could be considered as possible fields for professional entertainment, there now existed two developing towns (Kimberley and Johannesburg) in the interior whose demand for amusement was only too apparent.

This quotation points to several issues: the mining revolution unleashed modernity; the interconnection of the city and modernity; the demographic upheaval unleashed by modernity; the technological revolution of modernity; the necessity of instituting leisure spaces within modernity; the interconnection between the city and film; and that film culture is the central part of the inventiveness of the cultural forms of modernity and as such, should not be subsumed by other technological innovations and breakthroughs.

Clearly then, Gutsche posits the landscape of South Africa history as a dramatic clash between European modernity and European tradition. I need not mention here that by unintentionally displacing Africans from this historical drama, Gutsche by implication defined them by their absence in her narration as passive agents or subjects of European history. Given the racial divide in our country then, she could not have been aware that in the 1920s and 1930s there was a spectacular construction of South African modernity by a group of brilliant African intellectuals in the *Umteteli wa Bantu* newspaper: R.V. Selope Thema, H.I.E. Dhlomo, H. Selby Msimang, Sol T. Plaatje, Allan Kirklang Soga and others. Had she known of H.I.E. Dhlomo rather than Benedict

W. Vilakazi she may have been made aware of this astounding construction of South African modernity. But it is not accidental that she approached Vilakazi for he in many ways was more concerned with utilising the institutional forms of tradition to channel in cohesive order the chaotic maelstrom of modernity. In contrast, Dhlomo was more interested in celebrating the maelstrom of modernity. I, in turn, am here to celebrate Gutsche who has unfortunately not been allowed to inform our cultural imagination in South Africa.

The need to celebrate Thelma Gutsche is evident when one reads her classic text, *The History and Social Significance of Motion Pictures in South Africa*. From the moment of writing this text she was clear as to the nature of her future projects in the coming decades, for in the *Avant-Propos* of 1946 she theorised the necessity of writing about aspects of South African cultural history from a *comparative perspective*. It was clear to her that a history of film would not be fully realisable, let alone understood, without being articulated adjacent to the history of theatrical entertainment, radio and musicals. The main point here is that for Gutsche the history of cultural forms had to be comparative in approach and perspective. It is in this sense that all her historical works should be seen in relation to each other, particularly since she saw in this prolegomenon of 1946 that upon their realisation they would establish *a history of South African Manners and Customs*. It is thus perhaps not surprising that her work was centrally concerned with institutional forms that would give a sense of cohesiveness or ordering to reality. Even her biography of Sophia Wharton Myddleton, *The Bishop's Lady*, is characterised by a sense of ordering, finding regularities, patterns and forms in chaotic processes: the taming of chaos through cultural orders. Perhaps more important is the fact that this biography makes evident one other principal theme of Gutsche's historical vision: the intrusion and integration of Europe into Africa.

In a real sense the theme of the book on South African cinema is the intrusion of the United States and Europe into Africa. This may be the rationale for her not analysing any films made by South Africans in South Africa. For instance, *De Voortrekkers (Winning a Continent*, 1916) which looms so large in the history of South African cinema, and has recently been of particular concern to some historians of our cinema, is given only a minor mention in one of the later chapters (Strebel, 1979; Tomaselli, 1986).[4] Being primarily about the institutions that made the ordering of South African visual culture possible on a massive scale, *The History and Social Significance of Motion Pictures in South Africa* does not examine films as artistic objects whose expressive form articulates a particular aesthetics, but rather as cultural forms. Gutsche's perspective on South African cinema is that of a cultural historian rather than of a film historian, and consequently films for her are objects whose fundamental effect is a civilising one. Nowhere in the whole expansive terrain of her inquiry are films ever scrutinised as film texts or cultural forms possessing their own singular grammar and syntax. Instead of encountering the aesthetics of film in the book, one is more likely to stumble repeatedly on the effects of film in the making of the cultural fabric of South Africa. Perhaps this is because Gutsche seems more likely to have been influenced in the writing of this book by the nineteenth century double decker novels of George Eliot, Charles Dickens and others, than, for instance, by Sergei Eisenstein's theory of film montage or Bela Belazs' theory of film, whereby film progresses in its development by intensely differentiating itself aesthetically from theatre and other expressive forms preceding it.

Gutsche's book is not really about South African cinema, which is in fact almost absent in her book, but more about the entrance of European modernity into South Africa through film culture. There is a deep shock of realisation that until one encounters her dismissive contempt of the first South African film made in 1911, *The Great Kimberley Diamond Robbery/The Star on the South,* on page 125 of this densely detailed book, what one had been reading was not a captivating prelude leading to the great moment of the making of our first film, but rather how offensive it was to her that such an outcome could possibly even be contemplated. Again it is only on page 218 that one becomes aware that for her South African cinema was constituted by the social and cultural institutions that made the showing of foreign films possible, not by films made by South Africans in South Africa. This moment in the book is intriguing because for the first time Gutsche is talking about films of real quality which were shown in South Africa in 1928: Pudovkin's *Mother,* Fritz Lang's *Metropolis,* Robert Weine's *The Student of Prague,* William Wellman's *Wings,* Raoul Walsh's *The Last Command.* Both moments speak to the comprehensiveness and great narrative drive of this paradoxical book, in that although it is dismissive through its silence of South African films, it may be the best book written on South African film, an archival retrieval of the most extraordinary kind. Consequently a relatively detailed appraisal of the structure of *The History and Social Significance of Motion Pictures in South Africa* is in order.

Having established that the mining revolution and the subsequent industrial revolution gave new dynamism to the cultural formations of the late nineteenth century, Gutsche maps out the social and cultural history and structure of pre-cinematic entertainment forms in major South African cities. She analyses the complex web of the variety of entertainment forms adjacent to each other: theatre, concerts, music halls, vaudeville, and so on. Gutsche argues that these theatrical and musical entertainment forms could only have taken root in the new emergent cities: Cape Town, Port Elizabeth and Grahamstown, and later Johannesburg and Kimberley. Many of these cultural forms were given impetus by visiting European and American artists. She argues that the zeitgeist of this period was the invention of the new. The invention of electricity was one of the factors which gave tremendous impulse to the construction of cinematic culture: the invention of Panoramas, Cosmoramas, Magic Lanterns etc. Decrepit musical halls were being transformed into 'Graphophone Parlours' and 'Phonograph Concerts'. All of these inventions were slowly shaping the public imagination. The invention of Edison's Kinetoscope made possible the coming on a massive scale of a visual culture associated with modernity. Gutsche proceeds to give a remarkably detailed account of the first appearance of motion pictures in various parts of South Africa. For her, the making of visual culture in our country was inconceivable without the constant and continual importation of European modernist cultural expressive forms to refurbish that vision:

> Both kinetoscope and kinetophone were undoubtedly the mechanical wonders of the day and became known to a sizeable proportion of the public of the big towns where they were exhibited; but like all mechanical novelties, their attraction steadily faded and they were soon regarded as nothing more than transiently fascinating toys … Of far greater social importance were the variety turns and dramatic companies imported from overseas which continuously brought an air of novelty to South Africa.

From this observation of the early stages in the formation of our visual culture, Gutsche was to believe unswervingly that these imported modernist forms were to constitute the very foundations and fibre of South African visual culture. Given the role of foreigners in the 'making' of South African cinema in the first half of the twentieth century - such as Carl Hertz, who consolidated the South African motion picture audience through Zenomettascope; Edgar Hyman, who made searing documentary notes of the Anglo-Boer War of 1899–1902; W. Wolfram, who organised 'bioscopes' as professional entertainment through constructing permanent cinema houses; Charles Urban, who built a comprehensive film distribution system through his Warwick Trading Company; I.W. Schlesinger, who formed in 1913 the African Theatres Trust Ltd to save South African cinema from bankruptcy; Harold Shaw, the American film director of *De Voortrekkers* (1916); Lionel Rogosin, the director of *Come Back Africa* (1959) and so on – Gutsche's conviction may not be as far fetched as one may suppose. I would like to emphasise again that the book is very impressive and exemplary in its synthesis of diverse and complex material.

I would like to cite one more instance in which Gutsche develops her thesis of the importance of European cinematic practices in shaping our visual culture, to indicate that this was not based merely on dry archival material but on knowledge which comes from having viewed thousands and thousands of films that shaped our imagination.

A bewildering heterogeneity followed on the widespread popularity of the fiction film and the products of every European and American producer were shown in South Africa. American production continued to be typified by the 'Wild West', heavily-moral drama and sensational melodrama. The subjects for English production were frequently stage successes of every kind from Shakespeare to melodrama. French films continued to be largely historical and many dealt with Dickens's stories. Italian films dealt increasingly with scenes of historic debauchery produced with zest and extravagance, classical history being ransacked for suitable incidents. A few Swedish and German films completed many programmes. These films drew South Africans into the complex visual culture of modernity.

A large portion of the book is about the construction and placement of social, economic and cultural institutions which facilitated the formation of our modernist visual sensibility. The public capacity for wonderment which had been nourished by Panoramas and Cosmoramas, was to be deepened by subsequent inventions such as Vitagraphs, Mutoscopes and Zenomettascopes. Each of these mechanical forms of visual projection eventually necessitated special film houses. Many companies emerged and collapsed participating in this capitalist enterprise. Gutsche writes of the two companies, the Warwick Trading Company and the Biograph Company, that endured the longest in this enterprise of building the foundations of South African cinema: 'Both enterprises not only popularised the cinema in South Africa at this time but also succeeded in making considerable profits.' This was the beginning of the serious organisation of professional visual entertainment in South Africa. The conjunction of History and Cinema through the filming of the newsreels of the Anglo-Boer War of 1899-1902, ensured the immediacy of wonderment to one's lived existential experience.

It is interesting that the formation of the Union of South Africa in 1910 coincided with the first forms of South African cinema as an industry. The coincidence goes much further, even if in a contrastive way, for if in the formation of the Union England was relinquishing political power, the coming into being of the 'industrialisation' of moving pictures intensified English imperial cultural domination for it was the English who exploited the popularity of films in South Africa by establishing hegemonic structures of film distribution and built and owned the most viable cinema houses. In both spheres Africans were excluded from participating: the Union disenfranchised Africans, Coloureds and other groups, while film houses were constructed on racial lines, with cinemas for 'Whites Only' and those for 'Coloured People Only'.

Wolfram's empire of permanent cinemas was able to endure only because the good quality films, predominantly English, he obtained through the Warwick Trading Company would repeatedly be shown in the cinemas. One of the companies which collapsed during this era of high competition, was the Electric Theatres Company because it obtained poor quality films for rapid turnover. Gutsche emphasises three factors which laid the foundations of the South African cinema industry: construction of permanent cinemas in major cities such as Cape Town and Johannesburg; the formation of indigenous film companies, i.e. Union Bioscope Company; and the continuous performance of films on an hourly basis. Gutsche states that 'bioscope fever' thoroughly gripped South Africa.

The realisation of the institution of permanent cinemas made possible the organisation of South African cinema on a *rational* basis. This brought to an end the itinerant showmen showing films in many corners of our country. With this rationalisation process, cinema was given a sense of permanency and the audience could watch motion pictures on regular basis. Gutsche traces the emergence, making and possession of film culture by the audience. Their appreciation is indicated by their beginning to make demands as to the kinds of motion pictures they would like to see, such as films not only preoccupied with amusement but rendering instructive entertainment: films demanding respectability and freedom, not vulgarity and sensationalism as Gutsche so wonderfully puts it. Since practically all the films shown in permanent cinemas had continuous musical accompaniment, usually from a pianist, it is clear that the construction of visual culture went hand in hand with the refining of musical sensibility. Influenced by the audience, four features began coalescing: the length of motion pictures increased; the diversity of films enabled the audience to exercise its discrimination and cultivate taste through preferences; the audience became aware of 'stars' and also participated in their making through exercising its choice; and lastly, newsreels began to precede the actual feature presentation. The rationalisation of South African cinema also had an effect on newspapers, in that new columns were added reporting on theatres, and subsequently film reviews were added.

The development of cinema in South Africa was not, however, to be uniformly linear, for in the years 1910–1913 it suffered a crisis which nearly resulted in its bankruptcy. On its emergence from the crisis, it effected its self-reorganisation in five areas: the lengthening of fiction films; the publicising of stars; the construction of larger cinema houses; the making of cinemas into respectable family amusement areas; and the infusion of greater 'sound effects' in the films. In all of these endeavours, the films made in South Africa were attempting to emulate the popularity of American films which were shown on a larger scale. Gutsche states that French and Italian films which were largely based on literary and historical subjects were unable to compete with American films since the latter were mainly predicated on sensationalism and melodrama. In other words, the shaping of South African modernist sensibility through film was effected through European classicism and American sensationalism. It was at the time of this contestatory context that supposedly 'the first South African film' was made in 1911. The film was *The Great Kimberley Diamond Robbery* or *The Star of the South*. Extraordinarily, only a single sentence is devoted to this momentous occasion by Thelma Gutsche: 'The first South African film *apparently* taken locally and entitled either *The Great Kimberley Diamond Robbery* or *The Star of the South* was also shown but *inauspiciously*' (my italics). The great historical moment of the birth of the South African cinema holds absolutely no importance to her. I have emphasised two words to pause for a moment concerning Thelma Gutsche's astonishingly Europeanist or Anglophilic critical sensibility. Her words indicate that for her the very idea of a South

African film or cinema was not only inconceivable, but totally laughable. Consequently she does not consider the historical, cultural, and political factors that occasioned the making of the first South African film at this particular time, a year after the founding of the Union of South Africa. Was this merely a coincidence or significantly connected to this important event? Given her impeccable archival credentials and her serious belief in its protocols, it seems she announces this occurrence for historical purposes rather than for the significance it holds for South African intellectual and cultural history, or for that matter for commercial purposes, as an attempt to launch a blitzkrieg against the economic hegemony of American and European films.

The film was a failure commercially, and more importantly to her, culturally as well, for as she writes in the footnote to the above sentence, the film was 'conceived in the spirit of the current cinema,' which I take to mean she damns the film for having aligned itself with American sensationalism against European classicism. To Gutsche, these were the two greatest forces struggling against each other in the shaping of South African modernist cultural sensibility. I would like to quote the whole sentence in the footnote: 'Conceived in the spirit of the current cinema, the film does not appear to have made much impression, possibly through amateurish production.' This sentence is revelatory and fascinating for two reasons. I'm puzzled when she writes, 'the film does not appear to have made much impression', because given her astounding research skills, Gutsche was in a position to say definitively whether the film made an impression or not. I thus take this to be a subtextual way of saying: who cares whether the first South African film made an impression or not; I'm (that is Gutsche) not going to waste my invaluable research time trying to establish this definitively. As for the other segment of the sentence, 'possibly through amateurish production', this clearly means: I (meaning Gutsche again) have not seen *The Great Kimberley Diamond Robbery* to determine its artistic merits, nor do I intend to because it cannot possibly deserve serious attention from me. This is confirmed by a long footnote which consists of two summations of the plot of the film: one from the advertising of the film by its makers, the Springbok Film Company; and the other from a review of the film in the newspaper *The Star*. That there is no evaluation, analysis or summary of the film therefore is not accidental. From these observations a singular conclusion is inescapable concerning *The History and Social Significance of Motion Pictures in South Africa*: the book is largely a product of archival work, rather than familiarity through actual viewing of the films whose social history is appraised.

The mentioning of *The Great Kimberley Diamond Robbery* in the book as the moment of the emergence of South African cinema has paradoxically a disruptive effect on the real theme preoccupying Gutsche in this section of the narrative text: the struggle between European classicism and American sensationalism. The very fact that she disparages our first film because she perceives it to have emulated Americanism rather than Europeanism, is clear as to what has been the end result. I read Gutsche at this

narrative moment to be lamenting that South African cinema had been still-birthed, if
I may say so, by American sensationalism.[5] For her the struggle between these two
forms of filmic representation concerned matters of vital importance: ethics, behaviour, manners, social etiquette, national identity, cultural continuity, historical formation, etc. Interestingly, Gutsche examines the relationship between European classicism and American sensationalism, partly in the context of the relationship between
documentary films (she calls them actuality films) and fiction films.[6] At this moment
(1910-13) in the history of cinema in South Africa, fictional films were beginning to
exceed documentary films in popularity. She attributes the triumph of fiction films to
the appeal of the baseness of American sensationalism to a certain class of filmgoers,
and not to the intrinsic poetic form of this mode. Gutsche was analysing the historical
conjuncture of film history pre-*Birth Of A Nation* (1916), the fiction film which established the grammar, syntax and aesthetic style of world cinema. These associations and
condemnations reveal two issues about her critical sensibility: the aristocratism of her
artistic taste and the profound moralism of its nature. In a not fully articulated connection, she attributes the defeat of European classicism and documentary films as directly related to the triumph of American sensationalism and fiction form.

   Thelma Gutsche's hostility to American sensationalism was not due solely to its
supposed amoralism in her estimation, but also to the fact that it precipitated the first
attempts of censorship in South African film history. Commenting on this period,
Gutsche (1972) writes:

> During 1912, American sensationalism expressed in grotesquely exaggerated
> acting began to characterise moving pictures as a whole and to neutralise the
> values of other types of films... Apart from the gross improbabilities of plot
> which began to irritate even the least susceptible members of audiences, some
> of the scenes which the 'bioscope' portrayed could no longer be ignored. 'Night
> Life' and 'the Underworld' provided the excuse for exhibitions which surpassed
> vulgarity to the point of lechery and letters to the Press began to multiply until
> they became an almost daily occurrence throughout South Africa. So far from
> improving, the quality of films deteriorated more and more until every type of
> person implored the authorities to take action. The 'bioscope' was now the
> recognised amusement of the young but its evil effects were even more exten-
> sive... The odium which increasingly surrounded the bioscope from 1911 on-
> wards and which in 1913, compelled legislative action, was not founded only in
> the objectionable type of film which then characterised its programmes. It was
> founded too in the buildings themselves and in the conditions under which
> bioscope exhibitions were given ... women were molested in the best bioscopes
> and in the more impoverished districts, women themselves brought their ba-
> bies and attended to their comfort under most unhygienic circumstances. Unac-

companied children screamed, quarrelled and fought, running about as they pleased and coloured people frequently mingled with white. In an unventilated hall frequently packed with vociferous humanity, the fetid atmosphere was often almost unbearable.

The call from various organisations in civil society for the regulation of what was actually portrayed on the screen, and the policing of the consumption of popular culture in the public sphere did not result in immediate legislation. The licensing for the exhibition of films in the public sphere was made stricter. In the meanwhile, the First World War intervened.

Continuing with her perspective as a cultural historian of South African modernity rather than as a film historian per se, the latter since Andre Bazin mainly preoccupied with film texts, Gutsche, in considering the years 1914–18 (which she designates as 'The Great War Period') is mainly preoccupied with foreign artistic forms of representation in South African poetic imagination. She writes practically nothing on the evolutionary structure of South African cinema, its development, problematics, etc. The only thing she can bring herself to consider is the beautiful cinema houses which were being constructed at this time in major cities, particularly in Johannesburg. Without being totally cynical, I would venture to say that perhaps she marvels at the beautiful decor and the architecture of the cinema houses because presumably they were financed by foreign capital. The only context in which she mentions *De Voortrekkers/Winning a Continent* (made in 1916) is in her celebration of the film 'stars' who were popular in South Africa during this period. The reason she mentions the film is because a relatively well known English actress, Edna Flugarth, starred in it. Here we have a paradoxical situation that arguably the most important scholar of South African film culture was not really concerned with the films made by South Africans. To me this is the central fascination of the Thelma Gutsche enigma. This section of the book is slightly tinged with a melancholic tone as she recognises that the beginning popularity of American films meant that American populist realism would eventually supersede European classicism. Paradoxically, the most effective instrument of this process was a British born actor acting in popular American films: Charlie Chaplin. Gutsche posits the beginning hegemonic importance of the American films in South Africa to the greatness of David W. Griffith, the American who established the grammar of film. She emphasises the popularity of Griffith's *Intolerance* together with *Caribia*, the Italian epic which inspired Griffith to make his own film, among the South African film public. Concerning American cinema's hegemony, Gutsche was torn between her admiration for Chaplin and Griffith, and her unwavering hostility to American spy and thriller films which she found to be the epitome of American sensationalism. Given the convincing analysis of Sergei Eisenstein in showing the profound influence of Charles Dickens on Griffith, it would not be farfetched to postulate that Gutsche's real reason for her passion toward these incomparable artists was her belief that they were constructing, though in different ways, different forms of European classicism inside American modernity.

When Gutsche does now and then pull back from her 'Europeanism' to reflect on purely South African film matters, it is interesting to note her shifts from aesthetic and artistic matters to economic matters. To Gutsche the crucial matter concerning South African cinema in and of itself was its economic integration and rationalisation. But even in this sphere external forces were strong. Within the context of rationalisation, she observes that the programming of films was institutionalised: the 'institution' of the feature film and support programme were set in place. With this observation of the paradigmatic forms of the institutionalisation of film culture, one is made aware of the profound feel for the historicity of forms Gutsche had, be they social, cultural, economic, etc. Even though Gutsche may be criticised as not having been truly a historian of South African cinema, perhaps one of her greatest contributions to South African culture was an enrichment of our sensibility through her feel for the historicity of forms.

This deep awareness of the historicity of forms is especially evident in the 1920s when silent cinema was coming to its end and a national entertainment industry was emerging. At this time, the era of the perpetually new and novel, film had to vie with jazz for recognition within the cultural space of South Africa. Much like the New African intellectuals, the cultural organs of the white ruling establishment were violently hostile to the entrance of jazz into South Africa: 'Jazz' in South Africa was regarded with suspicion by the more serious-minded and thoughtful articles under headings such as dancing degradation, ballroom buffoonery, the 'jazz' epidemic, appeared in the daily papers. They were often characterised by puritanical invective against its sensual nature and its inevitable effect on war-weary soldiers; but there was no gainsaying its foundation in contemporary circumstances and its world-wide popularity. Originally an 'escapist' medium, jazz became a universal institution which has developed through various stages of 'syncopation', 'crooning', 'swing', 'boogie-woogie', 'jive', etc.[7] The African working class appropriated jazz as an artistic form that enabled them not only to make sense of their historical location, but also as a healing process enabling them to hold at bay the alienation of the proleterianization experience.

Gutsche not only has film and jazz vie with each other, but she also theorises cinema within a complex structure of modernity:

> In general therefore, the post-war period was characterised by the public's recovery from severe depression and the incorporation into the social structure of the advances of mechanical science. The cinema, the motor-car, the radio and the aeroplane had become integrated with the fabric of ordinary life and a little later, the cinema was further to entrench its position with the improvement of

sound. Inasmuch as the public accepted mechanical methods of transport and communication and later the thorough mechanisation of utilities (such as the traffic robot, the automatic telephone, the automatic lift, the frigidaire, the electric stove, the electric radiator, etc.), the tempo of life in general steadily increased and concomitantly accentuated the demand for 'escapist' recreation.

At this juncture she launches into a brilliant and detailed analysis of American films which embodied the sensationalism she so profoundly despised. She inveighs end-lessly against this cinema. In her defence, one could say she was politically correct (in the old non-American sense) in analysing American films because they were hegemonic, and were shaping the cultural sensibility of the South African imagination.

When Gutsche writes of the distinguishing features of South African cinema in the 1920s, these are not unique characteristics of our 'national' culture finding expressive articulation in film form as one would expect, but rather markers of the standardisation of visual film culture which was happening in many other 'national cinemas' under American hegemony: a phenomenon having more to do with the maximisation of profit than the development of aesthetics. Being located at the periphery of the cinema as a world system, Gutsche mentions that outstanding films were shown in South Africa months or even years after having been shown overseas. A second characteristic was that films were much shorter than the time advertised for; a program would speak of two hours of entertainment, whereas the viewing of films themselves would not be more than an hour. The third feature was the beginning predominance of 'trailers' and advertising for forthcoming films. And lastly, the process of 'block' or 'blind' booking which forced exhibitors to buy massive quantities for showing regardless of their quality. Given these structural features, Gutsche implies that the hegemony of American cinema in South Africa was to be expected. Britain, failing to challenge the hegemony of American cinema while imitating its sensationalism, called upon and in fact attempted to force commonwealth countries to impose quotas on Hollywood films. In support of Europeanism classicism, this gives Gutsche an opportunity to castigate Britain for imitating Americans, while renewing her hostility to American popular film culture. In this context, she speaks of the physical, physiological and psychological detrimental effects of American films on children. Here again, to her what was crucial were effects of films rather than actually analysing and showing the supposed poor aesthetic quality of these films. A question beyond this presentation emerges: to what extent has Gutsche's unwavering preoccupation with the social history of film devoid of aesthetic merit been detrimental to the subsequent emergence of film aesthetics in our country? Given her greatness as a film scholar, should we not put at her door the mediocrity of our cinema, rather than blaming apartheid for this disaster? With the coming of talking films in the 1927–31 period, Gutsche traces the institutional forms, practices and transformations which enabled the breaking of the

American hegemony in South African cinema. This chapter reinforces one's admiration for her command of the relevant material, and the dazzling interweaving of its many forms in constructing dense textural patterns of interpretation. Here I quote at liberty:

> The continued success of this enterprise which already held leases and options on a large number of theatres, made it clear that the film 'monopoly' operated by African Theatres and African Films for nearly fourteen years had at length been broken. Kinemas continued their policy of expansion apparently without limit and both organisations now entered on a phase of competitive development which was to provide South Africa with some of the best cinema entertainment ever presented. During the four years that the struggle lasted, the South African cinema developed most of its distinguishing characteristics – notably the subtle change from 'bioscope' to 'cinema'. The outstanding feature of this fierce competition was the countering of one company of every development announced by the other. Simultaneous with the publication of the share prospectus of Kinemas Ltd came the announcement of extensive building plans on the part of African Theatres which manifested great activity and prosperity... Every move on each side was watched and combated and the public soon sensed the tenseness of the situation ... The unqualified rivalry between African Theatres and Kinemas was constant with these unhappy circumstances. On the one hand, Kinemas had persuaded themselves and gave the public the impression that they were waging a kind of altruistic crusade to break a pernicius monopoly for the benefit of the public; on the other hand, African Theatres and its associated companies fought to save an industry which they alone had founded, consolidated and brought to prosperity. the issue therefore came to be fought without quarter, many disreputable incidents characterising its development.

A sense of mischievousness did not escape her: 'During these activities, competitive action continued along standardised lines. For instance, when Kinemas showed *The Rat* with Ivor Novello at the Astoria in Johannesburg in June 1928, African Theatres showed *The Bat* at the Palladium.' I could not resist the literary vividness of these passages; written so effortlessly, but based on painstaking research and enormous accumulated facts.

This competition between these two institutions eventually became impracticable for several reasons: the overseas production and distribution companies, knowing that they were bidding against each other, exploited and took advantage of both of them; the building of endless cinema houses was financially exhausting to both companies; cinemas were opened in cities whose populations could not support them; their financial situation was becoming worse and worse. This economically unsound competition eventually led to a merger of the two companies forming two new companies dealing with exhibition and distribution, African Consolidated Theatres Ltd and African Consolidated Films Ltd: 'The amalgamation was at first regarded with real regret by the general public. Competition had provided cinema entertainment of an unprecedently high order as well as innovations and variety which were previously impossible. Some considered that the bonds of 'monopoly' would clamp film entertainment within rigid limits and that the public would become passive victims of dictatorial caprice while others felt that the combining of resources would ensure progressive development.' In a central way, our visual sensibility was also structured by this competition of long ago.

One of the interesting theses that Gutsche develops in this section of the book is that while on the one hand sound film widened the aspect of social life it represented, on the other hand it homogenised the nature of film form: the extension of the social horizons of film were at the expense of its poetic lyricism. This belief seems to have been taken as self evident by many pioneering film scholars from Bela Belazs through Siegfried Kracauer to Andre Bazin. Gutsche was in many ways articulating a consensus view of the 1930s and 1940s among film scholars who had intimate knowledge of both the silent era and that of the advent of sound. To them the Eisenstein of *Battleship Potemkin* (1925) was more lyrical and had a deeper and complex emotive structure than *Alexander Nevsky* (1937).

As a consequence of the hegemony of American films on our national sensibility in the 1930s, Thelma Gutsche has two chapter headings that would seem more relevant to the history of American cinema than to the national history of our cinema: 'Advent of Metro-Goldwyn-Mayer And Union Theatres Ltd Impregnation Of The Cinema In The Social Structure'; and 'Advent Of Twentieth Century-Fox And United Artists The Film In Every Phase Of National Life'. It would seem that the history of South African cultural sensibility in this decade was more wedded to American entertainment and popular history than to its own nationalistic history. I extrapolate from this section that although Gutsche constantly and continuously inveighed against American sensationalism in film culture, this never blinded her to the fact that American cinema was a carrier of what could be called cosmopolitanism, however compromised and problematic it was, which to her was preferable than the fundamentalist Afrikaner nationalism which in her evaluation compromised the few films made by white South Africans. Clearly then, the reason why Gutsche in *The History and Social Significance of Motion Pictures in South Africa* is contemptuous of South African films made by whites for whites is that she sees it as a project of resentment intended to feed Afrikaner nationalism endlessly howling about the defeat of 1899–1902. Another remarkable thing about this extraordinary woman is that like Frantz Fanon she does not confuse nationalism with national consciousness. The fundamental lesson imparted is now obvious: film form and nationalism are simply incompatible with each other.

This lesson was never heeded from 1948: is it surprising that 'our', or more appropriately I should say, 'their' apartheid cinema has been one catastrophe after another of mediocrity?

I will pass over in silence the chapter on 'The History of Film Censorship in South Africa', even though in itself it imparts many invaluable lessons, as this theme has been exhaustingly considered by South African film scholars of later generations. But, in the next chapter, 'The History of Film Production in South Africa', I expect the matriarch of African Film Studies to say something more about South African films than she had in the rest of the book.[8] Here I would like to begin with a quotation because her voice is the most authoritative about the nature of our origins in the realm of film culture:

> The history of commercial film production in South Africa may be said to have begun in May 1896 when Edgar Hyman, manager of the Empire Palace of Varieties in Johannesburg, first saw the 'cinematographe' used by Carl Hertz and, fascinated by its possibilities, obtained from Charles Urban, managing director of the Warwick Trading Company of London, a cinecamera and supplies of unexposed film. Hyman continuously took films in South Africa as agent for the company and it would appear that, prior to the outbreak of the Boer War, Urban also sent one of his cameramen (possibly Joseph Rosenthal) to film scenes in South Africa on two separate occasions. The Warwick Trading Company's Film catalogue from 1899 onwards itemised a large number of South African films many of which were shown at the Johannesburg Empire from 1898 onwards and some to President Kruger (whom Hyman also filmed) early in 1899. It is evident that from 1896 to 1899, both Edgar Hyman and other cinecameramen were active in South Africa and that their films, distributed through the Warwick Trading Company, were shown throughout the world. The Boer war was systematically documented by three enterprises; but subsequently film production seems to have ceased in South Africa for some years except for the filming of Cecil Rhodes' funeral in April 1902 by J. T. Blake, the 'bioscope operator' attached to Fillis' Circus, then in Cape Town.

Although within six months of the invention of cinematography in France South Africa imprinted itself on this visual medium of modernity, Gutsche makes it clear, without seeming to be aware of the political implications, that South Africa was an object of imperial gaze rather than self defining: Gutsche speaks of film production *in* South Africa, instead of South Africa film production. From the moment of its inception in our 'national' territory cinematography was an instrument of imperial domination. South African film scholars have been lax in their historical responsibility in determining whether this petrifying imperial gaze was partly responsible for the subsequently debilitating gesture of making nationalism, precisely white nationalism, the undefined but 'naturally' articulated ideology of pre-1994 South African cinema.[9] The second critical point indicated by Gutsche is that extensive film documentation of the Anglo-Boer War of 1899–1902 brought to the consciousness of the world the profound importance of the intersection of film and history. Although writing respectfully on the surface of the worthy efforts in the making of *De Voortrekkers* and *Symbol of Sacrifice* (1918), the lack of extended consideration on her part of these historically important films would seem to indicate that she was weary of them for they were largely historical myths.

As already indicated, South African cinema of the Segregationist and Apartheid Era went down this tragic path,l showing *De Voortrekker* annually on December 16 ('Dingaan's Day') as a means of recharging nationalist passions by means of the invocation of historical myths. This could not but have the effect of narrowing the possibilities and options of our cinematic national imagination.

The extraordinary importance of Thelma Gutsche's classic book lies not in its unrivalled archaeological reconstruction of our visual imagination, but in enumerating the dangers that will always be debilitating in constituting a national cinema. Afrikaner nationalistic destruction of our cinematic visual imagination, with the connivance of English-speaking white South Africans, has made us pay a heavy price: in the almost a century of the encounter between the South African visual imagination and cinematography not a single film masterpiece has emerged from us. Where is our *Round-Up* (1965)? Where is our *Memories of Underdevelopment* (1967)? Where is our *Daughters of the Dust* (1991)?

A bibliography of the work of Thelma Gutsche

Gutsche, T. (1966). *No Ordinary Woman: The Life and Times of Florence Phillips*, Cape Town: Howard Timmins.

Gutsche, T. (1966). *Old Gold: The History of the Wanderers Club*, Cape Town: Howard Timmins.

Gutsche, T. (1968). *The Microcosm*, Cape Town: Howard Timmins.

Gutsche, T. (1970a). *A Very Smart Medal: The Story of the Witwatersrand Agricultural Society*, Cape Town: Howard Timmins.

Gutsche, T. (1970b).*The Bishop's Lady*, Cape Town: Howard Timmins.

Gutsche, T. (1972). *The History and Social Significance of Motion Pictures in South Africa, 1895-1940*, Cape Town: Howard Timmins.

Gutsche, T. (1979). *There Was a Man: The Life And Times of Sir Arnold Theiler, K. C. M. G., of Onderstepoort*, Cape Town: Howard Timmins.

Notes

1   This paper was originally presented at the African Studies Association in San Francisco in November 1996. The panel, 'Southern African Cinema: Politics and Aesthetics', was organised by Mark Beittel of Universita degli Studi di Trento. I would also like to thank the other panellist, Peter Davis.

2   All these books were published by Howard Timmins, Cape Town.

3   The book has its own prejudices against Africans and the Khoisan. For instance, in *No Ordinary Woman* she writes of 'the resentful and pillaging Basuto and the belligerent Matebele' in the context of the Great Trek, as though Africans should not be resentful at having been displaced from their land by the Afrikaners. On the following page (6), she writes: 'Their [Europeans] behaviour to non-whites and especially to the thieving Hottentots and Bushmen who as late as the seventies, were shot down as 'pests' by specially-organised commandos, was indefensible.'

4   Keyan Tomaselli, arguably the foremost historian of the South African cinema, states that the years 1916–1919, the era in which this film was made, were the golden era of South African cinema (1988, p. 32). If this is so, Thelma Gutsche's study does not register this fact at all.

5   What I mean by this is that Gutsche may never have actually seen the first film establishing our cinema *historically*, but much more importantly, she incapacitated herself by viewing it within the over-deterministic Manicheaniasm she was struggling with at this juncture in South African cultural history. What is interesting about this studied indifference is that *The Great Kimberley Diamond Robbery*, as the title implies, deals with the fundamental issue which precipitated the making of modern South Africa, a theme resonating in Gutsche's own work: the discovery of minerals in the late nineteenth century. Within the context of this discovery, it also deals with the intensification of frontier clashes between Europeans and Africans and the 'necessity' of the State to police lives to assure the triumph of white nationalism. However, although this film historically demarcated the beginnings of South African cinema, it was *De Voortrekkers/Winning a Continent*, made five years later, which gave ideological and artistic perspective to our cinema. In other words, the film, structuring the ideological perspective of our cinema, was implicated in fanatical white nationalism, bordering on proto-fascism. The mediocrity of South African cinema from its inception to the present is its failure to deal with this issue. The fatal mistake within the context of post-apartheid cinema in the process of being forged at the presently, would be for upcoming African filmmakers to think that these are skeletons of concern only to white South African filmmakers.

6   It does not follow that for Gutsche all European films embodied the classicism that was central to her critical imagination, as made clear by her condemnation of

French crime 'drama' which she characterised as immersed in 'American' sensationalism and sordidness. Her strenuous objection to these films was she that believed they glorified felony and made criminality triumph over law (126). It follows, of course, that she did not view all American films as carriers of sensationalism. What she objected to was an ideological morality which inhered in certain particular modes of films.

7   I make a similar observation in my essay, 'The TransAtlantic Connections of the New African Movement', in *United States and South Africa: The Historical Field of Social and Cultural Interaction*.

8   In an essay we attempted to trace the genealogical structure of African Film Studies: '*Presence Africaine* and the Emergence of African Film Criticism', 1–44. Elsewhere it will be necessary to attempt to integrate South African Film Studies with (or into) African Film Studies which for obvious historical reasons until 1994 were geared into mutually conflictive epistemological and ideological systems.

9   This will be criticised as a meaningless overgeneralisation, ill informed of the specificities of the South African cinema. I content myself with this statement by Tomaselli (1988, p. 11): 'Conventional sources of investment, both domestic and international, continue to produce bland, and often racist, feature films, films which legitimate current political processes or show American, colonial and white myths about Africa and Africans.'

References

Blignaut, J. and Botha, M. (eds) (1992). *Movies-Moguls-Mavericks: South African Cinema 1979-1991*, Cape Town: Showdata.

Masilela, N. (fortchoming). 'The TransAtlantic Connections of the New African Movement', in *United States and South Africa: The Historical Field of Social and Cultural Interaction*.

Masilela, N. (1996). '*Presence Africaine* and the Emergence of African Film Criticism', *Communicare*, 15(1).

Strebel, E. (1979). '*The Voortrekkers*: A Cinematographic Reflection of Rising Afrikaner Nationalism', *Film and History*, 9(2).

Tomaselli, K.G. (1986). 'Capital and Culture in South African Cinema: Jingoism, Nationalism and the Historical Epic', *Wide Angle*, 8(2).

Tomaselli, K.G. (1988). *The Cinema of Apartheid*, New York: Smyrna/Lake View Press.

CHAPTER TEN

Re-fashioning identity in post-apartheid South African music: a case for Isicathamiya choral music in KwaZulu-Natal

Angela Impey

The Beatrice Street YMCA in downtown Durban is a modest establishment. The upstairs hall is unadorned except for a few scattered rows of plastic chairs and several strips of flickering lights precariously fastened to warped and rotting ceiling-boards. At the far end of the hall there is a low wooden platform in front of which is positioned a wooden table and a single chair.

Every Saturday night, the YMCA is hive of activity. By mid-evening, the street is congested with minivan taxis delivering people from their hostels and township residences. Around midnight, they begin to drift off the dimly lit streets and into the hall. The majority of those who enter are men. They are Zulu migrant workers who live in the city for periods of up to eleven months of the year, working in factories, on the docks or in the dark shadows of the inner-city as night watchmen.

Upon entering the YMCA, they begin to congregate in tight circles, on the stairs, in the foyers. Leaning inward towards one another, hands behind their backs, they begin to sing softly, haltingly, in close 4-part harmonies, a cappella. They are preparing for a competition they call *isicathamiya*, which literally translated means 'in a stalking approach', descriptive of the soft, tiptoed dance styles, crouching actions and songs they perform. The choirs are made up of 'homeboys', men who share kinship or regional ties from rural KwaZulu Natal, a province in the north east of South Africa.

It is the stage of the evening they call 'iprakthisa': practice time. It is the time when each group has the opportunity to take its turn on the stage, to perfect voice parts, to make final corrections of lyrics and to remind themselves and each other of the finer details of their carefully choreographed steps.

Later they will compete in front of a judge and the choir that exhibits the most synchronized actions and the most creative song arrangements will be awarded a small sum of money. On a more prestigious night, a goat or a cow may be offered to the winning group, but it is the prestige associated with victory that is the incentive that attracts the participants to the competitions.

Each choir is immaculately dressed in matching suits and bow ties, two-tone shoes, white gloves, pocket-handkerchiefs and shining costume jewellery. The leaders of each choir wear white sashes across their bodies loudly announcing their group: The Harding Morning Stars, The Really Happy Singers, The NBA Champions, The Hundred Percent Brothers.

The audience is made up largely of women. They are the wives, girlfriends and supporters of the singers and their participation in the performance is essential. They clap enthusiastically and ululate; they discuss amongst themselves the finer details of the groups they favour, and loudly voice their disapproval of those they don't. Some run onto the stage, dramatically approaching a singer and, in a series of stylized gestures, declare: *this one is mine and don't any of you forget it!* Some drape scarves on their men, spray them with deodorant, or tuck paper money into their belts. Throughout the spectacle, the men remain stony faced, feigning indifference to the fuss and flattery, and concentrating only on their song and dance.

While the choirs prepare themselves for the competition, the atmosphere is thick with anticipation. Until recently, the adjudicator of the competition was always a white person; he should be unknown and therefore unbiased. During the practice, the leaders of each group would comb the city streets in search of a judge. He could be a hobo found sleeping under a bridge, or a rough city kid found slouched outside a late-night discotheque.

He would be approached with great humility and skillfully lured into the hall with offers of drink, cigarettes and a night of sweet music. He would be seated at the lone table facing the stage and told to select the three best choirs of the evening. For the remainder of the night, and often way into the following day, he would have to dedicate his attention respectfully and absolutely to the choirs.

With the establishment of the South African Traditional Music Association in 1991, the practice of white adjudication has been reviewed. SATMA, an organisation which presides over the standards and practices of *isicathamiya* in South Africa, has replaced the old system with one in which educated black persons (teachers, nurses, policemen, or members of a non-isicathamiya choral groups) are trained make an informed judgement by listening 'in the isicathamiya way'.

Competitions begin around four am. The singers will begin their performance from the back of the hall and will parade past the judge, subtly drawing his attention to themselves as they pass him by pointing out their matching cufflinks and socks, or the beaded badges of the new South African flag they may have pinned to their lapels. They will salute, smile and stare imploring at him, all the while maintaining, with absolute rhythmic precision, the delicate steps, shimmering hand movements and the respective vocal parts of their song.

Stylistic history of Isicathamiya

The origins of *isicathamiya* are rooted in American minstrelsy and ragtime, which entered South Africa in the mid-19th century by way of touring vaudeville groups from the United States. Troupes such as Orpheus McAdoo and his Virginia Jubilee Singers toured the country extensively from 1890, inspiring the formation of numerous black South African groups whose imitation of crude black-face minstrelsy performance and song repertoire signaled notions of cultural progress and self-improvement[1].

Prior to the adaptation of African American performance models, however, choral music had for some time been performed by the educated, landed black elite, whose missionary education instilled in them the desire to imitate all things British. One of the main symbols of identification with Victorian values was religious 4-part choral singing referred to as *imusic*. The Natives' Land Act of 1913 was the first law passed in the then Union of South Africa which proscribed territorial partitioning of the country. It was an extreme piece of legislation that prohibited black property ownership, regardless of educational, religious and class status, and forced thousands of indigenous peoples from their ancestral land. Consequently, religious hymns or *imusic* were no longer considered capable of accommodating emerging discourses of black social and political dissent and began to be blended with, or replaced by minstrelsy and other African American performance styles. The combination of multi-part hymnody and minstrelsy (and later, traditional musics) thus became the basis of much subsequent black popular music in South Africa.

By the 1920s, minstrelsy performances had gained widespread popularity throughout South Africa, extending deep into remote parts of the countryside. These shows particularly impressed Zulu migrant workers from the KwaZulu Natal regions, who combined stylistic elements of minstrelsy performance with *ingoma dance* (characterised by high kicking footwork) and *izingoma zomtshado* (wedding songs) to form the prototype of present-day *isicathamiya* song and dance. During the following decades, western popular song styles such as rock 'n roll and Jimmy Rogers' country music have found their way into *isicathamiya* performance and today it is not unusual to hear renditions of the Beach Boys enacted alongside a more traditional repertoire.

'We see people crying,' (they sing). The leader dances into a falsetto, from falsetto into yodelling lament, strumming his imaginative guitar. The Brothers cry 'ey! ey!' They cry 'tala tala'; they cry 'mmmmhh!' They lift their right legs across the bodies of the next in their choral line. They finger their neighbour's ankles, strum their neighbours' calves like guitar necks. 'Bam bam, ba bam bam bam' goes the bass, while they finger trumpet valves. Now they circle the stage. With upright bodies and raised hands they flick up their legs, stamp their feet.

Meintjes, 1990, p. 5

Isicathamiya forms and functions

The vast numbers of Zulu men who entered the migrant labour system during the early years of the century occupied the marginal spaces of the cities: squalid single sex hostels, compounds and impoverished locations. Although still rooted in rural identity, city dwelling inspired creative responses to the demands and new experiences of everyday life. With urban development in South Africa, so an infrastructure of trade unions, sports organisations and entertainment clubs became established amongst black urban dwellers. This cultural infrastructure became the framework around which Zulu *isicathamiya* groups modelled their weekly performances. Groups developed a complex network of all-night competitions which took place every weekend; they were stately occasions, and as had been the convention of competitions held at schools and missions, were organised around a fixed performance repertoire.

Erlmann (1996) contends that the organisation of choirs and the repertoire of song and dance which characterized *isicathamiya* performance do not merely represent creative adaptation of old and new, thus expressing rural-urban migration and the negotiation of traditional and western worlds. Rather, choirs, and the web of competitions that hold them in place, became an important strategy for survival for migrants who sought to root themselves in an increasingly fragmented and alienated world. As with countless similar semi-urban South African expressive forms that developed during the harsh years of apartheid rule, *isicathamiya* provided a dynamic medium through which a particular group was able to reflect upon itself and the rapidly changing environment. Ironically, its participants sought dignity through symbols that are centrally identified with those political and ideological forces which denied them self-respect. Like other African syncretic or hybridized musics, *Isicathamiya's* domestication and re-functioning of western symbols herein bear the imprint of a different, or even opposing, cultural logic (Lazarus 1999, p. 197).

> 'We're here and suffering,' sing the Nthuthuko Brothers, 'just as we come from difficulties in Zululand.' 'Sizula-zula,' we're going up and down, between town and homeland. Then 'Sikwhela sikhwela, time my baby.' 'We're going here and there, riding the train, see you later my sweetheart.'
> Meintjes, 1990, p. 4

The notion of concealment with regard to the development of *isicathamiya* is significant when considering the nature of its emergence in the post-apartheid era. For the most part, the development of *isicathamiya* occurred in a physically removed place, separated from others by racial laws, curfews and restricted access to public halls and clubs. In addition and perhaps more importantly, it evolved in an imagined cultural space. Over a period of a century, the genre has assumed an exclusive design and function, selectively blending and embracing new ideas, yet shielded from the forces and fads of popular culture as mediated by the state-controlled radio stations and white-owned record companies. Performances responded directly to the needs of those who created and consumed it, providing solace to Zulu city dwellers whose reality was characterised by dislocation from home, family and community. *Isicathamiya* perform-ance provided a space where meaning has been negotiated through the communal design of song and style; and where the loneliness, nostalgia and hardship experienced in the everyday life was able to be dramatized and temporarily discarded.

This notion of cultural space was as significant for the women consumers of *isicathamiya*, without whom the performance would be incomplete. Research conducted on *isicathamiya* to date has largely overlooked the essential role played by women as the emotional benefactors of the genre. Their dedication and zeal has supported and made meaningful the weekly moments of glory to male choristers whose status as migrants rendered them otherwise invisible and socially impotent. In addition, *isicathamiya* pro-vided an important economic space for Zulu women in the cities, many of whom had been denied access to formal employment by influx control laws during the apartheid years and more recently, have fallen victim to the staggering rate of unemployment in the province. Through *isicathamiya,* women could affirm their ties to a home commu-nity and they could meet and establish relations with men who would support them financially, either in the capacity as prostitutes, wives or lovers. The actual or desired nature of their relationships with particular male singers is enacted for the audience during the practice period by way of a complex sign language and the conspicuous presentation of gifts and money.

Isicathamiya's hybrid nature may be read as a creative response to social and political oppression, but so too does it reflect the complex hegemonic entanglements produced by colonial and neo-colonial power relations. In this regard, *isicathamiya* could be read as culturally and politically co-opted. This perception would have been corroborated by the way *isicathamiya* was presented on the South African Broadcasting Corporation's Bantu Radio Services, whose policy was to broadcast certain musics only to promote cultural difference and identification with rural 'tradition'. *Isicathamiya* satisfied the image of an apolitical, rurally orientated music and was thus featured regularly on the state-controlled airwaves. However, in deliberately avoiding overt political engagement, it could also be interpreted that *isicathamiya* practitioners relied on their relative seclu-sion and apparent submissive stance to circumvent and even subvert the pervasive restrictions of the government. While claiming to be apolitical therefore, *isicathamiya* song and dance provided a metaphor for social action. In the words of one of its main spokespeople, the late Paulos Msimango, '*isicathamiya* was our way of attacking with song' (personal communication, Durban 26/1/98).

Isicathamiya has not remained solely outside of the commercial and political arenas, however. One the most significant early exponents of the style was the celebrated composer, Reuben Caluza, whose composition, *Silusapho Lwase Afrika* (We are the children of Africa) was adopted in 1913 as the first official national anthem of the SAANC (the precursor of the African National Congress). The lyrics, written in the vernacular, translate as follows:

> We are the children of Africa
> We are crying for our land
> Zulus, Xhosas, Sothos unite over the Lands Act issue
>
> in Erlmann, 1991, p. 120[2]

In the 1980s, *isicathamiya* became linked with the workers movement in South Africa and was often featured at mass rallies for such organisations as the Congress of South African Trade Unions (COSATU).

The first commercial recording made of *isicathamiya* was by Solomon Linda. Linda worked as a packer for Gallo Record Company in Johannesburg in the 1930s. As one of the most innovative *isicathamiya* composers of his time, he caught the attention of the company's talent scouts and in 1939, Linda and his group, The Original Evening Birds, recorded the hit song *Mbube* (Singer GB829). *Mbube* has subsequently been recorded by a range of South African and international artists (under the title *Wimowe* or *The Lion Sleeps Tonight*) and remains one of the best known and most widely re-recorded South African songs to this day.[3]

From backyard to big business

Perhaps the real moment of emergence for *isicathamiya* occurred during the mid-1980s, with the advent of national television and its introduction of weekly programmes featuring traditional and neo-traditional South African musics. Television facilitated the visualization of *isicathamiya*, introducing to audiences its characteristic choreography and impeccable style and herein shifting its potential for display or self-representation out of the halls and into the national gaze. More significantly perhaps, was the international profile given to *isicathamiya* by Paul Simon's controversial Grammy Award winning album *Graceland* (Warner Brothers, 1986). While this purported collaboration between Simon and various South African artists raised meaningful concerns regarding cultural imperialism, it also served to place South African music and the celebrated *isicathamiya* group, Ladysmith Black Mambazo, on the world map.

South Africa's first democratic elections in April 1994 led the country back into the international arena after long years of cultural isolation. No longer propelled by the passion of struggle and opposition, the arts moved initially into a state of suspension. Artists required time to regroup, to refunction. They began to seek inspiration from the past and from images, sounds and characters perceived to be traditional, authentic and locally meaningful. Within this context, *isicathamiya* has emerged from the dark inner-city halls and become widely promoted as a 'traditional' South African expressive form. Rather than displaying the obvious symbols of traditional identification such as skins and feathers, beating drums and perspiring brows, *isicathamiya*'s claim to tradition references history, defiance, community, dignity and hope. Its prominence in emerging post-apartheid South African popular culture can herein be attributed to the way it has embodied the tenacity and resilience of black South African culture.

International responses to this imaginative practice are mixed, however, particularly amongst those consumers of world music for whom the discourse of authenticity is circumscribed and even militant. I have witnessed European audiences visibly offended by these immaculately styled, tiptoed performances, clearly annoyed that it is not what they perceive to be 'African' music and dance. To them, *isicathamiya* is derivative, westernised and coopted. Ironically, while the genre may be a complex amalgam of transatlantic characteristics, it is essentially and iconically linked to the notion of rooting, or, as Erlmann would have it, 'homing' (1996). In this regard, SATMA members have remained determined to maintain the shape and integrity of their performance practice, asserting that what was meaningful to *isicathamiya* in the halls and hostels of the past, must remain meaningful within the context of its international consumption in the present.

Isicathamiya's characteristic defiance does not speak for all 'new' South African popular music, however. A major trend of the post-apartheid era has been the blending and layering of local styles; a sort of 'peace making' gesture on the part of musicians across cultural categories that have been historically separated by racially determined marketing strategies and language- and culture-specific radio stations. In an attempt to seek a definitive, 'new' South African sound, some mbaqanga musicians have begun to collaborate with traditional Afrikaans accordionists; jazz musicians are bringing onto stage traditional mouth-bow players; Zulu maskandi are playing with head-banging rock musicians and some, inspired by the eclectic whole earth visions of world music, have resorted to sampling the musics of indigenous peoples (e.g. San/ Bushmen) and overlaying them with a pinch of African jazz, a dab of West African djembe and flavouring of Aboriginal didgeridoo. I argue that these explorations into new sounds are as much an exercise in post-apartheid self-discovery as they may be a statement to the world of an emerging national identity, re-fashioned at once on sentiments of reconciliation and the celebration of cultural difference.

Isicathamiya is becoming increasingly popular both locally and on the global music circuit. Choirs regularly tour international festivals, sing alongside major international stars, record in foreign studios and hold competitions in plush venues under the spotlight of international television cameras. In spite of the self-consciousness that inevitably results from such an emergent status, what is significant is their ongoing dedication to the essence of their genre. Despite the often lucrative opportunities that are being made available to them today, they religiously return every Saturday night to compete at the downtown Beatrice Street hall; to the space that contains the historical references of their performance; that continues to dignify its participants and feed their creativity, passion and identity.

Notes

1 For detailed research on the history of *isicathamiya*, see Veit Erlmann, 1996. *Nightsong. Performance, Power, and Practice in South Africa.* (Chicago, London: University of Chicago Press).
2 Caluza's composition was later replaced by Enoch Santonga's 'Nkosi Sikelel iAfrika', (God Bless Africa) a haunting, hymn-like melody which now serves as the South African National Anthem.
3 For further information about Solomon Linda and 'Mbube', see Veit Erlmann. 1999. 'Music, Modernity, and the Global Imagination' (New York, Oxford: Oxford University Press) and Rian Malan. 2000. 'Behind the Hits' (*Rolling Stone Magazine*, May 25). Original recording of 'Mbube' is available on 'Mbube Roots – Zulu Choral Music from South Africa, 1930s-1960s' (Rounder 5025).

References

Meintjes, Louise. (1990). 'The Hobo Judge Wears No Coat Tails: Zulu Choristers Do.' Austin, Texas: Unpublished paper.

Erlmann, Veit. (1991). *African Stars. Studies in Black South African Performance.* Chicago, London: University of Chicago Press.

– (1996). *Nightsong. Performance, Power, and Practice in South Africa.* Chicago, London: University of Chicago Press.

– (1999). *Music, Modernity, and the Global Imagination. South Africa and the West.* New York, Oxford: Oxford University Press.

Lazarus, Neil. (1999). *Nationalism and Cultural Practice in the Postcolonial World.* Cambridge: Cambridge University Press.

CHAPTER ELEVEN

The autobiography of a movement: trade unions in KwaZulu-Natal 1970s–1990s

Ari Sitas

Introduction

As a sociologist I have worked in 'qualitative' research environments in the past: trying to understand the explosion of trade union organisation on the East Rand during the early 1980s; trying to understand the cultural movement that emerged in KwaZulu Natal (KZN) in which I was a participant; trying to understand the volatile black youth movements in the area. In the early days, inspired by oral history methodologies, by Touraine's 'group self-analysis' (1984) and by workshop processes we had developed in the popular theatre of the 1970s (Orkin 1992; Junction Avenue 1995) I attempted to give systematic interpretations of the cultural formations of resistance and conflict that were emerging everywhere. The craft of the fieldworker as I had learnt from rule of thumb techniques and untold mistakes, was to facilitate multiple narrations: to allow the subjects interviewed to speak with others, with each other and in one to one encounters about themes brought to them by the researcher, and later to construct an 'experiential mosaic' (Sitas 1984).

In 1994 I was asked to facilitate the identification of the main themes that were to be pivotal in this study through a creative workshop. The workshop, which involved writers and cultural activists in COSATU, involved 16 people: Vusi Bhengu, Marrasta Shabalala, Dumbuzo Jwara, Alfred Qabula, Temba Mpungose, Petros Madlala, Max Masango, Gladman Ngubo, Thulani Ntuli, Nester Luthuli, Beauty Mahlaba, Wright Raboteng, Ellson Gcwabaza, Jabu Nkosi, Marjorie Njenje. They increased to 18 (Beauty Maningi, Elias Dumbuza) after the workshop: they were all people who were ready to write about their experiences in a collaborative way.

The participants were self-selected in so far as they constituted the network of cultural leadership in COSATU, all recognised to use a handy expression as 'grassroots intellectuals' (Bonnin 1988). The workshops distinguished three different areas for reflection: the traditions (or what Bourdieu (1989) has called 'symbolic capital') that socialised them – traditions, that is, which were available to them before they entered waged employment; the experiences of their life in the urban-industrial clusters of KwaZulu Natal; and finally, their struggles in the 1980s. Within each area there were sub-divisions and refinements. The identification of areas and therefore the writing and research that ensued had less to do with the 'sociologist' and more with the 'public consensus' of the participants at the workshop and the need to take the discussions further. Once the themes were identified each one of the 18 core people were supposed to use them as set topics around which they were to draft their personal experiences. They were to exercise absolute linguistic freedom (which translated into ten English and eight Zulu narratives which were cross-translated by Vusi Bhengu, Siyabonga Mngadi and Bekhisisa Nxasana). Then, each one of them was to interview a further six people: the first person that influenced them to join trade unions, the first shop-steward they elected, the most crucial person who influenced them culturally, and three workers from their immediate shopfloor: one around sixty, one around forty and one around twenty years old. Each one was to be interviewed on exactly the same themes the core people were writing about.

Black worker writing in South Africa has had some impact on the fields of poetry, short stories and autobiography. As Steve Kromberg (1992, p. 2) outlined:

> initiated by a small group of workers involved in The Dunlop Play, worker poetry has arguably the largest audience of any modern poetry in South Africa ... The poets enthusiastically engaged in stylistic innovation and reached out to embrace new audiences ... Although the poetry had been published before, new journals and anthologies which actively catered for their work began to appear and the worker poets were invited to submit their work to international journals. Local video crews focused their cameras on the performances, sound engineers offered their skills and sophisticated equipment to record the poems and the poetry began to find its way into university curricula.

From oral media, many black workers moved to writing. Such a transition brought forward a vigorous debate about the nature and competence of such writing as literature (Cronin 1987; Abrahams 1987; Kromberg 1992) The challenge at hand is more complex – can this collaborative effort produce reliable knowledge that is at once reflective and analytical? Some of the authors here have in the past produced collaborative stories, such as *The Man Who Could Fly* (1992), a story about the Natal violence.

Furthermore, the mixing of their narrations with oral ones elicited from people close to their 'struggles', brings to us the complex interrelationships between orality and literacy. If as Jeff Guy (1990) has argued, the gulf between the two forms of communicative practice is fundamental, what would such a distance do to analytical modes of cognition? Would it be possible to construct an 'autobiography' of a movement? What was brought into the workshop was a simple uncontroversial theoretical point that movements in general are challenges to the social or class orders of society and not mere responses to objective stimuli. And by the same token therefore, they brought with them new normative orientations, solidarities and, around their energy-points, generated novel ways of organising the world. This of course translated into questions around umadlandawonye - the kind of unity, solidarity, co-operation that was being created and further questions around the trade union movement's 'moral core'.

What this project has achieved in sociological terms, is a series of necessary adjustments to our understanding of identity and consciousness among black workers in KwaZulu Natal. However unfashionable the classing of experience might be in post-modern social theory, the feelings that words like umsebenzi/abasebenzi constitute a defining experience, and an experience that organises a world and its meanings, and constructs collectivities, is a central part of the narratives. Perhaps it could not be otherwise, in a network of labour leaders and militants. That such a classing also corresponds to a racing of experience also emerges from the narratives themselves. As shall be shown, the awareness that as blacks and as a distinctive majority, they were the only grouping to have been subjected to the Pass Laws, to the humiliations of Kwa-Muhle, to the racial hierarchies at work, to defective education, to all those experiences that they classify now as Apartheid.

The past in the present

The answer offered by all the participants is simple – black workers joined trade unions in the 1970s and 1980s because of the 'terrible wages', because they were 'treated like dogs' and using Zulu imagery, because they needed a 'shield' (Mcanyana, Khanyile). The emotive resources utilised were based on traditions groomed in the countryside, on religious beliefs, on political legacies, on the experience of apartheid strictures and plain common-sense on each shopfloor.

For most, it was less the 'warrior blood' that 'ran through Zulu veins' that led them to resist, although this was to be of vital import later, but a more humane communalism: traditions learnt in the 'mountains of Kwa Dwalshela' near Port Shepstone where, as Bhengu insists, 'my umbilical chord still lies'. 'It taught me,' claims Njenje 'to love and share with my people. It taught me that if you were disobedient, your ancestors would not bring you luck.' It was an ordered world where young people grew up under clear age-sets and hierarchies, where boys and girls knew their places, where according to Madlala, 'boys would play stick-fighting before eating meat while beautiful girls would be around singing.' At work in their narratives is a deep idealisation of countryside traditions: even when men walked around with sticks, they did so because of their manhood, 'they had never been a party to violent culture … no riots, no killings, no exploitation' (Dumbuza). There is a deep pride in Zuluness but also a worry in the way it has been used in contemporary mobilisations.

For most narrators there is a qualification whenever the more 'military', 'violent' elements of the past associated with Zuluness resurface. Whenever the image of struggle, mobilisation and conflict resurfaces it is deeply militaristic and is placed often within a continuum of the Zulu wars of expansion and resistance. Perhaps Bhengu captures the sense of difficulty in being both of a tradition and at a distance from it: 'I am proud of being a Zulu … I am proud of our history, of its spectacular events and our previous dignified way of life … I am ashamed though, about the current events and the misuse of our historical powers.' Perhaps here we are dealing with the most profound sense of a cultural schizophrenia: that struggles always conjure up both an active, fighting, heroic sense that calls on historical narratives of prowess, whilst at the same time it emphasises reciprocity, care and affect. And, given the violence in the areas most of the participants have come from and the intensive mobilisation of militaristic cultures that they animated, the communal and affective moments are revisited as a hope for transcendence.

Many, too, trace the threads of solidarity not only in a deeply humane past but also in a variety of Christianities. Here the reference is not only to the formal churches but also to the more grassroots Zionist ones. In a variety of anthropological essays the sense of community within such non-establishment black Christian congregations has been emphasised. What is emerging though from labour leaderships is another nuanced reworking of Christianity.

Reactions to religion have been rather varied: 'religion taught me to be honest and to love my neighbour.' For Mbonambi, Christianity sedated people whilst 'they', the colonists with the assistance of missionary clerics, 'were taking the wealth away from them'. At the same time, he admits, Christianity brought with it new types of gatherings, reciprocal obligations, symbols of transcendence and possibilities. In the Bible, 'it is said, a man will enjoy the fruits of his labour … also, in the Bible there must be no racial group that must be above any other.' In the new Christian congregations (Rounds 1969) and its arch-text, people thus found a language which was subversive of earthly powers.

Whereas 'culture' and 'religion' created a social disposition to resist 'being treated like dogs', there were also political traditions that were alive in family memory. What emerges here is not a formal ANC history, but a rich trove of particular struggles. For example, in Nongoma amongst the Madlakazi we are told of 'chief Bhekintika of Phumanyova (who) was against the oppression of the people. He was against the division of the land into pieces by the oppressors'. For Mncube, a worker leader and a 60-year old. this was a defining experience. For Gcwabaza further south, his childhood involved 'struggling for Chief Albert Luthuli, facing soldiers and policemen … gathering at the Lakhani Chambers ... belonging as a youth to the Vukuzenele organisation.' Both of them later would be recruited into Inkatha as a continuum of prior struggles; both later would find themselves targeted by Inkatha warlords because of their trade union involvements: they both turned, as a consequence, into ANC activists.

The sense of oppression was actively communicated through a variety of stories: indeed communal life entailed an intricate web of stories where socialisation occurred through their imagery and metaphoric nature – for Jwara, the image of colonisation with the 'oppressor fighting with Bibles on one hand and guns in the other' was not only a metaphor, it became a defining image. The stories heard by Raboteng in the rural areas during the early days of his childhood, about 'people who were on the hunt, hunting for people.

People were being ambushed and were sold to other people ...' could be referring to a prior instance of slavery, or something someone read somewhere, retold with the force of recent experience. The younger generation of twenty year olds were socialised 'during the darkest Apartheid years': 'we spent most of the time with friends and attended youth meetings, political meetings, places where we were not allowed to go, places like Halls to enjoy music and dancing.' There they learnt about the 'camps' in Mozambique and Angola, Tanzania and Zambia, where their contemporaries lived the dream of Umkhonto we Sizwe.

For Dumbuza hatred and distance was not based on stories but as he claimed, 'grit and experience': 'I saw that our people were treated badly by the white people and I wished to know how it happened that God allowed the white people to do all these awful things to us.' Dumbuza's story is common to most participants – they spoke of the same forms of dispossession occurring to themselves or their kin, or sometimes to people they knew. The fact that not all black people faced actual dispossession does not detract from the belief that most people did so: 'My parents,' Dumbuza adds, 'were living on their own land and they had cattle, sheep and goats. They had a space to keep their belongings. Then the white people took their land. They also put poison in the water where the cattle had to go and drink and they all died.' And he surmised that no God could have planned or tolerated that.

For all, racial discrimination and Apartheid – 'Verwoerd's dream' (Bhengu) – was a constitutive experience. The passes, pass-queues, influx control regulations, compounds and hostels, racism in the countryside and the city grated against their sense of dignity. The stories tell of 'blackjacks' and the 'kwela-kwelas', of the exhausting lines of waiting at Kwa-Muhle, being forced 'to expose our private parts'(Nzuza). Marjorie Njenje sums up Apartheid with a new found irony: 'heaven and the angels were meant for the whites only'. But so was the land according to Nhlengethwa, 'our people's land was taken by the Boers and our people were foreigners in their own country ...'

Most narratives started with a kind of origin: in the beginning there was the 'dreaded' Pass: 'the carrying of passes was one of the difficult things we had to do,' asserted Cele, 'it was demanded by the police wherever and whenever you moved. One had to always have it in one's pocket, with its tax paid up to date, and signed. If you could be found without a permit, you would be either arrested or sent back home or you would receive a fine.' Zungu agreed: 'if you happened to forget your pass you knew that you could be arrested at any one time. Through the pass,' he reminisces:

> you were given special permission to be in town for only seven days after which you would be expected to go back home in the rural area. We used to refer to this as ukusendwa (being sent away). If some people were failing to secure employment after fourteen days, they were forcibly taken to work in the potato garden as slaves and if this was not done, you would be issued with a ticket which could enable you to be transported back to your original home where you had to be tried by your original, tribal court. On being sent way, you would be under the guidance of the police, and when they reached your destination they would report that you had come back to look after your father's goats - this was an insult to men as it was only young boys who looked after goats.

Men and women from this project spent time detailing this frustrating and cruel game of the South African state, and of course their struggles to 'enter' the city at whatever costs. The administration of the rural side of this process by headmen and chiefs, the constant to and fro-ing from police vans and waiting lines, the constant fear of being apprehended, demands a study in its own right.

To get a permit was no mean feat either – Cele stated that 'we found that you had to bribe the clerks into giving it to you. For instance at Kwa-Muhle you could even pay a sheep for a bribe.' 'You had to be on the good side of a white person who was named Zinti. If you were successful, the queues at Kwa-Muhle, Durban's permit/pass office, were waiting for you once again. There were the doctors "opening up your penis" to check you in public. Then the emasokeni (womaniser department) where people were injected at King Edward the VIII hospital for sexually transmitted diseases' (Mcanyana).

Once through with Apartheid officialdom many found their homes in company compounds and hostels where their 'children and their mothers were not legally allowed inside'. It was part of 'the South African misfortune of being black'. There the strictures of urban controls and regulations, the regimented life of migrants became commonplace, a way of life, an inescapable marker of urban life. When Bhengu visited his father for the first time in the compounds of AECI at Umbogothwini he could not believe his eyes: 'out of this experience, I found myself bombarding my father with questions he would not answer ... I was querying a wrong person at the wrong place and the wrong time.'

Men could enter the urban system through either domestic labour or gardening. Cele remembers how he started from the gardens:

Westerhoff, my boss, was a true Afrikaner. I worked in the garden. I had to water the garden at six o'clock, I had to kneel down and polish the rooms of his palace. I was also required to clean the furniture. I was also required to clean the very big yard of the palace from whose trees leaves were shed every day. By ten o'clock it was tea time; my tea was put into an empty tin of milk and used to be accompanied by jam that was spread on the slices of brown bread. For lunch I was given samp without beans in it, and chicken bones. What used to happen was that when chicken was delivered all the meat thereof would be eaten up, and I would be given the bones, sometimes too the white bones of beef. There was a girl who was doing housework like cooking and making the beds as well.

Each narration presented its own Mr or Mrs Westerhoff with the relationship of dominance and reluctant subordination playing itself out in many contexts. For Hadebe the whole relationship was governed by fear, while for others like Mahlaba by 'tactical adjustments'. For all, 'apartheid is something that we are injected with, and it has become part of our blood stream.'

According to Bhengu, 'apartheid played a very big part at work impacting on race and gender'. It impacted on feelings of maleness and femaleness. For example Hadebe remembers how in the 1950s in the streets of Durban, 'when I walked down West or Smith street in those days I had to walk alongside the road avoiding cars on the one hand and on the other hand avoiding ... white people walking on the pavement. At the beaches we had to be divided as blacks from whites. As a black man you could not even look at a white lady otherwise they would ask you "what the hell do you think you are?" that you could cast your eyes on their lady.'

Finally, racial domination 'infected' everyone's life chances through its Bantu Education provisions: 'while we were still in our mothers' wombs, apartheid's masters had imagined and thought out for our fathers what kind of education we should get.' For most of them schooling was never completed. Economic need and homestead pressures found them in the labour market. For the few that had managed to complete their high-school education, prospects were also limited. According to Mahlaba: 'when I was working in the nursing home we had to sweep the floors, do some washing and even clean toilets. We had our Std 10 (school leaving) certificates but if an Indian person was employed, even if she had Std 2 she would become a nurse or a supervisor. All this was not good and we really did not like it.' For men like Bhengu it was marginally better: 'it is an open secret that Bantu education drove me into ending up as a poor clerk, not a highly educated figure I had dreamt of becoming. It was also an open secret that I had no alternative, I only had to take what was available. After completing my matric in 1979 I was employed as a clerk by the KwaZulu Government and I was stationed at Ulundi. This was my first direct exposure to the migrant labour system ... There at Ulundi I used to stay in a four roomed house with four other people. There was one person in each room. and four of us shared the kitchen.'

Whether the narratives belong to Dumbuza who still wears the marks of being 'whipped with a sjambok by the white farmer' or Qabula who was part of the Pondoland peasant revolt in the late 1950s who doubts if there 'is any black man who was not terrorised by it', the word 'apartheid' captures more than institutional, legal and power arrangements and their symbolic connotations. Alongside the cultural, religious and political memories, the experience of racial domination created powerful symbolic constellations that could not be reduced to the actual immediate experiences of wage labour. Any sense of identity and dignity was a negotiation between these constellations and the concrete experience in KwaZulu Natal's industrial life.

Black worker, white city

Most narratives speak of the experience of the city and of their workplaces as a maze of material hardships. Their pasts and already socialised dispositions allowed them to create a distance, indeed a dissonance from the goals others made them achieve, but their consciousness was deeply marked by the everyday realities. Proletarianisation is not considered an act of God, 'for our people not to live with their families was not an act of the creator' but rather an act of colonial violation (Dumbuza). They had to learn about life in factories, to learn from their bosses how to become 'greedy for money'. They learnt about 'long hours' (Mbhele), 'colour privilege' (Njenje) and the 'unity of the clock' (Ncanyana).

For Qabula, whose poetry and autobiography *A Working Life Cruel Beyond Belief* are a testimony to proletarianisation, migrancy and its implications, the choice was always twofold: the white farm and the plantation, or the mine and the factory: 'farms were all the same, they all did the same things to their workers no matter which farm it was. Workers were working without being paid or being paid very little and they were only given small amounts of food to eat. Apartheid was also playing a big part there. If you knew no one on the farm where you were working, you worked very hard, especially if you were from Pondoland. People started squatter camps when they were tired of workings, and staying on the farms. They started them at Inanda and Egoli and called them Emkhukehwini.'

In all their experiences, discipline and especially the discipline of the clock predominates. 'First you had to work just as you were told. Otherwise out you went, back to the farms. Into the kwelakwela for a good beating by the police. You were not to be cheeky, not talk back, call them the names they wanted - sir, baas, boss, mnumzane - laugh when they want you to, worry when they said so. Children or things, that's what we were. Then, the clock. Production, production, pressure to keep the score, faster and faster.' This contrasted radically with life on the rural homestead, where 'one's only thoughts were that we should have more cattle and bigger houses with vast lands to plough for food' (Raboteng). Yet the idealisation of the countryside stops short of the white farmers' fences. Even under the regime of a sympathetic boss, farmwork was about low wages and a 'sack of mealie meal'- 'we slept over the plank-beds with grey blankets, to earn 15 cents a day. Work from crack of dawn, eat porridge at 9:00, eat samp with a lot of water in it at 1:00 with white bones they called meat.' For some of the narrators, poverty on the farms was preferable to 'using machines' (Dumbuza), and the life of the 'rural area boy' (Raboteng) who had to tend cattle and goats was far better. But a 'woman was not allowed to go and work in big places or towns. Instead she had to look after her children and make sure the garden was neat and tidy' (Chala). Everyone commented on their thankless 'toil': 'we were working very hard and whites were sitting down watching us' (Nkosi).

In the cities, factory life was also punctuated by job reservation. 'Coloured' workers were seen to be both better workers and better trainees. Invariably on each shopfloor whites and Indians would be the people in constant mobility and promotion. 'If you are an African,' Cele asserts, 'you were automatically an operator, an Indian would become a supervisor from the time he joined the company. If you were a white you just automatically became a manager of some kind without qualifications'. In the KwaZulu Administration as well, 'regardless of qualifications a white man started as a senior clerk'. Everywhere race was a defining experience.

According to Masango, 'the bosses always made a point to use indunas or African supervisors as oppressors because they were promised increases and good working conditions.' Already there is a growing literature about how custom and tradition was used to rule people at work, but the usage of customary categories as indices and confirmations of being ruled, needs more emphasis. As Masango recollects: 'when I was working at Jacobs, there was one foreman, Mr James, a young man, every time he paid us, he would ask one African man to sing an African song before we got our pay! Can you believe it? He never asked any white person to sing when they collected their wages, to sing for his money! I always resisted so badly, he hated me so much that he tried on many occasions to fire me and told the bosses that I was rude with the whites.'

Related to race in ordinary experience was the demonstrableness of power: arbitrary dismissals, 'treatment like dogs,' demands for 'blind obedience'. But in each factory power was administered and distributed through a style of managerialism which was based on a colonial matrix: the induna system. This experience of tribal controls ranged from actual chiefs like Mngadi at Dunlops in the '50s (Mcanyana) to a paid system of management functionaries. In most accounts it was less the common tradition and authority that was highlighted but the issues of surveillance and control as the izinduna 'had to watch us in each and every step we took, it was even difficult to talk to the person next to you.'

This sense of an incarcerated experience of race, with its job grading hierarchies and humiliations, and exclusion of African people from industrial relations because as 'tribal people' they needed customary forms of representation and control, marked most responses to industrial life. Race mattered, shaping feelings, understandings and later ground-swells of discontent.

Many found their foothold at first in the city as domestic servants and toed their way into the growing industrial plants of Durban. Very little of that experience was described positively. The usual words are 'prison', 'privation', 'hell'. Everyday in front of the machines and under racist supervisors was a 'loss of dignity'. But it was also a turning of people into 'things', instruments', 'machines', 'kaffir pumps' - 'working like a machine whilst you are a human being,... the hardship of receiving and passing a product or material from the machine, with its pace, as the iron machine cannot get tired.' 'We were black instruments and not people' (Bhengu). There is a tiredness and weariness in the older workers after a life of functional effort, but a disbelief in the younger ones that their future will always be like this: 'machines working other machines'.

By the late 1960s and 70s African women began sharing this experience primarily in the clothing industry, but as the years rolled on in the metal and electrical trades as well. Beauty Mahlaba started from the clothing factories 'where all the white people were machinists and we as blacks were cleaners. Then blacks (male) were given a better position – machinists – but women still made tea'. By the time she left, in the early 1970s, black women moved to take over as machinists as the rest moved one category upwards. This according to male workers was not without its sexual pressures, as they 'were finding it hard to get jobs because before they were employed they had to sleep with the bosses and managers' (Nene). Beauty Maningi moved straight into machining and welding but 'because of gender discrimination I was paid half of my fellow male machine operators' wages ... there were no safety and protective measures which had to guide the behaviour of the fellow machine operators during the performance of this dangerous work ... many of us developed chest pains because of that coating powder... I was working as a welder operating machines, but I was not paid well. I was doing a man's work but I was not paid the same salary as a man, despite the fact we produced the same amount of work.'

By the 1980s employers could pick and chose. Raboteng, a product of the 1970s and the education struggles that wracked South Africa, entered textile work at Frame's, the largest employer in KZN. 'We were told that only matriculants would be employed. Fortunately I had what they wanted for entrance. The expectations were too high since matriculants were the only ones allowed. But we were devastated when they offered us labour jobs. My supervisor was illiterate. You can imagine – a blind man leading someone who can see!'

One of the commonest themes centred around wages, *asinamali?* – the lack of money. Beauty Mahlaba started factory work in the late sixties at Buffalo Salt earning

R2.30 a week. Mr Phakhathi earned R3.00 on a banana plantation for an Indian boss. Then, according to Mahlaba men had women ploughing the fields. By the 1970s he was earning R50 a month as a bus conductor. By the 1980s, Beauty was earning R150 per month and he was earning R170 per week. By the 1990s she was earning R400 per month and he was earning R300 a week as a welder. For both: 'peanuts'. Dumbuza remembers that in the '60s factories paid R6 to R12 a week. In the 1970s on the farms it was R15 to R30 per month, whilst at factories it varied from R10 to R20 a week. In the eighties on the farms it was R60 to R300 a month. In the nineties, the factories paid R120 to R800 per week. The consensus was that they survived by helping each other. They also noted how wages started climbing after the Soweto uprising in 1976. In short, being short-changed, exploited, taken advantage of featured strongly in every narrative.

Life in the urban areas was marked too by people's living spaces and arrangements – either by the location or the hostel. For example, according to Ntshengeza, who lived in the first squatter settlement of the 1950s, 'I was born at Mkhumbane where the kwela-kwela was always roaming about from Bank Road to Esinyameni. There were robbers hid there, there were prostitutes, killers, famous musicians, shebeen queens, gangsters and hawkers, and that is why police always frequented the place. Everyday people were being arrested for failing to produce passes and permits on demand. There also, our mothers were brewing traditional beer... There was also those who planted and sold marijuana'. And over beer brewing and the attempts to crush it by Durban's authorities one saw the explosion of women's anger. There were policemen killed, and residents killed and assaulted. By the late 1950s, the squatter areas were major centres of struggle against urban white authority.

By the early 1960s the 'spirit' of Mkumbane, the sprawling urban settlement that defied authority, was broken and people were relocated in the new apartheid townships of Umlazi and KwaMashu. The new, hybrid cultures and forms of interaction that were spawned in the settlement were replaced by regimented forms of life in the new functional and regulated townships. In the meantime the hostels of KwaDabeka and Kranzkloof near the textile mills of Pinetown, the Umlazi and KwaMashu hostels, and others became the home of tens of thousands of recent migrants, both men and women entering the growing industries of the 1960s.

Living arrangements were poor, but nevertheless after hours there was always the perennial competition between the cross and the bottle – whereas the church taught 'you could not touch blood' (Makhoba), the shebeen spilt it liberally. At the same time, within the walls of the urban homesteads, the shebeens and the few church-halls, almost in defiance of the poverty around them, emerged a profound and vibrant 'musicality'. Many of the songs were nuggets of experience, ciphers of resistance, coping mechanisms and also a celebration of extraordinary feats. Bhengu remembers how the strains of '*Thoko ujola mobani*' rose alongside underground and illegal feelings, as people burst into '*Tambo sithwele kanzima*'. These forms interacted freely, remembers Njenje, with the more rural songs of peace, reconciliation and responsibility. Mpungose describes how 'we spent our leisure hours by singing and dancing in those years. We were unhappy or grieved, singing was the only solution to our problems'. In the hostels, '*isicathamyia*' and in the halls, Zulu dance groups proliferated (Khanyile). These collective forms of singing, with their call and response codas and their participatory nature, enhanced the solidarity of poor black communities in the nooks and crannies of the city.

Further north a younger generation started learning from cassette technology too: 'we played our music. One would hear the sweet melodies by Miriam Makeba, Hugh Masekela, Bob Marley and others on those mountains of Mahlabatini. An outsider would be surprised to find out that under those asbestos roofs there was a lot of political debates which could only be interrupted by the sight of a stranger.'

There is a need to understand how the past with its irreducible constellations interacted with the urban milieu, its experiences and tensions and finally how both interacted with the experiences of conflict and militancy in the 1970s and 1980s. It is there that one will 'discover' the normative orientations and values that make movements the radical challenges they often are.

Struggled lives

'Somebody started a song,' Martha Sithole remembers, 'and then everything happened.' She is referring to the Durban strikes of 1973 that saw 60 000 or more workers downing tools and pouring into the streets of Durban and Pinetown to launch the new period of movements, trade unions and anti-Apartheid struggles. Sithole, a textile worker from Durban's mills, switched off her loom in January 1973 and joined the thousands of other women who streamed into the yard. The 'surge' was imitated by the women in the mill next door; this in turn spread to the mill further down the road. These were to be the initial ripples that turned into a strike-wave, better known as the Durban strikes, which announced the re-emergence of black militancy and democratic trade unionism. Sithole's memory is simple: 'somebody started a song and then ... everything happened!' This though is a *profound* simplicity. It can be retold as somebody, drawing from a unique cultural formation with its traditions and Zulu symbolism, striking up a song and as the call and response style demanded, people responded by singing back and switching off their machines.

Madlala describes how he found himself on the streets during the first few days of his thirteenth job. As part of an excitable crowd in 1973 he witnessed how 'workers united, spoke and planned together' throughout the strike-wave. Indeed his story is typical of black workers in Durban: the general strike poured thousands of workers into Durban's streets who demanded higher wages, better treatment, new conditions. Some marched, chanted and ran back to work; others ran to the emerging trade unions. The new democratic trade unions that were being formed in tandem grew between 1973–5 and then, facing opposition, bannings, harassment and intransigent managements, they shrank. It was only in the post 1980s period, that a second wave of unionisation turned them into the mass organisations we know today.

Trade unionism emerged from somewhere between the efforts of a committed leadership of organisers, white and black, and ordinary black workers' self-activity. What appears now as the actions of a small group of activists or a spontaneous explosion of militancy, involved slow, pain-staking work, and thousands of complications. The role of white intellectuals has been referred to often enough in the literature (Maree 1985; Friedman 1987).

Their impact on the grassroots was remarkable even a decade later: 'we are still surviving today because of that girl (Pat Horn) who put us under the union COSATU' (Hlongwane). The names of Erwin, Schreiner and many others are mentioned by a number of workers as examples of white commitment to the organisation of workers; so are the names of dozens of black grassroots leaders, shop-stewards from other factories, cultural workers like Qabula and ANC/SACP leaders including Harry Gwala.

There is a danger in any overarching narrative that complexity might be lost. Dambuza for example recollects how 'they' (the bosses) were 'casting an eye on my movements around the place of work...' Outside of the factory gates, policemen followed him. 'I was always praying, and hoping that one day the union would come.' But after a while, when this 'force' did not come, he took his own initiatives. He found the union offices and asked the organisers to start working on his factory.

Once rooted there, rumours of organisation spread rapidly through the 'hostel system.' They used to meet and teach each other songs, he recollected. and later. Many also formed cultural organisations, but he laments that they 'had no women to show our culture or expose our talents to!'

Unionisation was a complex process involving thousands of personal and collective initiatives. Jwara, like Dambuza, decided to sacrifice everything to the process. He joined the metalworkers union, MAWU, in the early 1980s after a period of frustration with a general workers' union. He became a shop-steward until his dismissal in the early 1990s and for him the union became his *mission*: 'I learnt that no matter how hard it is, (the struggle) is your life. But you need to stand up for truth and your comrades. Even apartheid was fought through togetherness and through being prepared to die.' And die he almost did as he was stabbed and left for dead by Inkatha-based vigilantes after a nightshift at the Umlazi station. Although the violence and its hardships will be discussed later, it is important to mention how dangerous it was to be 'standing up' throughout the 1980s. For Jwara this increased his resolve and he managed to be influential in the organisation of the Mobeni/Jacobs industrial areas and to spread his work near his home in Umlazi: 'I got experience of how to handle and direct illegal strikes. In the '80s there were many rights to demand. As from the day of my employment in 1980 my best tool of resistance was winning more friends than enemies in the place of work. That I achieved before I could even become a unionist. The shopfloor was the foundation of our struggle. I was labelled as a trouble maker.'

Madlala only joined the union (the Chemical Workers Industrial Union) in 1984 after a lot of 'pestering' by Charles Ngema, a shopfloor leader turned organiser. But for him, joining the trade union was not a solution, rather it was the *beginning* of his problems. He was victimised at work, blamed for workers' resistance around overtime conditions and followed by company spies. He also claims to have been 'sold out' to the Security Police, who beat him up and abused him after hours. His problems, like Jwara's, multiplied as Inkatha supporters started flexing their muscles and pointing their spears in the townships – he had to flee his home in 1986.

Whereas hundreds of Jwaras, Madlalas, Dambuzas and Ngemas were working away consolidating union power in Durban, the heartland of the 1973 strikes, Pinetown with its tens of thousands of textile workers experienced similar trends after a major union defeat in 1981 at the largest textile producer, Frame. The strike, which brought about division in worker ranks and caused the dismissal of many workers, 'seemed to be the beginning of the end.' Whilst the textile sector was in crisis, the Metal and Allied Workers' Union experienced a period of rapid expansion after 1982. Ronnie Coles recalled how 'comrade Willie Khanyile, Msibi and myself started to organise workers into MAWU in 1982/3. My feeling was that we must have a forum that would enable us to put our views forward. By the time I joined the union I had a hope that the exploitation situation was going to decrease or stop altogether, but there was that fear because even the unions were said to be illegal. They were said to be communist things. It was easy for the members to get arrested.'

Max Masango started as a textile worker only to find himself dismissed. It was, in his words, 'struggled lives, struggled times' as the textile bosses wanted to show who was boss. He joined the metalworkers' union drive through the networks of the area as union activity spread into township life as well. 'Though I got involved with the unions in 1985,' he recalls, 'the ground was well prepared by Max Xulu, the MAWU branch chair, Cyril Khawula, then our MAWU Pinetown Local secretary, Ronnie Coles, Joe Eckstein, Paulos Ngcobo (now the COSATU general secretary in the province) and Baba, then our local chair, invited me to catch up with this new and strange involvement I had landed myself in.' He also noted how crucial the trade union office was as a meeting, education and cultural centre and 'the clear-headedness and commitment of the 1970s union officials in Pinetown; from the union officials, people I found there who moulded me are the late Gordon Bailey and Ian Weir, both ex-MAWU organisers, Pat Horn, Monde Mfeka (from the Transport and General Workers Union).' They, alongside an emerging shopsteward leadership, 'inspired me with their conversations regarding their dealings in the factories.' By 1989, Pinetown seemed to be the most organised in the greater Durban area.

The difficulties in organising the public sector were greater still; from all accounts whether it was working in the Departments of National, Provincial and/or KwaZulu Government, worker leaders 'had to do things underground at times. We had house meetings and for mass meetings we used NEHAWU offices, mostly Justice Hall in town'. All of them concur that since the eighties all their efforts were 'about a living wage and how to fight for rights'. From the moment the song started to this day, hundreds of micro-initiatives and processes made sure that a shop-steward based movement emerged and strengthened in most factories.

For most, joining a trade union and struggling for rights was a tentative, cautious process; for many it was an act of pride as long as it was not in the public domain. Of course, there were the militant exceptions, ranging from women like Jabu Nkosi developing her own 'amazing spirit', from slow learning of how 'the union is not the key to all our problems' but that the 'union was its members' (Cele), to Ntuli who used to hide in the toilets each lunch-time to avoid being recruited and having to say 'no'. Some like Madlala, had a 'feeling of fear'. Ntuli was 'searching for a mouthpiece'. Shabalala was part of a strong oral culture in the north and was 'always waiting for the opportunity of becoming a member of the union. To me it was a blessing. My heart became white, like mountains under snow. It was as if I had reached the promised land, like the people of Israel.' In contrast, Ngubo heard from his father in the Underberg area that once again the 'amakomanisi' (communists) will take to the streets; all workers were using a cumulation of imagery from a symbolic granary of their pasts.

For an urban matriculant like Raboteng trade unionism was a sobering and alienating experience, 'first of all, I was sure that nothing was to make me lose my job. Secondly, I was never going to be led by someone who was illiterate. Instead it was me who was to lead, but I didn't bear in mind that I lacked experience. Thirdly, I told myself that the time of earning peanuts was over. Fourthly, I committed myself in everything comrades did, in order to be free from bad conditions at work.' For Shabalala, the 'promised land' led to suffering: he was shot through the head and miraculously survived. He also lost his job. Raboteng lost his job too, but before that, he lost his 'pride': inter-union rivalry turned into lack of trust for trade unionism.

Cele recalls how in 1975 he was employed at the Mondi papermill: 'In that factory I was teaching the whites who were called the fitters. Whilst I was teaching the work they were highly paid, much more than myself. What worried me mostly was the coming of the Portuguese running away from Mozambique, who knew nothing. I also taught them the work. I already had an idea of their attitude and treatment of people of our stature. That is where we found that Madlala had unions but there was one inside the factory which was a 'sweetheart union'. We had to fight to create real, democratic trade unions, accountable to us. For that, we had to suffer'. So did Qabula:

'participating in the struggles of 1984 brought me difficulties within my workplace and where I lived at eMawoti. But because I was sure of what I was doing, arrests and rough treatment by the police meant nothing to me. Instead, it gave me a reason to carry on. I was also encouraged to gain more members for the UDF. This also made me a very big antagonist to the members of other parties. They mentioned that if I wasn't killed, things were going to be worse at eMawoti. In those struggles I lost my best friend, comrade Toto Dweba, from Ntuzuma who was a Transkeiian by birth. After his death, it was difficult to get him buried here in South Africa. To send his body to Transkei was also difficult without a passport. We finally buried him in Transkei under the hard supervision of Mathanzima's police.

Nzuza explains that 'after we had joined the union, it was never easy for an employer to fire a worker. If they tried to, we used to go on strike with our shop steward. These strikes were not easily defeated.' He concedes that sometimes in the 1980s the 'employers would end up firing everybody,' but by then the summary dismissals of the 1970s had receded.

Alongside their everyday frictions on the shopfloor there were also the pressures of the township as Inkatha was flexing its muscles, recruiting members by force after 1985: 'one day in my residential area we were forced to join Inkatha. We refused and we were attacked by their members. Some were killed and others lost all of their property in fires. We ran away to other areas and the same thing happened. Up to now I have been renting a back room in a white man's yard.' From then on, the majority of worker leaders were forced into perpetual exile.

For Cele hardships began in the 1980s: 'things started changing when FOSATU changed to COSATU. This caused Inkatha to take part and said that COSATU was not good, they were accused of being with the ANC. Inkatha said that all the Zulu people should not join and those that have joined COSATU should resign and join the other union which was formed by the Zulu people and Zulu government. They did not succeed because there were few people who joined them. I was also a member of Inkatha and we said that we must work together with the ANC as we thought they were together, and that is how people started hating us.' Indeed Inkatha's most devastating mistake was to disrespect the value ordinary workers placed in their organisations. By creating an either/or situation in Natal, it forced people to defend their organisational gains. Once this was seen as resistance to Inkatha's aims, it was assumed to be an ANC stance. Whereas Inkatha was taking control of the streets, unions grew despite the violence hostile to their actions.

Ncayana was horrified by some of the forms of indiscipline and violence which were the direct consequence of their struggles. 'Late in the '80s people could burn each other with a tyre. The children could play around corpses, which did not happen in the past. They could kill a child or a woman. I grew up in a place of faction fights in the uMkomaas ... But it was never, never like this'.

The lessons they drew through these harsh years were two: on the one hand, patience was 'the mother of success' (Nester), on the other, they learnt to balance 'militancy and negotiation.' 'The more I attended the meetings,' reflected Bhengu,

the better it got. I became wiser and stronger. I looked at things differently. I learnt about the importance of unity for workers. I preached the gospel of unity. The more we were unified the better feelings I had. I felt that I was contributing. That made me feel better. Step by step the enemy no. 1 of human nature – 'fear' – was running away. I could hear some of my colleagues confiding in me. This in itself kept me searching for more about myself. I found myself committed in through practice all the time. The time for relaxation in the shebeens with a beer was no more. When it happened that I could visit the place, it was with a different feeling and aim. I was to preach the same gospel of unity and the need to fight for our rights. The stronger I became the best feeling I experienced, but even then I still could ask myself, 'why necessarily me?' More leaders were produced. I noticed that I was still I not alone. My first worker leader was always there. He was always ready to sacrifice. He was even prepared to die in saying and in practice in front of the enemy. He was so encouraging. I grew from strength to strength. The harder we worked the stronger I became. The rock of trust was cemented. We spoke in one language and in one voice. The enemy was isolated and we were one big strong family in harmony.

The religious fervour, the 'gospel', 'preaching', 'unity' and 'harmony' intermingled with an older Zulu imagery of militancy. Jwara's experience was similar, but such 'family' and 'harmony' implied the loss of all that at home:

I will be doing a bad thing if I failed to stress that in all my struggles I was never alone. This was the beginning of a serious struggle, from the struggle of Soweto in 1976, which escalated all over the country. Every province was vibrating with strikes, resistance and struggle. In my views, there is not even one black who was not a victim of apartheid. When I sometimes talked to other people, they never wanted to listen to me and say I am too forward and will end up in jail one day. All those things never hindered me from preaching the gospel of struggle for I knew that one day we would be free. Police were always harassing us whoever we were. The state laid a law stating that if there were two or more black people seen chatting, they were to be arrested. So whenever we saw the police approaching, we had to scatter all over the place and when they passed us, we gathered together again. So that's the kind of life we lived. I had to sacrifice myself more for the people who suffered than for my family and quarrelled a lot with my wife. I didn't blame her for being angry with me.

The communities of care that emerged, the networks of comradeship were real and manifold. Although not all households responded like Jwara's, the strains on the home proliferated. And so did friendships that were developed out of the trade union and political meetings of the area; also, reference groups and resource groups proliferated, creating an intricate web of co-dependencies.

The militancy of the 1980s was based on the solid foundations of the 1970s as Hlongwane remembers, 'by the time we started joining the union the special branch police were there. They took Mr Mnyandu and they hit him until he lost his mental capacity and then he was taken to Pietermaritzburg to be treated.' 'Workers got arrested,' confirmed Duma, 'if talking about politics, the police was after us.' Initially the confrontation was small scale, but as the confidence grew so did the determination: 'we struck for eight weeks for a living wage' and 'we did all this for negotiation purposes, for our unions to be registered, as well as the release of those who were in prison'.

Gcwabaza remembers how it all started for him in 1984 – the strike at Dunlops. 'The employers did not consider the recognition agreement. The workers were angry and began to strike. The employers translated the strike as illegal. The strike took four weeks. They dismissed us and our money was withdrawn from the bank and paid over to 'new' employees. Our sister companies like Slazenger and Dunlop Pillow supported us. There were countrywide strikes then. I contributed to those struggles although I was politically neutral then. Later the employers decided to recognise the union, not because they liked it but because they wanted a well-channelled way to negotiate or even tame the defeated leaders and the workers. They thought that this would also stop disturbing productivity.' For many the Dunlop strike was a turning point in the militancy of black workers in KwaZulu Natal. Not only was it the first trial of strength (Sitas 1984) but it was also the first to mobilise direct action by workers all over South Africa, especially in Dunlop subsidiaries and linked to community support, cultural initiatives and defiance of existing legislation. That they won their demands sent a message throughout the industrial areas that were soon to be experiencing a variety of strike waves.

Beauty Mahlaba's experiences throw light on the 1980s and the implications and burdens of grassroots leadership. While Mthethwa, Gcwabaza's strike leader and Dunlop co-worker, became the chair of COSATU in KZN, Beauty became his vice-chairperson. 'I joined the resistance,' she states, 'while staying in Lamontville. I remember the time of Msizi Dube when the situation was very tense as we were fighting for our communal rights. I fled to Chesterville but continued with resistance until I was elected as the regional vice-chairperson of COSATU. I was the first female person to hold that position. I was also a member of the United Democratic Front. We were also under the attack of Inkatha, the South African Police and the KwaZulu police. Between 1989-1993 I could not stay in one area but kept changing places.' She has settled in a squatter camp close to a hostel. Her writings and performances speak volumes of that experience of burnings, shootings and violence. Finally, dismissed from work, she became active in the Self-Employed Women's Union and runs a little sewing co-op.

'We were not there for fame or praise,' adds Bhengu. But the suffering has been extensive. 'I am still hiding. As a unionist I had to sacrifice any friendship with management for the sake of the truth. I was transferred from office to office. The councillors (who were IFP leaders) became my enemies ... They claimed that I was dangerous and I was about to organise the comrades from the place nearby the hostel called Uganda against Unit T. I was transferred. There, another councillor. He started to verbally intimidate me.' Then in broad daylight, by the Umlazi station, he was surrounded by councillors and hit squad members and was shot. He lived despite the seventeen bullets that entered his body.

For Hlabisa the lasting memory is one of 'teargas and how the police used to disperse us'; Zungu agrees and adds that, 'in our struggle the benefits were meagre, but others might benefit from them.' Russell Hadebe adds his log to the fire: 'Zulu police were just the servants of Inkatha as they sided with them. You could not oppose anything at these times, if you did not side with Inkatha or the councils, you were an obvious enemy of the Zulu police.' Khehla Makhaye felt similar forms of oppression: 'I had a tuckshop at Inanda. To make it official I approached the councillors at Inanda. ... Whilst we were talking, a woman came in crying and shouting that she had been intimidated by one of the councillors. She was asked – why can't you have sex with him? – and they all laughed. Mr Rogers wrote me a letter and said I won't be arrested anymore. Soon I was verbally informed that I was going to be attacked. I had to leave the place. Most of the time my life has been in danger.' According to Mpungose, 'we were harassed by the police without any valid reasons. We also experienced intimidation at our work places. We were victimised by the employers themselves ...'

Gasa attempts to sum up those years with some passion. 'Here I can refer to things like heroism in the struggle for human rights, fighting for our land taken by the Boers with cattle, demands for living wages and to strive and die for truth and what you are doing to be successful'. According to Mncube all this 'perseverance' was stirred by 'our brothers and sisters' who died. In the process there were lessons: Thombi Zulu, as a woman, learnt the lesson of 'struggle of tolerance in the community.' Others like Njenje were too scared to lose their job. For Gcwabaza, 'we need to respect the cultures of all the people. That I am a Zulu must not be a problem for anyone.'

To speak of a clear, 'boxed' consciousness that permeates the feelings of black workers in KZN might be desirable for sociologists and ethnographers. To speak of 'difference', 'multiple identities', 'complexity' will be equally pleasing to many postmodem theorists. But this would belie the moral core of this movement and the deep sense of horizontal solidarity that characterises it. Within such a solidarity the themes of Zuluness and Christianity persist in a variety of combinations, cf. Gcwabaza's dictum that 'Christianity was not good for me ... ' and his, 'that I am a Zulu must not be a problem for anyone', with the fact that he is intimately linked with people in both aspects. He has no problem with being a comrade of Zungu for whom 'Christianity was part of the unions because they are both fighting for human and social rights'; it does not perturb him that he should pray in all union gatherings. Nor does it stop him being a comrade with Nafthali Mathiwane, his retired co-worker, cultural activist and Moslem. They are all bound by a deeper moral core and solidarity.

This solidarity also accommodates both Mabeyakhulu's claim that 'women should be paid the same as men if they are doing the same work' and Jabu's claim that 'men will always control women and women will always listen to men'. It is elastic enough to include Gcwabaza's claim that 'there are traditionally things that we need to discuss privately as men before we can even tell our women. This does not mean gender discrimination.' as well as Nester's 'equality in everything, by everyone in the lives of God.' It even accommodates a variety of beliefs around white management: Nkosi rejects their styles and initiatives when she says that 'whites are sitting down doing nothing' while Chala is convinced that the tide has turned: 'the employers' attitudes have changed ... there is more concern on the working shopfloor.' It accommodates traditionalism too, with Jwara's declaration that 'there was nothing wrong with our religion' and that 'the missionaries were sent to soften us so that we did not resist or hit back ... whatever the Bible says will happen and change will come through hardship'. Bhengu synthesises: 'let our children respect our roots. The strength of any tree is its roots.'

What are the parameters then, and what is the moral core of this movement? It is about a new reciprocity which was learnt through *umzabalazo*, struggle. It is, according to Jwara, very difficult to define, more complex than kinship or ethnicity, yet something that will endure: 'the struggle will never end before the world comes to an end because there is always going to be greediness, jealousy and superiority and power.' If it is not religion or ethnicity as such, but ethnic and religious elements proliferate in its definition; if it is not exactly about class in general ('many workers are not comrades') or about race in particular ('many blacks are confused and part of the system'; whites and Indians can be comrades but they need new souls'), then what holds the movement together? Being a comrade, a part of the 'us' means at least two things: a way of behaving and interacting with others, and a way of speaking about the world. Although all the designations above are available for recruitment in the forms of language and behaviour, the word *umzabalazo* seems to be the qualifying authority for comradeship. This allows 'you to call others brother and sister and when they talk, to understand where they belong.'

This sense is also future-looking and cautiously optimistic. To quote Cele: 'I have discovered that there is no day that passes without me knowing and without remembering that I am exploited and that I am coming from a community that is oppressed.

What you need to do,' he comments, 'is to pose questions. We must problematise things for workers in order that they solve their problems. If I may refer to education, our education had been a kind of domestic education ... so that at the end of the day they had the animal they wanted to have. We need to be critical and teach people what is relevant to them.' He advocates the study of the workplace and the 'design of our own machines and instruments and to share our own experiences. Maybe we can end up with answers to the questions.' Cele's 'lessons' are echoed by many others. 'I think the workers should own the industry because they are the people who are producing everything.' 'We need,' adds Qabula, to leave our societies 'run by fear and find something new'. Others advocate partnerships with employers, while many share none of the visionary hopes but rather, instrumentally, want to earn as much a possible. All of them, though, share with Jwara a sense of belonging, harnessed through *umzabalazo* and its multiple solidarities.

Sharing experiences, collectively exploring the new and learning is a theme Jwara elaborates on with didactic force: 'do not dictate to others because you might be wrong and it might be easy to rectify your mistakes. Do not allow yourself to be used. Try to negotiate peacefully but accept mistakes. Do not take things for granted. Be patient. Do not allow people to exploit you... we are used to those who think we do not see them. Let us in COSATU do as we were doing in FOSATU. Allow our unions to be controlled by workers and not organisers as it is now.' Nester Luthuli agrees: 'We are to think of the future and to concentrate on the past, but to know this for future references. In the struggle I learnt to respect, to keep the past, and to face our living standards but not concentrate on useless things that do not build, but destroy'. The narrations here point to some profound conclusions. These are the voices of a crucial politico-cultural leadership in organisations that cater for over 200 000 members in KZN and these voices span age, gender and sectoral divides. It is remarkable how the discourses produced highlight within this comradeship a class and racial distinctiveness with clear unambiguous tones. The word *abasebenzi* (workers) denotes layers of meaning and pride. Simultaneously the class sense and experience is bounded by feelings of racial oppression. But although 'bounded' by it, it does not express the central project embedded in their narrations – that they are building a nation. This slippage from race to nation and back, and its co-existence with a class perspective makes and has made for a volatile challenge to any status quo. In the words of Mbonambi: 'we did bring down the monster to eye-level and chased it away, didn't we?'

Notes

— This text is part of a lengthier manuscript: a grassroots sociology of the trade union movement between 1985–1995, the first decade of COSATU's existence in

KZN, by eighteen workers for whom writing had become a habit by the 1990s; and, through them the recording of another 108 voices and testimonies by co-workers in their immediate environments. This analytical paper attempts to achieve two things: firstly, it brings to discussion insights gleaned from a qualitative exploration of experience and consciousness. Secondly, it attempts to bring to voice the main themes of the research and writing process, for debate and discussion within the trade union movement.

References

Abrahams, L. (1987). Letter to the Editor, *Weekly Mail*, April.

Bonnin, D. (1987). 'Class Consciousness and Conflict in the Natal Midlands: The Case Study of BTR Sarmcol Workers', MA thesis, University of Natal, Durban.

Bourdieu, P. (1989). *Distinction*, London: Routledge and Kegan Paul.

Cronin, J. (1987). 'New Poets Rising', *Weekly Mail*, April.

Friedman, S. (1987). *Building Tomorrow, Today – African Workers in Trade Unions*, Johannesburg: Ravan Press.

Junction Avenue Theatre Company, (1995). *Up the Junction*, Johannesburg: Witwatersrand University Press.

Kromberg, S. (1993). 'A Study of Worker Poetry in Natal', MA dissertation, University of the Witwatersrand.

Maree, J. (1985). 'Democracy and Oligarchy in South Africa's Independent Trade Unions', PhD thesis, University of Cape Town.

Moore Jr, B. (1967). *The Social Origins of Dictatorship and Democracy*, Boston: Beacon Press.

Orkin, M. (1992). *The Theatre and the State in South Africa*, Johannesburg: Witwatersrand University Press.

Qabula, A. (1984). Interview, *South African Labour Bulletin*, April.

Qabula, A. (1991). *A Working Life – Cruel Beyond Belief*, NUMSA 7, Culture and Working Life Project, Durban.

Shabalala, N.M. et al (1991). *The Man Who Could Fly and Other Worker Stories and Poems*, The Culture and Working Life Project, Durban.

Sitas, A. (1984). 'African Worker Responses on the East Rand to Changes in South Africa's Metalworks, 1960-1980s', PhD thesis, University of the Witwatersrand.

Sitas, A. (1990). 'The Making of the Comrades Movement', *Journal of Southern African Studies*, Winter.

Sitas, A. (1995). 'Neither Gold Nor Bile: Industrial and Labour Studies and Socio-Economic Transformation in KwaZulu Natal', Inaugural Lecture, University of Natal.

Sitas, A. (forthcoming). *The Flight of the Gwala-Gwala Bird: Essays on Politics, Culture and Labour in Natal*, Madiba Press.

Skopcol, T. (1979). *States and Revolution*, New York: Cambridge University Press.

Tilly, C. (1979). *From Mobilisation to Revolution*, Reading: Addison-Wesley.

Touraine, A. (1981). *The Voice and the Eye: An Analysis of Social Movements*, Cambridge: Cambridge University Press.

CHAPTER TWELVE

Have culture, will travel

Rehana Ebr.-Vally

786
Bismillahir Rahmanir raheem
In the Name of Allah, the Most Kind, the Most Merciful

The N1 highway connects the two cities of Pretoria and Johannesburg in the Gauteng province in South Africa. Popularly regarded as the busiest route in South Africa, this stretch of highway (±60 km) is reputed to carry an average of 120 000 cars per hour during peak hours (and increasing). This represents a substantial increase in the number of users of this route between Pretoria and Johannesburg, for this highway was initially built to carry a maximum of 100 000 cars per hour. Not only are these two cities part of the most affluent province, but they are also home to core governmental, business and financial institutions.

In the imagination of many people in and beyond South Africa, these two cities assume an almost mythical importance in the affairs of the country. This reputation is in a way borne out by the fact that the traffic on the N1 highway illustrates the reality that these two cities live and feed off each other. Many people living in, or moving into, Gauteng choose or accept to live in one city and work in the other.

I am no exception to this. I too have made the choice to live in Pretoria and work in Johannesburg. The N1 highway, which is the shortest and fastest route between these two cities, has come to acquire a meaning other than that of the functionality of highway routes. To many, it has in some ways become an extension of their familiar home surroundings. It is becoming a part of a known and recognisable area to commuters who use it daily. How this comes about, forms the basis of this paper.

How do commuters appropriate the distance covered daily to make it recognisable and part of their environment? How do commuters succeed in 'owning' a stretch of highway whose fundamental function is to link two cities?

Let me begin by saying that the time commuters spend in moving from home to work or vice versa depends on the density of the traffic on the N1 highway. They could spend anything from thirty minutes to two hours or more depending on the number of vehicles and/or problems, like accidents and breakdowns. When traffic is dense and commuting becomes difficult, observing the surrounding areas or other vehicles become ways of breaking the monotony of the journey. An activity which can be done simultaneously to listening to the radio or conversing on the mobile phone.

Observing how other users negotiate difficulties on the highway by straddling lanes, reading the various bumper stickers, deciding to count the number of cars of a certain colour or make that pass by, become ways of making an otherwise impersonal and boring routine interesting. In doing this, not only have I succeeded in making the journey between these two cities interesting, but I have also noticed an emerging pattern which explains how different commuters use symbols and signs to drive and parade certain chosen aspects of their identity themselves.

The vehicle, an extension of the home

Cars have become more than just commodities used by individuals to travel to destinations. Aside from the marketing strategies used by manufacturers to sell their brand of cars, users today have their own ideas for the cars they drive. In addition to the cup holders, the comfortable and adjustable seats that wrap around the body, the purring of the engine that would not interfere with the sound system (which in many cars is a regular feature), the tinted windscreens or the sophisticated anti-theft devices, car owners can add features to personalise their vehicles. The choice of these additional features serve the purpose of transforming the car as a commodity into a unique car.

It is in this way that the car can become an extension of the home. Like the home made of brick, mortar, mud or wood, the car has a body made of steel or aluminium with room for a fixed number of users, an engine and wheels. In the home, the choice of colour and furniture, for example, serve both a utilitarian and an aesthetic function. How furniture and other objects are arranged express the inhabitant/s idea of comfort and aesthetics. The home is recognised by the owners and by others through its geographical location – address – and its decor. Moreover, the title deed entrenches the idea of the building belonging to someone.

Ownership of the car is strictly regulated by the state. At any moment, like for the house, ownership of the car should be determinable. The car registration number indicated on the numberplates as well as on the licence affixed to the windscreen represents accepted state regulations confirming ownership of the car. Thus, in a case where the driver is not the legal owner of the car, the onus of using the car in accordance with the prescribed rules of the road remain the legal responsibility of the legal owner. Like for the home, additional insurance becomes an added safety measure for car owners to negotiate their rights and/or obligations in situations of litigation. Paying of the annual licence fee can further be equated to paying rates and taxes by homeowners.

The car and the home are private properties, formally controlled by the state. While the purchase of the car and the home as personal possessions is determined by the amount of monies available to one, the use of these objects is subject to strict codes laid down by the state. Thus, where the state can determine whether an addition to a home is viable or not, organising the living space in terms of colour and décor for example is the right of the individual. Only in cases where the tastes or designs of an owner may infringe on the rights of a neighbour can the state be asked to mediate and resolve the issue. Again, this form of resolution would require strict adherence to principles and regulations forming part of state legislation.

Similarly, the car is subject to an array of rules and regulations conceived to allow all users the maximum advantages. In this way the legislation is a framework meant to ensure safe and convivial use of all public routes. In addition to the compulsory regulations regarding ownership, any modification to the car on a public route is controlled. This is done to allow each public route user equal and maximum benefit of the road.

Given the formal rules regulating the use of vehicles on a public route, how is it possible for individual vehicle owners to 'appropriate' the N1 highway?

To examine how car owners/drivers use the car as an extension of their home, requires us to reconsider the relationship person-car. The car as a mode of transport, to get from one point to another using the public routes specified for this purpose, is in our opinion constantly being reinvented. Increasingly in South Africa, the car is becoming an object of necessity: a fundamental item in the range of objects used by individuals. It, today, goes beyond being a luxury item, becoming a necessary object required for everyday life. Like the proverbial roof that is fundamental to a person's well being, transport is becoming fundamental to a person's livelihood. Thus, the car used in a public or private capacity fulfils an important aim in allowing people to travel to and from work and to other desired destinations. [1]

Landscape, carscape: democracy in motion

The numerical computation of numberplates is the method the authorities use in regulating the use of the car. The purchase of a car, new or second hand, carries an obligation to document who the owner is, or any change of ownership. While the number printed on the plates is to most people just a tag that differentiates between two identical cars, it nonetheless allows the state and other interested persons or parties to identify the car as the legal property of a person or an institution. To regulate ownership of vehicles through the use of numbers the licensing authorities, as part of the state bureaucratic institutions, are the only institutions authorised to allocate these numbers. Each allocated number is legally used for a single vehicle. In other words, no two vehicles can have identical numberplates.

Until the latter part of the 1990's, identification numbers followed a fixed pattern. The numbers were preceded by a series of either two or three letters. The letters indicated the town or city of the fixed domicile of the owner of the vehicle. Thus, TAZ 123 indicated the owner of the car was a resident of the town of Brits in the province of Transvaal, CA 456-323 was proof of the owner living in Cape Town, in the Cape Province and ND 456 321 that the owner was a resident of Durban in the then province of Natal. Car numberplates changed as often as the owners.

The introduction of computer generated numbers in the latter part of the 1970's allowed the Transvaal authorities to introduce a different method of car registration. The vehicle identification plates took on the following form – TBP 080 T – and no vowels were used. The three letters and the three numbers became the digits identifying the vehicle and the T indicated the province of Transvaal and made it almost impossible to know which town or city the vehicle came from. To emphasise their town/city of origin on an otherwise anonymous numberplate, many a parochial car owner from the Transvaal used bumper stickers with the symbol of their town or city.

Roughly twenty years after the introduction of provincial plates in the Transvaal, it became necessary to review the process, for two reasons.

1   The plates had reached the letter X and it meant that another system needed to be implemented soon.
2   The reconfiguration of the country into nine provinces also laid the erstwhile province of Transvaal to rest. Renamed Gauteng, the 'Transvaal' has become part of South Africa's apartheid memory and as such no longer finds a place in the democratic dispensation of the country.

The rearrangement of the South African landscape as part of the democratising process had a very direct and definite influence on local authorities in this country. To give credence and visibility to this democratic découpage of the South African territory meant that this socio-political and geographical reality is tangible and visible to all. To this extent the numberplates, because they are issued by the different local authorities within the provinces, become the visible carriers of democratic South Africa.

With South Africa now divided into nine provinces, cars from each of these provinces carry an alphabetical computation to indicate the relevant province. Vehicles from the province of Gauteng that inform this study carry the letters GP. Examples of this pattern are the Free State province, recognised by the letters 'FS', Mpumalanga is indicated by MP, the Northern province by an N, the Eastern Cape by the letters EC, or

North West by the letters NW. The common factor which signals a distinctive departure from the old system of numberplates as symbols of origin is the introduced uniformity. This uniformity manifests itself by the fact that all provinces now follow systems that closely resemble each other. Moreover, as will become evident in this paper, the introduction of personalised numberplates also acts as a feature to introduce high degrees of similarity between the nine provinces of South Africa.

All local authorities are responsible for the registration of vehicles at a prescribed fee. They are also responsible for the annual renewal of licences at a fee. In addition to this, local licensing authorities have now acquired the expertise to allow for two types of vehicle registration. The first type is a continuation of an existing form where owners registering their vehicles are given an aleatory number. The second type of registration introduces a new form in that it allows owners to choose their personal numbers and letters. It should be pointed out that the use of the facility to personalise numberplates is at a considerably higher cost. The personalised numberplates are more expensive for the initial registration and thereafter the set tariffs regulating the annual renewal of the licence apply.

The numberplates in present day South Africa have the same computational form. The identification aspects of the numberplate replicate the following pattern: the numberplate is divided into two distinct sections. The letters GP on the right stand for Gauteng Province. The left side of the numberplate can be regarded as the side of identification. On this side three letters, with the exception of vowels, are used and are followed by three numbers. Together they make up the personal allocated number of the vehicle. JNX 952 GP or CDM 654 NW are examples of numberplates illustrating this aspect.

In democratic South Africa, the motorised vehicle successfully represents the moving and tangible reality of the reconfiguration of the landscape and this even when plates are personalised.

Documenting and overseeing good neighbourliness

Where owners choose to use their personal letters and numbers, the format of the numberplate somewhat changes. To illustrate that the number complies with the formal requirements, the three numbers appear before the letters. Thus, numberplates 786 MSM GP, 007 JMB GP or 888 LCK FS would without doubt belong to a vehicle owner who opted to pay the extra fee attached to such numberplates. An interesting detail concerning personalised plates is the format used in KwaZulu Natal. In this province, individuals can decide to use only letters. Thus numberplates in KwaZulu Natal reflect names and other personal attributes that individuals choose as signs of distinction. It is consequently usual to see the following DOLLY ZN or CNP1 ZN or

PREM ZN or FAIZAL ZN.

Soon after 1 January 1997, entrepreneurs recognised a niche in setting up business acting as intermediaries between individuals and/or businesses and the Department of Transport. At a fee almost always included in the price these entrepreneurs would deal with the administrative requirements and deliver a finished product to their clients. This niche in the market probably came about as a result of the tedious procedure involved in obtaining Special Vehicle Registration Numbers.

The procedure is elaborate and as the Director of the Department of Transport and Public Works in Pretoria indicated, is *culture and religion sensitive.* This translates to all combinations for Special Vehicle Registration being subject to approval. The approval is given by a committee, which meets regularly to examine the combinations applied for. This committee made up of representatives from each of the official language groups and religious leaders, reserves the right to grant or refuse combinations applied for. In addition, this committee also has the right to veto numbers already allocated. The equivalent of the four letter word f*** in another language would theoretically be refused. But, should it slip through, the committee upon having received complaints from the public retains the prerogative to retract the combination. This right to retract a combination according to the Director, came to pass in the Western Province where the public complained about the combination STN 666 WP. The public apparently objected to the Satanist implications of the registration.

In reality, the application subject to the approval of the committee translates into time spent waiting. The private companies specialising in Special Vehicle Registration can be seen as able to gain time or short circuit the process. However, the Director was quite adamant in stating that the procedure for the intermediary company was the same as for the lay person. The argument is that since every Special Registration Number (SRN) is subject to approval, all applicants have to wait for the Committee to meet and review their applications. The Committee is made up of lay persons and meets upon sufficient demand. The fact that the introduction of Personalised Registration Numbers (PRN) in the Gauteng area is in its inception phase, explains why the Committee's meeting schedule is demand-driven.

The Committee's decisions are relayed to the applicant in writing. The Director was able to give me the terms of reference but was unable to indicate the size of the Committee. She nonetheless indicated that every official language group would be represented and this means that a polyglot could represent various linguistic concerns. She stated - as a fact - that the committee's mandate is to rule out all swear words in all languages as well as four-letter words and words that people from a religious or cultural perspective would find offensive. This applies to special numbers containing vowels and amounts to the committee acting as a watchdog to ensure that the choices made are as inoffensive as possible. The Gauteng Department of Transport and Public Works has inserted a clause of protection and equality for the people it represents.

Expecting a tremendous demand for Personalised/Special Registration Numbers, it issues these numbers under specific conditions. A form PRN1-GP needs to be filled out. The applicant indicates that s/he is applying for a PRN/SRN combination. Three choices of combination in order of preference are to be indicated. Depending on the availability, the committee would allocate a combination or refer it back. Should the applicant be successful, he/she has 21 days to submit payment. On payment, a certificate is issued indicating that the applicant is the registered user of the number. After the delivery of the certificate, the Traffic Administration will instruct the approved manufacturer to manufacture the set of numberplates. The manufacturer is to deliver these plates within 72 hours to the Traffic Administration. The applicant applies to have the numbers allocated to a vehicle licensed in his/her name at his/her appropriate registration authority (normally where he/she resides). As soon as the number is allocated to a vehicle and the motor vehicle is licensed, the registering authority will hand the set of registration plates to the user.

In the case of PRN plates, the set will consist of the plates and a replica thereof as a sticker. The sticker is affixed to the inside of the left bottom corner of the rear window. If the vehicle does not have a rear window or, if it is not transparent, the sticker is affixed as prescribed for a clearance certificate.

These measures are introduced to ensure – as far as possible – an equal chance for all. They are meant to rule out fraud and corruption where plates could be sold fraudulently. However, the Special Registration plates can be transferred to another vehicle belonging to the owner of the plates. This can be done upon payment of a R100.00 for an internal transfer (same owner, different vehicle). The rules do not mention the sale of the plates to another person, but it is possible to return the plates to the Traffic Department, in which case they would probably be returned to the pool of numbers available.

Understanding the market and the proliferation of requests for Special Vehicle Registration, intermediary companies began business well before the actual implementation of such legislation. In the case of the Plates Company, it advertised the Special Registration Plates as from 1 May 2000 which according to the Department of Transport and Public Works, came into operation on 26 June 2000. To date there are four companies operating in Pretoria of which the Plates Company exclusively operates on the Web.

The date of 1 May was presumably introduced to allow interested people to apply for personalised plates as well as have the possibility to perform an internal audit of the combinations applied for, thus avoiding embarrassment vis-à-vis their clients. Noting this, we have browsed the website of the Plates Company to extract information relevant to our purpose.

Excluding special combinations

Before the introduction of personalised numbers, the Gauteng Department of Transport and Public Works had already drawn up a list of numbers and alpha characters to be blocked. They are:

- Triple letters (e.g. BBB, CCC, DDD ... ZZZ) excluding AAA, GGG, ZZZ
- BMW, DKW, FRD, HND, KDT, LND, MBZ, MRC, MZD, NSN, PCS, SZK, and ZCC
- Triple figures (e.g. 000, 111, 222, 333 ...999)
- 090, 110, 130,140, 150, 160, 180, 200, 230, 240, 250, 260, 280, 300, 302, 306, 316, 318, 320, 323, 325, 335, 340, 341, 380, 405, 400, 420, 500, 525, 530, 540, 600, 601, 602, 605, 606, 626, 740, 750, 786, 850, 900, 944 and 960.

Blocking out these particular numbers and letters is interesting. They are in more ways than one linked to a vehicle. Either they indicate a vehicle brand as is the case with BMW, or the brand is inferred: e.g. HND could be either Honda or Hyundai; KDT= Kadett (Opel); MBZ= Mercedes Benz: MRC= Merc (abbreviation for Mercedes Benz); MZD= Mazda; FRD=Ford, PCS=Porsche or NSN= Nissan. An example of the numbers related to the vehicles or to the engine capacity of the vehicle:

1   200, 230, or 500 could refer to a specific engine capacity of Mercedes Benz.
2   316, 318, 525, 540, or 740 could refer to specific BMW vehicles
3   as a final example, the numbers 911, 928 or 944 together with the alpha PCS could be Porsche 918 or Porsche 944.

Categories of class / the price of vanity

Setting aside numerical and alpha characters and creating the possibility for indiviuals to invent their own combinations implies a particular reading of social stratification. It is aimed at individuals and businesses that desire to stand out. This the various Provincial authorities have grasped well and are eager to promote with the aim of generating revenue for the Provinces. The Gauteng Department of Transport and Public Works has introduced categories of Personalised Registration Numbers (PRNs) that allow interested parties to showcase the fact that they own numbers and/or alpha characters. From the type of PRN on a vehicle, it is possible to determine the amount a vehicle owner has spent.

These plates range from R400 to R1 900, while the cost for an ordinary registration is R50. In other words, a personalised plate in Gauteng could cost eight times more if the least expensive plate is purchased at R400.00 or thirty eight times the price of an ordinary registration if the most expensive plate is bought. Meaning that the auctioned price of certain names could be anything more than five thousand times R50, if the Western Province is used as a marker of what people are prepared to pay.

In the Western Province the prices for personalised registration numbers range from R1 500 to R50 000. From the fee structure for Special Vehicle Registration Numbers in the Western Province, we see two distinct categories emerging. They are the Personalised Registration Numbers and the Special Discreet Registration Numbers. For R50 000 with an annual fee of R500.00, the applicant can choose one alpha or numeric character e.g. 8-WP or Q-WP. Two alpha or numeric characters e.g. B2-WP would cost R25 000 (annual fee: R350) and three alpha or numeric characters (e.g. WIN-WP) R10 000 (annual fee: R200). All other combinations of alpha and numeric characters up to a maximum of six (e.g. PIERRE-WP) would set a person back for R1 500 with an annual fee of R200.

The discreet category prices range from R16 000 to R600. Under this category, interested persons are allowed to buy the alpha letters used under the old system to indicate cities and towns. For the sum of R16 000 (annual fee R350), a person can buy three letters and numbers e.g. CA 7. R8 000 buys four letters and figures (annual fee R300) e.g., CA 16 or CPT 7. For five letters and figures one needs to pay R4 000 (annual fee R250) e.g. CA 567 or CBS 89. The cheapest category is six letters and figures for R600 (annual fee R125) e.g. CDG 123 or CG 1232.

Upon the question why the province of Gauteng did not have a R50 000 category, I was informed that the Department of Transport and Public Works has the intention of auctioning certain names which are in great demand. The names BEETLE or PAJERO, for example, are in such demand that they have been blocked in Gauteng and are to be auctioned in the near future. The modalities need to be finalised.

The Gauteng Province also has both categories of Personalised and Special Vehicle Registration Numbers; the PRNs and the SRNs or Personalised Registration Numbers and Special Registration Numbers. They are markedly less expensive that their WP counterparts. They range from R400 to R1 900.

These represent the basic cost respectively to which is added a fee of R100.00 payable for allocation of personalised or 'special' number to a motor vehicle. I was told that the annual renewal fee is equal to that of a vehicle of the same calibre registered ordinarily.

To give an idea of the cost of the plates we cite examples of mid to low-income category earners in South Africa. R50 000 is what a mid-level state employee earns per annum and R24 000 is what a salesperson in South Africa earns per annum before tax. According to Census 1996, from a population of 40 million, 26% of employed people earn R500 per month or less, 62% of the employed earn less than R1501 per month and only 10% of the overall employed population earn more than R4500 per month.

The highest income bracket of R30 001 and more represents 0.2% of the population. Unemployment is at 34% for the country as a whole of which 42,5 % are African and 4,6% are White.

'Plates.co.za'; filling the niche

From the Internet site www.plates.co.za the system applicable to our question of numberplates is further explained. The Gauteng Province has blocked specific combinations at the initial introduction of GP numbers on 1 January 1997. These numbers form part of the Ordinary Registration Number (ORN) category. An ORN according to the definition on the plates site is 'a unique combination of 3 alpha and 3 numerical characters followed by the Provincial coat of arms and the suffix GP.' Meaning that the numbers blocked out can be purchased from the Plates company which has entered into an agreement with the Gauteng as well as the Western Province authorities and certain car manufacturers.

The second category of plates is the SRN or the Special Registration Number. For the moment the SRN plates are only available in the Gauteng Province. The SRN plates are a combination of 3 numeric and 3 alpha characters followed by the Provincial Coat of Arms and the suffix GP. Examples of these plates are 007 MAY – GP. They are the same price as the ORN plates and as of 1 May 2000 (a contentious date) alpha characters may include vowels.

The Personal Registration Number (PRN) category, to use cars as a measure of distinction would be the 'Rolls Royce' or the 'Porsche' of all plates. This category is the most expensive in Gauteng Province and comprises of 'a maximum of six alpha and/or numeric characters followed by the Provincial suffix'. Either the sentence is not clear or buyers of this plate could choose both six numbers and six letters thus making it twelve. Further, it would seem that the suffix GP is all that is required to indicate the Province of origin. For unlike the ORN and SRN categories, no mention is made of the Coat of Arms of the Gauteng Province.

The PRNs are advertised as plates that 'afford motorists the opportunity to use their numberplates to showcase their personalities, nicknames, brands or sense of humour'. This form of displaying one's nickname or sense of humour comes at a price of R2995.00 with the same regulatory annual fee of R295.00. Examples of PRNs 'showcased' on the net are BARBIE – GP, IXLR8- GP, NIKE- GP or MTN-GP. There is a mobile telephone number indicated for businesses interested in buying PRNs.

The appearance and visibility of these personalised numberplates has introduced a new vocabulary. They are the ORNs, SRNs, and the PRNs. They are also commonly referred to as vanity plates. From the marketing strategy on the Plates Internet site, we get a sense of why the choice of the colloquial use of the term 'vanity' is appropriate.

These perceptions of the use of personal plates are well understood when juxtaposed with dictionary definitions. The noun 'vanity' in the Chambers English Dictionary is defined as 'the quality of being vain: that which is vain'. The adjective vain in the same dictionary carries meanings of 'without real worth: futile: thoughtlessness: empty minded: pettily self-complacent: valuing oneself inordinately on some trivial personal distinction: futility.'[2] If we follow the dictionary definitions of vanity and vain, we get the sense that those who choose to use the personalised plates are either empty minded or prone to display an excessive self-image. Which at first glance can be interpreted as a class distinction where the fee paid for these plates can determine a person's class position.

The advertising strategy of the Plates Company emphasises the categories 'fun, personal and branded' as reasons for buying these plates. Appealing to ideas that persons have of affluence, wealth, humour or business, the company has perspicaciously chosen vehicles and other brands to advertise their product. The NIKE - GP plate is affixed to a Jeep and the MONTY plate to a BMW. The message created is 1) 'taming' the outdoors in a Jeep in NIKE accoutrements or 2) the ladies' man baring it all like in the film *The Full Monty* MONTY- WP.

The slogans used to advertise their products are closely related to specific brands, movie characters and personal and physical prowess. *Just do it, The Better Connection, Sheer Driving Pleasure, We Try Harder, Forever Young, The Full..., Wear your heart on your bumper* or *Bond. James Bond;* are examples of how the advertising campaign capitalises on and suggestively plays on selected subliminal desires and aspirations of people and future clients. Making their illustrations: 007, BARBIE, BOKKE, a phrase I DO (on the old Beetle) or MADIBA on the different plates is an astute method of capitalising on current vain, senseless or pointless fashionable ideas floating about.

Through the introduction of what is commonly known as vanity plates, the Gauteng and Western Province authorities have understood that vanity is a commodity that sells well. To the effect that they have succeeded in attaching figures to the vanity of increasing numbers of car owners by creating a spectrum of plates that emphasises their social class and standing in society.

The use of PRNs or SRNs became possible when the new system of GP plates was launched in Gauteng. The blocking of a specific range of characters demonstrates the Provincial authorities' understanding of the monetary value these predominantly vanity characters represent. In this way, sales initiatives specialising in the commercialisation of these numbers in the form of a package commenced and coincided with the introduction of the present system. Mr. Mbhazima Shilowa, the Premier of Gauteng was the first recipient of the Personalised Registration Numberplate. He chose LOWANI, the name of his ethnic group, so as 'not to upset his forefathers'. As Premier he urged residents of Gauteng to give vent to vanity and status symbols and purchase these numberplates. According to the Premier, the PRNs have the capacity to generate an additional income of R3,6 million for the Province. The money, he states, would be used for victims of car accidents, trauma centres and other welfare organisations.[3]

Phantasmagoria

The characters chosen in the various combinations appeal to a self-image a person wants to project. The list of blocked characters can be used to create combinations substantiating the vanity aspect of the numberplates. The one exception to this rule though, is the number '786', which is developed further down. The manner in which the Gauteng Provincial authority blocked characters endorses the idea that they closely scrutinised the Provincial market to ascertain which characters would be in demand and sell well. How did they choose these characters? How did they identify these characters? To answer this question, we examined a few examples. Character samples were chosen by the frequency of which they were observed on the N1 highway between Pretoria and Johannesburg and in the two cities. Where it was possible, I stopped motorists at service stations, at shopping malls, in parking bays, at mosques and sometimes fleetingly at red traffic lights and interviewed them about their choices of characters. Some were surprised, others rolled up their windows and some took the time to answer questions as diligently as possible.

1   The power of numbers

What do the combinations 786, 007, 888 or 001 have in common? We know from our observation that 1) they are numbers that have been blocked out by the Gauteng Provincial authority, 2) interested people are prepared to pay large sums of money to obtain ownership of these numbers in some way or the other, 3) they have some meaning for the buyer and 4) they are to be seen on our roads. In addition to this, we would argue that the choice of character combination can be interpreted as a bird's eye view of the buyer's/motorist's world. By affixing the PRN, SRN and ORN numberplates to the bumper of the vehicle, the motorist is sending a message to other road users. These messages carry the potential of being interpreted as vain, presumptuous, funny or sometimes serious.

2   The name is Bond. James Bond.

On the highway and in the cities of Pretoria and Johannesburg, I saw the following James Bond variations on personal numberplates: A yellow BMW

Z3 with the plate JMB 007-GP; BND 007-GP, JMZ 007-GP and a JMS 007-GP. The blocking of the combination 007 means that a few people are able to use the number matched with those letters that read James Bond. Others would have to be content with using the combination of 007 with other letters. Not being able to use the combination that automatically reads James Bond, many have chosen to use their initials or other letters they cherish, for example, VDW 007-GP or JFK 007-GP.

Ian Fleming's character is generally regarded as the most successful spy on the silver screen. His is a success story that those who carry his name on their bumpers emulate. James Bond has a licence to kill, oozes charm and is worldly wise to the extent of recognising the vintage and brand of brandy by a single sip. Women can't resist his charm! In short he is a modern day hero: the unrivalled master in the art of living and the science survival in any circumstance. He is admired and emulated to the extent that his '007 - licence to kill' number, affixed on vehicles as a licence plate, allows the 'Bond, James Bond' PRNs or SRNs to imagine their cars as the skin of 007, which they adorn every time they take the wheel.

3 Triple digits

Triple characters can be divided into the two categories of letters and numbers. However, insofar as the triple digits are used, I have noticed a predominance of 666, 777 and 888 over the others. These sets of numbers seem to carry a very special meaning for the users. We shall consider some of these independently.

4 666

The triple six, or six hundred and sixty six (666), is a palindromic number generally regarded by the larger public as the number of the devil. By flouting this number on personalised numberplates, the impression created is that owners of this number are Satanists, or just indulging in senseless humour to irritate other commuters. Commuters likely to be irritated by this popularly accepted display of Satanism are those who carry their religiosity on their cars. These can be in the form of symbols on bumper and rear windscreen stickers or prayer beads and other religious symbols dangling from the rear view mirror.

Yet this number, popularly interpreted as the number of Satan, forms part of the history of Christianity where it is regarded as the number of the Antichrist. It is the apocalyptic number, the number of the Beast. It is also the mystical number 666, spoken of in Revelations 13:18: '*This calls for wisdom: let him who has understanding reckon the number of the beast, for it is a human number, its number is 666'.*

Pope Clement V (1305-1314) was the first pontiff to adorn the triple crown with a frontal sash carrying the inscription *Vicarius Fili Dei* (Vicar Son of God). The enemies of papacy took the numerical values of the seven Latin letters contained in the inscription and came to a sum of 666. Since the Church prohibited the use of Arabic numerals, they used Roman Numerals instead (example I=1, V=5, X= 10, L=50, C=100, D= 500, M= 1000). In this way the pope, as *Vicarius Fili Dei,* was transformed into the Antichrist. The method used was to take the corresponding Roman numerals of *Vicarius Fili Dei* and add them to yield 666. The sum of 666 however is controversial, in that to some it should read 616.

Moreover, in the XVIth Century, Lambert Daneau, a Protestant pastor, affirmed that the Pope was indeed the Antichrist since the numerical values formed by the two following sentences once added corresponded to a total of 666: *Vicarius Fili Dei* and *I Vescovi papali e clericato ecclesiastico.* The Reformationists had also affirmed that 666 was contained in the name of Pope Paul V (1552-1621). The tiara or Triple Crown was suppressed under John XXIII who died in 1963 and the blasphemous crown replaced by the bishops' mitre.

Nonetheless, the controversy surrounding the origins or authenticity of 666 as the number of the Antichrist is largely ignored in the popular imagination of South Africans. To them it represents the number of Satan and as such has meaning for them. For this reason, I have opted to include the use of 666 as part of the highway of phantasmagoria.

5 888

Triple eight is also a widely used number. The Director of the Gauteng Department of Transport and Public Works maintained that 888 is popular with Chinese. According to her, it is a lucky number for them. However, I have noticed this number being used by people other than Chinese and would argue that it can be grouped with all palindromic numbers. According to Eloise Mozzani[4], numbers read alike backward and forward are carriers of luck. An obvious exception to this is the number 666.

6 Teasers or pointless humour

Teasers are generally humorous messages. In this category, individuals play with the characters in a way that is supposed to capture the attention of the onlooker. An illustration of this is 000 PSY-GP that contains the exclamation 'oops' of apology for a mistake. Furthermore, with the introduction of PRNs in Gauteng it is possible to use (as in the Plates Company advert) combinations like 4U2NV-GP i.e. for you to envy or IXLR8-GP = I accelerate. All combinations are allowed on condition they are not offensive.

7 Other examples of phantasmagoria

Numbers and letters can be used in many different and ingenious ways to create a message. For some, the use of personal registration numbers is a way of flaunting specifically chosen aspects of their identity document as a means of recognising their vehicle in a parking lot. They use elements in their date of birth juxtaposed with their initials to create a personalised number. 210 MHG-GP reads Marion Hedda Goosen born on October 2.

Some people own more than one car and wish to advertise it ... or remind themselves. CAPRA- ZN and CAPRA1- ZN are examples of this. In Gauteng, I had the opportunity of interviewing the owner of 001 JFK-GP. His initials are JFK and he owns five vehicles. All his vehicles carry personalised registration numbers ranging from JFK 001 to JFK 005. He revels in the idea of being 'confused' with the American president John F. Kennedy but is also quick to prove that his initials are the same.

Many vehicle owners are proud to reinforce the make and model of their vehicle as part of their registration numbers. Thus, we find plates reading BMW 540-GP or SLK 500-GP. These are obvious choices reflecting a BMW and a Mercedes Benz sports. Where alpha characters have already been allocated, owners use the model of the car and their initials or other alpha characters dear to them as identification on plates. We therefore find 318 HSM-GP on a BMW or a 300 CNP-GP on a Mercedes Benz.

Business and identification

Business too has recognised the impact of personalised registration plates. The mobile telephone company of MTN in South Africa, has registered vehicles that display their acronym. In Gauteng we see cars carrying plates that read 083 MTN-GP or 518 MTN-GP since only one car would be allocated the 083 prefix. Small businesses are also using the plates as a form of added visibility. 007 VMS-GP is an interesting example. The vehicle was spotted at the mosque and it belonged to Value Motor Spares, hence the VMS. Spotting it at the mosque on a Friday (the most important prayer for Muslims) among cars in the parking space of the mosque was an obvious indication of the person being a Muslim. However, the owner of the car added stickers that made it possible to identify the car on a public route as belonging to a Muslim.

Meaning that whomever driving behind this car and who understands something about symbolism in Islam would be in a position to recognise the car as a 'Muslim car'.

786: symbolic expression of an Islamic identity

Not all personalised numberplates are vanity plates. In the following example, we will see how religious identity marker are also expressed on numberplates. The idea of this research arose from my observation of the sudden proliferation of a 786 combination on obviously personalised numberplates. Understanding what 786 represents to some Muslims, I began a series of pictures and interviews to understand what this number means to those who have effectively bought it. From interviewees, invariably Muslims, I realised the symbolic importance this number occupies in their expression of a Muslim identity. This was corroborated by many interviewees spontaneously declaring that their cellular phone number and where possible their home and business telephone numbers also contained a 786 sequence. Some were quick to inform me that in their personal correspondence they would always put a 786 on the upper-most part of the page. Whilst I do not have copies of such letters, I spotted an exam script in my class at university adorned by 786 on each page, which corroborates this practice.

Intrigued by the proliferation of 786s on the highway and in the erstwhile so-called Indian areas of Pretoria and Johannesburg, where a significant portion of the Muslim population resides, I conducted a series of interviews hoping to establish the different perceptions that Muslims have of this number and their understanding of the origin of 786. I simultaneously started researching the meaning and origins of the numerical sequence.

Without exceptions, Muslims told me that it means '*Bismillah*', 'In the Name of Allah' and by extension an expression of Grace bringing protection and luck. Many times I was reminded that 'whomever reads 786 takes the name of God, whether they know it or not. This is the beauty of 786, whether you are Jewish, Christian or Muslim, when you read 786, you take the Name of Allah'. The student who wrote 786 on the top of each page of her exam paper told me it is "*a lucky number, that helps to pass*".

Why is *Bismillah* so important? Why not another verse? *Bismillah* is the essence of the Holy Qur'an and is to be recited before commencing any activity. In '*Bismillah and its Blessings*'[5], it is stated that 'the Prophet recited *Bismillah rahmaanir raheem* before doing any work' and 'he advised the Ummah to do the same'. For example, 'reading before shutting the door for the night, before putting out the light, before taking meals, before drinking water, before boarding a conveyance and when alighting any conveyance'. Furthermore, the reciting of *Bismillah rahmaanir raheem* imparts good fortune and abundance. Carrying a 786 numberplate means for some car owners that, should they be in trouble on the highway or anywhere else for that matter, they would readily obtain assistance from fellow Muslims who recognise the personalised 786 as definitely belonging to a Muslim.

This raised a myriad of questions in my mind and I began to wonder if 786 was a proselyte tool, how 786 came about, how a whole range of Muslims agreed on the meaning without ever being able to explain its origins. For some, it was regarded as controversial and not to be used, for they located its origins in India. This refers to a current evolution of Islam in South Africa, which aims at purging Islam of its Indianness.

Observing 786s on numberplates and being told about special cellular phone numbers, I interviewed the Director of the Gauteng Department of Transport and Public Works and the Sales Director of one of the two cellular network suppliers in South Africa, Vodacom.

The Gauteng authorities confirmed that the numbers 786 are blocked out and they are aware that only Muslims would apply for them. This is the only sequence of numbers that is directly related to a religious identity, in this instance, to the Muslim faith. From my interviews, I learnt from a used car dealer – himself the owner of several 786 plates – that prior to the introduction of the Personalised Registration Numbers, arrangements used to be made with 'sympathetic officials' from the Department of Transport in the then Transvaal, to have as many 786 sequences as possible allocated to Muslims. The booking of this number was subject to two conditions: 1) the car had to be new and 2) the car had to come from another province. Whenever a 786 sequence was available, the understanding official would phone a contact person and quietly inform them of the availability of the sought-after number. The interested party, often on an unofficial waiting list, then had to act swiftly to ensure the car registration. My well-informed interviewee remarked: 'All those 786s on yellow T numberplates, they belonged to Muslims'.

Vodacom started operating as a cellular network supplier in 1994 with 082 as a prefix and seven digits, or 10 million numbers at their disposal. 8.5 million numbers can be allocated to the wider population. Service providers are given blocks of numbers of about 100 000 (082 55 ....). One of the service providers at the time, in 1994, was a company called TTC (Trust Telephone Company) which has since folded. TTC had requested and obtained numbers starting with 082 78. They further broke this down to 082 786, which gave them 10 000 numbers to sell to Muslim clients. The Vodacom Sales Director remarked that 'this was their killer ad'.

Vodacom did not have a policy on number allocation and merely reacted to a demand in the 786 case. Vodacom has a few short codes composed of 082 and only three digits, allocated on the basis of need. Short codes are used for their customer care line and their emergency services for example. An affluent Muslim user, noticing these short codes and lured by the possibility of obtaining an 082 786 short code, applied for the number, which translated into blocking 9 999 potential numbers. The network supplier refused. With this exception maybe, network operators and cellular phone retailers have identified this niche in the market and some even use 786 as an added sales strategy to attract Muslim clients. Whilst the 786 cellular phone numbers were originally only sold by Muslim retailers to Muslim customers, some retailers now know the added value of being able to supply such a sequence of numbers.

786 as an expression of Muslim identity is more than often not displayed on its own. Cars, especially, but also Muslim homes, display other accoutrements depicting verses from the Qur'an or prayer beads dangling on the rear view mirror and stickers on the inside of the rear windscreen. It often carries the verse 'Allah is One and Mohammed is His Messenger', or a Prayer (Du'a) for security, protection against accidents. Muslim retail shops even sell 'plasticised prayers' for use in the home, in the car and pocketsize cards for carrying on oneself. Often, the owner of a vehicle carrying a Personalised Registration Number includes one or more of the above signs inside the car, thus reinforcing his/her identity as a Muslim.

Arabic, a Semitic language, is written from right to left. Some car owners, believing that since 786 means *Bismillah* in Arabic, the number should be written from right to left and pushed the zeal as far as applying for a 687 numberplate instead of 786. The reality is that numbers in Arabic, are written from left to right.

Intrigued by the origins of this widely used numerical computation, I researched the origins of 786. I searched the libraries and the Internet. To no avail. I then interviewed an Arabic scholar, Professor of Arabic at the University of South Africa. He pointed me towards 'A New Arabic Grammar of the Written Language'[6]. According to him, the use of encapsulated verses of the Qur'an in the form of numerical computation is ancient. There is a tradition amongst Muslims to wear verses of the Qur'an or the entire Qur'an as a charm or amulet. Since the verses are obviously bulky to wear, the computed forms are easier and more practical. The old Semitic form of the Arabic alphabet was differently arranged to the present one.

The current Arabic alphabet groups letters by shape. The old form followed a numerical value system, from the lowest (1 for *alif*) to the highest and last letter (1 000 for *ghain*). The old Semitic alphabet was called the *hurufu l-'abjad*. The computational value of 786 derives from the *hurufu l-'abjad*. 786 is a short code for seven hundred and eighty six, which is the sum of all letters composing the entire verse of '*Bismillaahir rahmaanir raheem*', meaning 'In the Name of Allah, the Most Kind, the Most Merciful'.

This demonstration of the origin of 786 thus proves that this numerical computation affixed to many cars and used by many Muslims in various ways has become a commodity acting as a medium of mutual recognition, regardless of the way and reasons for its origins. None of the interviewees, except for the Arabic scholar, were able to point out the numerical computation of the verse and everyone limited it to 7-8-6, not understanding that it should read seven hundred and eighty six and limiting the meaning to an abridged version of the verse. It is however known, recognised, used and understood as a means of mutual recognition and at the same time, we could argue, as a means of Othering. Those, like the officials of the Department of Transport or the cellular network suppliers for example, who have knowledge of the use of 786 amongst Muslims are able to recognise it as such without needing any further explanation.

They readily accept it as a symbol of Islam. One of the ideal supports for this commodified number amongst affluent Muslims is their car numberplate. We saw that the ownership of a personalised numberplate supposes financial means beyond those of the vast majority. These numberplates are in their large majority affixed to luxury cars. On a Friday afternoon, outside the mosque in Laudium, a Pretoria former Indian township, about 20% of the approximately 100 cars parked outside the Mosque carried a 786 numberplate and were luxury cars.

Conclusion

To be part of the Highway tribe means initiation through observation. Whilst I have deciphered many signs, some might have totally escaped me, like a 786 numberplate without any other signs on or inside the car would escape a non-initiate.

My highway initiation has reinforced my conviction that one can no longer confine the study of identity and its variegated forms of expressions to fixed sites and spaces. Though some of the expressions used are situated in history, they can now be extracted from their historical context and made to travel. The highway is generally regarded as an impersonal space, a necessary evil, connecting two geographical spaces. It is seen as a functional space. Yet today, because of its extensive use, people experience the need to express themselves through visible and transportable signs. The moving car with its adornments roots itself into the highway, transforming an eluding space into a more palpable and appropriated space.

The car becomes the focus of attention and gives the driver a sense of ownership of the highway. There is no mixing and no fusion, but people attract each other's attention through fugitive glimpses, hoping to recognise each other, share a joke, or display their affluent status and phantasmagoria. The highway becomes the route on which value and belief systems are transported and for every inch travelled, personalised registration drivers root themselves into the impersonal road by displaying their plates of personification. Numberplates can be customised to an individual's purpose thanks to digital technology and the collaboration of the State, which now allows anyone with sufficient financial means the possibility of buying and exhibiting their cherished fragment of identity.

Notes

1   In South Africa, in the absence of an efficient public transportation system, all people without cars - the majority - are obliged to use some form of vehicle transport. The privately owned collective transport system – the minibus taxis – is at present fulfilling this gap. The government's attempts thus far unsuccessful, to regulate this industry and the fact that it responds to real needs of people who do not own vehicles, emphasises the need for South Africans to have access to a vehicle in different ways: as owners or as commuters.

2   Chambers English Dictionary; 1988: pp.1629 and 1631, Cambridge University Press

3   Kruger, T. 'Stamnaam van Gauteng se premier ry oral saam' in *Naweek Beeld*, 23–24 June, 2000, p. 7.

4   Mozzani, E; 1997 (1995). *Le Livre des Superstitions: Mythes, Croyance et Légendes.* Robert Laffont, Collection Bouquin: Paris. p. 1657–8.

5   'Bismillah and its blessings', a pamphlet distributed at mosques and published by Islamic Publications, Johannesburg, South Africa.

6   Haywood, J. A. & H. M. Nahmad. (1976). *A new Arabic Grammar of The Written Language*, London: Lund Humphries.

CHAPTER THIRTEEN

How cultural policy creates inequality: the case of the Greater Johannesburg Metropolitan Council and its Biennale project

Jane Duncan

> The less you eat, drink and read books; the less you go to the theatre, the dance hall, the public house; the less you think, love, theorise, sing, paint, fence, etc., the more you save – the greater becomes your treasure which neither moths nor dust will devour – your capital. The less you are, the more you have; the less you express your own life, the greater is your alienated life – the greater is the store of your estranged being.
>
> Karl Marx, *Economic and Philosophic Manuscripts of 1844*, 96

'There must be an end to white monopoly on political power and a fundamental restructuring of our political and economic systems to ensure that the inequalities of apartheid are addressed and our society thoroughly democratised'. These words were uttered by Nelson Mandela on his release from prison in 1990. In the light of the tremendous sacrifices that Mandela and many others made, one would imagine that once they came to office, the organisations that comprised the liberation movement, including the African National Congress, would have done all in their power to bring about these objectives.

Yet, it seems that a number of new South African policies are creating rather than reducing inequality, a claim which – in the words of a well-known educational activist – could be considered 'heretical'[1]. This article suggests how and why this reversal has happened in relation to arts and culture: in other words, why a country fresh from a liberation struggle is acting in ways that undo the gains of this struggle. This reversal is evident in many areas of life, including the visual arts, where a growing emphasis on promoting the country's international competitiveness is marginalising key development needs in the sector; in spite of this, the government is arguing increasingly that the realities of globalisation leave South Africa with no option but to join the race to be 'competitiveness race, and to use its benefits to address the country's huge social needs (an approach termed 'progressive competitiveness').

While this article considers how this reversal has restructured general cultural policies, it focuses specifically on Johannesburg's Biennale project which has been sponsored largely by Johannesburg's local government, the Greater Johannesburg Metropolitan Council (GJMC). Biennales have grown in popularity recently as prestigious art
events that elevate the status of the host country in an increasingly globalising and
competitive artworld, and Johannesburg's Biennale project clearly began to play this
role. Yet, anyone with at least a passing acquaintance of this project will be aware of the
voluminous criticism it has been subjected to. Key detractors have argued that the
project benefits a few already-established artists, and therefore has very little relevance
to the country's need to address the huge disparities in the arts carried over from
apartheid. Its praise singers have argued that South Africa as a whole, including artists,
will inevitably benefit from Johannesburg's growing prestige as a cultural hub, as this
elevated status will allow it to attract more investment: therefore, affairs like the Biennale
are not only justified, but necessary at the moment on the grounds that '..it would be
impossible to produce a populist exhibition that was at the same time of international
significance'[2]. In fact, they argue, there is no alternative to joining the race for global
relevance, and that everyone, including artists, should be prepared to contribute as the
consequences of being left behind are too ghastly to contemplate. Meanwhile, the
GJMC wavers between the two positions, and has yet to make a clear statement on the
Biennale's future.

If we value art in a society such as ours and if we value the principles of equality and
social justice, then surely we should evaluate these claims to assess whether we want
state resources to be used in the service of global competitiveness, and to engage the
government accordingly. Even if the Biennale project does not continue, we need to be
able to take the lessons learned from its short existence and use them to evaluate the
growing body of local government-related cultural policy proposals promoting the
competitiveness agenda.

Cities and deepening inequality: the context of Biennales

In order to evaluate the above claims, it is necessary to unpack some of the underlying
assumptions of the competitiveness approach, progressive and otherwise. It is common knowledge that while globalisation is leading to greater integration of national
markets, it is also leading to greater inequality between rich and poor. The policy
bouquet of privatisation, de-regulation, liberalisation, international competitiveness
and government downsizing (generally termed 'neo-liberalism'), has been largely
blamed for this growing inequality, as these strategies tend to advantage developed
countries in the North at the expense of developing countries. The competitiveness
ideology ensures that resources are deployed to turn economies outward, with the

result that each country specialises in areas where they are believed to hold a comparative advantage. Changes in the nature of production made possible by the information technology revolution are leading to fewer people being needed to run this competitiveness-driven, 'high-tech/high-value-added/high-wage'[3] global economy: as a result, countries with labour intensive heavy industries have been undergoing de-industrialisation. Some commentators have termed this new productive order the 30%/70% society, where a relatively privileged labour aristocracy participates in economic activities while the vast majority are shut out, leading to apocalyptic projections about 'the end of work' as we know it.[4]

The African continent has found itself in a particularly precarious position. Generally, sub-Saharan Africa is being increasingly marginalised in relation to trade opportunities, and even though the continent accounts for 39% of the world's population, it accounts for only 3% of output in cash terms.[5] This extremely uneven distribution of resources is increasing regional disparities, which could well be a causal factor in the bitter conflict witnessed in the African great lakes region in recent years.[6]

The competitiveness logic requires governments to 'crowd in' resources to industries and areas capable of meeting the competitiveness challenge. For this reason, cities have been identified as the productive engines of the world economy, as they generally enjoy highly developed infrastructures essential for the efficient production of goods and services: small wonder that they have been referred to as '... the international growth machines of the new [global] economy ... cities are the workhorses of the world'.[7] However, this 'crowding in' of investments in particular areas leads to the 'crowding out' of investments in others, resulting in the creation of small, well-resourced centres and huge, sprawling peripheries locked out of the global economy. Even within 'global' cities, the strategic re-positioning of resources in particular internationally competitive areas and activities – often called 'Spatial Development Initiatives' – has resulted in the deliberate running down of communities left out of the globalisation process.[8] Neo-liberal urban development strategies are difficult to apply in most African cities, as they simply lack the infrastructure to compete in the global economy[9]: those with the potential to make the grade, such as Johannesburg and Cape Town, are under enormous pressure to upgrade key facilities to attract foreign investment.

The formation of new global, regional and local centres and peripheries is also being fuelled by the downsizing of the state in many countries: a trend that is especially evident at local government level given that this tier of government is arguably 'closest to the people' with respect to delivery of services. According to neo-liberal logic, public sector roll-back is necessary to make space for greater private sector involvement in the affairs of government. Neo-liberal policies have advocated a shift in thinking from 'government' to 'governance', as the former is apparently unable to respond to current realities and is therefore outdated: instead, the vertically-integrated state which governs on its own should be replaced by governing partnerships involving government, the

private sector and civil society organisations. These partnerships should take joint
responsibility for the delivery of social services.[10]

In phasing in these public/private partnerships, local governments have argued
that they are as serious as they ever were about the delivery of services: the only change
is in the method of delivery. Yet growing evidence from cities where they have been
implemented for some time suggests otherwise. For example, in studies of cities like
Birmingham in Britain and Baltimore in America, commentators have identified profound problems with the partnership approach. Local governments are accountable to
their electorate through the democratic mandate, whereas private business is not, so
obliging the latter to implement the policies of the former can result in substantial
changes in the outcomes of those policies. In the above mentioned cities, partnership-
based governance has led to a gradual loss of accountability, even to the point in
Birmingham where powerful multinationals 'captured' the policy-making process, leading to the '... general externalisation and globalisation of influence over strategic decisions in the city': as a result, local and economic elites have benefited at the expense of
the cities as a whole.[11] Also, ironically, local government activities tend to expand rather
than contract in managing these partnerships, resulting in huge expenses that may
even be in excess of the amounts saved through the cutbacks.[12] As service-specific
partnerships are implemented, services that were incorporated into an integrated bureaucracy are separated from one another, resulting in the gradual fragmentation of
local government; in the process, it becomes more difficult to implement the sorts of
coherent plans that increase political accountability. The most serious problems, though,
relate to the declining quality and rising cost of service delivery, since private sector
companies will deliver services only to the extent that it is profitable. If communities
are unable to afford services, they are simply left out of the development loop.[13]

Given the strong critiques of neo-liberal policies, the compromise strategy of progressive competitiveness or 'fiscal populism' has been developed by some governments in an attempt to give neo-liberal policies an acceptable face. Many governments
have argued that there is no alterative to these strategies, and that the most realistic
approach is to ensure that at least some of the benefits derived from international
competitiveness will be channelled to social upliftment programmes: an argument that
has been used by these governments to encourage key social groups to 'buy in' to neo-
liberalism, as it provides them with the tools to unite traditional liberal/left concerns
around social delivery with right-wing fiscal ideology.[14] According to Leo Panitch, this
approach '...ends up being not an alternative to, but a subsidiary element in, the process of neo-liberal capitalist restructuring and globalisation', and as a result, becomes all
too easily a cosmetic attempt to reconcile the irreconcilable.[15] Even the progressive
approach has to accept that corporatist arrangements inevitably exclude significant social groups ('disproportionately the young, women, immigrants or minority groups,
and the unemployed'[16]), in the hope that they will benefit from a general growth in the

economy once competitiveness begins to pay off. However, the recent trend worldwide towards 'jobless growth' suggests that there is no necessary link between growth and redistribution.[17] In fact any attempt by governments to fashion this link may be thwarted by speculative attacks on their economies, given that their social justice strategies are premised on accepting the inevitability of an outward-orientation. As a result, they may find themselves being forced to react in the same ways as non-progressive governments, cutting social spending even further and fostering mass unemployment to promote capital-intensive industries even more vigorously[18] Small wonder that neo-liberal governments – even so-called 'progressive' ones – walk a tightrope between co-determinism and outright repression, as their policies are recipes for social instability: if the one approach fails, then the other is always an option.

Arts policies in the context of neo-liberalism and the rise of Biennales

The ascendence of neo-liberal policies has placed enormous pressure on government departments to demonstrate their relevance to the competitiveness drives of their respective countries. This is especially so in relation to departments with national, especially social welfare, agendas,[19] as they are required to attune their activities to the exigencies of global competitiveness and fiscal restraint, or risk marginalisation.[20] Given that arts and culture is an especially soft target for government cutbacks, these departments have fought back by re-casting their activities in neo-liberal clothing.

Welfare states have provided arts funding on the basis that these activities were necessary for active participation of citizens in social life. In response to neo-liberal budget cuts, governments are being enjoined to strike up partnerships with the private sector and non-profit organisations to diversify their sources of funding. Cultural policies are expected to promote these funding shifts, and to act as a guide to which 'mix' is best depending on local circumstances. Also, governments are engineering aspects of the arts that increase private sector investment, foreign exchange while promoting their countries' international competitiveness. Policy-makers are enjoined to develop arguments for government support for the arts that are based on its potential as an economically productive sector, rather than relying on 'pleading of a more subjective nature'.[21] Craft has become a key area of government support in developing countries. India for example has industrialised its crafts sector to encourage its success in international markets: policies promoting the economic viability of such sectors have become known as 'cultural industries growth strategies', and can qualify for trade and industry incentives if they promote the country's macro-economic objectives.[22]

According to John McGuigan, these strategies have been adopted in European and American cities as part of urban regeneration programmes to counter the effects of deindustrialisation. Tracing their implementation in various English cities, he notes that over time, the cultural content of the programmes was gradually marginalised by commercial priorities. Yet in spite of this evolution, there is a paucity of evidence of these programmes' direct economic benefit, and the few jobs that are created by the cultural industries have not ameliorated the huge levels of unemployment. Also, instead of challenging the exclusionary effects of 'city edge' development (where capital and the middles classes invested in areas outside city centres), these strategies further marginalised mainly inner city-based workers and the growing pool of unemployed. This was because local governments prioritised the development of the sorts of facilities that would draw back middle class consumers: small wonder that 'race riots' and other forms of social unrest ironically became features of cities targeted for such 're-generation'.[23]

In spite of these contradictions, cities around the world are still putting into practice cultural strategies to boost their international competitiveness. 'International' mega-exhibitions, and specifically Biennales have come to assume a prominent role in these strategies, with new ones being launched by different countries virtually every year. Countries as diverse as South Africa, Cuba, Turkey, Korea, France, Australia and Chile have responded to this trend by launching their own Biennales.

The oldest Biennale by far is the Venice Biennale, dating back to 1895. The largely government-funded mega-exhibition Documenta X has not been in existence for nearly as long – in fact it dates back to 1955 – and occurs once every four to five years. In spite of the fact that nearly half a century separates these exhibitions, and the impulses behind setting them up were different, their approach has been largely the same: to host art from other countries in the context of national pavilions. Put crudely, these exhibitions started out as trade fairs which functioned as propaganda tools for countries seeking to demonstrate their levels of technological, scientific or cultural advancement.[24]

Since the 1990's though, there appears to have been a complex shift in the role of these mega-exhibitions. In their quest for global relevance, countries have identified particular cities for further development, especially those that have the capacity to specialise in fields relevant to the global economy. Cultural activities linked to tourism strategies are attractive propositions for cities with already-established, distinctive identities. For example, the Istanbul Biennale builds on the city's identity as a 'golden gateway between Asia and Europe'.[25] Singapore has signalled its intention to vie for the status of 'global city for the arts' by exploiting its historically important position on the Straits of Malacca to attract international tourists to its government-backed artistic facilities.[26] Both Kwangju and Johannesburg have built on their histories of struggle against oppression to host Biennales that turn quite fittingly on themes of cultural domination and identity.[27] Even cities with no presence at all in the global consciousness can rise to prominence through a strategic development of cultural facilities, possibly the most startling example of recent times being the attention being enjoyed by the Basque city of Bilbao after the Solomon Guggenheim Foundation built a satellite of the New-York based Guggenheim museum there.[28] These events have also been linked to urban regeneration strategies for cities whose centres have become run down through the de-industrialisation of local economies, coupled with the 'suburbanisation' of finance capital.

The shifting global terrain is also evident in how other Biennales and mega-exhibitions are motivated and organised. This shift is particularly conspicuous in relation to the Venice Biennale and Documenta X, as they have been around longer. Both exhibitions have changed their curatorial approach from exhibiting the art of different countries in their own national pavilions to curating according to themes: in terms of the latter approach, the criterion for contributing to a particular exhibition would be the relevance of a particular artist's work to the theme, rather than his or her country of origin. In motivating this change, the curators have argued that globalisation is rendering the national approach to mega-exhibitions less and less relevant.[29]

The newer Biennales have embraced this approach with a flourish. The Kwangju Biennale adopted this approach both for its inaugural exhibition in 1995 and in the second one in 1997. This government-funded initiative was set up after Korea established its presence at the Venice Biennale in the early 1990s. The first Biennale, entitled 'Beyond the Borders', attracted a staggering 1.7 million visitors over the two month period: however, concern was raised about the fact that the overwhelming majority of visitors were from Korea, for '.... as an international event and potentially one of the most important art events in the Asia Pacific region more foreign visitors would have been welcomed.'[30] In fact, the Minister of Culture and Sports, Kim Young-su, identified the Biennale as a focus for developing Kwangju's tourist facilities to help attract more foreign visitors.[31] The importance of gearing the event for international participation was underlined by the Korean Overseas Information Service in 1996, when it stated that 'the globalisation of the local art world means the survival of the local art industry. In this respect, the main goal is to rationalise the Korean art industry in line with international standards. This is crucial in the face of the opening of the art market to foreign competition.'[32] This survival strategy was deemed necessary in the light of a post-boom recession, where investments needed for the continued expansion of the arts were contracting.[33] The second Biennale, entitled 'Unmapping the Earth', attempted to entrench its competitive edge as the leading Asian showcase for contemporary art. The exhibition also followed the thematic approach.[34] Five 'internationally known' curators were invited to curate these exhibitions, who – according to one commentator – could explain the inclusion of artists that '... could be found in any number of international group shows'.[35]

The Instanbul Biennale – which began in 1987 – is rather different from the ones discussed above in that the bulk of its funds come from the private sector: in fact, early on the organisers took a decision to distance it from the government so that it could not capture the event for its own nationalistic ends.[36] In spite of this, the Biennale has largely followed the trends evident in other recent Biennales. The first two exhibitions were organised on the basis of national pavilions. However, the third Biennale was based on a theme, the 'Production of Cultural Difference', around which the national pavilions were curated.[37] The fourth Biennale, however, eschewed national pavilions entirely in favour of exhibitions curated around a theme 'Orientation: The Vision of Art in a Paradoxical World': artists were selected depending on the extent to which their works related to the theme, not on the basis their national origins (although the bulk of the artists were drawn from various diasporas). According to the curator, Rene Block, organising Biennales on a national basis was an outdated nineteenth century approach.[38]

The fifth Istanbul Biennale, entitled 'On Life, Beauty, Translations and other Difficulties', focussed on Istanbul as a metaphoric gate between the East and West generally, and Asia and Europe specifically. Site-specific works were set up in the airport, the train station, the Bosphorus Bridge that connects Asia to Europe, the historic walls and the old city gates.[39] The exhibition claimed to explore 'the borderlines that separate art and life...the differential spaces, the places of 'others' and the fluidity and difficulties of translation between different contexts [as a means] of reinterpreting our position in the contemporary world'.[40] This emphasis on the uncovering of repressed identities through the act of travel bears a strong resemblance to the theme of the second Kwangju Biennale, which concerned itself with '... the niches, the places in-between, the points of convergence, which are only to be found of the revelations and articulations ...' 'Unmapping the Earth' is intended to expose vigorous forces, interstices, ruptures, and singularities, activated in the complex diversity of problems current confronting the earth'.[41] Themes of travel, migration, transit sites, mapping the global terrain and the fracturing of identity in the context of globalisation have emerged in the Northern mega-exhibitions as well: as early as 1993 in the case of the Venice Biennale, and to a lesser extent in the last Documenta X.[42] These themes also formed the focus of the second Johannesburg Biennale, which will be dealt with below.

In choosing these loose (even amorphous) themes, the curators have not only been able to circumvent having to dwell on issues of national concern, but they underscore the relevance of the Biennales in the context of globalisation. The veneer of contemporaneity invariably rubs off on the host city, which helps to project it as a globally relevant cultural centre: this approach has been termed the 'glocal', which is identified as '... the most pressing issue for curators today, at least to the extent that success at integrating one's local realities with those of the world at large is fast becoming the only sure way to maintain a community's standing in the race for global relevance'.[43] The rise in global status of the host cities is clearly in the interests of governments and local businesses seeking a foothold in the global economy, so it is not surprising that to varying degrees, the public and private sectors have entered into partnerships to sponsor most of the above events.

It seems fair to say from this brief discussion of a number of Biennales that they have (either deliberately or unwittingly) begun to intertwine in very complex ways with the neo-liberal interests in their host countries. These developing relationships are really not well understood, in relation to Biennales, as well as a host of regional travelling exhibitions aimed at the 'global' artworld: in fact, Mari Carmen Ramírez has warned that the absence of such critiques is leading to the manipulation of artists and curators by local neo-liberal economic elites.[44]

With respect to travelling exhibitions of Latin American origin, she notes that a few artists have been 'mainstreamed' as 'marginal', resulting in the further marginalisation of many more artists who are excluded from exhibitions on the grounds that the 'marginal' has already been catered for.

However, as a number of these events shifted to reflect the new 'realities' of globalisation, they have suffered from the kinds of contradictions mentioned above in relation to neo-liberal urban development projects. For example, although the auxiliary exhibitions of the second Kwangju Biennale had a specifically Korean focus, the Biennale as a whole was accused of not engaging sufficiently with the country's culture, preferring to provide a platform for foreign artists at the expense of domestic ones. As a result, the Biennale was criticised for being too Western in its artistic view, and failing to differentiate itself from the other famous art fairs it seemed to want to compete with, such as Kassel or Venice.[45]

Even an event like the Havana Biennale in Cuba has found it difficult to resist being sucked into the slipstream of global competitiveness, with all the attendant contradictions. This Biennale was originally set up in 1984 to bring together the works of artists that were marginal to the cultural centres, in the process establishing mainly South-South art networks.[46] However, concerns have been raised that the Biennale organisers may be seeking to transform the Biennale into an 'alternative Biennale of the First World', which acts as a feeder of 'peripheral' art to the cultural capitals of the North (with all the commercial kick-backs involved).[47] These developments have raised questions abut the extent to which these events critique or promote neo-liberal agendas.

However, nowhere has the contradictions been more starkly evident, or more consistently articulated, than in relation to the Johannesburg Biennale.

Arts and culture in South Africa: from the RDP to GEAR

South Africa has not been immune to the pressures of globalisation, although its full exposure to them was retarded somewhat by the isolationist character of apartheid. The increasing influence of neo-liberal policies has been especially evident in how Johannesburg's Biennale project has evolved since its inception in 1995. To understand why this is so, it is necessary to map out some key developments in the South African political and cultural landscape since the demise of apartheid and transition to democracy in 1994.

The first Biennale was held just after the first democratic elections had taken place, and transformation was proceeding according to the then newly-adopted Reconstruction and Development Programme (RDP). The RDP had its origins in the trade union movement prior to the elections, and was developed mainly by the ANC as a programme of action that 'belonged to everybody', including historically opposed social forces like business and labour. The real result, though, was an uncomfortable (even incoherent) mix of Keynesian and neo-liberal strategies, largely based on a 'growth through redistribution' approach where development of domestic industries in marginalised communities was the key to growing the economy.

In the wake of the world's 'honeymoon period' with South Africa immediately after the elections, the ANC soon found itself exposed to the tough reality of integrating into the global economy. The reality hit particularly hard in 1996, when speculators attacked the Rand, resulting in a rapid devaluation and marked exchange rate instability. In what has been described as a 'panic response'[48], the government sought to restore investor confidence by drafting an economic strategy that took advantage of the weak Rand, called the Growth, Employment and Redistribution Programme (GEAR). GEAR seeks to solve the unemployment problem by setting targets for growth, which are to be achieved through promoting an export-oriented economy and attracting foreign investment. This is to be achieved by promoting privatisation, de-regulation and liberalisation, and the resultant growth would then be used to deliver on RDP objectives (in other words, 'redistribution through growth', which could be related to the 'progressive competitiveness' approach): in fact, if the private sector is harnessed to deliver on the RDP via public/private partnerships, the government will be able to spread the costs of social delivery and infrastructure development.[49] In addition, government savings are encouraged and strict targets are set to reduce the country's deficit, consisting of debt inherited mainly from apartheid: these measures are to be achieved by cutting social spending, rather than raising taxes. Once the debt has been amortised, the country will be able to turn the corner towards greater prosperity. The logic is clear: the country needs to tighten its belt before it can loosen it.

While it would appear that at the outset GEAR was an emergency measure brought in to rescue an ailing economy, in reality the ANC leadership had been subjected to relentless pressure for some time by powerful domestic and international forces to favour an investment-led export orientated growth strategy. Lobbies in the organisation that favoured state-interventionist economic approaches were weakened by the collapse of the Soviet Union and later on, by the centrist compromises the organisation was called on to make to conclude negotiations successfully with the apartheid government. Negotiations had ensued because neither 'side' was strong enough to resolve the conflict on their terms alone, but the ascendence of neo-liberal interests internationally gradually strengthened the centrist elements in the ANC's leadership.[50] As a result, embracing neo-liberal orthodoxy by these elements was decisive and led to an economic trajectory that gave rise to GEAR. By the time it was adopted as the government's overriding framework, the ANC leadership clearly believed that the reality of globalisation presented them with no alternative but to make the best of an export-led approach. Also, any signs of retreat from the programme would result in punishment being meted out by the world financial markets in the form of further speculative attacks and decreasing investor confidence.

GEAR has been roundly criticised by the trade union movement and civil society organisations for increasing rather than decreasing inequality and has been likened to the much-maligned structural adjustment programmes of the International Monetary Fund and the World Bank. To bear out this argument, critics point to the fact that unemployment has increased markedly since its implementation, and the country is now formally in recession. Two of the key criticisms are that there is no necessary relationship between growth and redistribution, given that the phenomenon of capital-intensive 'jobless growth' has become all too common in other countries and a private sector-driven export-orientation will not necessarily create more jobs that a public sector-driven inward-orientation. Small wonder that GEAR has been termed 'voodoo economics' as it is based on highly dubious assumptions that have increased inequality when implemented in other developing countries as part of structural adjustment packages.[51]

In order for GEAR to succeed, its writers noted that policy co-ordination is needed as inconsistent approaches '... have the potential to destabilise the credibility of the overall macro-economic framework'.[52] Since the release of GEAR, the government has set about restructuring sectors capable of achieving GEAR's growth targets, especially those that could generate exports, attract foreign investment and cut back the state's role in economic activities and the provision of social services.

Arts and culture have also been affected by the shift from the RDP to GEAR. The former set clear targets for the sector: for example, everyone should have access to resources, facilities and education for the production and appreciation of the arts, which should be seen as a fundamental component of development.[53] The RDP also calls for the affirmation of the country's richness and diversity, while at the same time promoting a unified national culture and common heritage in the context of a nation-building programme.

Although GEAR does not mention arts and culture specifically, since 1996 a shift has been evident in the priorities of the Ministry of Arts, Culture, Science and Technology to foreground activities consistent with GEAR objectives. The Ministry's budget has been cut gradually since then.[54] In response, the Ministry's Department has stated that funding at provincial and local government levels will make up the shortfall.[55]

Also, there has been a subtle shift in Ministerial rhetoric from a nation-building para-digm to a more monetarist approach, where those aspects of its portfolio capable of earning income, especially on an internationally competitive basis – have been foregrounded. The Department has dedicated itself to '... effecting a paradigm shift in understanding the role of arts and culture', which includes working with the Depart-ments of Trade and Industry and Labour to include culture in their industrial and employment strategies.[56] This shift in thinking is being developed in a Cultural In-dustries Growth Strategy, where industrial strategies are being implemented for each of the 'cultural industries', which are confined to film and television, music, crafts, publishing and multi-media:[57] in the words of the Minister, '... the cultural industries focus on the production of cultural products for commercial purposes'.[58] The arts are also being linked to cultural tourism strategies in the context of spatial development initiatives, identified by the government as areas capable – with some investment – of becoming internationally competitive.[59]

Given that arts and culture tend to be seen as 'soft targets' for government cut-backs, it is hardly surprising that South Africa's Ministry has chosen to foreground those activities that may position it more favourably for government funding. The Ministry has also started to cast its role increasingly as an enabling one rather than as cultural investor, where it facilitates activities in public – private partnerships (either wholly or partially funded by the private sector) rather than initiating and funding activities itself.[60] To facilitate these partnerships, the Ministry established Business Arts South Africa in 1997 as a conduit for joint funding of the arts by the government and business.[61] According to its promotional material, it will promote private sector sponsorship of the arts '... to enhance high-profile marketing strategies, brand particu-lar products, build corporate image and market share, or break into new markets'[62] While it is too early to identify any discernable sponsorship patterns, it should not be surprising, given the above, if high-profile, publicity-generating events are favoured over and above longer-term and ultimately more demanding community develop-ment and educational activities. Also, logically, artforms and activities that are incapable of corporate image-building will struggle to attract sponsorship.

The Johannesburg Biennale and the localisation of neo-liberal policies

In terms of the interim and final constitutions, culture is listed as a concurrent national and provincial responsibility. However, provincial governments have also sought to extend this responsibility to local governments.[63] Local governments have been strug-gling to transform themselves generally from serving a white minority to all residents regardless of colour. This transformation has been governed up to this point by an interim constitution drafted during multi-party negotiations in 1993, which said very little about the responsibilities of local government. The Gauteng Provincial Government exploited this lack of clarity by devolving a wide range of responsibilities on the Johannesburg Council as soon as it was proclaimed in 1994: these included the onerous task of managing and developing the RDP for the area and, in fact, managing the whole transformation process. It was also charged with passing a budget for the whole Greater Johannesburg area and setting minimum standards for service delivery.[64]

When the interim constitution was replaced in 1996 by a more permanent constitution drafted by a constitutional assembly, a GEAR-influenced shift in thinking about the role of local government was evident. The list of services to be offered by local governments was greatly expanded, as was the potential for greater central government control over local governments.[65] Yet at the same time, local governments are expected to generate greater revenues from the collection of service payments, rather than relying on funding from provincial and national governments.[66]

In the same year, funding allocations for local government decreased by 47 percent. Councillor for the Democratic Party, Ian Davidson, interpreted this move as a 'major shifting of the responsibility for the financing of local government from the central fiscus to the local ratepayer'.[67] This twin approach of devolving services from central government coupled with fiscal restraint has led to the accusation that local councils are being forced to do more with less, and has raised a controversial debate about the constitutionality of unfunded mandates being imposed on these councils.[68] Johannesburg has been especially hard hit by this cutbacks, given that its population has nearly trebled to almost seven million people.[69]

These fiscal pressures became evident in the GJMC's approach to arts and culture. The first Biennale in 1995 was couched explicitly in a RDP framework, at least on a rhetorical level, and dealt with the global repercussions of colonialism on Africa especially, as well as with issues related to cultural difference and marginalisation. This Biennale occurred one year after the country's first democratic elections, and aimed to celebrate South Africa's reintegration into the global community after decades of apartheid isolation.

As a result, the emphasis was on inviting as many countries as possible: in fact, sixty-three countries were represented in eighty-three exhibitions.[70] The Biennale was a Janus-faced affair, where attempts were made to reconcile the international trade fair approach with local development needs, and the event was heavily criticised for prioritising the former at the expense of the latter.[71]

The shift to a monetarist approach in justifying arts expenditure could already be seen in the GJMC's report-back on the first Biennale. The report points out that the total media coverage locally was worth over R2 million. Also, the approximately 500 overseas visitors to the exhibition in February alone accounted for R1.25 million. The report also notes that approximately 17 direct jobs and an additional 33 indirect jobs were created by the tourism spin-off of the Biennale.[72] Most tellingly, though, the controversies about the Biennale's development role (or lack of it) were barely mentioned, so clearly the GJMC's assessment of the event was not based on the full picture.

The second Biennale, entitled 'Trade Routes: History and Geography' was markedly different from the first, in that it was organised on a thematic basis. The Biennale was divided into six exhibitions, each dealing with a series of sub-themes based on the above overarching theme. Four took place in Johannesburg and two in Cape Town (given that this article focuses on the GJMC, the Cape Town exhibitions will not be discussed). A total of 160 artists were included in the exhibitions, including 35 South Africans.[73] The shift between the two Biennales needs to be understood in the context of the adoption of GEAR, and the strengthening of local and international neo-liberal influences on local government.

In 1996, the GJMC underwent profound restructuring on the basis of an investigation undertaken by Joint Negotiating Council into the powers and functions of the GJMC. The changes were effected by a Provincial Proclamation, and led to the establishment of clusters and sub-clusters of activities. Arts and culture were included in the cluster 'metropolitan sport, arts, culture and economic development', which incorporates tourism, sport, museum and library services, and parks.[74] Vision statements were drafted for each cluster: for economic development, the vision was to be '... to promote economic growth and job creation for all citizens of Greater Johannesburg by establishing an integrated, growing and globally competitive economy and by investment and development which will enhance the Metropole's international, national and regional hub and gateway function'.[75] The clustering together of these areas is telling, especially given the neo-liberal undertones of the first vision statement, and set in place a structure that facilitates the application of monetarist principles to arts and culture.

This clustering of economic and cultural considerations became especially evident in relation to the second Biennale in 1997. The Chief Executive Officer of the GJMC, Professor Nicky Padayachee, identified the Council's support for arts and culture as part of Johannesburg's 'localisation' of the RDP, as it contributes to the upliftment of the city. He also noted that '... the integrated approach employed by the GJMC recognises the importance of cultural tourism to the economy of the region and the necessity for international cooperation in achieving a climate conducive to social and economic investment.'[76]

This statement points to the extent to which GEAR logic had become internalised at local government level, especially the way in which it is projected as a seamless extension of the RDP. According to the Executive Officer of Arts, Culture Development and Facilities, Victor Modise, the Biennale was supposed to put the city of Johannesburg, and the country as a whole, firmly back on the world map, in the process hitching the event to the country's drive for international competitiveness.[77]

'Trade Routes' and the rise of Johannesburg as a marginal centre

At first blush, *Trade Routes* would not have served the GJMC's neo-liberal turn very well, as it focussed largely on the victims, rather than the beneficiaries, of economic globalisation: it therefore threatened to expose the consequences of the very economic strategies that the GJMC had so recently embraced. For example, its exploration of the theme of travel focussed mainly on forms of forced travel engendered by globalisation – such as displacement, exile and economic immigration – rather than the tourism of the leisured classes. In exploring these themes, the exhibition's curator, Okwui Enwezor, steered away from nationalist representations on the basis that given the realities of globalisation, national identity is becoming increasingly associated with exclusion, xeno-phobia, coercion and even violence. According to Enwezor, more and more people are unable to fix their identities to notions of citizenship and nationality. For this reason, he wanted to explore what constitutes 'home' for diasporan communities especially, arguing that 'belonging is always a matter of choice, never coerced'. In his introduction to the exhibition catalogue, he maps out conditions for a new 'global citizen' as a 'mobile, itinerant group' that does not respect borders or subscribes to one notion of citizenship, and is therefore more closely connected to the notion of 'diaspora'.

These themes were most clearly elaborated in the flagship exhibition entitled 'Alter-nating Currents'. According to its curators, this exhibition focussed on the impact of '... new era of capitalist restructuring' on the 'non-West'. It sought to examine how globalisation gives rise to new forms of colonialism or ethnocentrism, as the West seeks to inscribe the Third World as well in a global monoculture. Yet, this part of the world is more concerned with claiming agency to counter the concrete experiences of globalisation, such as war, migration, exile, racism and poverty: hence the title 'alternat-ing currents', which foregrounds the ways in which globalisation generates its own opposition.

A number of the works exhibited were fairly literal 'illustrations' of the themes; for example, Theresa Serrano's video entitled *The Grass is Always Greener on the Other Side of the Fence*, which superimposed images of migrating swarms of insects on the mass migration of displaced people. Carlos Uribe exhibited a rows of 'wooden boxes for trading and sowing' (in the artists words) under the title *Landscape 1*. Most were filled with seed, with a rough diagonal row of boxes containing crude oil cutting across the arrangement, suggesting the life and death role that oil has come to play in global trade. Peter Spaan's grouped photographs draw unremarkable parallels between differ-ent cities in their juxtaposition of 'old' and 'new' architecture, pointing to the ways in which globalisation creates urban spaces that are increasingly similar to one another in appearance. Vivan Sundaram's installation entitled ... is a more outrightly critical piece, as it is an explicit examination of the effects of globalisation on India. The installation consists of number of objects associated with industrial mass production – including tin boxes carrying photographs of decrepit Singer sewing machines – arranged in a ring around a series of tin sheets attached to a wall. The sheets are stamped with 'Made in India' industrial production stamps, with superimposed text outlining the effects of globalisation and trade liberalisation on the third world generally, and India specifically, where the labour is paid starvation wages in the interests of international competitiveness.

Such artworks, which are relatively easy to access by audiences as clear statements on globalisation, could be made to complement the GJMC's attempts to project Johannesburg as an outward-oriented city eager to shed its parochial apartheid-era skin. The critical tone of some works did not necessarily disrupt this exercise in image building, though: in fact they could serve this purpose even better than celebratory ones, as the former could be used to portray the event as a platform representing marginal interests, and an event with a critical 'edge' could play this role better than an outrightly propagandistic one. As a result, one critic could comment that, in the light of the 'potential for social explosion in South Africa today', given the still-existing apartheid legacy of economic inequalities, '… Johannesburg seems ideally suited to bring into focus the problems of globalisation'.[78]

Many of the works, though, were more nuanced and personalised: photographic installations by Santu Mofokeng and Cho Duck-Hyun, and photographs by Seydou Keita all focussed on the colonial tradition of the posed photographic portrait, with the first two raising explicit questions about the impact of this mode of representation on the identities of the colonised. The personal toll of colonisation was also developed in exploring the theme of 'home', interpreted with varying degrees of literalness in works by artists like Pat Motlau, Zwelethu Mthetwa and Esko Männikö. This element of nuance allowed one critic to praise the exhibition as 'international art at its most profound', and as 'state of the art' work that required 'a little more intellectual engagement than toe-tapping to *Do You Wanna Be My Lover?*'[79], the implication being that even though the host was a local government, it had the foresight to allow an exhibition that rose above being a simple government propaganda exercise. The fact that the works were overwhelmingly multi-media installations, videos and photographs – and in fact all the Trade Routes exhibitions steered away from 'Modernist' media like painting and sculpture – also contributed to the exhibition's contemporaneity. This suppression of painting and sculpture – as media that are arguably more popularly accessible as 'art' – was heavily criticised as 'neither demotic nor democratic'[80], alienating to South Africans[81], and 'excluding an untold number of artists and artworks', apparently in an attempt to conform to 'valid' international exhibitions such as Documenta'[82] The exclusive thrust of the Biennale was further reinforced by how the underlying concept was presented, which was described by one critic as 'scholasticism gone rampant'[83], and by another as 'over-intellectualisation' that could leave '… John Citizen … gasping for clarity'.[84]

The choice of artists as well helped to reinforce the 'high art' tenor of the Biennale, in spite of the fact that the event was used to promote Johannesburg's image as an emerging 'marginal centre' of culture, which in the words of Armin Medosch, 'appears to be a model for the hybridisation of the world'.[85] Many of the artists included in 'Alternating Currents' could be considered to be established names of 'marginal' art, such as Ghada Amer, Eugenio Dittborne, Coco Fusco, Cho Duck-Hyun and Seydou Keita. Some of the pieces had been exhibited before, such as Yinka Sonibare's installation 'Victorian Philanthropist's Parlour'[86], and some were even quite dated: Pepón Osorio's *Badge of Honour,* dates back to 1995, when it made its debut in a vacant store in downtown Newark and was subsequently installed in the Newark Museum.[87] Many of Esko Männikkö's portraits of Finnish men had already been exhibited, and featured in art publications.[88] The black and white photographic portraits by Seydou Keita date back to the 1950's[89], pre-dating the very contemporary themes addressed by the exhibition. Eugenio Dittborne adapted his concept of airmail paintings for the Biennale, which he pioneered as far back as 1984 to keep contact with a friend who left Chile in the wake of the then-President Pinochet's brutal repression.[90] Called 'Southern Cross', the piece consists of his trademark envelopes – this time addressed to the Biennale in Johannesburg – exhibited next to their contents, namely large cuniform-shaped pieces of cloth adorned with images relating to slavery and colonial expansion on the African continent. Duck-Hyun Cho extended on his use of colonial Korean portrait photography incorporated into installations[91], in his piece entitled 'Our Theory of the 20th Century': the installation consisted of a circle of six large crates, five of which contained life-size sepia portrait photographs of several generations of Koreans. The inclusion of these 'marginal heavyweights', some of whom either exhibited already-known works, or had adapted well-established styles, suggests that the opposition to globalisation that the exhibition aimed to showcase was in fact part of an existing, institutionalised network with its own well-established codes and conventions.

This anomaly was even more stark in Gerardo Mosquera's exhibition 'Important and Exportant', in that it aimed to explore the assumptions behind labelling certain artists important, as this terms tends to be '... related to the mainstream or broad international recognition, which, in its turn, depends on established circuits'.[92] Instead, the exhibition strove towards a more diversified, 'international' definition of importance, while working inside the structures [of the exhibition], but against the mainstream'[93]. Yet the exhibition includes what could be considered well-known artists with established reputations, like Sophie Calle and Ana Mendeita. Mendeita's inclusion is especially noteworthy, as her relationship to 'the mainstream' had been complex even when she was alive, given her attempts to reconcile her Cuban background with her art training in an American university. This she attempted to do by using her acquired skills in performance and photography to 'become one with the earth', where her body, or representations of her body, are inscribed on the earth in sites in several countries outside America, including Mexico and her birth-place, Cuba (some of these works were shown in the exhibition). Also, the fact that she aligned her work with feminist and Hispanic communities of interest '..led to her work to be seen as fulfilling two minority quotas [ethnic and feminist], and the U.S. mainstream's quota system accounts for the velocity of her short career'.[94] These difficult questions were largely effaced by Mosquera. The curator also did not engage sufficiently with the venue in which the exhibition was held (the Johannesburg Art Gallery, which in spite of its name, is actually a museum). Given that a museum is generally taken to be a key institution in the conferring of the status of 'importance', one would have thought that Mosquera would have found ways of confronting the ironies of holding the exhibition in this venue.

This lack of critical enquiry was carried over into other exhibitions, especially 'Hong Kong Etc.', where the curator Hou Hanri almost acted as a praise singer for Hong Kong as a model 'postcolonial' global city, and therefore a 'metaphor for a universal future'. This extreme naivety was also evident in Yu Yeon Kim's introduction to his exhibition 'Transversions', where in exploring the incredible speed of life ushered in by the digital revolution, he stated that 'it is no longer a question of cultural dominance, or even multicultural dilution, but of transactions that elude geographic, historical, political, and time-zone limitations. In the digital age we have all become colonisers and are in return colonised'[95] It should not be surprising then, that – unlike 'Alternating Currents' – both exhibitions contained work that at best was vague on the negative impact of globalisation, and at worst openly celebratory. Some notable exceptions could be found in 'Transversions', though, especially, Keith Piper's video entitled 'The Exploded City', consisting of three screens showing videos based on a parallel between London as a 'global' city and the Tower of Babel, which explores how globalisation produces both urban integration and fragmentation. Afredo Jaar also pointed to these disparities in his photographic installation based on the Rwandan massacres, entitled 'The Eyes of Gutete Emerita', which successfully confronted the viewer with the human dimension of the tragedy.

As mentioned earlier, works such as the above can both critique and complement neo-liberalism at the same time, and the curatorial shift to a thematic approach rather than one based on national pavilions strengthened this contradiction. While the former allowed room for more coherent exploration of the kinds of themes germane to Enwezor's exhibition, the suppression of the national origins of the works allowed the GJMC to promote Johannesburg's credentials as a marginal centre far more effectively: after all, it was not using its own platform to build the images of other countries through the hosting of national pavilions. The city's credentials were further enhanced by playing host to an exhibition that has been described as '..a model of South-South curating', which apparently gave life to Gerardo Mosquera's plea for the movement of art '... to be South-South, so that we can establish dialogue without mediators, as well as South-North, so that we can offer our own views to the centres'.[96] Yet as should be evident from the discussion above, that in achieving these ends, 'Trade Routes' remained blind to the ways in which new centres and peripheries have been generated even within the South, organised essentially around class.

In fact, as noted rather astutely by critic Jen Budney, questions of class barely surfaced in the exhibition, except in relation to one or two performances that were 'excessively ignored'.[97] According to Budney, had these questions been more prevalent in the content of other works and the themes of the exhibition generally, they could have been used to trigger a discussion about how a Biennale should be conceptualised in the South. The claim that the event represented the interests of '... excluded cultures and polities'[98] should have been examined critically, especially in relation to the event's accessibility.

While what constitutes 'accessible' art is clearly a vexed question, the very nature of the event's claims meant that the question should have been posed rather than ignored. For example, the exhibition failed to engage critically with the preponderance of installations, videos and photography. The debate on what constitutes 'accessible artforms' is a highly complex one. It has been argued by incorporating the language and content of contemporary visual culture, these artforms are easier for viewers to relate to than paintings, drawing and sculpture.[99] These 'traditional' artforms have also been identified with Western imperialist culture, given their canonisation as 'art' in the Italian Renaissance period; hence their being treated with a good dose of scepticism especially by artists from Third World Countries and the diaspora. However, the turn away from these artforms has led to another set of contradictions, where the alternatives risk being appropriated by the artworld as a '... a closed shop of aesthetic intrigues and jangling politics'.[100]

These complexities were not foregrounded to any significant degree in the Biennale: as a result, the event's silence on the question of access, and the class basis on which it rests, meant that the organisers fail to distinguish themselves sufficiently from the neo-liberal interests of the host.

The GJMC's commitment to the Biennale: why the contradiction?

One would have thought, though, that given the sophisticated image-building exercise that the Biennale was for Johannesburg, that it would have been much more committed to its continued existence. In fact, Biennale staff had argued for ongoing support in language that government should have understood, given its current direction. For example, its Project Co-ordinator, Clive Kellner, said that the Biennale could be used to build an alternative to Johannesburg's image as a crime-ridden city. Instead, by pursuing an 'export-led' growth approach through the project, the city could be presented through the Biennale as a place that offers culture 'in a civilised metropolis' enhanced:

> It increases tourism and offers employment in areas related to the Biennale. It brings professional people from various parts of the world. This in turn creates opportunities in which South African art and artists can be promoted; their work then reaches a larger audience via published articles and overseas exhibitions. The demand for South African art thus increases often providing new impetus for commercial galleries. What all this means is that a viable, sustainable infrastructure can be developed.[101]

In spite of the fact that Kellner and others argued that the Biennale could complement rather than contradict the government's current macro-economic framework, the project has been put on hold by the GJMC for financial reasons.

In fact, even at the time of 'Trade Routes', the GJMC's financial commitment to the project was in doubt, with its contribution being cut from the R5 million for the first Biennale, to R3 million. According to the organisers, the budget was certainly not sufficient to do justice to the Biennale, and key functions like publicity and education suffered as a result.[102] To compound the problem, the GJMC announced several weeks before the Biennale's closure that its funding to the exhibition would be terminated, which reportedly would have saved the Council between R670 000 and R1 million (although these amounts were disputed): the closure was averted when the Biennale staff managed to raise sufficient funds to keep the exhibition going.[103] Several commentators criticised the GJMC at the time for its bad judgement in withdrawing the funding, as the image crisis it would cause for the city far outweighed the saving it would make.[104]

Why the seeming contradiction in attitude? According to Victor Modise, some project staff mismanaged Biennale funding, resulting in a shortfall that the GJMC did not budget for.[105] Financial crises specific to the GJMC also played an important role determining the fate of the Biennale. Central government funding cuts coupled with the crippling effect of a rates boycott by residents of the wealthy suburb of Sandton led to a negative cashflow of R130 million per month. In response, the Gauteng Provincial Government stepped in in October 1997 and issued a Proclamation creating a management committee to deal with the financial crisis by introducing stringent fiscal discipline, and began preparing certain services for management through public/private partnerships or full privatisation.[106] This move has been interpreted as a top down effort to force the GJMC to restructure in line with GEAR objectives.[107]

The impact of this proclamation was evident in the GJMC Executive meeting that took the decision to curtail the Biennale's funding, as this decision was qualified with a directive that '...the Executive Officer: Arts and Culture Development and Facilities ensures that future Biennales be sponsored on a Public/Private Partnership basis in which the Council plays a facilitative and co-ordinative role involving minimal funding.'[108] To interpret such a move as a 'lack of commitment' is a misnomer: rather the project was being brought into line with GEAR thinking, which states that '[municipalities'] main task should not necessarily be the operation of such services but, instead, their regulation'.[109]

This approach to service delivery in culture and other areas has been formalised in a recently-released strategy document entitled 'iGoli 2002' (or Johannesburg 2002), which is to act a blueprint for the GJMC's transformation for the next three years. Igoli 2002 starts with the slogan 'it cannot be business as usual', and provides for '... the foundation for professionally run utilities, agencies and corporatised units. Non-core activities and non-strategic assets of the Council will be privatised'.[110] Arts and culture will now function within a 'client-contractor' framework, where the central administration, or 'client' will issue contracts for the delivery of these services. Culture has been defined as low priority in terms of expenditure priorities, on the basis that 'income generating activities are to be given priority, while revenue-absorbing services are given reduced emphasis'.[111]

No Biennale took place in 1999, as the GJMC does not have funds to organise one. The GJMC has been sensitive to the public criticism of the project, and Modise expressed concern that it had done very little to transform itself to serve all Johannesburg's residents: these factors also influenced the decision not to fund another one. If the project is to be revised in the future, then Modise envisaged that it may have to be set up as a Trust, Foundation or Section 21 company. Both the government and the Biennale's private sector sponsors would be represented in the company as partners, which could run a range of developmental activities culminating in a Biennale once every two years: in other words, the Biennale needed to be re-cast in a 'progressive competitiveness' mould to qualify its blatantly outward-orientation. Another GJMC-funded festival, Arts Alive, may also be run on this basis.[112] In Modise's words, the GJMC would act as a facilitator of cultural activities, but the activities themselves will take place outside the government bureaucracy. These developments imply that funding for arts and culture will be pared down to a bare minimum, and those activities relating to the GJMC's public mandate will be 'privatised'.

Recent proposals for the regeneration of the Newtown area reinforce this view. The area has been declared a Spatial Development Initiative by the Gauteng Provincial Government, which will probably draw heavily on the area's existing arts activities to develop a 'cultural district'. Apparently, this concept originates from America in the 1970's, where '... there was a coming together of interests of local politicians (who wished to regenerate downtown areas and increase their tax base), developers looking for new profits, preservationists and arts organisations looking for new homes'.[113]

The film and television industries have been earmarked for development in the Initiative, as have music, multimedia and crafts. The intention behind the proposal is to assist Johannesburg in becoming a globally competitive city in relation to the 'cultural industries', which will be developed by a roject management team. The team will be responsible for implementing the plans in line with iGoli 2002, which includes organising the necessary institutional arrangements such as companies, associations, public/ private partnerships, and the like.[114]

The GJMC has also announced that it is bidding for a satellite of the Guggenheim museum to be built in Newtown. The satellite would be similar to the one built in Bilbao. Discussions are proceeding with the New York-based Solomon R. Guggenheim Foundation and the World Bank's development arm to formalise these plans. According to the GJMC''s inner-city manager, Graham Reid, 'The impact for Bilbao was sigificant. We expect it to have a similar level of economic impact in Johannesburg in a whole range of ways, such as through job creation and generating economic viability in the area. And the indirect spin-off could be phenomenal. It will contribute significantly to economic growth and reinforce Johannesburg's position as a leading cultural centre.'[115]

What is evident from these proposals is that the Minister of Arts and Culture's vision of local governments compensating for the shortfall in national arts budgets has become a pipe-dream in the GJMC. Even art projects that promise to promote the country's competitiveness may not attract funding, a contradiction generated by fiscal austerity, ironically enough resulting in the starvation of GEAR's own machinery. Also, given the international experiences with the alternative modes of service delivery outlined above, some controversial outcomes could be predicted. The 'progressive' development aspects of these projects may struggle for survival even more than they did when they were government-funded, as public accountability will be weakened. Also, private sector sponsors will be able to influence the direction of these projects far more than in the past, possibly with the result that they begin to take the shape of publicity platforms for commercial interests. The Biennale project especially is potentially a powerful image-building exercise for neo-liberal corporates seeking a foothold in global markets, so it is very possible that such 'partners' could pull the project even further away from a local development focus. It should not be surprising, under these circumstances, for these events to continue acting as platforms for largely inaccessible artforms, which could be considered the art equivalents of 'high-tech/ high-skill' economic production. Also, given the need for these projects to be commercially viable, they may start charging entrance fees, effectively making the events unaffordable to ordinary people. Given that the private sector will be participating in the project both as a funder and as a partner, government representatives may find it very difficult to pull the project back towards RDP objectives, especially if it is not contributing financially. In essence, the real danger of the GJMC's new approach towards arts and culture is that vast numbers of Johannesburg's residents may be marginalised in favour of the needs of local economic elites, and government's participation in these 'privatised' projects will effectively sanction this shift.

With respect to the plans for Newtown, the brief overview of similar initiatives in other cities suggests that the 'crowding in' of resources to selected industries can lead to a gentrification of specific 'leisure' spots at the expense of working class residential areas. This should not be surprising as such plans are implemented in the name of 'economic growth', without any specific indications of how the benefits of that growth will trickle down to the city's residents. Also, artforms that lend themselves to 'industrialisation' are prioritised, with the result that the remaining artforms such as art, theatre and creative writing risk falling off the public policy agenda.

Conclusion: building an alternative, developing our creative capacities

> The negative, the tearing down, can be decreed; the building up, the positive, cannot. New territory. A thousand problems. Only experience is capable of correcting and opening new ways. Only unobstructed, effervescing life falls into a thousand new forms and improvisations, brings to light creative force, itself corrects all mistaken attempts ... The whole mass of people must take part in it. Otherwise, socialism will be decreed from behind a few official desks by a dozen intellectuals.
>
> Rosa Luxemburg, *The Russian Revolution*

Artists are faced with a difficult dilemma in motivating for government support. There are competing demands on the fiscus, and government may well argue in response that the limited resources at its disposal must be used to meet more pressing needs. As a result, it may be quite tempting to back off from arguing for support, or to argue in ways that would complement the government's neo-liberal macro economic framework. In arguing the latter point, artists may project partly mega-exhibitions like Biennales as being beneficial both for governments and for artists: they can be used to enhance the global standing of their host cities, and to 'grow' local artworlds. Admittedly, the number of artists who benefit in the short term may be limited, but in the long term, the artworld's increasing international status should benefit ever-increasing numbers of artists.

However, when the above arguments are translated into reality, they exhibit similar contradictions to those generated by neo-liberal economic policies. Biennales in South Africa and other countries have promoted small pockets of artists who are associated increasingly with an artworld discourse about globalisation. In doing so, these artists have helped develop a veneer of contemporaneity for their host cities, with positive spinoffs for governments and local neo-liberal elites. Even Biennales that attempt to situate themselves as alternatives to the existing mainstream cultural centres have found it difficult to distance themselves from neo-liberal interests locally, nationally and globally. It is difficult not to conclude that the 'export-led' nature of Biennales make these events inherently incapable of addressing the needs of 'excluded cultures and polities', even when they claim that they do: in other words, there can never be a 'Biennale of the 70%'. This is because even 'progressive' Biennales – like the one in South Africa – largely reproduce a definition of 'contemporary art' that is premised tacitly on exclusion, as it does not make space for the creative production of people in a multiplicity of genres. As a result, these exhibitions remain blind to class questions around the organisation of cultural resources in their host countries: there is no space for 'national questions' in 'global' mega-exhibitions.

The second Johannesburg Biennale was especially guilty of these oversights, as its organisers did not engage in a systematic examination of the assumptions underlying the prevailing discourse of Biennales.

As mentioned earlier, it is unclear whether the Biennale project will continue. What is clear, though, is that the export-led approach to cultural activities has firmly taken root, and indications are that it will continue driving a host of other activities in Johannesburg. Art in the interests of economic growth has become the logic of the moment. International experiences with this logic should force us to ask: growth for whom?

Recent evidence suggests that even in terms of its own targets, GEAR is a disastrous failure. Instead of increased employment, there have been massive job losses, with unemployment reaching record highs. The private sector – supposedly the main engine of job creation in terms of GEAR – has been mainly responsible for destroying jobs. Instead of growing, the country's economy has been plunged into recession, and the growth in the country's Gross Domestic Product is well below the rate of population growth. The level of private sector investment has fallen, government expenditure on the debt has increased, and domestic savings have shrunk. While foreign investment has increased, jobs have been lost rather than created as investors intensify rationalisation programmes in the name of improved productivity.[116] In fact, there is more than enough evidence that the GEAR strategy is in need of urgent review.

In spite of this evidence, in spite of the sheer scale of human suffering caused by neo-liberal policies in this country and in others, the government persists. No aspect of government is being left untouched, including arts and culture. So government restructures its financing of creative activities to support an anti-human economic strategy; it massacres jobs by the thousand, and then links arts and culture to 'development' strategies whose job creation records in other countries are shaky to non-existent. In spite of the RDP, government policy is actively encouraging the provision of arts and culture activities for the few, in the interests of fostering economic 'growth'.

Nowhere is this shift more evident that in Johannesburg, where the race is on for the GJMC to pip other cities to the post in establishing itself as South Africa's first truly 'global' city.

It is clear, though, that there are progressive elements within governments that cast their support for arts and culture in the 'competitive austerity' mould, in the belief that it represents the only alternative to dealing with the realities of globalisation. So, in line with this belief, they implement policies and activities that increase inequality in the hope that these disparities will be reversed once and for all at some stage in the future. The problem with this approach is that the very generation of South Africans who were made to bear the brunt of apartheid are now being forced to pay the costs of the reintegration in the global economy. Given the huge social cost of even this strategy, it is essential that we do not surrender to such fatalism: as a matter of sheer survival, there *must* be an alternative.

It is extremely difficult, though, to map out the contours of such an alternative. What is clear is the necessity of breaking with the competitiveness logic entirely. In the words of Canadian trade unionist Sam Gindin, '... the overwhelming power of competitiveness as an ideology means that we do not just need an "alternative" but a truly independent alternative. Trying to modify or qualify competitiveness (progressive competitiveness, competitiveness-with-a-human-face) will inevitably fail and fail dangerously. We must base any challenge to competitiveness on a clearly different set of assumptions and principles'.[117]

In doing so, perhaps we need to start from a very basic point, which is to ask what the purpose of human production is, including artistic production. A fundamental aim of emancipatory theory and practice is to realise a society where we all can live as whole human beings. Democracy and equality are merely organising principles to help us operationalise this ideal. Productive activity organised on these principles becomes both an end and a means: we produce in order to become fully human, and our quest for humanity drives us to produce. Production is, in essence, life-activity. Given that life-sustaining activity must, of necessity be both manual and intellectual, these facets of production should be inextricably intertwined: so, creative and manual activities can and should be undertaken by everybody, and should not be the preserve of specific individuals. Production can also give rise to a sense of community, as it brings individuals together in collective activity for their own benefit. If we are to realise our full productive capacities, and by extension, our full humanity, then society must be organised to support what Gindin has called 'the democratic development of capacities'.[118] As Gindin has noted, international competitiveness undermines this development as it pits worker against worker for the benefit of their employers. In the process, it marginalises whole areas of life-activity as 'non-productive' if they do not have the potential to be turned into competitive industries. Artistic activity especially runs the risk of becoming marginalised by the competitiveness logic, as it is less easy to exploit for financial gain than many other aspects of human production.

It will be possible to determine what constitutes useful and meaningful production only if the political space has been created to do so. It could be argued that a
country like Malaysia has done just that by pulling up the drawbridges and 'de-
globalising' through the re-introduction of exchange controls. The problem with this
approach is that – as attractive as it may seem to countries devastated by the vagaries of
tumultuous money markets – it does not guarantee that the resources salvaged will be
redistributed within those countries. A more effective approach could be encapsulated
in Samir Amin's term 'de-linking', which involves '...the subordination of outside
relations to the logic of internal development and not the reverse'[119] This approach is
based on the recognition that neo-liberal 'development' strategies applied universally
result in increasing wealth gaps between and within countries. Ironically enough these
realities make the case for de-linking strategies, as globalisation of key industrial centres can only succeed through the creation of peripheries. Given that it is still largely the
state that acts as a gatekeeper to the global economy, de-linking will inevitably involve
struggles around how the state is organised: in other words, they may take the form of
national liberation struggles or nation-building movements with an internationalist
undertone.

The reorganisation of local governments like the GJMC could be considered the
start of the wholesale privatisation of public life, leading to the fragmentation and
marginalisation of communities left out of the competitiveness loop. The social consequences could be devastating. In order to counter this trend, communities will need
to organise themselves on the basis of their needs and aspirations: in fact, in mobilis-
ing against the GJMC's iGoli 2002 plan, the South African Municipal Workers' Union
has argued that it has been foisted on the city in an undemocratic manner, and that
'..the restructuring of Johannesburg is the task and responsibility of all who live and
work in the city'.[120] Residents could organise themselves into user groups, tenant
action groups, civics and the like: these would need to be linked to trade unions
organising in the public sector. The sternest test of a community's organising strength
will be at local government level, as the coalface of government delivery to its electorate: this tier of government, especially, cannot be allowed to disintegrate under the
weight of fiscal austerity. Residents will need to develop a vision for local government,
and insist on their involvement in its implementation. This vision would need to
make a clear case for the continued relevance of the public sector, and should include a
public education drive to promote its defence. It should emphasise the interrelated-
ness of different services, and promote forms of integration that privatisation breaks
down. Support for arts and culture should be included in this integrated vision, to
counter any arguments that artists are seeking support on a self-interested basis, and at
the expense of more pressing social needs (arguments that are a logical consequence of
the competitive austerity approach). In fact, service-specific strategies on their own

could well exacerbate fragmentation, and should be avoided. Such support would also promote the development of creative capacities of all residents, not just those generally considered 'artists': after all, specialisation is a logic that drives international competitiveness. It would be important, though, not to promote creative activities on a parochial basis: given the realities of globalisation, their vision should be both local and internationalist. The difference between these activities, though, and Biennale-like arrangements is that global cultural exchange would be encouraged to the extent that it develops local capacities. Ultimately, though, the precise shape of the 'alternative' to GEAR will (and should) develop only through struggle: it cannot be decreed from above.

As resistance to the GJMC's restructuring mounts, it will be important to pose practical alternatives to government's competitive austerity measures: they would need to point out that attempting to save the country money by slashing services will have such an enormous social price that the short term fiscal benefits will soon be swept away. Costing the implications of increasing marginalisation, inequality and alienation of large sections of South African society will be difficult, but we need to rise to the challenge. If we do not, then the following words of South Africa's new president, Thabo Mbeki, may become prophetic: 'When the poor rise up, they'll rise up against us all. They will do to us what they did to apartheid'. [121]

Notes

—   The title is an adaptation of a paper by Jonathan Jansen, entitled 'How Policy Creates Inequality', and is inspired by both its title and contents. The paper deals with how apartheid inequalities have been exacerbated by the South African government's approach to educational restructuring. See Jansen, J. 'How Policy Creates Inequality', Centre for Education Research, Evaluation and Policy, Faculty of Education, University of Durban Westville, March 1998.

1   Jansen, J. 'How Policy ...', p. 1.

2   Geers, K. (1997). 'Being Topical Doesn't Mean that it's Art', *Sunday Independent,* 13 November, p. 19.

3   Panitch, L. (1996). 'Rethinking the Role of the State', in Mittleman, J. *Globalisation: Critical Reflections,* Colarado: Lynne Reinner Publishers, p. 104.

4   Martin, H.P and Schumann, H. (1997). *The Global Trap: Globalisation and the Assault on Democracy and Prosperity,* Johannesburg: HSRC, Pluto Press and Zed Books, p. 4.

5   Cheru, F. *New Social Movements*, p. 150.

6   Cheru, F. (1996). 'New Social Movements: Democratic Struggles and Human Rights in Africa' in Mittleman, J. (ed.) *Globalisation: Critical Reflections,* Colarado:

Lynne Reinner Publishers, p. 147.

7   Hank Savitch quoted in Bernstein, A. (ed.). (1996). *Cities and the Global Economy: New Challenges for South Africa*, Johannesburg: Centre for Development and Enterprise.

8   This matter is explored further in Goetz, E. and Clarke, S. (ed.)(1993). *The New Localism: Comparative Urban Politics in a Global Era*. London: Sage Publications, p. 78.

9   Noted by Halfani, M. in 'The Challenge of Urban Governance in Africa', in Swilling, M. (ed)(1997). *Governing Africa's Cities*, Johannesburg: Wits University Press, p. 18.

10   Swilling, M (ed)(1997). *Governing Africa's Cities*, Johannesburg: Wits University Press. pp. 3–7.

11   Goetz and Clarke. p. 71.

12   Goetz, E. 'The New Localism from a Cross-National Perspective', in Goetz, E. and Clarke, S., pp. 205–207.

13   Van Niekerk, S. (1997). 'Private Gain, Public Loss? Service Delivery in the New SA', in *Southern Africa Report*, September, pp. 135–138.

14   Hula, R. (1993). 'The State Reassessed: The Privatisation of Local Politics', in Goetz, E. and Clarke, S. (eds) *The New Localism: Comparative Urban Politics in a Global Era*. Newbury Park: Sage Publications, p. 31.

15   Panitch, L. 'Globalisation and the State', http://www.aidc.org.za/archives/gl_and_state.html, pp. 15–16.

16   Robert Cox quoted in Panitch, L. *Ibid*.

17   'Why "Growth" May Not Produce Jobs?' in *The Great Debate: A Special Supplement Dealing with the Economy, Sponsored by Catholic Justice and Peace, ESSET and Fair Share*, July 1997. p. 2.

18   Leo Panitch makes this point succinctly in relation to the relatively well advantaged North American and European economies, in a section entitled 'A Progressive Competitive Alternative?' in 'Rethinking the Role of the State ...' pp. 103–108.

19   Robert Cox, quoted in Panitch, L. 'Rethinking the Role of the State', in Mittleman, J. (1996). *Globalisation: Critical Reflections*, London: Lynne Reinner Publishers, p. 92.

20   Leo Panitch makes this point in critiquing Cox's understanding of the neo-liberal state. See Panitch, L. 'Rethinking ...' pp. 93–94.

21   Isar, Y. R. 'On the Financing of Culture: More Questions than Answers', in Oliphant, A (ed). (1995). *Bringing Cinderella to the Ball: Papers Presented at a Conference on Arts and Culture in the New South Africa*, Johannesburg: National Arts Coalition/Congress of South African Writers, p. 25.

22   *Ibid*, 29.

23   McGuigan, J. (1996). *Culture and the Public Sphere*, London: Routledge, pp. 74–115.

24   Haupt, G. 'Interview with Gerardo Mosquera', 6th Biennial of Havana, http://www.kulturbox.de/univers/car/havanna/opinion/e_mosq.htm.

25   Bosch, G. (1997). 'Rosa Martínez: Artistic Director of the 5th International Istan-

bul Biennale (interview), *Flash Art*, May/June, p. 77.

26 Gumpert, L. (1997). 'A Global City for the Arts? Report from Singapore', *Art in America*, December, p. 41.

27 A point noted by Staniszewski, M.A. (1997). 'Charting of Course', *Artforum*, September.

28 Bradley, K. (1997). 'The Deal of the Century', *Art in America*, July, pp. 48-55, 105.

29 For the Venice Biennale, see Hanru, H. (1993). 'Bi-Biennale: The Venice Biennale and the Biennale de Lyon', *Third Text*, 24, Autumn, p. 94. For Documenta X, see Storr, R. (1997). 'Kassel Rock' (Interview with Catherine David), *Artforum*, May.

30 'Korean Contemporary Art'. Korean Overseas Information Service, 1996, http://korea.emb.washington.dc.us/kios/News/Features/1996/socil.html, p. 1.

31 Kim Young-su. Minister of Culture and Sports. 'Kwangju Biennale is a National Event ...' Biennale Magazine, First Edition, http://www.Kwangjubiennale.org/eng/bienmag/mag1/mag1_01.html.

32 'Korean Contemporary Art ...' p. 2.

33 Kontonva, H., S. Nagoya and C. Park (1998) 'Kwangju Biennale: Unmapping the Earth', *Flash Art*, 31, (198), January/ February, pp. 70–73.

34 Staniszewski, M. (1997). 'Charting of Course', *Artforum*, September, p. 79.

35 *Ibid.*

36 Volk, G. (1996). 'Between East and West: Report from Istanbul', *Art in America*. May, p. 39.

37 'History of the Istanbul Biennials'. 5th International Istanbul Biennial, http://www.istfest.org/events/biennail.html, p. 1.

38 Volk, G. (1996). 'Between East and West: Report from Instanbul', *Art in America*. May, p. 39.

39 See 'On Life, Beauty and other Translations': Conceptual Framework of the 5th Instanbul Biennale, http://www.istfest.org/events/bconcept.htm. Also see Bosch, G. (1997). 'Interview with Rosa Martínez: Artistic Director of the 5th International Istanbul Biennale', *Flash Art*. May/ June, p. 77.

40 'On Life, Beauty ...'

41 'Unmapping the Earth: Main Exhibition'. http://Kwangjubiennale.org/eng/97bien/main/main.html.

42 For the Venice Biennale, see 'Bi-Biennale ...' For Documenta X, see Storr, R. (1997). 'Kassel Rock: Interview with Documenta's Catherine David', *Artforum*, May, pp. 129-131.

43 Cameron, D. (1997). 'Glocal Warming', *Artforum*, December, p. 17.

44 Ramirez, M.C. (1996). 'Brokering Identities: Art Curators and the Politics of Cultural Representation', in Greenberg, R., Ferguson, B.W. and Nairne, S. (eds) *Thinking about Exhibitions*, London: Routledge, p. 30.

45 Young-sup, K. 'Kwangju Biennale Gains Mixed Reviews; Critics Say it has Failed to

Differentiate Itself from Foreign Fairs', *Korea Herald: Culture/Lifestyle*, http://www.koreaherald.co.kr/kh1127/m1127c01.html. Also see Kontonva, H.

46 See Haupt, G. 'Interview ...', p. 1, and Camnitzer, L. (1994). *New Art of Cuba*, Austin: University of Texas Press, pp. 120-121.

47 Camnitzer, L. (1994). 'The Fifth Biennale of Havana', *Third Text*, 28/29, Autumn/Winter, pp. 147-154. This warning has also been made by Gerardo Mosquera in Haupt, G. 'Interview ...' pp. 1-2.

48 Adelzadeh, A. (1996). 'From the RDP to GEAR: The Gradual Embracing of Neo-Liberalism in Economic Policy', National Institute for Economic Policy, NIEP Occasional Paper Series, 3. August, p. 5.

49 Ramos, M. 'In Defence of GEAR: Comment from the Department of Finance', *Indicator SA*, 14 (3), Spring.

50 Murray, M. (1994). *The Revolution Deferred: The Painful Birth of Post-Apartheid South Africa*, London: Verso, pp. 21-22.

51 Adeldzadeh, A. (1997). 'From the RDP ...' pp. 7-16. Also see Osborn, E. 'Why GEAR Isn't Working: An Update', *Indicator SA*, 14 (3), Spring, pp. 26-30 and (1997). 'Why "Growth" May Not Produce Jobs?' in *The Great Debate*, Fair Share, July, p. 2.

52 '1. Policy Coordination', GEAR ... p. 19.

53 '3.4. Arts and Culture', in African National Congress. (1994). *Reconstruction and Development Programme*, Johannesburg: Umanyano Publications, pp. 69-70.

54 In terms of the Medium Term Expenditure Framework, the budget allocation for the Department was R740 million , of which arts and culture received R274 million. The budget has been reduced to R247 million in 1999/2000, but would be increased in 2000/01 to R254 million. So in real terms the budget for arts and culture is declining. Information from the South African Institute of Race Relations, *South Africa Survey 1997/98*, p. 342.

55 Friedman, H. (1997). 'Arts Budget Revealed', *Mail & Guardian*, 25 April.

56 Ngubane, Dr B.S., Minister: Arts, Culture, Science and Technology. (1999). 'Investing in Creativity and Innovation', 1999-2000 Budget Address, 4 March, p. 8.

57 'Arts Culture and Religion', in Burger, M. (ed)(1998). *South African Yearbook 1998*, Pretoria: Government Communication and Information System, p. 409.

58 Ngubane Dr B.S. 'Investing in Creativity ...' p. 8.

59 *Ibid*. Also see 'Arts, Culture and ...' p. 408.

60 Mtshali, L.P.H.M. (1998). *Budget Speech by the Minister of Arts, Culture, Science and Technology*, 1 June. p. 5.

61 'Business and Arts South Africa', in *The Cultural Weapon*, May 1997, pp. 3-4.

62 Shevel, A. (1997). 'To Sponsor Art or to Sponsor Sport, that is the Question', *The Star*, 5 November.

63 White Paper on Local Government, http://www.polity.org.za/govdocs/white_papers/localgov/wpindex.html.

64 Emdon ... p. 2.

65 Pimstone ... p. 9.

66 Pimstone, G. (1996). 'The Constitutional Basis of Local Government in South Africa'. p. 11.

67 'Decrease of Grant Allocation Causes Concern', *The Star*, 8 June.

68 Department of Development Planning and Local Government, Gauteng Provincial Government. (1996) 'White Paper on Local Government Transformation in Gauteng' (discussion paper, draft 1), 15 October, p. 6.

69 Van Driel, M. (1998). 'Gear "Will Make the Poor Poorer"', *Sowetan*, 30 July.

70 'Africus, Johannesburg Biennale 1995: Report-Back', Greater Johannesburg Transitional Metropolitan Council, p. 4.

71 Atkinson, B.(1997). 'Johannesburg Biennale: Good Works, Heated Debate', *Mail & Guardian*, 31 October.
Hynes, N. (1997). 'Biennale raises questions of SA's identity', *Business Day*. 28 November.
Diawara, M. (1998). 'Moving Company: The Second Johannesburg Biennale', in *Artforum*, 3, pp. 89-96
Haye, C. 'Spin City: The Istanbul, Johannesburg and Kwangju Biennales', in *Frieze*, 2, pp. 48-51
Medosch, A. (1997). 'The Second Biennale of South Africa: Digital Diaspora in the Cape of Good Hope', in Telepolis, http://www.heise.de/tp/inhalt/sa/3125/1.html. pp. 1-11

72 *Africus, Johannesburg Biennale 1995: Report-Back*, Director: Culture, Greater Johannesburg Transitional Metropolitan Council, pp. 5-6.

73 'Message from the Press Office and Introduction to 2nd Johannesburg Biennale 1997' (Press Information), p. 3.

74 'Administrative Structure of the Greater Johannesburg Metropolitan Council', GJMC, p. 3.

75 Vision statement for Metropolitan Sport, Arts, Culture and Economic Development, GJMC.

76 Padayachee, N. (1997). In Enwezor, O. *Trade Routes: History and Geography*, Johannesburg: Greater Johannesburg Metropolitan Council, p. 4.

77 Modise, V. in *Ibid*.

78 Mendosch, A. The Second Biennial of South Africa: Digital Diaspora at the Cape of Good Hope', http://www.heise.de/tp/english/inhalt/sa/3125/1.html, p. 2.

79 Geers K. 'Being Topical ...' p. 19.

80 Leary, R. and Bayley, D. (1997). 'Onan Slays the Barbarians at the Johannesburg Banal', in *Sunday Independent*, 19 October, p. 19.

81 Diawara, M. (1998). 'Moving Company: The Second Johannesburg Biennale', in *Artforum*. March, p. 88.

82 Preller, K. 'The 1995 and 1997 Johannesburg Biennales as a "Reflection" of Con-

temporary South African Art', *De Arte*, 57, pp. 28–47.

83 Cruise, W. Review of the Information on the Theme and Programme for the Second Johannesburg Biennale 1997, *De Arte*, p. 40.

84 Dewar, J. (1997). 'Verbal Gymnastics to Leave Art Lovers Gasping for Clarity', *Business Day*, 25 July.

85 Mendosch, A. 'The Second Biennial ...' p. 2.

86 Enwezor, O. (1997). 'Yinka Sonibare', in *Flash Art*, 30 (197). November/December, p. 96.

87 Feldamn, R. (1996). 'Pepon Osorio', in *Artforum*, November, pp. 97–98.

88 See, for example, Schjeldahl, P. (1995). 'Finnish Gilt: The Photography of Esko Männikkö', *Artforum*, November, pp. 66–69, and Herbstreuth, P. (1996). 'Esko Männikkö', *Flash Art*, January/February, pp. 114–115.

89 Enwezor, O. and Zaya, O. (1996). 'African Art International', in *Flash Art*, March/April, p. 65.

90 Cubitt, S. (n.d.). 'Eugenion Dittborn: Travels on the Picture Plane'.

91 Fraser, R.J. 'Duch-Hyun Cho and the Art of "Memories" ', *Third Text*, pp. 73–84.

92 Mosquera, G. 'Important and Exportant', in Enwezor, O. *Trade Routes ...* p. 268.

93 *Ibid.*

94 Camnitzer, L. (1994). *New Art of Cuba*, Austin: University of Texas Press, pp. 91–92.

95 Yu Yeon Kim ... p. 348.

96 Mosquera, G. (1994). 'Some Problems in Transcultural Curating', in Fisher, J. Global Visions: *Towards a New Internationalism in the Visual Arts*, London: Kala Press, p. 136.

97 Budney, J. 'Whos's It For?: The Second Johannesburg Biennale', *Third Text*, pp. 93–94.

98 Enwezor, O. 'Introduction', in Enwezor ... p. 12.

99 Walker, J. (1994). *Art in the Age of Mass Media*, London: Pluto Press, pp. 71–81.

100 Tuer, D. (1995). 'Is It Still Privileged Art? The Politics of Class and Collaboration in the Art Practice of Carole Condé and Karl Beveridge', in Felshin, N. (ed)(1995). *But is it Art? The Spirit of Art as Activism*, Seattle: Bay Press, p. 199.

101 Cruise, W. 'Second Johannesburg ... p. 51.

102 Cruise, W. 'Second Johannesburg Biennale', *De Arte*, 57, pp. 50–51.

103 Grieg, R. (1999). 'Jo'burg Torpedoed the Role of Cities in the Arts when it Scuttled the Biennale', in *Sunday Independent*, 11 January, p. 11.

104 Gieg, etc.

105 Interview with Victor Modise, Executive Officer: Arts and Culture, Greater Johannesburg Metropolitan Council, 5 June 1999.

106 Emdon, E. (1998). 'Greater Johannesburg Metropolitan Area' (Chapter 7), in Sutcliffe, M. (ed) Further Research into Metropolitan Government Systems.

107 Van Driel, M. 'GEAR "Will Make ..." '

108 Report on the early closure of the 1997 Johannesburg Biennale, GJMC Executive Committee and Council Decisions Post-Elections 1996/97. 18 November 1997.

109 'Guidelines for Private Sector Participation in Municipal Service Delivery', Department of Constitutional Development, p. 2.

110 Fihla, K. 'Foreword', *iGoli 2002*, Greater Johannesburg Metropolitan Council. p. 3.

111 *iGoli 2002* ... p. 24.

112 Interview with Victor Modise, 5 June 1999.

113 'The Creative City: Creative Industries and their Contribution to Greater Johannesburg (Proposals for the Development of Newtown)', Creative City People, SQW (SA), February 1999, p. 4.

114 'The Creative City ...' p. 190.

115 Jacobs, C. (1999). 'Jo'burg's Bid to Join Guggenheim Club', *Sunday Times Metro.* 29 August, p. 1.

116 Adelzadeh, A. 'The Cost of Staying on Course', Ngqo!

117 Gindin, S. (1995). 'International Competitiveness and the Democratic Development of Capacities', *South African Labour Bulletin,* 19 (3), July, p. 41.

118 Gindin, S. 'International Competitiveness ...' Also see Gindin, S. 'Socialism "With Sober Senses": Developing Workers' Capacities'. http://www.iaf.regards.fr/EspMarx.utres%20contributions/Gindin.html.

119 Amin, S. (1997). *Capitalism in the Age of Globalisation: The Management of Contemporary Society*, Zed Books: London, p. 40.

120 'iGoli 2002 – Who Will Restructuring Really Benefit?', South African Municipal Workers' Union, 7 April 1999, p. 5.

121 Ray, M. (1999). 'RDP's ideals swamped by harsh economic reality', *Sowetan,* 9 April, p. 9.

CHAPTER FOURTEEN

The burden of the present

Abebe Zegeye and Ian Liebenberg

Any contextualisation of South African socio-political transformation and its relation with emerging (or salient) social identities has to take into consideration major structural changes since 1994. These changes include

1   Transition-through-negotiation since 1991, culminating in free elections and the implementation of the final South African Constitution.
2   Greater implied constitutional freedom following the institutionalisation of provinces that facilitated new interregional dynamics.
3   Greater freedom in public debate (or freedom of speech, consciousness and association in its various manifestations) since 1991 when political liberalisation started.
4   More developed elements of social dialogue, such as the National Economic Development and Labour Council (NEDLAC) and community police forums. However, the attainment of democracy and what the democratic theorist Held calls 'democratic autonomy', extends further than formal structures and processes. In terms of discussing social identities in South Africa, these have to be noted.

Change in South Africa has however brought about both good and bad elements. The good is mostly linked to the fact that an extremely authoritarian and racist minority regime known for its brutality has departed from the political scene and South Africans have become free to choose their own destiny as citizens. The bad side is that South Africans also inherited what the historian Harrison Wright refers to as 'a burden of the present'. The country and its people tend to suffer from the legacy of 'waves of colonialism', apartheid and separation (a colonialism of a special type) and neo-colonialism (the New Global (dis)Order), a lack of development and potential economic stagnation, as well as unacceptably high levels of crime. The latter is due to many factors, including a recent past of armed protest politics, the militarisation of youth and sub-optimum socio-economic conditions (widespread poverty being one phenomenon responsible for the ongoing occurrence of widespread crime and violence). Over time, various contending ideologies rooted in the contextual material conditions of South Africans have evolved. These morbid symptoms are not particular to transitional societies, but have to be noted here.

We would argue that historically exclusive and seemingly incompatible political and cultural paradigms have developed in South Africa over time. The specific material historical struggle over scarce resources – land, minerals, water, livestock – combined with a socialised fear of the 'other' (and in the case of European settlers, eurocentrism) brought forward a society and its accompanying civil-society belief systems that became historical prisons. The potential for unity and commonality was shelved or restricted to create a material and cultural reality that defied human experience. Notions of common humanity and common cultural heritage violated the logic of colonialism and apartheid. Moreover, apartheid required a suspension of reason and what Wilfred Desan calls 'unity of origin' or what Neville Alexander calls a 'common core of humanity'.

Apartheid had many such exclusive paradigms, with the most prominent intellectual one being cultural exclusivity. Culture was not simply an instrument for constructing communities or allocating material resources, but was marshalled as an ideological weapon for both apartheid beneficiaries and the dispossessed. Though culture was used as such with strategic and tactical fluidity, it still tended to freeze thought. In the Gramscian 'war of position and war of manoeuvre' the purpose of communication was domination and coercion.

Even in its most subtle aspects, maintaining culturally distinct and constructed communities was a project of gaining political hegemony. Those striving after political hegemony collaborated with culture only to the extent that culture could procure something for the former. Thus culture as influenced by ideology became exclusive and static in its attempt to dominate or wrest power from the 'other'. People acting in terms of these exclusive paradigms representing the interests of opposed communities eventually tried to transplant each other with force. Consequently, from the 1960s to the 1980s, thinking was static.

Apartheid relied on the consequences of material scarcity and so quite easily imposed nations and sub-nationhood from above. People socialised within one entity were encouraged to fear the culture and manifestations of the culture of 'others'. Added to this were supremacist philosophies such as ethnocentrism and eurocentrism that concretised differences between groups. Not only did the supporters of the apartheid *Weltanschauung* use apartheid as a tool for their own ethnic mobilisation, an attempt was also made to make the paradigm fit all South Africans – hence the nation building from above. Though apartheid failed to create viable self-sufficient nations for the majority of people in society, it did create the cultural ethos associated with defending those nations and groups.

Ultimately, the most critical burden of the present is a cultural and artistic ethos that transcends this prior linkage of culture with political hegemony and cultural exclusivity. Because both the resistance to inequities and the justification for inequities revolved around this critical belief in political hegemony and culturally exclusive groups, the new culture must be a culture of consensus, adaptation, process and dynamism. In other words, the new cultural direction must reflect the complexity of human relationships.

The good news is that not all definitions of culture are static. Neither are cultural goods, the products of human activity, static. Most often, culture effectively problematises stock-in-trade discourses of progress, computerisation and globalisation. Culture interrupts these debates as it is an 'open system of rules' and thus the 'great dynamic learning process of mankind'. Included in this definition of cultures are also 'manifestations of culture'. Accordingly we can move away from the idea of irreconcilably different 'cultures'. Alexander's argument on the 'common core of humanity' informs our position. In this way, we are abandoning the historical prisons created by static views of culture, opting instead for an ongoing mapping of the fluidity, interaction and mutations of 'manifestations of culture'. Moreover, if one keeps mapping culture, it becomes clear that it is not a 'state of affairs already attained, a status quo, but a historical process' (Van Peursen). Hence our opting for a dynamic interpretation of culture. Ultimately, a new culture can include desires for self-rule and the redistribution of rights to historiography, rights to material resources, rights to representation and rights to collaborating culturally with the 'other'.

An open-ended definition of culture creates certain tensions that need to be taken into account, such as the persistence of violence and contempt. In our attempt to account for the presumed need for a cultural strategy we point to the negative manifestations of culture inherent in crime, xenophobia, authoritarianism, homophobia, sexism, fundamentalist interpretations of religion, exploitation of the poor and other forms of violence. Thus, the intervention of this volume has been to reassert the social and cultural manifestations of commonality that have emerged in the process of dismantling apartheid. Our project points to the process and procedure of cultural practice without fear of the final destination because, after all, the destination is both daily made and remade.

Moreover, in this dynamic interpretation of culture we must envision a route past and between the cultural traditionalism and the cultural relativism – and thus may find ourselves between a rock and a very hard place. The former, cultural traditionalism, is a static attempt to move back to the past. It suffers from an intense longing for a perfect hierarchically ordered community. However, to negotiate a way out facing the cultural relativism is certainly just as tricky. Cultural relativism, like its younger intellectual cousin, post-modernism, often becomes a cover for secondary conservatism. It has a tendency to become a defence and bulwark for the powerful.

Our open-ended system of rules will not be complete unless they can speak to the conflict and chaos created by these negative tendencies. These negative tendencies can and will impact on our common core of humanity in the post-apartheid society and might well breed contempt, tension and eventually violence again (structural on the side of the 'haves', violence for equality or autonomy on the side of the 'have-nots'). But the new cultural project as demonstrated by the contributors to this volume can address sexism, homophobia, authoritarianism, xenophobia, crime, fundamentalist interpretations of religion, exploitation of the poor and other forms of violence.

South Africans still find themselves in a semi-third world country, albeit a regional power, but with serious social maladies. The legacy of colonialism, apartheid and neo-colonialism is still prevalent. A new set of political values were introduced during transition, firstly by the introduction of the Interim Constitution and later by the acceptance of the New Constitution and Bill of Rights with a Constitutional Court as final arbitrator. The notion of regionalism, through the introduction of provinces and a Council of Provinces, brought about new inter-regional socio-dynamics and in political terms, the need to build intergovernmental relations. Land reform and resti-tution became an implied constitutional imperative. Affirmative action (a controversial notion in some quarters) became government policy at various levels. Language equity is also a set ideal in the new constitution.

This all happened in a country where there are substantial rural-urban differences, where a duel economy marks society and poverty is rife. Poverty, like crime but unlike affirmative action, has become a pervasive non-racial phenomenon. South Africans currently need more than the challenge of a non-static cultural approach, such as cul-tural traditionalism, cultural relativism or post-growth, coupled with a culture of de-mocracy, commonality and tolerance to provide the essential economic outlook, houses and development. There is also a need to creatively allow various cultural manifesta-tions, through free association and a deepening of social dialogue to interact while strengthening the minimum social consensus on equality, eliminating poverty and reconstruction through growth. Does this not imply a planned and managed cultural strategy? In his opening speech at a symposium on Culture, Communication and Development (1996), Dr Ben Ngubane, then Minister of Arts, Culture, Science and Technology, argued that:

> South Africa is faced with the challenge of ensuring two equally important social [and may we add, cultural – A.Z. & I.L] imperatives. Firstly we must gain genuine support for cultural relativism, by which all cultural systems are afforded equal value. Yet we also have the urgent political imperative of building a national consciousness based on acceptance and celebration of diversity.

He qualifies this statement by adding that 'surely our overriding objective must be the movement of popular culture to centre stage' and 'articulating human rights through culture (and the consolidation of democracy) that has to do with the nation as a whole'. If Ngubane's interpretation is correct, this implies that South Africans have to accept some elements of cultural relativism. The qualification is that cultural relativism is not to be understood as a secondary tool of conservatism, but rather as a pragmatic possibility, which is concurrently underpinned by a sceptical progressiveness.

We know that the whole or universal without the particular is not all encompassing and in order to avoid destructive tension and violence, the interdependent relationship (and thus power-dependence relationships) need to be grasped in both culture and politics. Arguments about the reflective images and existence-dependence of the universal seem of particular relevance here. What is new is to be reflectively enhanced through 'culturally-being'.

To build such a cultural entity of high democratic values, tolerance, commonality and human rights together with economic equality will require constant interaction and negotiation on the definition of key concepts. In a democracy, *every* concept needs to be constantly negotiated and renegotiated. Once applied within the broader South African social sphere and the market square *(Khotla)*, the implication is constant transformation towards greater accommodation. This deepening of the process of democracy is a given for a society that aims at the consolidation of democracy, political transparency and socialisation (or economic democracy). Thus, having opted for culture as *an open-ended process*, citizens of a democracy still have to give communication and the communicative praxis priority in their natural and cultural beings. This also applies to the needed discussion and dialogue concerning the potential value of a directed cultural strategy and the extent to which state and civil society should complement each other in the 'bottom-up' search for such a strategy.

Only if people engage in this democratic process will it be possible to move beyond lip service to the notion of culture. But beware of a strong-handed, one-sided top-down approach. Strategies tend to become centralised and then will also have to be resisted as this may bring about a culture of kitsch. And even if, as Kundera states, kitsch may be an integral part of the human condition, one should nonetheless be aware of the danger of lurking 'totalitarianism' – and learn to laugh at it, thus 'moving it into the realm of the non-kitsch, making it lose its authoritarian power and becoming as touching as any other human weakness' (Kundera 1982).

Acceptance of the open-ended process or dialogue, even if there is only a limited degree of participatory strategy, may be necessary:

> If we are to further transform ourselves and transform our human environment, we must plan, be powerful, be adaptive to the least winds of challenge or change. We are already becoming refreshed with keen noses and sharp eyes and

agile movements for the adaptational dance that we call life. Eventually we shall be happily startled to realise that the evolution-revolution is not a transient event which will one day be over as we settle into a new cultural routine; rather evolution-revolution describes our future state of constant, fluid, never-ending adaptation which is the playful manner in which the (human) race finally learns to live.

Hanna 1970

If one can wish this for South Africans and others with whom we are in interaction within the paradigm of a new mutant culture *en route* to a more democratic and inclusive, commonality-directed society that yet celebrates its diversity in peace, then one would be satisfied that simple mapping may provide a first but hopefully useful rough map for our future cultural being. This does not imply that we will reconstruct 'truth' and 'memory' to become a kind of therapy to appease and flatter insecure erstwhile minorities – rather it calls for a dialogical, discursive multiperspectival reconstruction of truth and history. It also does not imply a morbid, guilt-ridden process, a fearful response to demographic trends, a charitable gesture or a course correction, but rather a conscious project directed towards greater democracy and justice.

The authors herein aimed to reclaim the cultural contributions from above and below and make them speak to each other. This volume unmasks the static of apartheid and reminds us that the struggle against it has had a long history of cultural interaction. Moreover, this collection represents the fluidity that has been claimed in resistance, redevelopment and reconciliation. The care and affection required to hear multiple voices explain the meaning of a shared experience is the same care that individuals, families and organisations must use to protect the vitality of democratic South Africa. The South African struggle has generated enormous creativity and inspiration for people world wide. At some point, the legacy of the present must become a celebration of what this transition means for South Africans themselves. That is to say, the new dynamic cultural process must involve an emphasis on intergenerational communication; passing on the dignity, elegance, innovation and aesthetic character that was a part of the persistent struggle for liberation. In these profound representations of human interaction, hopes, foibles, follies, negotiations, collaborations and triumphs an honest legacy can be the rich living history of the present and the future.

References

Alexander, N. (1985). *Sow the Wind: Contemporary Speeches*. Johannesburg: Skotaville Press.

Desan, W. (1987). *Let the Future Come: Perspectives for a Planetary Peace*. Washington DC: Georgetown University Press.

Kundera, M. (1986). *The Art of the Novel*. London: Faber & Faber.

– (1982). *The Book of Laughter and Forgetting*. London: Faber & Faber.

Index